British Women Poets
of the 19th Century

This anthology will, for the first time, reveal the incredible breadth and richness of women's verse written during this key period. Readers will find here many poems on traditional women's subjects—love, death, spirituality, and nature—but they will also uncover ironic resistance to stock images of femininity and women's work. Besides conventional romance, these writers celebrate maternal love and "mother-want," sisterly devotion, and (by the end of the century) the bonds of lesbian passion. There's even a mock heroic poem entitled "Sappho Burns Her Books and Cultivates the Culinary Arts" by Elizabeth Moody. The women writers in this volume, whether driven to compose by artistic ambition, economic necessity, or moral conviction, sharply etch the defects of the social order around them in verse that is often highly political. But these poets also find much to praise and celebrate and do so with unparalleled emotion, observation, and lyricism. This is a breathtakingly rich collection, and one that will continue to resonate and reward for years to come.

Margaret Randolph Higonnet is professor of English at the University of Connecticut and an Affiliate of Harvard's Center for European Studies. She is the prize-winning author of numerous titles from university presses in the areas of nineteenth-century and children's literature. She lives in Cambridge, Massachusetts.

British Women Poets of the 19th Century

edited by

Margaret Randolph Higonnet

A MERIDIAN BOOK

MERIDIAN
Published by the Penguin Group
Penguin Books USA Inc., 375 Hudson Street,
New York, New York 10014, U.S.A.
Penguin Books Ltd, 27 Wrights Lane, London W8 5TZ, England
Penguin Books Australia Ltd, Ringwood, Victoria, Australia
Penguin Books Canada Ltd, 10 Alcorn Avenue, Toronto, Ontario, Canada M4V 3B2
Penguin Books (N.Z.) Ltd, 182–190 Wairau Road, Auckland 10, New Zealand

Penguin Books Ltd, Registered Offices: Harmondsworth, Middlesex, England

First published by Meridian, an imprint of Dutton Signet,
a division of Penguin Books USA Inc.

First Printing, December, 1996
10   9   8   7   6   5   4   3   2   1

 REGISTERED TRADEMARK — MARCA REGISTRADA

LIBRARY OF CONGRESS CATALOGING-IN-PUBLICATION DATA:
British women poets of the 19th century / edited by Margaret Randolph
Higonnet.
        p.   cm.
    ISBN 0-452-01161-2
    1. English poetry—Women authors.   2. English poetry—19th century.
3. Women—Poetry.   I. Higonnet, Margaret R.
PR1177.B75   1996   96-14411
821'.808—dc20   CIP

Printed in the United States of America
Set in Garamond No. 3
Designed by Eve L. Kirch

BOOKS ARE AVAILABLE AT QUANTITY DISCOUNTS WHEN USED TO PROMOTE PRODUCTS
OR SERVICES. FOR INFORMATION PLEASE WRITE TO PREMIUM MARKETING DIVISION,
PENGUIN BOOKS USA INC., 375 HUDSON STREET, NEW YORK, NEW YORK 10014.

For there is no friend like a sister

Contents

Introduction

When the beautiful, witty, and scandalous radical poet Mary Robinson surveyed the literary landscape in 1799, she proclaimed: "Poetry has unquestionably risen high in British literature from the productions of female pens."[1] Throughout the nineteenth century British women poets continued to flourish and win fame, as Robinson foresaw. Over the long span from the French Revolution to World War I, they rose to fresh educational opportunities, shifts in literary fashion, and changing expectations about women's roles. Working within this frame of dramatic social transformation, they formed a sisterhood that shared issues and disagreements—as siblings do. In this chorus of voices we hear different class origins, politics, and self-understandings as poets. If we listen carefully to the full range of their poetry, we hear the ring of their anger, their desires, and their laughter.

In the wake of the Revolution, which inspired Olympe de Gouges's *Declaration of the Rights of Women* (1791) and Mary Wollstonecraft's *Vindication of the Rights of Woman* (1792), many women pursued the right of citizenship in the republic of letters. While women were legally excluded from the political public sphere, female readers including servants "often took a more active part in the literary public sphere than the owners of private property and family heads themselves."[2] An overview of poets in 1792 observed that "the most sensible women are more uniformly on the side of Liberty, than the other sex."[3]

Enlightenment philosophy, with its twin ideals of knowledge and self-understanding, had encouraged women's desire for learning and self-expression. By the end of the eighteenth century increasing numbers of male mentors and critics conceded that it was "no longer a question, whether woman *is* or is *not* inferior to man in natural ability," and they instead focused on delimiting for aspiring writers the "properly female subject."[4] The burning question then became not *whether* women should write but *what*: Should they be restricted to a "feminine" topic such as nature, home, or morality?

The Romantic revolution in poetry that made both spontaneity and democratic realism acceptable in serious verse nurtured this flowering of writing by women. In reaction against neoclassical forms mastered through formal education (an education often denied to women), poets like Robert Burns, Anna Barbauld, and Helen Maria Williams cultivated vernacular forms, such as ballads, verse letters, and hymns—forms in which women were understood to excel. The Romantic turn toward the private self and the language and feelings of the common people, celebrated in William Wordsworth's "Preface" to *The Lyrical Ballads*, was also important, since it legitimated the everyday events of domestic life that filled the "feminine" sphere.

The achievements of these writers often came in a struggle against poverty. Ideally, it was thought, women should not market themselves or their literary work; nevertheless, many of these poets were forced to assume modern attitudes toward the production of poetry as a commodity. Both Charlotte Smith and Mary Robinson wrote when imprisoned for their husbands' debts, in the hope that sales of their poetry might repair their family fortunes. At the turn of the century, writers in modest circumstances still relied on advance subscriptions by family friends or patrons who might be persuaded to support the oddity of a "milkmaid" poet or a carpenter's wife as a poet, like Ann Yearsley or Christian Milne. Within a few years, however, a more modern grasp of the literary economy is shown by Jane Taylor and her sister, who drew on their experience in their father's engraving shop to publish their own works and retain the profits. Such writers understood poetry as a business—at the very moment when Romantic theorists like Wordsworth and Coleridge were stressing the esthetic purity of inspired geniuses singing to themselves in spring showers.

Over the course of the century, lending libraries, periodicals, and annual gift-books sought female poets in order to reach a growing audience of literate young women. They gathered women's poems in the printed equivalent of a drawing room conversation or girl's keepsake book. As Elizabeth Barrett Browning's heroine Aurora Leigh argues, women know the "trifles" by which young girls grow; but a poet withers who must write magazine verse for "light readers." Felicia Hemans and Letitia Landon (who discreetly signed her poems L.E.L.) addressed this need by acting the role of domestic icons who incarnated feminine beauty and respectability. A fresh professionalism becomes evident in the way such women undertook to market themselves and to repackage their troubled personal lives; they rivaled even Byron in popularity.[5] Literacy campaigns and journals aimed at workers also fostered poetry by a broader group of women. Janet Hamilton, a weaver who learned late in life how to write in crude letters, began at age fifty-four to publish in the *Working Man's Friend*; even as she went blind she produced three volumes of poetry and prose.

The emergence of a youthful "feminine" audience required the formation of a canon of appropriate authors. To provide proper reading matter, anthologizers like Sarah J. Hale compiled "wreaths," "garlands," or "gleanings" selected from "the female poetic writers."[6] The new tradition proved a capacious envelope that held many poets. Robinson's radical politics and sexual liaisons precluded her inclusion in most anthologies for family consumption, as did Helen Maria Williams's defense of the French Revolution. But others such as Jane Taylor,

Felicia Hemans, L.E.L., Elizabeth Barrett Browning, Christina Rossetti, and Jean Ingelow became household names.

The pens of these nineteenth-century women were not simply prolific and celebrated in their day. Alexander Dyce, whose *Specimens of the British Poetesses* (1825) included brief lyrics by seventy-six women, argued that growing opportunities would facilitate the ascent of even greater female genius. Frederic Rowton's *Female Poets of Great Britain* (1848) sought to bring them the honor that they "unquestionably deserve." Elizabeth Sharp's *Women Poets of the Victorian Era* (1891) included fifty-four "really fine" writers who promised yet greater accomplishments in the future; about the same number figure in Clarence Stedman's 1895 collection of Victorian poetry. And by the end of the century Emily Dickinson's would-be Pygmalion, Thomas Wentworth Higginson, had amassed a vast "Galatea" library of British and American women's poetry as well as fiction and nonfiction.[7]

The formation of a female canon served editors' desire to shape a narrative of progress and national identity. George Bethune held that the multiplication of superior female poets was proof of "moral advancement" in British society. Elizabeth Sharp believed that the Victorian era offered women an "ever-widening field for the exercise of their powers," enabling them to transcend the "socially fettered condition" in which their predecessors had lived, when "the house, with its unrelieved monotony of small daily duties, was still held to be the only sphere in which a woman's life should revolve," and "writing for publication was looked on as unwomanly."[8] Victoria's accession to the throne marked the "Modern Era," which would free women from the sentimentality imposed by earlier fashions.

Only three of the names common in nineteenth-century anthologies, however, survive today in general collections: Elizabeth Barrett Browning, Emily Brontë, and Christina Rossetti. In the twentieth century, the thread of women's poetic tradition has been lost. As Barrett Browning put it, many of "the worthiest poets have remained uncrowned" (*Aurora Leigh* 2.28).

What factors were responsible for the effacement of the female tradition? Dyce suspected that women had been "carefully excluded" from earlier anthologies; he pointed also to the "small quantity of female effusions, and their concealment in obscure publications." While he praised women's "genius" in the expression of sensibility, tenderness, and grace, he nonetheless doubted that they might rise to "the grander inspirations" of sublimity or to masculine epic history that stamps "the character of nations" (iii–iv).

Writing even by recognized poets was often given such patronizing attention. Some critics, like Dyce, stressed what women had *not* done. Bethune faulted women for not applying the pruning knife. Others perceived women as the objects rather than the creators of art—the sisters, wives, or mistresses of Romantic and Victorian men.

The very successes of women writers undoubtedly seemed dangerous to some misogynists; Thomas Mathias and Thomas Polwhele held the French Revolution responsible for the "*unsexed* female writers" who "now instruct, or

confuse, us and themselves in the labyrinth of politics."⁹ The burden of these at-
tacks can be seen in the case of Anna Laetitia Barbauld, who, while acknowledg-
ing that she herself had "stepped out of the bounds of female reserve in
becoming an author," warned that "the thefts of knowledge in our sex are only
connived at while carefully concealed."¹⁰ Yet Mary Wollstonecraft and Mary
Robinson were quick to deny that education or poetic composition could unsex
a woman. Half a century later, Christina Rossetti's friend Dora Greenwell con-
tinued the debate, citing John Stuart Mill's argument that "the proper sphere of
all human beings is the largest and highest which they are able to attain to."¹¹

The most famous exchange between poets on this subject is the correspon-
dence of the young Charlotte Brontë with poet laureate Robert Southey. When
Brontë sent her poems to Southey in 1836, he replied, "Literature cannot be the
business of a woman's life, and it ought not to be. The more she is engaged in
her proper duties, the less leisure will she have for it, even as an accomplishment
and a recreation." He warned that her poetic "day dreams" were "likely to in-
duce a distempered state of mind" and "unfit" her for ordinary life. Although
Brontë appeared to acquiesce in the rule of duty, her response to Southey under-
scored her intense desire "to pursue that single, absorbing, exquisite gratifica-
tion"—poetry.¹²

The notion that men and women had separate spheres of poetic practice,
corresponding to their public and private duties, had been firmly established by
the didactic poet Hannah More among others. More's "prefatory Letter" to Ann
Yearsley's *Poems on Several Occasions* (1785) reminds the author that "the making
of verses is not the greatest business of human life, and that as a wife and a
mother she has duties to fill, the smallest of which is of more value than the
finest verses she can write." More's *Essays* (1777) reserved "the steeps of
Parnassus" (epic, tragedy, and satire) to the male sex, and her *Strictures on the
Modern System of Female Education* (1799) urged women to survey "home scenes"
from their own garden, while men might gaze on the world from their "loftier
eminence."¹³

One way to counter the opposition between a woman's duty and poetry was
to assert that they were really the same thing. In the same decade that Southey
instructed Brontë to subordinate her thirst for poetry to the fulfillment of her
duties, the anthologist Sarah Hale argued that "the feeling of devotion or piety
is inseparable from real genius in a woman." A poet herself, she assigned female
poetry the tasks of "purifying the literary atmosphere" and exalting "the house-
hold affections." Although she recognized that the rose "offers more varieties
than the oak," she nonetheless restricted "the appropriate domain of woman" to
love lyrics, poetry for children, devotional hymns, and "the music of nature."
Hale did not believe that a true woman's taste could admit "the unholy passion
of animal appetite" or the "heathen" realm of epic deeds, war, and violent pas-
sions (4–7). As this volume will show, the record proves otherwise.

Most Victorian anthologies such as George Bethune's *British Female Poets*
(1848) or *The Home Book of Verse* foregrounded sentimentality, a love of flowers,
and spiritual uplift in women's writing. The genius of woman, Bethune ex-
plains, yields "peculiar delight when its themes are love, childhood, the softer

beauties of creation, the joys or sorrows of the heart, domestic life, mercy, religion, and the instincts of justice" (iii). The works of women, Aurora Leigh might respond, "are symbolical"; and what they symbolized, once they had passed through this sieve of values, were society's preconceptions about womanliness. These preconceptions became both frame and ironic filigree in the poetry that women wrote. Forced to conceal their "thefts," as Barbauld put it, women transformed the subject matter to which they had been assigned.

Victorian editors in turn screened women's poetry for propriety, by and large excluding humor, politics, and long narratives from periodicals and anthologies. As Elizabeth Sharp complained, "Women have been represented by their most indifferent productions" (xxviii). Reduced to a single note, voices were ironed out through selection to make them more domestic and palatable. Felicia Hemans was remembered for the patriotic effusions favored in school exercises; Barrett Browning for the simplest of her love poems. Because women's long poems were not reprinted, femininity became identified with lyric brevity and especially with poetry about feelings. Isolated and simplistic selections invited autobiographical readings that undervalued women's artistic inventiveness and their use of ironic masks. Tradition identified women poets with nature, love, and religion.

Then in the twentieth century, the modernist values of irony, skepticism, and difficulty further obscured our view of women's accomplishments, because these had become synonymous with the straitlaced Victorian values of the anthologies. Just as Aurora Leigh feared, writing magazine verse for "light readers" was fatal to the gifts and reputation of women poets. When a new generation of critics revived interest in lyrics by male Romantics, they left women's poetry in the attic. Even Barrett Browning and Rossetti were dismissed as "writers of lyric, of facile movement, and of simple, sometimes mawkish sentiment."[14] Caught in this backlash against the very virtues women had been exhorted to display, many of their most interesting and rebellious poems fell out of circulation.

Of course, the topics of "nature," "love," and the "spirit" were important to women, since each carried a powerful ideological charge transmitting concepts of femininity. Women writers have had to struggle against the dictum that Woman is to Nature as Man is to Culture—that she is passive, ignorant beauty in need of cultivation and artistic form, and that (in Poe's phrase) "the death of a beautiful woman is, unquestionably, the most poetical topic in the world."[15]

The dark side of the identification of woman with nature can be seen in a ballad by Rosamund Mariott Watson, who translates the war between the sexes into a haunting confession by the man who loves but unwittingly kills his bird-bride and her children; in their final flight, they elude him. In a classical register, Dora Greenwell and Caroline Fitz Gerald retell the Greek legend of the earth goddess Demeter and her daughter Persephone, abducted by the lord of the underworld, to reveal the sustained power of bonds between women to resist male violence.

Throughout the century, women published poems that suggest their bodies are works not of nature but of art. Mary Robinson, for example, in her poems on fashion calls attention to the corseting and construction of both the male and the female body. As an actress herself, she pointedly describes the social farce of painted faces and cross-dressing masquerade. "Mirror" poems by Rossetti, Augusta Webster, and Mary Elizabeth Coleridge remind us that women compose themselves for consumption, but cannot entirely repress the Medusa-like other within.[16] The doubled image of the woman and her mirror self provokes a reflection that unsettles any notion of essential or natural femininity.

As a living example of the woman identified with nature, Dorothy Wordsworth struggled to find her own voice as a poet. She was so close to nature, her brother William suggested, that her journal observations could serve as raw material for his poetry. Dorothy collaborated in this self-effacing project, even eliminating the "I" in her diary entries. But modern readers have come to admire her few poems in their own right, discovering her intense observation of isolated, glistening details. Unlike her brother, who works through his crises by turning scenes into mental landscapes, she visualizes a shifting, manifold world that is virtually independent of the human observer, who is cut off like a "floating island."[17]

For a woman inspired by Enlightenment thought, a stereotype that denied women the powers of scientific analysis and reason was troubling. Charlotte Smith's most interesting poetic experiment produced the topographical and botanical descriptions that structure the narrative line of her epic, *Beachy Head* (1807). There she boldly positions herself high above the British Channel to observe the natural and political landscape from a sublime yet localized perspective. Her ability to bring scientific observation to life made one reviewer think her poems well adapted to children. Charmed by what he took to be sugarcoated didacticism, he entirely overlooked the political implications of her rural scenes. He could not grasp the ironic double vision provided by her footnotes on Linnaean classification and by the topographical traces of a history that reaches back to the "concussion" of tectonic plates, through Viking invasions and the Battle of Hastings, to contemporary war and imperialist conquest. Smith used her scholarly botanical annotations to lay claim to the authority of immediate observation and common sense as well as poetic license. She refused to "adjust" her observations to the "objects of Natural History." A scientific theory that does not jibe with pragmatic observation, her note implies, may itself require adjustment.[18]

Other writers focus on the rural world's everyday interaction with its human inhabitants, in the tradition of Virgilian georgics. Thus Joanna Baillie's realistic slices of rural life describe in simple language the movement of a winter or a summer day from cockcrow to evening prayers; she juxtaposes barnyard animals' meals and labors with those of their masters. And Anna Barbauld's sophisticated poem "The Caterpillar" combines whimsy, pragmatism, and politics, as she balances between the housewife's "persecuting zeal" and the celebration of an "individual" existence that curls around her finger beneath her curious gaze.[19] The pastoral world may betray a rift in its midst, as Barbauld's pesticidal warfare hints. Within the rural idyll, Elizabeth Hands discovers not peaceful procreation but a mad heifer on a rampage, or an incestuous rape that ruptures the peace of a woman's life, as in *The Death of Amnon* (1789).

Later Victorian poems inspired by Charles Darwin underscored the indifferent and harsh nature of power in the natural world observed from a distance. In the murky wood of a poem by Agnes Mary Robinson, "Selva Oscura," ravens prey, eagles circle overhead, and "through the boughs a bird drops dead." Darwinian evolution may signify progress, of course, as Robinson foresees in "Darwinism," which tells of an aching unrest that goads us to the invisible goal of perfection; Emily Pfeiffer's "Chrysalis" likewise argues: "The sea-level rises." But progress is not the whole story, as we learn from May Kendall's comic conversation between a trilobite and homo sapiens about evolution and imperialism. The Briton who greets natives of an alien land "with hymnbook in one hand / And pistol in the other" may not mark much of an advance over the trilobite.

Not science, however, but passion is the dominant motif of women's nature poetry in this century, thus exploiting the Romantic turn toward expressivity and the identification of women with "the affections." Charlotte Smith's *Elegiac Sonnets*, which were considered models by contemporaries such as Wordsworth and Coleridge, fuse landscape descriptions with an outpouring of the observer's feelings. Sonnet 44 ("Written in the Churchyard at Middleton"), for example, draws on the force of a storm, the moon, and tidal waves to depict not only the destruction of a cemetery on the coast but the confusion of past and present moments in the irruption of a woman's passion. Through dynamic natural images like these, Smith, the Brontë sisters, and Augusta Webster's Circe subtly identify a woman's voice with tempestuous power, irregularity, and freedom rather than with the domesticated rose and sheep of nursery rhyme. Louise Bogan later worried that "women have no wilderness in them," but nature undoubtedly provided romantic release for many a woman's inner wilderness.

In an infamous polemic, *The Unsex'd Females* (1798), the misogynist poet Richard Polwhele recognized the power of Smith's sonnets, which combine a "romantic air" of wild sorrow with original images "drawn from nature." But he feared that Erasmus Darwin's *Loves of the Plants* might convey "illicit knowledge" arousing prurience and encourage women to "point a pistill" with unblushing cheek. For Polwhele, to fondly gaze at titillating pollen was tantamount to surveying "liberty's sublimer views," i.e., the wreck of kingdoms.[20] Picking up the gauntlet, Elizabeth Moody's poem "To Dr. Darwin on Reading His *Loves of the Plants*" playfully responds to the erotics of plant life and the "gossip tales" of Darwin and Linnaeus, who "pried in every blossom's fold, / And all he saw unseemly—told." The male prurience she points to, of course, permits her to allude to taboo matters with impunity.

The encoding of women's sexuality in natural images afforded rich material for the exploration of female desire, especially among the later poets. Suffusing that desire is a sustained thirst to be free, to join "all things that freely course, that swim or leap," as Emily Pfeiffer writes. The speaker of Dora Greenwell's "Scherzo" seeks to pursue "things that are chainless," "anywhere, out of this room." Charlotte Mew runs away from a tea party, to lie beneath trees and "watch a red squirrel run over my knees, / Very still on my brackeny bed" ("Afternoon Tea").

The free play of desire frequently seeks expression in fluidity. Tidal waters in the poetry of Katherine Bradley and Edith Cooper (fin-de-siècle collaborators known collectively as Michael Field) eddy and fan weeds "to plumy forests" that spread, untwine, and undulate ("Ascending and Descending"). Afloat with seaweed, erotic tides in Alice Meynell's love poems fill the rivulets among the inland hills ("Regrets," "The Visiting Sea"). The fantastic brookside realm of Rossetti's *Goblin Market* entices our senses, as we glimpse a sinister natural revelation through a glass darkly. "Bloom-down-cheeked peaches, / Swart-headed mulberries, / Wild freeborn cranberries" tempt us to transgression and lure Laura from the domestic tasks she abandons.

Strong nature poems by Dorothy Wordsworth and Charlotte Smith, Christina Rossetti, Dora Greenwell, and Michael Field magnify details to evoke intensity of passion. Like the hypernaturalistic images of Georgia O'Keeffe's paintings, flower and fruit images open up vaginal depths. In "The Black Wallflower" Fanny Kemble unfolds unexpected beauty recognized only by a child; a rich and sacrificial blood red spreads mantling "through the velvet tissue" around a golden throat that throbs and breathes "strange fragrance, like a silent prayer." Greenwell's "Scherzo" follows an intoxicated wasp into "the innermost heart of a peach," the trout into the dark pool, and the fernseed into the chink of a tree. Intoxicated bees trail "up the napes" of sunken flowers and probe "to wildering depths" in poems by Kemble, Field, and Pfeiffer.

The active synesthesia of some poets may remind us of Keats's luxuriant pleasure in the savor of colors and textures as well as of Gerard Manley Hopkins's celebration of nature. Charlotte Mew "knew how jewels tasted." Michael Field showed exceptional inventiveness in translating natural images into sexual code. Within an iris the reader discovers kinetic seeds "in a thousand vermilion beads / That push, and riot, and squeeze, and clip, / Till they burst the sides of the silver scrip" ("Unbosoming"). Drenched in sensuality, Field's sonnets accumulate sensuous layers of "scale, or sheaf, or tissue of armed wings." We discover a world within the heart, first seen as a Platonic cave dripping tedious stalactites of despair, then woken to startling life by burgeoning maidenhair fronds that crack open rifts and "lift the great stones of its rock apart" ("Maidenhair").

Among the most shocking of Field's nature poems for its reversal of conventions is "Your rose is dead," where the speaker takes "vague, prodigious pleasure" in the majestic "recession" of the rose "from flesh to mold." These erotically charged poems about the natural world were one important way that women in the nineteenth century revised both their identification with nature and their traditional role as the objects of love poetry.

Throughout the century the development of complementary gender roles, assigning reason and warfare to men and love and "the household affections" to women, made the love poem a significant channel of women's creativity. The heartache was held to be "woman's special, proper ache," as we learn from Aurora Leigh's quarrel with Romney over woman's proper role (II.113). The topic became so central that Elizabeth Barrett Browning complains, "All sounds of life assumed one tune of love" for the quintessentially "feminine" poet, Letitia Landon ("L.E.L.'s Last Question"). In the *Venetian Bracelet* (1829) Landon herself asked, "For a woman, whose influence and whose sphere *must* be in the affections, what subject can be more fitting than one which it is her peculiar province to refine, spiritualize, and exalt?"[21]

As Charlotte Smith's *Elegiac Sonnets* had shown, one way to "refine" love was to make it melancholy. Landon frankly avowed, "I have ever endeavored to bring forward grief, disappointment, the fallen leaf, the faded flower, the broken heart, and the early grave" (vi). Indeed, hopeless, passive passion came to seem such a commonplace of femininity that Alice Meynell at the age of eighteen confided to her diary, "Whatever I write will be melancholy and self-conscious, as are all women's poems."[22]

A number of poets convert this conventional theme, however, into material for self-conscious irony. Letitia Landon herself translates the theme from tragedy to comedy by doubling the betrayals in her acidly Poe-esque "Revenge," where the speaker "feeds" upon her lover's pain at being rejected by another; sardonic rage runs through Caroline Lamb's bitter address to a false lover ("Would I had seen thee dead and cold"). Felicia Hemans's sculptress, Properzia Rossi, recounts in her dramatic monologue how she translates herself into a stone figure of Ariadne abandoned by Theseus, thus turning her pain into artistic capital. And a number of Edith Nesbit's poems wittily proclaim the contradictions of passion for a fickle lover: "I desire you, despise you, deny you, / Am false to myself and to you" ("Bewitched").

In order to escape the conventional poetic structure in which the woman is the object of desire, many writers deliberately revised the models inherited from masters like Dante and Petrarch. The *Sonnets from the Portuguese*, in which Barrett Browning explores the hesitancies and surprises of her relationship to Robert, respond to the traditional love lyric by giving a voice to female desire. The poet searches for a shared "level" and everyday union with her lover amid grief and need as well as through passion. With their sharp stops and reversals these powerful sonnets refute the equation of a woman's love with passivity. And in her other great tribute to love, *Aurora Leigh*, Barrett Browning follows a pattern familiar from novels like *Pride and Prejudice* and *Jane Eyre*, representing courtship as a process of education. Aurora's cousin Romney must first be refused in the great dialogue of Book II; later he is twice refused by the seamstress Marian Earle in a motif that adds a class resonance to the poem, before he finally wins Aurora.

With somewhat different aims, Christina Rossetti in the preface to her sequence of fourteen sonnets, *Monna Innominata*, also cites the long tradition of "unnamed ladies" who were sung by the poets but whose own poetic voices remained silent. "Had such a lady spoken for herself, the portrait left us might have appeared more tender, if less dignified." Rossetti's concern for transcendence causes her to distance herself from Barrett Browning: "had the Great Poetess of our own day and nation only been unhappy instead of happy, her circumstances would have invited her to bequeath to us, in lieu of the 'Portuguese Sonnets,' an inimitable 'donna innominata' drawn not from fancy but from feeling, and worthy to occupy a niche beside Beatrice and Laura." Rossetti foresees a moment beyond death, when her Beatrice-like speaker will lead her reborn lover to a mother country where "all is love."[23]

A shift in perspective may be one of Rossetti's most striking accomplishments. In several of her most famous love lyrics, Rossetti's speaker turns herself prophetically into a corpse, suspended in the "soul sleep" that precedes the Last Judgment, to achieve a reversal of power and provoke her errant lover to remember and regret. The roles in the traditional elegy of speaker and object, the living and the dead, are transposed in Rossetti's hands. These dramatic scenarios aimed at the lover from the perspective of death lend a sinister eroticism and edge to the form.

In fact, the forms into which the theme of love flowed were various, ranging from pathos to comedy, and the dramatic strategies are often ambiguous. Whereas the nineteenth-century novel seems to rely heavily on a marriage (or death) to close the plot, poetry offers a wide array of moments in women's affective lives: not only courtship but betrayal, rape, or marriage, sisterhood and childbirth. Shorter lyrics often give us just a snapshot, while many of the longer poems—above all *Aurora Leigh*—allow progression through stages of growth, disillusionment, and transformation of love to self-understanding.

The darkest side of woman as object of male desire and exploitation is captured in poems about rape. The epic *Death of Amnon* (1789) by Elizabeth Hands finds even the daughter of King David subject to incestuous abuse. Hands revises the Biblical narrative to win psychological insight both into the victim Tamar and into Amnon's violent reaction of self-hatred and disgust. Rape as the desecration of desire sets an outer limit to the motif of love.

In her two great poems about rape, Barrett Browning focuses on the mother's response to her child. "The Runaway Slave at Pilgrim's Point" (1848) argues dramatically that the system of slavery perverts maternal love. The slave mother's child wears the whiteness of the master on his face, a hallucinatory reminder of her violation that drives the mother to infanticide and madness. To convey the crushed lives of the slave and her child she condenses the four-stress lines of this poem into a blunt, all-encompassing statement in which every word but one must carry a beat: "I am black, you see." By contrast, Barrett Browning chose in *Aurora Leigh* to show the power of Marian Earle's love for the child of her rape and her proud rejection of social prejudice, which proves a turning point in Aurora's education. When Aurora Leigh visits Marian with her baby, she learns from watching Marian, whose "kisses are all melted on one mouth."

Beyond conventional romance and marital relations, then, these women writers celebrated maternal eroticism and sister love. When Ann Yearsley prepares the pregnant Mira for the task of nursing her child, she evokes the "flow" of her pleasures in breastfeeding. Anna Barbauld recognizes the narcissistic pleasure in a mother's longing for the unborn child—a part of herself "yet to herself unknown." Similarly, Joanna Baillie records the pleasures of satisfying children's hunger and curiosity, penetrates the sensuousness of dimpled flesh, and invests the power of gratifying infantile narcissism. And in a series of sonnets on the theme, *Mother and Daughter*, Augusta Webster captures moments when her daughter's love transforms her sense of self.

Thus, at the very moment when the ideal of companionate marriage was gaining currency, some writers found that marriage itself threatens to destroy romance through confinement. Marriage, Aurora Leigh bitterly remarks, is "a current coin / Which men give women," and for their purposes, "Anything does for a wife." Marriage is a marketplace. In the words of "The Modern Wedding Day," an anonymous newspaper poem of 1800, "It is a day of sordid thought, / Where liberty is sold and bought!"[24] Jane West, a farmer's wife, in a jaunty epistle to a newly wed friend announces in "plain English" that the woman's empire in courtship ends with marriage, after which she must remain "mumchance" and darn old clothes while her husband rides off to socialize.

When we read the soft-spoken poetry of Dora Greenwell next to the plain-spoken comedy of West, ironic tones become audible. On the surface, Greenwell paints in "Home" a scene that exemplifies the ideology of separate spheres and the cult of domestic felicity. The poem begins by singing of "two birds within one nest," joined in "love and prayer." One waits at home, the other hastens home to rest. The home shuts a world of care and strife out; there we also find "a world of love shut in." These neat but slippery pairings by Greenwell (who herself never married) create a poem with a double voice: an official one that celebrates the clichés of Valentine's Day cards, and a more sinister one that notes the power of home to confine women and to deny the world.

Amy Levy's dramatic monologue "Xantippe" (1880), which gives voice to Socrates' supposedly shrewish wife (perhaps for the first time in history), casts light on the painful disillusionment of an intellectually ambitious woman joined in marriage to the greatest philosopher of her time. In a clever transposition of Platonic doctrine, Xantippe recounts the metamorphosis of her youthful romantic desires into intellectual desire as she came to know Socrates. Her marriage, however, has turned her into a domestic servant at the beck and call of male philosophers.

Love between sisters takes on a suggestively heroic form in *Goblin Market* (dedicated by Christina Rossetti to her sister, Maria), while its opposite, "sororophobia," grates in the voice of Webster's "castaway" prostitute. The erotic dimensions of Laura's relationship to Lizzie in Rossetti's poem suggests that we should reread other works with an eye to gender ambiguities and the acting out of sexualities.

The comic side of courting occasioned much wit and subversion of male narratives. Anna Dodsworth's brashly farcical verse letter to her brother-in-law, "On a Noble Captain," describes an intoxicated youth, "brimful of frolic," who will not take no from the kitchen-maid until at last he receives an untoward injury. How the "lame" limb was broken, it turns out, depends on who tells the tale. A similar scenario lurks in a nursery rhyme by Christina Rossetti in which a gentleman pig with a wig has a tail that "chanced to fail." Rossetti here challenges Lewis Carroll on his own turf, playfully picking up the visual joke in *Alice*, in which the mouse's tale trails off in the shape of his own tail. What should one do? Send the pig to a "tailoress"—or woman teller of tales, perhaps even a Jane Taylor—to get a new one.

By the end of the century, some writers openly moved beyond marriage as a frame for love. Amy Levy forecasts a day, "in a million years at most," when the gender system will disappear: "Folk shall be neither pairs nor odd," she proposes ironically, once "marriage has gone the way of God" ("A Ballade of Religion and Marriage"). It had always been possible, of course, for women poets to assume male personae that permitted poetry of same-sex desire, a strategy that Charlotte Mew apparently drew on. But some writers looked to Sappho for what Virginia Woolf would paradoxically call "pure, uncontaminated, sexless" writing. Michael Field, who was particularly innovative in devising a language of desire, assumes the voice of a mummy that invokes the soul to come down, to "prick with pores this crust" so that it may "fall apart, delicious, loosening sand." Field wittily appropriates a philosophical model to achieve an ungendered eroticism and make it resonant. As in romantic Hellenism, historical displacement and pagan settings gave airy space to Michael Field's sexual themes. Although Katherine Bradley and Edith Cooper translated Baudelaire and knew the group of decadent writers linked to *The Yellow Book*, their lighthearted gaiety and unrestrained labial imagery project in a very different tone from that of the decadent male poets.[25] It is in the evocation of sexuality that the transformation of women's poetic options over the course of the century is most apparent. And their revision of the traditional love lyric in the masculine voice makes women's comic genius and wit flash out most clearly.

Besides nature and love, the third domain assigned to women poets was that of morality. Called upon to purify, to teach, and to reform, many writers turned to private themes in order to project indirectly their social and spiritual vision. Their moral mission in part explains the preference for hymns, prayers, and children's poems, forms that legitimated their public vision by their piety and didactic thrust. These genres may also have drawn writers seeking an anonymous or depersonalized voice with deeply familiar oral rhythms.

The secularization of twentieth-century culture has deflected attention from women's religious poetry; its poignancy and narrative power deserve fresh attention today. From Barbauld's delicate "Fragment" describing her yearning to go "home" as a child longs to depart from school to the anguished prayer of Emily Brontë "for the time when I shall sleep / Without identity" ("The Philosopher") to Dora Greenwell's pilgrim on a "homeward" lane, death—the outer frame of life—is constantly held in view. Alice Meynell in "The Launch" leads us forward through shipbuilding metaphors to consider a final passage "to keep the incalculable tryst."

The most powerful religious poetry by an Englishwoman in the nineteenth century was undoubtedly that of Christina Rossetti, who composed hymns, meditations on lines from the Bible, and taut explorations of the tension between doubt and faith. Thus Rossetti fuses traditional quest romance, the woman lover's voice of desire in the Song of Songs, and the classical story of Psyche's search for Cupid in her allegorical vision "From House to Home." The earthly paradise must be left behind if the speaker is to follow her angel home-ward, and the twists of delight, self-deception, and painful separation that she experiences in the course of her travels give dense actuality to Rossetti's spiritual argument. The voyage inward traces the separation of the individual from society; at the final moment of release from this world it occasions hymns of praise rather than elegies.

The spiritual impetus was not just otherworldly, however. Within this earthly life, a primary locus of women's spiritual power was the home, where they received full social recognition for their capacity to educate through love.[26] Thus Ann Yearsley urges the mother of an infant: "Plant thyself true virtue in his mind."

Maternal duty, generalized beyond actual maternity, becomes a springboard for social criticism and powerful polemic. The pain and confusion experienced by abused and orphaned children, such as Aurora Leigh and Marian Earle, are the subject of some of Barrett Browning's most memorable writing. In the eloquent protest poem "Cry of the Children," Barrett Browning asks to whom the victims of social injustice can cry out. Through her epigraph referring to Medea's destruction of her own children she suggests that bourgeois women are implicated in the social order as unworthy symbolic mothers to the children of poverty.

Women's social vision constitutes a significant component of their poetic tradition. As moral arbiters, they asserted the right to speak out not only on domestic issues such as child abuse but on public issues such as urban poverty, slavery, and imperialism. Impelled by conviction, a number of these writers sharply etch the defects of their society. The tears of the prophets, critics of their own age and people, are the legacy claimed by a poet who must "weep and write," in the phrase of Barrett Browning's "A Curse for a Nation."

The French Revolution was the political event that defined Romantic thought and set the agenda for nineteenth-century social change. Edmund Burke accused "jacobins," or partisans of the revolution, of being sympathetic to its "excesses"—not only terror, but divorce, state recognition of natural children, and redistribution of property. For him, women who participated in politics were harpies. In the notorious satire, *The Pursuits of Literature* (1794), already quoted, Thomas Mathias expresses the fear that literature is an "engine" by which civilized states might be overthrown: "Our peasantry now read the *Rights of Man* on mountains and moors. . . . Our *unsexed* female writers now instruct, or confuse, us and themselves in the labyrinth of politics, or turn us wild with Gallic frenzy."

Many British radicals like Mary Robinson, Charlotte Smith, and Helen Maria Williams welcomed the promise in 1789 of major reforms: the abrogation of aristocratic privilege and the accession to new freedoms and rights for women and slaves. Some, like Williams, went to Paris to see this world-historical event for themselves. Williams, famous for her prose letters from France reporting on Revolutionary events, celebrated the Fall of the Bastille. She records in her verse letter "To Dr. Moore" the downfall of French aristocratic privilege through the image of a harvest feast shared by young and old, where all the laborers around the soup "a circle make, / And all from one vast dish at once partake."

The political picture is not simple: One could be critical of the allied war against the French but also write a poem on Marie Antoinette. A significant number of women, even those sympathetic to the Revolution, focused on figures of exile. The breakup of the domestic circle by sickness, poverty, and war, the nostalgic longing for what Williams calls "images of home," and the loss of civil rights were motifs in the emigration of aristocrats that struck a resonant chord among women across lines of political allegiance. In "January 1795" Mary Robinson balances bleeding schoolboy soldiers with fugitives seeking shelter; "The Fugitive" (1800) traces a parallel between the sufferings of a French émigré priest and the calamities and social alienation that are the portions of others, including the woman poet.

Poetry on the costs of war also cut across political alignments and class lines. Jane West, from a conservative farmer's family, attacks the Jacobins as warmongers. The "milkmaid" Ann Yearsley sets the war with France, in which "millions sink," in opposition to the constructive realm of the nursing mother. Charlotte Smith, whose third son lost a leg at Dunkirk in 1793, deprecates "the horrors of war." In *Beachy Head* and in her notes to "The Forest Boy," she denounces "the folly and wickedness of those who make nations destroy each other for *their* diversion, or to administer to their senseless ambition."

Another poet of the Napoleonic era, Anna Barbauld, foresaw that British militarism and imperialism would impoverish the working class. Her vigorous dystopia, *Eighteen Hundred and Eleven*, which prophesies the ruin of Britain as cultural capital of the world, was attacked as "unpatriotic" by critics who objected to "the intervention of a lady-author."[27] Because it was comic, Caroline Lamb's Byronic satire on the apocalyptic destruction of London did not rouse such ire.

The urban working class draws the attention of many of these poets. Jane Taylor (who had herself labored for years setting type in her father's printshop) uses a pair of portraits to level false distinctions between the classes. The continuity of working-class oppression is a foil to the factitious changes of politics, in which "war follows peace" only in appearance, as fresh enemies are shuffled into place and fresh imperial conquests vary a narrative of commercial exploitation.

The traditional genre of diverse city "cries" gives voice to urban workers at their daily occupations. In Robinson's "London's Summer Morning," as in Baillie's rooftop view of "London," we take esthetic pleasure in the richly orchestrated individual sounds, but we must also note the sordid poverty in which so many of those lives are played out. A later urban image anchored in the industrial revolution, George Eliot's "In a London Drawing Room," pessimistically condemns a world of "multiplied identity," in which the "monotony of surface and of form / Without a break to hang a guess upon" produces "one huge prison house and court." The slums of St. Margaret's and St. Giles produce some of Elizabeth Barrett Browning's harshest and bitterest descriptions, not so much of the miasmic conditions, but of human degradation.

Perhaps most important for us is not the particular politics of the moment but the fact that these writers assumed a public, sometimes cosmopolitan voice. They claimed the right to speak on issues of world politics and economic policy. The result is a body of work that often erodes the Romantic esthetic barrier between high art and low, or between the esthetic and the practical. Short lyrics as well as major epics are devoted to political satire rather than more "feminine" private topics.

Yet lyrics about the private world, as we have already seen, engage issues of ideology. Politics penetrates the parlor as well as the parliament. Domesticity can trigger the rebellious laughter of poets who threaten to burn the house down. Domesticity, of course, looks different from the perspective of "domestics." Frances O'Neill's mock epic on two servants, Mr. Kelly and Mrs. Sangster (presumably a self-caricature), violates every convention of decorum and feminine refinement, as tea is poured on the heads of the protagonists. Elizabeth Hands ironically reminds us that some of the women at the tea table may be servants, not consumers, and that they are reduced to silence while the ruling class gossips; tea things are set and removed by hands that are visible only on the title page.[28] Critiques of gender conventions about the separate spheres produced satirical poems on tea parties by Charlotte Nooth, Jane Taylor, and Charlotte Mew. At the same time, many poems hint that teatime gossip itself is closely allied to the masculine genre, satire. Their authors wield penknives as well as teaspoons.

In a poem of feminine "accomplishment," Jane Taylor argues against the production of elegant young women at the expense of "costly materials and capital tools." The economic metaphors in Taylor, Barrett Browning, and May Kendall underscore the distinction between real and false productivity, between "woolwork" or cross-stitch and the vocation to expose public suffering. Taking rebellion to its limit, Augusta Webster's courtesan flees from ices, teas, and social sheep who "baa" hymns, into the dangerous world of men; a "castaway," she herself casts the prim world of bourgeois women aside.

The boundaries between masculine and feminine spheres fade under a comic light with perhaps most startling effect in O'Neill's invocation to a male muse who has satire in his "pregnant pen." With witty diffidence and more familiar gendering, Anna Barbauld calls upon her "domestic Muse" to inspire her "slip-shod measure loosely prattling on" about a washing day. Her mock-heroic housewife, stretched on the rack of accidents (the clothesline snaps, thundershowers threaten), banishes everyone in order to organize the sequence of labor. Seen from the perspective of a child who takes refuge at a grandmother's knee, the mother's work resembles the public sphere of business, not the private one of family. Similarly, Elizabeth Moody invokes an "adventurous muse" to accompany her along the slippery epic path of Homeric feats, to describe how her female hero violently force-feeds and slaughters animals to bring "rebellious food" under control. Ancient manuscripts can authenticate pies as well as poems. Her comic verses ("The Housewife's Prayer," "Sappho Burns Her Books and Cultivates the Culinary Arts," and "The Housewife") celebrate the housewife's toils and vast bounds of "women's knowledge," while it turns presuppositions about domestic tranquillity topsy-turvy.

Comedy, it can be argued, is the domain that gave women most poetic freedom to revise political as well as poetic conventions. In verse that is boldly critical and delicately ironic they subvert the ideological patterns inscribed in lyric conventions—whether those of the elegy, the love poem, or the epic. They regender the voice of the speaker, invert foreground and background figures in received legends, and refuse to stay in their assigned place in the literary hierarchy of genres.

Central to women's effort to expand their poetic repertoire to include public topics was a reassessment of their own roles and possibilities as poets. This self-analysis rested to a large extent on the recognition that their forgotten literary grandmothers had paved the way. Elizabeth Barrett Browning asks the famous question: "England has had many learned women . . . and yet where are the poetesses? . . . I look everywhere for grandmothers and see none."[29] This of course does not mean that she was unaware of women's accomplishments. As a teenager, she had invoked Mme. de Staël along with Comnena as proof of women's capacities. But like Virginia Woolf, who had to drive out the "angel in the house" with her inkpot, she and Christina Rossetti had to combat the oppressive ideals of domestic femininity they found in the work of Felicia Hemans and L.E.L.

Tributes such as Browning's addresses to George Sand mark these women's sense of belonging to a female tradition that they self-consciously worked to create. Mary Robinson catalogued the great women writers of Europe; Barbauld included women in her fifty volume edition of British novelists; and Matilda Betham wrote a *Biographical Dictionary of the Celebrated Women of Every Age and Country* (1804). Charlotte Brontë edited her sisters' work and sketched their brief lives; Alice Meynell edited the works of Barrett Browning, Christina Rossetti, and Jean Ingelow. Matilde Blind composed a biography of George Eliot; Amy Levy wrote an essay on Christina Rossetti; and Agnes Mary Frances Robinson wrote critical studies of Felicia Hemans, Barrett Browning, and Emily Brontë.

Indeed one major contribution of recent critics has been to record women's poetic conversations and quarrels with their literary mothers and grandmothers. As Ellen Moers noted in *Literary Women* (1976), echoes and responses to their contemporaries Mme. de. Staël and George Sand also reverberate through the works of Barrett Browning and other poets. We can now see clearly the strengths that writers like Charlotte Nooth, Jane Taylor, Felicia Hemans, and L.E.L. drew from their encounters with Staël's *Corinne*.[30] Staël and Sand, latter-day Sapphos, crystallized the professional choices that the woman poet confronted. Most obviously, Staël and her heroine Corinne, an improvisationist, stood for the social condemnation of a transgressive woman who rejected confinement in a domestic sphere and chose instead fame as a public poet in Italy.

Set against the sublime ambitions of a Corinne or a Sappho are the more realistic models of creativity that arise from the domestic realm. Joanna Baillie confesses, "Whene'er I aim at heights sublime / Still downward am I called to seek some stubborn rhyme," but she believes that simple words and rugged verses will best avail "to tell my tale." Here on the comic plane of everyday life we find the kitchen Sappho of Elizabeth Moody and the "domestic muse" of Anna Barbauld, who sings in "slipshod measure" of tea tables, lines of linens, and nursing infants. Mary Robinson identifies her muse with a "tuneful puss," who "sings her love song soft, yet mournfully" in a squalid London attic. This unpretentious muse inspired some of the best poetry written by women in the nineteenth century, including *Aurora Leigh*, dedicated to depicting "this live, throbbing age."

For many of these writers, it was a struggle to find their predecessors. Today, it is possible to see links between them as artists that they themselves could not know. Their history necessarily remained incomplete so long as we approached them as their male contemporaries did, foregrounding what was saccharine rather than what was delightfully acid. In the preface to her volume, Elizabeth Moody expressed the fear that her muse might remain "stationary" in a bookseller's shop window before being delivered "(without habeas corpus) to the pastry cooks" to wrap food. The vast majority of the poems in this volume did remain undisturbed for a century, and it was long thought that they contained mere empty puff paste or sugared didacticism. When we open up the page, however, we hear again the lively echoes of women's tuneful laughter, their tearful curses, and their thoughtful questions.

NOTES

1. Optimistically she continues, "many English women have produced such original and beautiful compositions, that the first critics and scholars of the age have wondered, while they applauded." Her shortlist includes among contemporaries herself, Helen Maria Williams, and Charlotte Smith. *Thoughts on the Condition of Women and on the Injustice of Mental Subordination*, 2d ed. (London: Longman, 1799), 95–96.

2. Jurgen Habermas, *The Structural Transformations of the Public Sphere*, tr. Thomas Burger with Frederick Lawrence (Cambridge, MA: MIT Press, 1993), 56.

3. George Dyer, *Poems* (1792), 36–37, cited with disquiet by Richard Polwhele, *The Unsex'd Females: a Poem* (London: Cadell and Davies, 1798), 16–17. Dyer gives as examples "a Macaulay, a Wollstonecraft, a Barbauld, a Jebb, a Williams, a Smith." The more misogynistic Polwhele attacks the "Wollstonecraftians" for their "Gallic frenzy."

4. Reviews by Ralph Griffiths and William Woodfall, cited by Roger Lonsdale in his "Introduction," *Eighteenth-Century Women Poets* (Oxford: Oxford University Press, 1990), xxi, xxxiii.

5. See Anne K. Mellor, *Romanticism and Gender* (New York: Routledge, 1993), 112–13; and Angela Leighton, *Victorian Women Poets: Writing Against the Heart* (Charlottesville: University Press of Virginia, 1992), 26–44.

6. Sarah J. Hale, ed., *The Ladies' Wreath, a Selection from the Female Poetic Writers of England and America . . . Prepared Especially for Young Ladies*, 2d ed. (Boston: Marsh, Capen, Lyon and Webb, 1839); Clara Hall, ed., *The Poetic Garland: A Collection of Pleasing Pieces, for the Instruction and Amusement of Youth* (London: Edward Lacey, [1830?]).

7. Alexander Dyce, ed., *Specimens of the British Poetesses* (London: T. Rodd, 1825), iii; Frederic Rowton, *The Female Poets of Great Britain* (Philadelphia: Carey and Hart, 1849), iv; Mrs. William Sharp, ed., *Women Poets of the Victorian Era* (London: Walter Scott, 1891), xxx–xxxii. Higginson never completed the publication series planned for this collection, now housed at the Boston Public Library, but it became the basis for the "History of Women" microfilm series.

8. George Bethune, ed., *The British Female Poets* (Philadelphia: Lindsay and Blakiston, 1848), iii; Sharp, *Women Poets*, xvii, xxx.

9. Thomas James Mathias, *The Pursuits of Literature, a Satirical Poem*, 13th ed. (London: Becket, 1805), 244.

10. Cited by Lucy Aikin in her "Memoir," *The Works of Anna Laetitia Barbauld* (London: Longman, Hurst, 1825), xviii–xix.

11. Dora Greenwell, *Essays* (London: Strahan, 1866), 26.

12. Both letters quoted in Winifred Gérin, *Charlotte Brontë: The Evolution of Genius* (London: Oxford University Press, 1967), 110–11.

13. *Poems on Several Occasions* (1785), xi; *Essays* (1777), 14, and *Strictures on the Modern System of Female Education* (1799), 30, cited in Lonsdale, "Introduction," xxxv, xl.

14. B. Ifor Evans, *English Poetry in the Later Nineteenth Century*, rev. ed. (London: Methuen, 1966), 352.

15. Edgar A. Poe, "The Philosophy of Composition" (New York, 1984), 19. See Sandra Gilbert and Susan Gubar, *The Madwoman in the Attic* (New Haven: Yale University Press, 1979), 3–44, and Elisabeth Bronfen, *Over Her Dead Body* (New York: Routledge, 1994).

16. On mirror images in women's writings, see Gilbert and Gubar, *Madwoman*, 15–17.

17. Cf. Margaret Homans, *Women Writers and Poetic Identity: Dorothy Wordsworth, Emily Brontë, and Emily Dickinson* (Princeton, NJ: Princeton University Press, 1980); and Susan Levin, *Dorothy Wordsworth & Romanticism* (New Brunswick, NJ: Rutgers State University Press, 1987).

18. Marilyn Butler argues that Darwin himself "uses the paraphernalia of modern learning . . . to unsettle and even unseat what the reader may take for received wisdom." "Culture's Medium: The Role of the Review," in *The Cambridge Companion to British Romanticism*, ed. Stuart Curran (Cambridge: Cambridge University Press, 1993), 129. On footnotes, see Shari Benstock, "At the Margins of Discourse: Footnotes in the Fictional Text," *PMLA* 98 (1983): 204–22.

19. On natural detail and the moral meaning invested by Romantic women poets in the quotidian, see the pathbreaking essay by Stuart Curran, "Romantic Poetry: The I Altered," in *Romanticism and Feminism*, ed. Anne K. Mellor (Bloomington: Indiana University Press, 1988), 185–207.

20. Polwhele, *Unsex'd Females*, 8–9.

21. Landon, *The Poetical Works*, vol. 4 (London: Longman, Orme, 1839), v–vi.

22. Quoted in June Badeni, *The Slender Tree: A Life of Alice Meynell* (Padstow, Cornwall: Tabb House, 1981), 29.

23. *The Poetical Works of Christina Georgina Rossetti* (London: Macmillan, 1928), 58. See Antony H. Harrison, *Christina Rossetti in Context* (Brighton: Harvester, 1988), 157, and Jerome J. McGann, *The Beauty of Inflections: Literary Investigations in Historical Method and Theory* (Oxford: Clarendon, 1985), 244.

24. *Morning Post*, January 31, 1800.

25. Leighton, *Victorian Women Poets*, 211, 229.

26. On the way in which romantic culture was saturated by domestic values, see Susan Wolfson, "Gendering the Soul," and Isobel Armstrong, "The Gush of the Feminine: How Can We Read Women's Poetry of the Romantic Period?" in *Romantic Women Writers: Voices*

and Countervoices, ed. Paula R. Feldman and Theresa M. Kelly (Hanover, NH: University Press of New England, 1995), 13–32, 33–68.

27. Cited in *The Poems of Anna Letitia Barbauld*, ed. William McCarthy and Elizabeth Kraft (Athens: University of Georgia Press, 1994), 310.

28. I am grateful to Katharine Capshaw Smith for this insight.

29. *Letters*, ed. Frederic Kenyon (London, 1898), 1.230.

30. See Ellen Moers, *Literary Women: The Great Writers* (Garden City, NY: Doubleday, 1976); Leighton, *Victorian Women Poets*, 3–34, 88–91; and Isobel Armstrong on women's "expressive tradition" in *Victorian Poetry: Poetry, Poetics, and Politics* (London: Routledge, 1993), 318–77.

Note on the Text

The goal of this edition is to present a readable text rather than preserve all the irregularities of a manuscript or particular edition. Spelling and punctuation have been lightly modernized; where capitalization and italics play a substantive (often satiric) role, they have been preserved. Unstressed vowels elided by the author or printer have been restored.

The textual basis for selection has as a rule been the last edition published in an author's lifetime, or the latest manuscript. Yet, as Susan Levin has pointed out in her study of Dorothy Wordsworth, manuscripts revised by an author who was perplexed by self-doubt or in mental decline may not provide the best text. Where editions differ in significant ways I have indicated these in editorial notes.

Some base texts were printed posthumously. Lucy Aikin wrote that she worked from "corrected copies" her cousin Anna Barbauld prepared from previously printed versions of her work. Posthumous materials pose their own difficulties: neither Emily Brontë's unpunctuated manuscript, nor Charlotte's cut-and-paste version, nor a Victorian edition may be acceptable for a readerly text. In such cases I have compared several editions and noted substantial variants. For George Eliot and Dorothy Wordsworth I have drawn on recently printed editions of manuscripts.

Because the lives of many of these writers were obscure, the dates of composition and of early periodical publication often remain unknown. Where available, the date of composition follows the poem, separated by a slash from the dates of first publication and of any significantly revised edition. Authorial notes appear at the bottom of the page; notes explicating dialect, foreign phrases, and allusions appear at the back of the volume.

Acknowledgments

This volume would not have been possible without the books, suggestions, and help of scholars working on the nineteenth century. Stuart Curran, U. C. Knoepflmacher, Mitzi Myers, Judith Pascoe, Judith Plotz, and Linda Shires have been particularly generous with their time, knowledge, and recommendations. My father, Guy Cardwell, and my colleagues Matthew Bray, Janet Gray, Charles Mahoney, and Jean Marsden shared information and materials with me. Called on for advice, Regina Barreca, Mary Carpenter, Paula Feldman, Susan Levin, and Rajeswari Sunder Rajan encouraged me, as did my editor, Julia Moskin, who recognized the importance of these writers. Diane Cleaver's life was cut off before she could guide this project to completion.

In my search for rare (and often crumbling) books, librarians at the Houghton and Widener libraries of Harvard University, the Boston Public Library, the Beinecke Library of Yale University, and the interlibrary loan office at the University of Connecticut patiently worked to locate what I needed and supplied the plastic cradles that nurse the lives of these books. Throughout, the invaluable Brown University Women Writers Project gave me and my students in exploratory seminars access to reams of poems by little-known writers.

The University of Connecticut Research Foundation and Teaching Institute both supported work on this volume. I also want to thank my students at the University of Connecticut, especially Katharine Rodier, Katharine Capshaw Smith, Katie Girard, Bradley Johnson, Matthew Simpson, Nina Lomando, and Ellen O'Brien. When stacks of photocopies threatened to block the entrance to my office, Kathy and Kate marshaled them into order; they helped me hear poetic measure.

British Women Poets of the 19th Century

Anna Dodsworth

née Barrell (c.1740–1801)

Dodsworth's mother died when she was young; she was educated by her father, Francis Barrell. She began writing verse by 1755, when she composed an elegy on her brother's death at seventeen. A few years later she married Frank Dodsworth, a vicar at Doding-ton in Kent, who described their forty-three years together as "uninterrupted felicity"; they appear to have had no children, but she exchanged lively comic verse with her extended family as well as friends such as the Duchess of Chandos. She also wrote several poems for a prize competition on topics such as "dissipation." She describes herself as "artless, open, and sincere," with a "gaunt form, and lank, long meagre face." After her death, Frank Dodsworth printed her sole volume of poetry, Fugitive Pieces, in 1802 for private distribution only. In the preface, he expressed the fear that the domestic topics that had invited her comic pen were "not likely to engage the attention of the public."

To Matthew Dodsworth, Esq.
On a Noble Captain's Declaring That His Finger Was Broken by a Gate

The tale which I send will, I'm sure, hit your fancy,
Of Sandy the Captain and kitchen-maid Nancy;
The youth, by friend Colin's good liquor made gay,
Met the damsel, and brimful of frolic and play,
He romped with and kissed her, and though he'd his gun,
In vain the poor lassie attempted to run;
She pouted and scolded, and liked not the joke,
And at last, in the struggle, his finger she broke.
Ah! who, my dear brother, would ever believe,
That a swain with a look so demure could deceive?
We ladies, kind creatures, devoid of suspicion,
Were each very ready to play the physician;
By Mackay, his sore finger in spirits was laid,
And a bag, by my orders, was carefully made.

For it neither by one, nor the other was thought
That with Nancy, instead of a gate he had fought.
But now the poor maiden has told us the truth,
As we cannot ourselves have a laugh at the youth;
We entreat that from us, you the hero would tell,
In his frolics he ne'er should forget to bribe well;   20
For had but his kisses been seasoned with gold,
How he got his lame finger—had never been told.

                                                    1802

Badinage

On Recovering from a Bad Fit of Sickness at Bath, July 1794

When I first went to Bath it was thought I should die;
So the maidens and widows determined to try
To console my poor husband, should that be the case,
By showing he soon might get one in my place;
And as nothing had made me so loathe to quit life
As knowing how truly he'd miss his old wife,
I was pleased to behold them exert all their wit,
The friendship of good Mr. Dodsworth to get.
The first who began was my friend Mrs. H——,
Who desired, when I was not disposed for a jolt,   10
She in landaulet open might sit by his side,
As of all men with him she delighted to ride:
So up hill and down hill they trotted together
In spite of the dust and the heat of the weather.
The pleasing, polite, and the gay widow N——,
His equipage praised, and thought no one drove so well;
And though up the hills she quite trembled to go,
If he'd take her no symptoms of fear would she show;
But should strive all she could to enliven his mind,
And make him forget, he'd a sick wife confined.   20
A lady, who oft had been civil before,
Was quite grieved to behold me afflicted so sore;
And though I declared that I nothing could eat,
Insisted we'd come and partake of her meat;
She'd give me a chick—Mr. D. beef and wine—
Whenever we'd do her the favor to dine;
Her ladyship's meaning, I plainly could see,
Was, if Death that grim tyrant should seize upon me,
For herself or her daughter to gain Mr. D.
Mrs. T——, whose charms he in youth had oft sung,   30
And who thought she'd a chance to obtain him when young,
As he came to her brother's by night and by day,

And seemed happy with her to laugh, prattle and play,
Was in hopes, though at that time her art had proved vain,
As a partner for life the dear man to obtain,
If wise heaven decreed, I from earth should depart,
That the love he once felt might revive in his heart:
So she came every day, with a "How do you do?"
And flattered herself that her hopes would prove true.
Mrs. G——pronounced Mr. D. a good man,   40
And her sisters, dear creatures! adopted her plan;
They protested they thought him of husbands the best,
And that I was a wife, of all wives the most blessed.
If of parting the pangs I was doomed to endure,
As they'd all make good mates I was perfectly sure,
I felt I could die quite contented indeed,
Were I certain that one to my place would succeed.
The way which they took to accomplish their end,
Was by earnestly begging a doctor to send;
To this I unwillingly gave my consent,   50
So themselves they must blame if the deed they repent:
For instead of destroying (strange is it to tell),
The doctor at once made me hearty and well;
And my husband, God bless and preserve his dear life!
Is, I know, so attached to his queer, odd, old wife,
That so long as I live, I can ne'er be afraid,
Of his being caressed by wife, widow, or maid.

1794 / 1802

Anna Laetitia Barbauld

née Aikin (1743–1825)

Niece of the poet Anne Hunter and daughter of a Dissenting schoolmaster in the circle of Joseph Priestley, Anna Aikin was trained by her father and his colleagues in classics and modern languages. Her first volume, Poems *(1773), was reprinted five times by 1777. In 1774 she married Rochemont Barbauld, a Nonconformist clergyman, who suffered from an increasingly violent mental disease that eventually forced his confinement and ended with suicide in 1808. When the marriage proved childless, they adopted one of her nephews. Samuel Johnson lamented the waste of her talents on "small beer" when she and her husband founded a boys' school, but her work led to publication of her influential* Lessons for Children *(1778) and finely lyrical* Hymns in Prose for Children *(1781). Her brother, John Aikin, encouraged her to write, and her circle of literary friends included the Bluestocking group, Joanna Baillie, and later the Edgeworths, Scott, Wordsworth, and Coleridge.*

Like many of her contemporaries, she made poetry part of her friendships, using it to celebrate a gift or to teasingly refer to a chess game. At the same time, she aimed at serious pedagogical and political ends. An enlightened radical and abolitionist, she wrote on slavery in her Epistle to William Wilberforce *(1791). She opposed the Continental wars in* Sins of the Government, Sins of the Nation *(1793), as well as in her most important political poem,* Eighteen Hundred and Eleven *(1812). This satiric prophesy that imperialist Britain was on the brink of decline was denounced by hostile reviewers as "unpatriotic." Southey in the* Quarterly Review *complained about her dashing down her knitting needles to compose a pamphlet in verse: "We had hoped that the empire might have been saved without the intervention of a lady-author." Richard Polwhele likewise regretted that she had on occasion abandoned her "chaste and elegant" vein for politics. In 1810, she launched* The British Novelists, *eventually comprising fifty volumes, prefaced by an essay, "The Origin and Progress of Novel Writing." She edited works of Akenside, Collins, and Richardson, and in 1811 a selection of prose and poetry for girls,* The Female Speaker.

Religious hymns and political polemic mingle with descriptive and witty verses in her work. An early poem "in praise of old maids" did not save her from Mary Woll-

stonecraft's critique of later lines affirming that a lady's "sweetest empire is—to please."
To Elizabeth Montagu, Barbauld wrote that "the thefts of knowledge in our sex are only
connived at while carefully concealed"; she was convinced that "to have a too great fond-
ness for books is little favorable to the happiness of a woman." S. T. Coleridge mocked
"bare Bald" in his lecture on Milton and notes to the Rime of the Ancient Mariner,
but the variety of her voices elicited the admiration of Fanny Burney, William
Wordsworth, Mary Robinson, Henry Crabb Robinson, Leigh Hunt, and Walter Savage
Landor. According to Crabb Robinson, Wordsworth called her "the first of our literary
women"; Maria Edgeworth praised her "melancholy elegance and force of thought."*

The Rights of Woman

Yes, injured Woman! rise, assert thy right!
Woman! too long degraded, scorned, oppressed;
O born to rule in partial Law's despite,
Resume thy native empire o'er the breast!

Go forth arrayed in panoply divine;   5
That angel pureness which admits no stain;
Go, bid proud Man his boasted rule resign,
And kiss the golden specter of thy reign.

Go, gird thyself with grace; collect thy store
Of bright artillery glancing from afar;   10
Soft melting tones thy thundering cannon's roar,
Blushes and fears thy magazine of war.

Thy rights are empire: urge no meaner claim—
Felt, not defined, and if debated, lost;
Like sacred mysteries, which withheld from fame,   15
Shunning discussion, are revered the most.

Try all that wit and art suggest to bend
Of thy imperial foe the stubborn knee;
Make treacherous Man thy subject, not thy friend;
Thou mayst command, but never canst be free.   20

Awe the licentious and restrain the rude;
Soften the sullen, clear the cloudy brow:
Be, more than princes' gifts, thy favors sued—
She hazards all, who will the least allow.

But hope not, courted idol of mankind,   25
On this proud eminence secure to stay;
Subduing and subdued, thou soon shalt find
Thy coldness soften, and thy pride give way.

Then, then, abandon each ambitious thought,
Conquest or rule thy heart shall feebly move,   30

In Nature's school, by her soft maxims taught,
That separate rights are lost in mutual love.

1792 / 1825

To a Little Invisible Being
Who Is Expected Soon to Become Visible

Germ of new life, whose powers expanding slow
For many a moon their full perfection wait,
Haste, precious pledge of happy love, to go
Auspicious borne through life's mysterious gate.

What powers lie folded in thy curious frame—
Senses from objects locked and mind from thought!
How little canst thou guess thy lofty claim
To grasp at all the worlds the Almighty wrought!

And see, the genial season's warmth to share,
Fresh younglings shoot, and opening roses glow!   10
Swarms of new life exulting fill the air—
Haste, infant bud of being, haste to blow!

For thee the nurse prepares her lulling songs,
The eager matrons count the lingering day;
But far the most thy anxious parent longs
On thy soft cheek a mother's kiss to lay.

She only asks to lay her burden down,
That her glad arms that burden may resume;
And nature's sharpest pangs her wishes crown,
That free thee living from thy living tomb.   20

She longs to fold to her maternal breast
Part of herself, yet to herself unknown;
To see and to salute the stranger guest,
Fed with her life through many a tedious moon.

Come, reap thy rich inheritance of love!
Bask in the fondness of a mother's eye!
Nor wit nor eloquence her heart shall move
Like the first accents of thy feeble cry.

Haste, little captive, burst thy prison doors!
Launch on the living world, and spring to light!   30
Nature for thee displays her various stores,
Opens her thousand inlets of delight.

If charmed verse or muttered prayers had power,
With favoring spells to speed thee on thy way,

Anxious I'd bid my beads each passing hour,
Till thy wished smile thy mother's pangs o'erpay.

C.1795 / 1825

Washing Day

and their voice,
Turning again towards childish treble, pipes
And whistles in its sound.

The Muses are turned gossips; they have lost
The buskined step, and clear high-sounding phrase,
Language of gods. Come then, domestic Muse,
In slipshod measure loosely prattling on
Of farm or orchard, pleasant curds and cream,
Or drowning flies, or shoe lost in the mire
By little whimpering boy, with rueful face;
Come, Muse, and sing the dreaded Washing Day.
Ye who beneath the yoke of wedlock bend,
With bowed soul, full well ye ken the day   10
Which week, smooth sliding after week, brings on
Too soon—for to that day nor peace belongs
Nor comfort; ere the first gray streak of dawn,
The red-armed washers come and chase repose.
Nor pleasant smile, nor quaint device of mirth,
E'er visited that day: the very cat,
From the wet kitchen scared and reeking hearth,
Visits the parlor—an unwonted guest.
The silent breakfast-meal is soon dispatched;
Uninterrupted, save by anxious looks   20
Cast at the lowering sky, if sky should lower.
From that last evil, O preserve us, heavens!
For should the skies pour down, adieu to all
Remains of quiet: then expect to hear
Of sad disasters—dirt and gravel stains
Hard to efface, and loaded lines at once
Snapped short—and linen-horse by dog thrown down,
And all the petty miseries of life.
Saints have been calm while stretched upon the rack,
And Guatimozin smiled on burning coals;   30
But never yet did housewife notable
Greet with a smile a rainy washing day.
—But grant the welkin fair, require not thou
Who call'st thyself perchance the master there,
Or study swept, or nicely dusted coat,

Or usual 'tendance; ask not, indiscreet,
Thy stockings mended, though the yawning rents
Gape wide as Erebus; nor hope to find
Some snug recess impervious: shouldst thou try
The 'customed garden walks, thine eye shall rue   40
The budding fragrance of thy tender shrubs,
Myrtle or rose, all crushed beneath the weight
Of coarse checked apron, with impatient hand
Twitched off when showers impend; or crossing lines
Shall mar thy musings, as the wet cold sheet
Flaps in thy face abrupt. Woe to the friend
Whose evil stars have urged him forth to claim
On such a day the hospitable rites!
Looks, blank at best, and stinted courtesy,
Shall he receive. Vainly he feeds his hopes   50
With dinner of roast chicken, savory pie,
Or tart or pudding—pudding he nor tart
That day shall eat; nor, though the husband try,
Mending what can't be helped, to kindle mirth
From cheer deficient, shall his consort's brow
Clear up propitious—the unlucky guest
In silence dines, and early slinks away.
I well remember, when a child, the awe
This day struck into me; for then the maids,
I scarce knew why, looked cross, and drove me from them: 60
Nor soft caress could I obtain, nor hope
Usual indulgencies; jelly or creams,
Relic of costly suppers, and set by
For me, their petted one; or buttered toast,
When butter was forbid; or thrilling tale
Of ghost or witch, or murder—so I went
And sheltered me beside the parlor fire:
There my dear grandmother, eldest of forms,
Tended the little ones, and watched from harm,
Anxiously fond, though oft her spectacles   70
With elfin cunning hid, and oft the pins
Drawn from her ravelled stocking, might have soured
One less indulgent. . . .
At intervals my mother's voice was heard,
Urging dispatch: briskly the work went on,
All hands employed to wash, to rinse, to wring,
To fold, and starch, and clap, and iron, and plait.
Then would I sit me down and ponder much
Why washings were. Sometimes through hollow bowl
Of pipe amused we blew, and sent aloft   80
The floating bubbles; little dreaming then

To see, Mongolfier, thy silken ball
Ride buoyant through the clouds—so near approach
The sports of children and the toils of men.
Earth, air, and sky, and ocean, hath its bubbles,
And verse is one of them—this most of all.

1797

To Mr. S. T. Coleridge
1797

Midway the hill of science, after steep
And rugged paths that tire the unpracticed feet,
A grove extends; in tangled mazes wrought,
And filled with strange enchantment: dubious shapes
Flit through dim glades, and lure the eager foot
Of youthful ardor to eternal chase.
Dreams hang on every leaf: unearthly forms
Glide through the gloom; and mystic visions swim
Before the cheated sense. Athwart the mists,
Far into vacant space, huge shadows stretch,   10
And seem realities; while things of life,
Obvious to sight and touch, all glowing round,
Fade to the hue of shadows—Scruples here,
With filmy net, most like the autumnal webs
Of floating gossamer, arrest the foot
Of generous enterprise and palsy hope
And fair ambition with the chilling touch
Of sickly hesitation and blank fear.
Nor seldom Indolence these lawns among
Fixes her turf-built seat and wears the garb   20
Of deep philosophy, and museful sits,
In dreamy twilight of the vacant mind,
Soothed by the whispering shade; for soothing soft
The shades and vistas lengthening into air,
With moonbeam rainbows tinted. . . . Here each mind
Of finer mold, acute and delicate,
In its high progress to eternal truth
Rests for a space, in fairy bowers entranced;
And loves the softened light and tender gloom;
And, pampered with most unsubstantial food,   30
Looks down indignant on the grosser world,
And matter's cumbrous shapings. Youth beloved
Of Science—of the Muse beloved—not here,
Not in the maze of metaphysic lore,
Build thou thy place of resting! Lightly tread

The dangerous ground, on noble aims intent;
And be this Circe of the studious cell
Enjoyed, but still subservient. Active scenes
Shall soon with healthful spirit brace thy mind;
And fair exertion, for bright fame sustained,   40
For friends, for country, chase each spleen-fed fog
That blots the wide creation.
Now Heaven conduct thee with a parent's love!

1797 / 1799

The Caterpillar

No, helpless thing, I cannot harm thee now;
Depart in peace, thy little life is safe,
For I have scanned thy form with curious eye,
Noted the silver line that streaks thy back,
The azure and the orange that divide
Thy velvet sides; thee, houseless wanderer,
My garment has enfolded, and my arm
Felt the light pressure of thy hairy feet;
Thou hast curled round my finger; from its tip—
Precipitous descent!—with stretched out neck,   10
Bending thy head in airy vacancy,
This way and that, inquiring, thou hast seemed
To ask protection; now, I cannot kill thee.
Yet I have sworn perdition to thy race,
And recent from the slaughter am I come
Of tribes and embryo nations: I have sought
With sharpened eye and persecuting zeal,
Where, folded in their silken webs they lay
Thriving and happy; swept them from the tree
And crushed whole families beneath my foot;   20
Or, sudden, poured on their devoted heads
The vials of destruction. This I've done,
Nor felt the touch of pity; but when thou—
A single wretch, escaped the general doom,
Making me feel and clearly recognize
Thine individual existence, life,
And fellowship of sense with all that breathes—
Present'st thyself before me, I relent,
And cannot hurt thy weakness. So the storm
Of horrid war, o'erwhelming cities, fields,   30
And peaceful villages, rolls dreadful on:
The victor shouts triumphant; he enjoys
The roar of cannon and the clang of arms,

And urges, by no soft relentings stopped,
The work of death and carnage. Yet should one,
A single sufferer from the field escaped,
Panting and pale, and bleeding at his feet,
Lift his imploring eyes—the hero weeps;
He is grown human, and capricious Pity,
Which would not stir for thousands, melts for one   40
With sympathy spontaneous: 'Tis not Virtue,
Yet 'tis the weakness of a virtuous mind.

                                          1816 / 1825

Eighteen Hundred and Eleven

Still the loud death drum, thundering from afar,
O'er the vexed nations pours the storm of war:
To the stern call still Britain bends her ear,
Feeds the fierce strife, the alternate hope and fear;
Bravely, though vainly, dares to strive with fate,
And seeks by turns to prop each sinking state.
Colossal power with overwhelming force
Bears down each fort of Freedom in its course;
Prostrate she lies beneath the despot's sway,
While the hushed nations curse him—and obey.   10

Bounteous in vain, with frantic man at strife,
Glad Nature pours the means—the joys of life;
In vain with orange-blossoms scents the gale,
The hills with olives clothes, with corn the vale;
Man calls to Famine, nor invokes in vain,
Disease and Rapine follow in her train;
The tramp of marching hosts disturbs the plow,
The sword, not sickle, reaps the harvest now,
And where the soldier gleans the scant supply,
The helpless peasant but retires to die;   20
No laws his hut from licensed outrage shield,
And war's least horror is the ensanguined field.

Fruitful in vain, the matron counts with pride
The blooming youths that grace her honored side;
No son returns to press her widowed hand,
Her fallen blossoms strew a foreign strand.
Fruitful in vain, she boasts her virgin race,
Whom cultured arts adorn and gentlest grace;
Defrauded of its homage, beauty mourns,
And the rose withers on its virgin thorns.   30
Frequent, some stream obscure, some uncouth name,

By deeds of blood is lifted into fame;
Oft o'er the daily page some soft one bends
To learn the fate of husband, brothers, friends,
Or the spread map with anxious eye explores,
Its dotted boundaries and penciled shores,
Asks where the spot that wrecked her bliss is found,
And learns its name but to detest the sound.

And think'st thou, Britain, still to sit at ease,
An island queen amidst thy subject seas,   40
While the vexed billows, in their distant roar,
But soothe thy slumbers, and but kiss thy shore?
To sport in wars, while danger keeps aloof,
Thy grassy turf unbruised by hostile hoof?
So sing thy flatterers—but, Britain, know,
Thou who hast shared the guilt must share the woe.
Nor distant is the hour; low murmurs spread,
And whispered fears, creating what they dread;
Ruin, as with an earthquake shock, is here,
There, the heart-witherings of unuttered fear,   50
And that sad death, whence most affection bleeds,
Which sickness, only of the soul, precedes.
Thy baseless wealth dissolves in air away,
Like mists that melt before the morning ray:
No more on crowded mart or busy street
Friends, meeting friends, with cheerful hurry greet;
Sad, on the ground thy princely merchants bend
Their altered looks, and evil days portend,
And fold their arms, and watch with anxious breast
The tempest blackening in the distant west.   60

Yes, thou must droop; thy Midas dream is o'er;
The golden tide of commerce leaves thy shore,
Leaves thee to prove the alternate ills that haunt,
Enfeebling luxury and ghastly want;
Leaves thee, perhaps, to visit distant lands,
And deal the gifts of Heaven with equal hands.

Yet, O my country, name beloved, revered,
By every tie that binds the soul endeared,
Whose image to my infant senses came
Mixed with religion's light and freedom's holy flame!   70
If prayers may not avert, if 'tis thy fate
To rank amongst the names that once were great,
Not like the dim, cold Crescent shalt thou fade,
Thy debt to science and the muse unpaid;
Thine are the laws surrounding states revere,

Thine the full harvest of the mental year,
Thine the bright stars in glory's sky that shine,
And arts that make it life to live are thine.
If westward streams the light that leaves thy shores,
Still from thy lamp the streaming radiance pours. 80
Wide spreads thy race from Ganges to the pole,
O'er half the western world thy accents roll:
Nations beyond the Appalachian hills
Thy hand has planted and thy spirit fills:
Soon as their gradual progress shall impart
The finer sense of morals and of art,
Thy stores of knowledge the new states shall know,
And think thy thoughts, and with thy fancy glow;
Thy Lockes, thy Paleys shall instruct their youth,
Thy leading star direct their search for truth; 90
Beneath the spreading platan's tent-like shade,
Or by Missouri's rushing waters laid,
"Old father Thames" shall be the poet's theme,
Of Hagley's woods the enamored virgin dream,
And Milton's tones the raptured ear enthrall,
Mixed with the roaring of Niagara's fall;
In Thomson's glass the ingenuous youth shall learn
A fairer face of Nature to discern;
Nor of the bards that swept the British lyre
Shall fade one laurel, or one note expire. 100
Then, loved Joanna, to admiring eyes
Thy storied groups in scenic pomp shall rise;
Their high-souled strains and Shakespeare's noble rage
Shall with alternate passion shake the stage.
Some youthful Basil from thy moral lay
With stricter hand his fond desires shall sway;
Some Ethwald, as the fleeting shadows pass,
Start at his likeness in the mystic glass;
The tragic muse resume her just control,
With pity and with terror purge the soul, 110
While wide o'er transatlantic realms thy name
Shall live in light, and gather all its fame.

Where wanders Fancy down the lapse of years
Shedding o'er imaged woes untimely tears?
Fond moody power! as hopes—as fears prevail,
She longs, or dreads, to lift the awful veil;
On visions of delight now loves to dwell;
Now hears the shriek of woe or freedom's knell:
Perhaps, she says, long ages passed away,
And set in western waves our closing day, 120

Night, Gothic night, again may shade the plains
Where Power is seated, and where Science reigns;
England, the seat of arts, be only known
By the gray ruin and the moldering stone;
That time may tear the garland from her brow,
And Europe sit in dust, as Asia now.

Yet then the ingenuous youth whom Fancy fires
With pictured glories of illustrious sires,
With duteous zeal their pilgrimage shall take
From the Blue Mountains, or Ontario's lake,   130
With fond adoring steps to press the sod
By statesmen, sages, poets, heroes trod;
On Isis' banks to draw inspiring air,
From Runnymede to send the patriot's prayer;
In pensive thought, where Cam's slow waters wind,
To meet those shades that ruled the realms of mind;
In silent halls to sculptured marbles bow,
And hang fresh wreaths round Newton's awful brow.
Oft shall they seek some peasant's homely shed,
Who toils, unconscious of the mighty dead,   140
To ask where Avon's winding waters stray,
And thence a knot of wildflowers bear away;
Anxious inquire where Clarkson, friend of man,
Or all-accomplished Jones his race began;
If of the modest mansion aught remains
Where heaven and nature prompted Cowper's strains;
Where Roscoe, to whose patriot breast belong
The Roman virtue and the Tuscan song,
Led Ceres to the black and barren moor
Where Ceres never gained a wreath before.[1]   150
With curious search their pilgrim steps shall rove
By many a ruined tower and proud alcove,
Shall listen for those strains that soothed of yore
Thy rock, stern Skiddaw, and thy fall, Lodore;
Feast with Dun Edin's classic brow their sight,
And "visit Melross by the pale moonlight."

But who their mingled feelings shall pursue
When London's faded glories rise to view?
The mighty city, which by every road
In floods of people poured itself abroad;   160
Ungirt by walls, irregularly great,

---

1. The historian of the age of Leo [William Roscoe] has brought into cultivation the extensive tract of Chat Moss.

No jealous drawbridge, and no closing gate;
Whose merchants (such the state which commerce brings)
Sent forth their mandates to dependent kings;
Streets, where the turbaned Moslem, bearded Jew,
And woolly Afric met the brown Hindu;
Where through each vein spontaneous plenty flowed,
Where Wealth enjoyed, and Charity bestowed.
Pensive and thoughtful shall the wanderers greet
Each splendid square and still, untrodden street;   170
Or of some crumbling turret mined by time,
The broken stairs with perilous step shall climb,
Thence stretch their view the wide horizon round,
By scattered hamlets trace its ancient bound,
And, choked no more with fleets, fair Thames survey
Through reeds and sedge pursue his idle way.

With throbbing bosoms shall the wanderers tread
The hallowed mansions of the silent dead,
Shall enter the long aisle and vaulted dome
Where genius and where valor find a home;   180
Awe-struck, midst chill sepulchral marbles breathe,
Where all above is still, as all beneath;
Bend at each antique shrine and frequent turn
To clasp with fond delight some sculptured urn,
The ponderous mass of Johnson's form to greet,
Or breathe the prayer at Howard's sainted feet.

Perhaps some Briton, in whose musing mind
Those ages live which time has cast behind,
To every spot shall lead his wondering guests
On whose known site the beam of glory rests: 190
Here Chatham's eloquence in thunder broke,
Here Fox persuaded, or here Garrick spoke;
Shall boast how Nelson, fame and death in view,
To wonted victory led his ardent crew,
In England's name enforced, with loftiest tone,[2]
Their duty—and too well fulfilled his own:
How gallant Moore,[3] as ebbing life dissolved,
But hoped his country had his fame absolved.
Or call up sages whose capacious mind
Left in its course a track of light behind;   200
Point where mute crowds on Davy's lips reposed,
And Nature's coyest secrets were disclosed;

2. Every reader will recollect the sublime telegraphic dispatch, "England expects every
man to do his duty."
3. "I hope England will be satisfied" were the last words of General Moore.

Join with their Franklin, Priestley's injured name,
Whom, then, each continent shall proudly claim.

Oft shall the strangers turn their eager feet
The rich remains of ancient art to greet,
The pictured walls with critic eye explore,
And Reynolds be what Raphael was before.
On spoils from every clime their eyes shall gaze,
Egyptian granites and the Etruscan vase;   210
And when midst fallen London they survey
The stone where Alexander's ashes lay,
Shall own with humbled pride the lesson just
By Time's slow finger written in the dust.

There walks a Spirit o'er the peopled earth,
Secret his progress is, unknown his birth;
Moody and viewless as the changing wind,
No force arrests his foot, no chains can bind;
Where'er he turns, the human brute awakes,
And, roused to better life, his sordid hut forsakes: 220
He thinks, he reasons, glows with purer fires,
Feels finer wants, and burns with new desires:
Obedient Nature follows where he leads;
The steaming marsh is changed to fruitful meads;
The beasts retire from man's asserted reign,
And prove his kingdom was not given in vain.
Then from its bed is drawn the ponderous ore,
Then Commerce pours her gifts on every shore,
Then Babel's towers and terraced gardens rise,
And pointed obelisks invade the skies;   230
The prince commands, in Tyrian purple dressed,
And Egypt's virgins weave the linen vest.
Then spans the graceful arch the roaring tide,
And stricter bounds the cultured fields divide.
Then kindles fancy, then expands the heart,
Then blow the flowers of genius and of art;
Saints, heroes, sages, who the land adorn,
Seem rather to descend than to be born;
Whilst History, midst the rolls consigned to fame,
With pen of adamant inscribes their name.   240

The Genius now forsakes the favored shore,
And hates, capricious, what he loved before;
Then empires fall to dust, then arts decay,
And wasted realms enfeebled despots sway;
Even Nature's changed; without his fostering smile
Ophir no gold, no plenty yields the Nile;

The thirsty sand absorbs the useless rill,
And spotted plagues from putrid fens distill.
In desert solitudes then Tadmor sleeps,
Stern Marius then o'er fallen Carthage weeps; 250
Then with enthusiast love the pilgrim roves
To seek his footsteps in forsaken groves,
Explores the fractured arch, the ruined tower,
Those limbs disjointed of gigantic power;
Still at each step he dreads the adder's sting,
The Arab's javelin, or the tiger's spring;
With doubtful caution treads the echoing ground,
And asks where Troy or Babylon is found.

And now the vagrant Power no more detains
The vale of Tempe, or Ausonian plains; 260
Northward he throws the animating ray,
O'er Celtic nations bursts the mental day:
And, as some playful child the mirror turns,
Now here now there the moving luster burns;
Now o'er his changeful fancy more prevail
Batavia's dykes than Arno's purple vale,
And stinted suns, and rivers bound with frost,
Than Enna's plains or Baia's viny coast;
Venice the Adriatic weds in vain,
And Death sits brooding o'er Campania's plain; 270
O'er Baltic shores and through Hercynian groves,
Stirring the soul, the mighty impulse moves;
Art plies his tools, and Commerce spreads her sail,
And wealth is wafted in each shifting gale.
The sons of Odin tread on Persian looms,
And Odin's daughters breathe distilled perfumes;
Loud minstrel bards, in gothic halls, rehearse
The runic rhyme, and "build the lofty verse":
The muse, whose liquid notes were wont to swell
To the soft breathings of the Æolian shell, 280
Submits, reluctant, to the harsher tone,
And scarce believes the altered voice her own.
And now, where Cæsar saw with proud disdain
The wattled hut and skin of azure stain,
Corinthian columns rear their graceful forms,
And light verandas brave the wintry storms,
While British tongues the fading fame prolong
Of Tully's eloquence and Maro's song.
Where once Bonduca whirled the scythed car,
And the fierce matrons raised the shriek of war, 290
Light forms beneath transparent muslins float,

And tutored voices swell the artful note.
Light-leaved acacias and the shady plane
And spreading cedar grace the woodland reign;
While crystal walls the tenderer plants confine,
The fragrant orange and the nectared pine;
The Syrian grape there hangs her rich festoons,
Nor asks for purer air, or brighter noons:
Science and Art urge on the useful toil,
New mold a climate and create the soil,   300
Subdue the rigor of the northern Bear,
O'er polar climes shed aromatic air,
On yielding Nature urge their new demands,
And ask not gifts but tribute at her hands.

London exults—on London Art bestows
Her summer ices and her winter rose;
Gems of the East her mural crown adorn,
And Plenty at her feet pours forth her horn;
While even the exiles her just laws disclaim,
People a continent, and build a name: 310
August she sits, and with extended hands
Holds forth the book of life to distant lands.

But fairest flowers expand but to decay;
The worm is in thy core, thy glories pass away;
Arts, arms, and wealth destroy the fruits they bring;
Commerce, like beauty, knows no second spring.
Crime walks thy streets, fraud earns her unblessed bread,
O'er want and woe thy gorgeous robe is spread,
And angel charities in vain oppose:
With grandeur's growth the mass of misery grows. 320
For see—to other climes the Genius soars,
He turns from Europe's desolated shores;
And lo, even now, midst mountains wrapt in storm,
On Andes' heights he shrouds his awful form;
On Chimborazo's summits treads sublime,
Measuring in lofty thought the march of time;
Sudden he calls: " 'Tis now the hour!" he cries,
Spreads his broad hand, and bids the nations rise.
La Plata hears amidst her torrents' roar;
Potosi hears it, as she digs the ore: 330
Ardent, the Genius fans the noble strife,
And pours through feeble souls a higher life,
Shouts to the mingled tribes from sea to sea,
And swears—Thy world, Columbus, shall be free.

1812

The First Fire
October 1st, 1815

Ha, old acquaintance! many a month has past
Since last I viewed thy ruddy face; and I,
Shame on me! had mean time well nigh forgot
That such a friend existed. Welcome now!—
When summer suns ride high, and tepid airs
Dissolve in leasing languor; then indeed
We think thee needless, and in wanton pride
Mock at thy grim attire and sooty jaws,
And breath sulphurous, generating spleen,
As Frenchmen say—Frenchmen, who never knew   10
The sober comforts of a good coal fire.

—Let me imbibe thy warmth, and spread myself
Before thy shrine adoring—magnet thou
Of strong attraction, daily gathering in
Friends, brethren, kinsmen, variously dispersed,
All the dear charities of social life,
To thy close circle. Here a man might stand,
And say, This is my world! Who would not bleed
Rather than see thy violated hearth
Pressed by a hostile foot? The winds sing shrill;   20
Heap on the fuel! Not the costly board,
Nor sparkling glass, nor wit, nor music, cheer
Without thy aid. If thrifty thou dispense
Thy gladdening influence, in the chill salon
The silent shrug declares the unpleased guest.

—How grateful to belated traveler
Homeward returning, to behold the blaze
From cottage window, rendering visible
The cheerful scene within! There sits the sire,
Whose wicker chair, in sunniest nook enshrined,   30
His age's privilege—a privilege for which
Age gladly yields up all precedence else
In gay and bustling scenes—supports his limbs.
Cherished by thee, he feels the grateful warmth
Creep through his feeble frame and thaw the ice
Of fourscore years, and thoughts of youth arise.

—Nor less the young ones press within, to see
Thy face delighted, and with husk of nuts,
Or crackling holly, or the gummy pine,
Feed thy immortal hunger: cheaply pleased   40
They gaze delighted, while the leaping flames

Dart like an adder's tongue upon their prey;
Or touch with lighted reed thy wreaths of smoke;
Or listen, while the matron sage remarks
Thy bright blue scorching flame and aspect clear,
Denoting frosty skies. Thus pass the hours,
While Winter spends without his idle rage.

—Companion of the solitary man,
From gayer scenes withheld! With thee he sits,
Converses, moralizes; musing asks   50
How many eras of uncounted time
Have rolled away since thy black unctuous food
Was green with vegetative life, and what
This planet then: or marks, in sprightlier mood,
Thy flickering smiles play round the illumined room,
And fancies gay discourse, life, motion, mirth,
And half forgets he is a lonely creature.

—Nor less the bashful poet loves to sit
Snug, at the midnight hour, with only thee
Of his lone musings conscious. Oft he writes,   60
And blots, and writes again; and oft, by fits,
Gazes intent with eyes of vacancy
On thy bright face; and still at intervals,
Dreading the critic's scorn, to thee commits,
Sole confidant and safe, his fancies crude.

—O wretched he, with bolts and massy bars
In narrow cell immured, whose green damp walls,
That weep unwholesome dews, have never felt
Thy purifying influence! Sad he sits
Day after day, till in his youthful limbs   70
Life stagnates, and the hue of hope is fled
From his wan cheek.

                          —And scarce less wretched he—
When wintry winds blow loud and frosts bite keen—
The dweller of the clay-built tenement,
Poverty-struck, who, heartless, strives to raise
From sullen turf, or stick plucked from the hedge,
The short-lived blaze; while chill around him spreads
The dreary fen, and Ague, sallow-faced,
Stares through the broken pane. Assist him, ye
On whose warm roofs the sun of plenty shines,   80
And feel a glow beyond material fire!

1815 / 1825

Fragment

As the poor schoolboy, when the slow-paced months
Have brought vacation times, and one by one
His playmates and companions all are fled
Or ready; and to him—to him alone—
No summons comes; he left of all the train
Paces with lingering step the vacant halls,
No longer murmuring with the Muse's song,
And silent playground scattered wide around
With implements of sports, resounding once
With cheerful shouts; and hears no sound of wheels   10
To bear him to his father's bosom home;
For, conscious though he be of time misspent,
And heedless faults and much amiss, yet hopes
A father's pardon and a father's smile
Blessing his glad return. . . . Thus I
Look to the hour when I shall follow those
That are at rest before me.

1823 / 1825

ELIZABETH MOODY

née Greenly (d. 1814)

Probably born before 1750, Elizabeth Greenly married Christopher Moody, vicar of Turnham Green, and like her husband contributed notices of fiction to the Monthly Review *between 1789 and 1808. One of her earliest poems carries a date of 1760; others were published anonymously in the 1780s and 1790s. Her early mentor was the minor poet Edward Lovibond, whose work her husband also knew; apparently under Lovibond's tutelage she studied Dante, Petrarch, Tasso, and the satirist Aretino, lines from whose poetry provided several of her epigraphs. Her verse was collected with fresh contributions in* Poetic Trifles *(1798). Her preface notes that "this is no period favorable to the Muse," since war sharpens the pen "to make it like a two-edged sword." Contemporary politics informs several of her pieces, including a poem on Marie Antoinette, "Anna's Complaint, or The Miseries of War" (1796), "Thoughts on War and Peace," "To the New Year, 1796," and "Speeches in the French Convention." She was praised for the ingenuity and wit of mock heroics she wrote in the voice of a kitchen Sappho.*

To Dr. Darwin
On Reading His Loves of the Plants

No bard e'er gave his tuneful powers,
Thus to traduce the fame of flowers,
Till Darwin sung his gossip tales
Of females wooed by *twenty* males;
Of *plants* so given to amorous pleasure;
Incontinent beyond all measure.
He sings that in botanic schools,
Husbands[1] adopt licentious rules;
Plurality of wives they wed,
And all they like—they take to bed;
That lovers sigh with *secret* love,
And marriage rites clandestine prove;

1. See classes of Flowers, Polygamy, Clandestine Marriage, etc.

That fanned in groves their mutual fire,
They to some Gretna *Green* retire.

Linnaeus things no doubt revealed,
Which prudent *plants* would wish concealed;
So free of *families* he spoke,
As must that modest race provoke.
Till he invaded Flora's bowers
None heard of marriage among flowers;   20
Sexual distinctions were unknown,
Discovered by the Swede alone.
He blabbed through all the listening groves
The mystic rites of *flowery loves*.
He pried in every blossom's fold,
And all he saw unseemly—told.
Blabbed tales of many a *feeble* swain,[2]
Unmeet to join in Flora's train;
Unless appointed by her care,
Like Turkish guards to watch the fair.   30
These *vegetable monsters* claim
Alliance with the eunuch's name.
In every herb and tree that grows,
Some frail propensity he shows.

But then in prose Linnaeus prattles,
And soon forgot is all he tattles.
While memory better pleased retains,
The frolics of poetic brains.

So when the Muse with strains like thine
Enchantment breathes through every line,   40
That Reason pausing makes a stand,
Controlled by Fiction's magic hand,
Enamored we the verse pursue,
And feel each fair delusion true.

Luxuriant thought thy mind o'ergrows;
Such painting from thy pencil flows;
Warm to my sight the visions rise,
And thy rich fancy mine supplies.
Thy themes rehearsing in my bower,
From those I picture every flower;   50
With thy descriptive forms impressed,
I see them in thy colors dressed;
Remembering all thy lays unfold,
The snow-drop *freezes* me with *cold*.

2. See class Vegetable Monsters and Eunuchs.

I hear the *love-sick* violet's sighs,
And see the hare-bell's *azure eyes*.
See *jealous cowslips* hang their heads,
And *virgin lilies*—pine in beds.[3]
The primrose meets my tinctured view,
Far paler than before—she grew.   60
While woodbines *wanton* seem to twine,
And reeling shoots the *maudlin*[4] vine.

If e'er I seek the *cypress* shade,
Whose branches contemplation aid,
Of learned lore my thoughts possessed
Might dwell on mummies in a chest.
Unperishable chests, 'tis said,
Where the Egyptian dead were laid
Are of the cypress timber made.
And gates of Rome's famed church, they say,   70
Defying moldering time's decay,
From Constantine to Pope Eugene,
Eleven hundred years were seen
In perfect state of sound and good,
Formed of this adamantine wood.
Then, DARWIN! were it not for thee,
I sure must venerate this tree.
But as his boughs hang o'er my head,
I recollect from you I read
His wife he exiles from his bed.[5]   80

Since thus thy fascinating art
So takes possession of the heart,
Go bid thy Muse a wreath prepare

3. How snow-drops cold and blue-eyed hare-bells blend
Their tender tears as o'er the stream they bend;
The love-sick violet and the primrose pale
Bow their sweet heads and whisper to the gale.

With secret sighs the virgin lily droops,
And jealous cowslips hang their tawny cups
                    —Darwin's *Loves of the Plants*
4. "Drink deep, sweet youths," seductive Vitis cries,
The maudlin tear-drop glittering in her eyes.
                                        —Darwin
5. Cupressus dark disdains his dusky bride,
One dome contains them—but *two* beds divide.
                                        —Darwin

"To bind some charming Chloe's hair,"
But tune no more thy lyre's sweet powers
To libel harmless trees and flowers.

1798

The Distempered Muse

At the foot of Parnassus a bard was complaining
   His Muse much disease did endure;
That a rickety babe she had been from her training,
   And no permanent aid could procure.

Great critical doctors this parent had tried,
   For this Muse was the child of his heart;
And these often wished in her youth she had died,
   As her maladies baffled their art.

But empirics and quacks among critics are found,
   As well as in medical schools;   10
They insisted that *she* at the bottom was sound,
   And might trust for relief from *their rules*.

Then remedies various by turns were applied,
   Till so *feeble* at length she was grown,
Whenever she *moved* for assistance she cried,
   Not able to *stand* when *alone*.

The poet now heard of a doctor of verse,
   So famed in poetical cases
His art could the Muse's worst humors disperse,
   And of Pegasus temper the paces.   20

When his rod of correction he took in his hand,
   The bands of Apollo withdrew;
Not the *boldest* of metaphors this could withstand,
   Whole legions of figures it slew.

To this doctor the poet with ardor repairs,
   On his skill for success he depends;
"It is you, Sir," he cries, "can dispel all my cares,
   Fair renown on your counsel attends.

"My Muse has attempted so crazy a flight,
   No limits her fury could bound;   30
She has soared to the clouds beyond all mortal sight,
   And is *lost* from not knowing her ground.

"With Minerva herself she dares run such a race
   (For though lame she is swift as the wind)

Nor wisdom nor rhyme can keep up with her pace,
  They come lagging and limping behind.

"In labyrinths of ethics she wanders *unseen*;
  There perplexed and perplexing she strays;
No mortal can tell what her *rambles* would mean,
  Or find any clue to her *maze*."   40

The doctor looked grave, and his gestures betrayed
  He suspected a desperate case.
"Had your Muse sooner sought my assistance," he
      said,
  "She had never encountered disgrace.

"This vial containing a drop from the skies
  I caught ere it fell to the ground,
Of essence celestial the nostrum I prize,
  Since a balm for all ills it is found.

"Take this then, *poor poet*, with confidence take it,
  I here a specific dispense;   50
Important the use is of which you may make it,
  And the name it is known by, is SENSE.

"Those vapors of fancy that fly to the brain,
  And with empty conceits swell the mind,
If this be applied will ne'er rise again
  But will vanish like smoke before wind.

"This the flower of Parnassus will show from the weed,
  Which sometimes grows close to her side;
This, the Muse will instruct how to manage her steed,
  And when timid or boldly to ride.   60

"In this dip your pen when resolving to write,
  It will quench all the poet's false fires;
It will chase those delusions that dazzle the sight,
  And will tell when true genius inspires."

                                                            1798

To the New Year, 1796
Who Made His First Appearance
When the Weather Was Uncommonly Fine

Gentle stranger kindly smiling,
Cheat us not with looks beguiling;
Be these smiles that now appear,
Propitious to the infant year.

Features mark thy newborn face,
Tempered with a milder grace
Than those thy grandsires wont to show,
Frowning with threatening clouds of snow.

It seems as if with Taurus playing,
Already thou had'st been "a-maying,"   10
Disdaining Winter's rugged bed,
By sullen Capricornus led.

For see, the impatient violet springs,
Nor waits for Zephyr's tardy wings;
The meadows still are clothed in green,
Their russet garments yet unseen.

E'en birds frequent accustomed groves,
And meditate on future loves;
Prepare to quit their state supine,
And practise songs for Valentine.   20

Not such thy parent's wayward birth:
Hard icy shackles bound the earth,
Bleak Boreas nipped the infant grain,
And famine loitered in his train.

Mars in the ascendant shook his spear,
Prophetic of the slaughtering year;
While Winter aided savage war,
And drove the fury in her car.

Around he waved his iron hand,
Extending frost through every land.   30
By snow transformed each level stream
Did like an Alpine mountain seem.

But most terrific was his power,
And most disastrous was the hour
When, forging these obdurate chains,
He bade them fetter hostile plains.

To Belgium's climes he gave command,
And bade the waters form a land;
Bade ice restrain the friendly tide,
Where peaceful currents foes divide.   40

The pitying rivers now no more
Protection give the affrighted shore;
Their hardened bosoms now sustain
The fury of the ensanguined plain.

Each stream bedyed with crimson hue
Brings the Egyptian flood to view,
While all around the carnage spread,
And earth and waters groan with dead.

Be then abhorred thy parent's name!
Let annals blot his guilty fame!   50
O may his direful scenes be o'er,
And like his hours—return no more!

Come thou with blessings in thy hand;
Distinguish this my native land;
Let Heaven-born Ceres wait thy reign,
And plenty bring her stores again.

Yet let not patriot love confine
My prayers within a circle's line;
To every clime thy smiles extend,
And every mourner's sorrows end.   60

O come with virtue from the skies,
And bid a golden age arise;
Bid universal discord cease,
And charm the jarring world to peace.

1798

The Housewife's Prayer
On the Morning Preceding a Fête

To Economy

Goddess adored! who gained my early love
And formed my mind thy precepts to improve;
Taught me to practice each penurious rule
And made my heart a pupil of thy school;
Taught me that waste is an atrocious sin
And bade me cull from dust the scattered *pin*:
Remembering this thy maxim to revere:
"One pin a day collects a groat a year."
Thou value stamp'st on every rag I wear,
And show'st that patchwork makes an elbow chair;   10
Bid'st me respect the dyer's useful trade
That gives new being to my old brocade,
Restores my Persian to its pristine hue,
Or makes my faded red celestial blue.
Source of my health thy indurating power,
Inspired by thee I brave the threatening shower;

Nor seek defense against the winter's wind,
But scorn the cloak with costly ermine lined.
Let the blue current stagnate in my veins
And age come on with all his rheums and pains: 20
Nor hood nor bonnet will I deign to wear,
Nor aught that Nature will consent to spare;
In these privations still adoring thee,
All-*saving* Power! divine Economy!
This night impart thy parsimonious grace
To all that wasteful tribe, the vassal race;
Vouchsafe protection to each sacred hoard,
And grant no lavish hand profane my board.
Infuse thy spirit in the chosen fair
Ordained the tea and coffee to prepare;   30
May she distribute both with frugal hand,
And patient let the *brewing* teapot stand!
May blundering John his careless steps control
And heed the frailty of the china bowl!
Cakes, lemonade, orgeat, do thou defend!
And guard, O Goddess, guard each candle's *end*!

1798

Sappho Burns Her Books and
Cultivates the Culinary Arts

Companions of my favorite hours,
By winter's fire, in summer's bowers,
That wont to chase my bosom's care
And plant your pleasing visions there!
Guarini, Dante, honored names,
Ah, doomed to feed devouring flames!
Alas, my Petrarch's gentle loves!
My Tasso's rich enchanted groves!
My Ariosto's fairy dreams,
And all my loved Italian themes!   10
I saw you on the pile expire,
Weeping I saw the invading fire;
There fixed remained my aching sight,
Till the last ray of parting light
The last pale flame consumed away,
And all dissolved—your relics lay.

Goddess of Culinary Art,
Now take possession of my heart!
Teach me more winning arts to try,

To salt the ham, to mix the pie;   20
To make the paste both light and thin,
To smooth it with the rolling-pin;
With taper skewer to print it round,
Lest ruder touch the surface wound.
Then teach thy votary how to make
That fair rotundo—a plum cake;
To shake the compound sweets together,
To bake it light as any feather,
That when complete its form may show
A rising hillock topped with snow;   30
And how to make the cheesecake, say,
To beat the eggs and turn the whey;
To strain my jelly fair and clear,
That there no *misty fog* appear,
But plain to view each form may rise
That in its glassy bosom lies.

Now fancy soars to future times,
When all extinct are Sappho's rhymes;
When none but cooks applaud her name,
And naught but recipes her fame;   40
When sweetest numbers she'll despise,
When Pope shall sing beneath *minced pies*,
And Eloise in her *tin* shall mourn
Disastrous fate and love forlorn;
Achilles too, that godlike man,
Shall bluster in the *patty-pan*;
And many a once-loved Grecian chief
Shall guard from flames the roasting beef.

Then, when this transformation's made,
And Sappho's vestments speak her *trade*;   50
When girt in towels she is seen,
With cuffs to keep the elbows clean:
Then, Sorceress, she'll call on thee!
Accomplish thou thy fair decree!
If, like your sisters of the heath,
Whose mystic sound betrayed Macbeth,
Fallacious charms your arts dispense,
To cheat her with ambiguous sense;
Severest torments may you prove!—
Severest—disappointed love.   60

1798

The Housewife

Or, The Muse Learning to Ride the Great Horse Heroic

Addressed to Lysander

O Thou that with deciding voice oft sways
The doubtful wanderings of the adventurous Muse,
And oft directs her wavering feet where best
To tread, whether to climb the steep Parnassian
Mount—that slippery path where Numbers slide
And fall—or tread with firmer step Prosaic
Ground—accept this verse! And should the Muse
All insufficient to so new a theme
Fail in her song—if not thy smile, at least
Thy patience give! And with unruffled face,   10
Stern critic furrows banished from thy brow,
Attend her flight through regions sacred
To domestic use, where she, guided by truth,
In search of that fair nymph Economy,
Must now explore—and quit for these, the more
Inviting paths of fiction—her once loved
Haunts, where she was wont to cull poetic
Sweets, and lure thy fancy to more pleasing dreams.

Now when the sun in Sagittarius rides,
And Morn, her dusky brow in misty vapors   20
Clad, with lingering beams unfolds reluctant
Day—e'en though the awful monitor of time
Proclaims the seventh hour; yet sleep his drowsy
Poppies waves o'er all the house, and wraps
The *snoring* maids in gossip dreams, of *sweet*
Hearts, *shows*, and *fairs*!—all but the wakeful Housewife!
She late and early plies her busy cares
And preparation makes for Christmas cheer.

Before the dawn emits one ray of light,
Forth from her couch she springs; her pregnant mind   30
Alert: for *she* has things of great concern
In view. Sleep on ye idle fair! ye time
Destroyers! who live to dress, and flaunt,
And flirt, and waste your silly lives 'mid scenes
Of dissipation! This useful maid to deeds
Of more importance gives her day and scorns
The dainty modes of polished indolence.

In garb of russet brown and round-eared cap,
With bib and apron of an azure hue,
And bunch of pendant keys that graced her side,   40

Which *she* by thrifty rules of prudence warned
Ne'er from her side would trust, for she was versed
In tricks of *vassal-kind*, and knew full well
That those whom we mistaking *honest* call
Are oft disloyal to the faith they owe
And swerve from their allegiance—tempted
By paltry gains of little price! Thus with
Her economic ensigns decked—say, Muse!
If thou wilt deign to aid so mean a song?
And thou hast not disdained to sing in days   50
Of yore of culinary arts—both when
The beauteous Mother of mankind regaled
Her Angel guest, and from sweet kernels pressed
The dulcet creams—and when the Grecian chiefs
Reserved a portion of the victim slain,
And Agamemnon helped to *roast the beef*.
Say then where first the Housewife bends her steps!
Whether to that sequestered pile, where the cool
Dairy, guarded from summer's noontide beams
Stands in a grove retired? Or to the bright   60
Illumined Kitchen, whose chimney issuing
Furious smoke denotes the approaching feast
And fills the passing traveler, I ween,
With many a hungry thought? These, and
Departments many more than these, each in their
Turn, will her attendance claim—for method
And due order ruled her ways; but prisoners
Kept for luxury's repast, require their food
As soon as morning breaks—and haply if not
Fed—would pine and *die*, which *she*, I trust,   70
A sore mischance would deem. Her visitation
First to these she pays, and to the Poultry
Court with speed repairs. There, nourished by
Violence and cruel art, a group of feathered
Monsters round her stand, misshapen *fowls*,
With *maws protuberant*! There the crammed turkey
Groans beneath her care, and loathes the hand that
Ministers to life. *She*, calm spectatress
Of the woes she makes, repeats her barbarous
Task; down each reluctant throat the food   80
She thrusts, then with discerning and unpitying
Eye inspects their bulk—blows the light feathers
From their snowy breasts—proclaims their fitness
For the circling spit, and signs the warrant
That shall end their pains. The Dairy next demands
Her frugal care. There from the surface of the

Richest milk, the cream she skims; this with due
Labor and unwearied toil she *churns*, till
To a firm consistence it is wrought, and *bears*
The name of *Butter*. Then with some light   90
Fantastic mold the tiny pats she prints,
And in a china vase, filled with clear water
From pellucid spring, her workmanship deposits.

    Now with the nimble step of busy haste
She to the storeroom turns her active feet,
To the known manuscript of ancient fame,
Where from a copious line of eating ancestors
Are culled a hoard of choice receipts, and where
In Grandam spelling of no modern date
Recorded stands full many a dainty   100
Culinary art, she turns the *time-worn* page
To find that celebrated *pie*, which from the
Season takes its honored name. Then on the board
With noisy din the savory meat she chops,
And in some vessel fit blends the ingredients.
Spice odoriferous, and luscious plums,
With moistening juice of apple, extracted
From the golden rinds of fairest fruit, then
With that potent spirit, sought on Gallia's
Shore, whose power medicinal from indigestion   110
Guards rebellious food—the dangerous *mass*
She tempers, and in the patty pans and
Pliant paste, in circling folds envelops.
Cakes too she fashioned of fantastic forms,
Oblong, round, and square; some in the diamond's
Shape compressed—some in the heart's; some from the
Coriander seed their flavor take—some from
The plum—*cakes* of all names! Pound, saffron, lemon,
Orange—and those far famed for sweet delicious
Taste, that from the fair Salopia take their   120
Name. High above the rest majestic stood,
In size preeminent, with sugared top,
Graced by a royal pair, and studded o'er
With choice confection of the citron's fruit,
That mirth-inspiring *cake* all *children* hail,
When on Twelfth–tide they meet, with festive glee,
And dance and song, and sportive tricks to close
The gambols—time-honored gambols of the Christmas scene!

    What more this busy active dame performed,
In the *next Canto* shall the Muse rehearse.   130
The Housewife's toils an ample theme supply,

Returning toils that rise with every sun.
O days of Albion! happier far I ween,
When Woman's knowledge owned its boundary *here*!

1798

CHARLOTTE SMITH

née Turner (1749–1806)

❧

Orphaned at three by the death of her mother, Charlotte Smith was raised in comfort, formally educated, and taught landscape painting as well as other artistic accomplishments. When her father decided to remarry in 1765, she "unconsciously plunged" into a ruinous marriage (at fifteen) to Benjamin Smith, the dissolute son of a wealthy West Indian merchant and director of the East India Company. To her sister she wrote, "The more my mind expanded, the more I became sensible of personal slavery." She worked as accountant in her father-in-law's shipping firm; her poem "To My Lyre" embeds a rich commercial vocabulary drawn from this experience. During his lifetime, her father-in-law kept the family afloat. When he died in 1776, however, the trust he had drawn up to protect his grandchildren from his son's profligacy created a legal snarl that was not untangled for nearly four decades, leaving little for the surviving heirs.

By December 1783, the couple were imprisoned for debt; after their release several months later, Benjamin's further imprudence forced Charlotte to flee from creditors by taking her growing family to France. Eight of her twelve children survived, and she was forced to find employment; although she separated from her husband in 1787 she continued to support him, becoming "the slave of the Booksellers." While still in Marshalsea debtors' prison in 1784 she printed the first volume of Elegiac Sonnets, and Other Essays; its success led to eight expanded editions subscribed to by the Wartons, Horace Walpole, Cowper, and Charles James Fox. Jane West, Bowles, and Coleridge were among those who imitated her infusion of pathos into descriptions of nature. Readers have identified her with the morose voice of many of these poems ("frequent allusions to her own melancholy story"), forgetting that a number are spoken in the persona of Goethe's Werther, or invert the gender of Petrarch's rejected lover. Wordsworth, who sought a letter of introduction from her to Helen Maria Williams when on his way to Paris, wrote that English verse was "under greater obligations" to her work than were likely to be either acknowledged or remembered. She was, however, translated into French and Italian.

In supporting her family, even more important than poetry were her ten novels, starting with the gothic Emmeline, the Orphan of the Castle (1788) and Ethelinde, or The Recluse of the Lake (1789), followed by the more political Desmond (1792) *and* The Old Manor House *(1793), which was admired by Scott; she received an average of £50 a volume. Sympathetic at first to the French Revolution, she veered to a more conservative position in response to the Terror, as recorded in her blank verse epic* The Emigrants *(1793) as well as in her novels and other poems. Her third son, Charles, lost a leg at Dunkirk in 1793; she deprecated "the horrors of war" waged for "senseless ambition." Her fiction attacks lawyers, the laws of inheritance, and arranged marriages. Like her sister, Catherine Ann Dorset, she wrote books for children:* Conversations Introducing Poetry *(1804) and* The History of Birds *(1807). She also translated the Abbé Prévost's* Manon Lescaut *(1785) and* The Romance of Real Life *(1787), based on French criminal trials. A play,* Who Is She?, *was never performed.*

By 1800 an edition of her sonnets had grown from twenty to ninety poems in two volumes. The full range of Smith's powers is most apparent in her posthumous volume, Beachy Head, with Other Poems *(1807), whose title poem is a blank verse epic that redefines the function of solitary meditation in Romantic poetry. Scott praised the "sweet and sad effusions" of her poetry, while Wordsworth, who borrowed phrasing from her, praised her "true feeling for rural nature." Her close observation, attributed by Stuart Curran to her myopia, supports her depiction of a teeming natural world into which the human speaker is folded.*

Sonnet 44
From Elegiac Sonnets

Written in the Churchyard at Middleton in Sussex[1]

Pressed by the moon, mute arbitress of tides,
    While the loud equinox its power combines,
    The sea no more its swelling surge confines,
But o'er the shrinking land sublimely rides.
The wild blast, rising from the western cave,
    Drives the huge billows from their heaving bed,
    Tears from their grassy tombs the village dead,
And breaks the silent sabbath of the grave!
With shells and seaweed mingled, on the shore
Lo! their bones whiten in the frequent wave;   10
    But vain to them the winds and waters rave;
They hear the warring element no more:
While I am doomed—by life's long storm oppressed,
To gaze with envy on their gloomy rest.

1789

1. Middleton is a village on the margin of the sea, in Sussex, containing only two or three houses. There were formerly several acres of ground between its small church and the sea, which now, by its continual encroachments, approaches within a few feet of this half-ruined and humble edifice. The wall, which once surrounded the churchyard, is entirely swept away, many of the graves broken up, and the remains of bodies interred washed into the sea: whence human bones are found among the sand and shingles on the shore.

Thirty-eight

ADDRESSED TO MRS. H——Y

In early youth's unclouded scene,
The brilliant morning of eighteen,
With health and sprightly joy elate
   We gazed on youth's enchanting spring,
   Nor thought how quickly time would bring
The mournful period—*thirty-eight*!

Then the starch maid, or matron sage,
Already of the sober age,
We viewed with mingled scorn and hate;
   In whose sharp words, or sharper face,   10
   With thoughtless mirth we loved to trace
The sad effects of—*thirty-eight*!

Till, saddening, sickening at the view,
We learned to dread what time might do;
And then preferred a prayer to fate
   To end our days ere that arrived,
   When (power and pleasure long survived)
We meet neglect and—*thirty-eight*!

But time, in spite of wishes, flies;
And fate our simple prayer denies,   20
And bids us death's own hour await!
   The auburn locks are mixed with gray,
   The transient roses fade away,
But reason comes at—*thirty-eight*!

Her voice the anguish contradicts
That dying vanity inflicts;
Her hand new pleasures can create,
   For us she opens to the view
   Prospect less bright—but far more true,
And bids us smile at—*thirty-eight*!   30

No more shall scandal's breath destroy
The social converse we enjoy
With bard or critic, *tête à tête*—
   O'er youth's bright blooms her blight shall pour,
   But spare the improving, friendly hour
Which science gives at—*thirty-eight*!

Stripped of their gaudy hues by truth,
We view the glittering toys of youth,
And blush to think how poor the bait
   For which to public scenes we ran,   40

And scorned of sober sense the plan
Which gives content at—*thirty-eight*!

Though time's inexorable sway
Has torn the myrtle bands away,
For other wreaths 'tis not too late:
   The amaranth's purple glow survives,
   And still Minerva's olive thrives
On the calm brow of—*thirty-eight*!

With eye more steady we engage
To contemplate approaching age,   50
And life more justly estimate;
   With firmer souls and stronger powers,
   With reason, faith, and friendship ours,
   We'll not regret the stealing hours
That lead from *thirty-* even to *forty-eight*!

1788 / 1791

Sonnet 83: The Sea View

From Elegiac Sonnets

The upland shepherd, as reclined he lies[1]
   On the soft turf that clothes the mountain brow,
Marks the bright sea-line mingling with the skies;
   Or from his course celestial, sinking slow,
   The summer sun in purple radiance low,
Blaze on the western waters; the wide scene
   Magnificent, and tranquil, seems to spread
Even o'er the rustic's breast a joy serene,
   When, like dark plague-spots by the demons shed,
Charged deep with death, upon the waves, far seen,   10
   Move the war-freighted ships; and fierce and red
   Flash their destructive fires. The mangled dead
And dying victims then pollute the flood.
Ah! thus man spoils Heaven's glorious works with blood!

1797

1. Suggested by the recollection of having seen, some years since, on a beautiful evening of summer, an engagement between two armed ships, from the high down called the Beacon Hill, near Brighthelmstone.

Apostrophe to an Old Tree[1]

Where thy broad branches brave the bitter North,
Like rugged, indigent, unheeded worth,
Lo! Vegetation's guardian hands emboss
Each giant limb with fronds of studded moss,[2]
Clothing the bark with many a fringèd fold
Begemmed with scarlet shields and cups of gold,
Which to the wildest winds their webs oppose,
And mock the arrowy sleet or weltering snows.

But to the warmer *West* the woodbine[3] fair
With tassels that perfumed the summer air,   10
The mantling clematis, whose feathery bowers
Waved in festoons with nightshade's[4] purple flowers,
The silver weed,[5] whose corded fillets wove
Round thy pale rind, even as deceitful love
Of mercenary beauty would engage
The dotard fondness of decrepit age;
All these, that during summer's halcyon days
With their green canopies concealed thy sprays,
Are gone forever; or disfigured, trail
Their sallow relics in the autumnal gale;   20
Or o'er thy roots, in faded fragments tossed,
But tell of happier hours, and sweetness lost!

Thus in fate's trying hour, when furious storms
Strip social life of pleasure's fragile forms,
And awful *Justice*, as his rightful prey
Tears Luxury's silk and jeweled robe away,
While reads *Adversity* her lesson stern,

1. The philosophy of these few lines may not be very correct, since mosses are known to injure the stems and branches of trees to which they adhere; but the images of Poetry cannot always be exactly adjusted to objects of Natural History.

2. The foliage, if it may be so called, of this race of plants, is termed fronds, and their flowers, or fructification, assume the shapes of cups and shields; of those of this description, more particularly adhering to trees, [are] *Lichen pulmonarius*, lungwort lichen, with *shields*; the *Lichen caperatus*, with red cups; and many others which it would look like pedantry to enumerate.

3. The woodbine and the clematis are well known plants, ornamenting our hedgerows in summer with fragrant flowers.

4. *Solanum lignosum.* Woody nightshade is one of the most beautiful of its tribe.

5. The silver weed, *Convolvulus major* (Raii Syn. 275) or greater bindweed, which, however the beauty of the flowers may enliven the garden or the wilds, is so prejudicial to the gardener and farmer that it is seen by them with dislike equal to the difficulty of extirpating it from the soil. Its cord-like stalks, plaited together, can hardly be forced from the branches round which they have twined themselves.

And *Fortune's* minions tremble as they learn;
The crowds around her gilded car that hung,
Bent the lithe knee, and trolled the honeyed tongue,   30
Desponding fall, or fly in pale despair;
And *Scorn* alone remembers that they were.
Not so *Integrity*; unchanged he lives
In the rude armor conscious honor gives,
And dares with hardy front the troubled sky,
In Honesty's uninjured panoply.
Ne'er on Prosperity's enfeebling bed
Or rosy pillows he reposed his head,
But given to useful arts, his ardent mind
Has sought the general welfare of mankind;   40
To mitigate *their* ills his greatest bliss,
While studying *them*, has taught him *what he is*;
He, when the human tempest rages worst,
And the earth shudders as the thunders burst,
Firm, as thy northern branch, is rooted fast,
And if he can't *avert*, endures the blast.

                                          1800

The Heath

Even the wide heath, where the unequal ground
Has never on its rugged surface felt
The hand of industry, though wild and rough,
Is not without its beauty; here the furze,[1]
Enriched among its spines, with golden flowers
Scents the keen air; while all its thorny groups
Wide scattered o'er the waste are full of life;
For 'midst its yellow-bloom, the assembled chats[2]
Wave high the tremulous wing, and with shrill notes,
But clear and pleasant, cheer the extensive heath.   10
Linnets in numerous flocks frequent it too,
And bashful, hiding in these scenes remote
From his congeners (they who make the woods
And the thick copses echo to their song),
The heath-thrush makes his domicile; and while
His patient mate with downy bosom warms

---

1. *Ulex.* It is in some countries called gorse, in others whin. It is sometimes sown for fences, and to make coverts for the protection of game; but is naturally produced on heaths and waste grounds. There is a dwarf sort of it—it is sometimes chopped small and given to horses to eat, and is cut and stacked up, to burn lime with.

2. Whin chats, *Motacilla rubetra*; stone chats, *Motacilla rubicola*.

Their future nestlings, he his love lay sings
Loud to the shaggy wild—
               the Erica[3] here,
That o'er the Caledonian hills sublime
Spreads its dark mantle (where the bees delight   20
To seek their purest honey), flourishes,
Sometimes with bells like amethysts, and then
Paler, and shaded like the maiden's cheek
With gradual blushes; otherwhile, as white
As rime that hangs upon the frozen spray.
Of this, old Scotia's hardy mountaineers
Their rustic couches form, and there enjoy
Sleep, which beneath his velvet canopy
Luxurious idleness implores in vain!
Between the matted heath and ragged gorse   30
Wind natural walks of turf, as short and fine
As clothe the chalky downs; and there the sheep
Under some thorny bush, or where the fern
Lends a light shadow from the Sun, resort
And ruminate or feed; and frequent there
Nourished by evening mists, the mushroom[4] spreads
From a small ivory bulb, his circular roof,
The fairies' fabled board—

              Poor is the soil,
And of the plants that clothe it few possess
Succulent moisture; yet a parasite   40
Clings even to them; for its entangling stalk
The wire-like dodder[5] winds, and nourishes,
Rootless itself, its small white flowers on them.
So to the most unhappy of our race
Those on whom never prosperous hour has smiled;
Towards whom Nature as a step-dame stern
Has cruelly dealt; and whom the world rejects,
To these forlorn ones, ever there adheres
Some self-consoling passion; round their hearts
Some vanity entwines itself, and hides,   50

3. Common heath, *Erica vulgaris*; cross-leaved heath, *Erica tetralix*; fine-leaved heath, *Erica cenerea*. Of these last there are varieties, pink, blush colour, and white. Cornish heath, *Erica*, is found only, I believe, in that county.

4. *Fungus Agaric.* Of these there is an infinite variety, but one only is usually eaten in England. Though the Italians, French, and more particularly the Russians consider as very excellent food many Funguses which we think unwholesome and turn from with disgust. It is certain, however, that several of them are of a poisonous quality.

5. *Cuscuta.* There are of this plant two sorts, the greater and lesser dodder. It supports itself on the sap of the plant to which it adheres.

And is perhaps in mercy given to hide,
The mortifying sad realities
Of their hard lot.

1804

To My Lyre

Such as thou art, my faithful lyre,
For all the great and wise admire,
  Believe me, I would not exchange thee,
Since e'en adversity could never
Thee from my anguished bosom sever,
  Or time or sorrow e'er estrange thee.

Far from my native fields removed,
From all I valued, all I loved;
  By early sorrows soon beset,
Annoyed and wearied past endurance,   10
With drawbacks, bottomry, insurance,
  With samples drawn, and tare and tret;

With scrip, and omnium, and consols,
With city feasts and Lord Mayors' balls,
  Scenes that to me no joy afforded;
For all the anxious sons of care,
From Bishopsgate to Temple Bar,
  To my young eyes seemed gross and sordid.

Proud city dames, with loud shrill clacks,
"The wealth of nations on their backs,"   20
  Their clumsy daughters and their nieces,
Good sort of people! and well-meaners,
But they could not be my congeners,
  For I was of a different species.

Long were thy gentle accents drowned,
Till from the Bow-bells' detested sound
  I bore thee far, my darling treasure;
And unrepining left for thee
Both calipash and calipee,
  And sought green fields, pure air, and leisure.   30

Who that has heard thy silver tones—
Who that the Muse's influence owns,
  Can at my fond attachment wonder,
That still my heart should own thy power?
Thou—who hast soothed each adverse hour,
  So thou and I will never sunder.

In cheerless solitude, bereft
Of youth and health, thou still art left,
   When hope and fortune have deceived me:
Thou, far unlike the summer friend,   40
Did still my faltering steps attend,
   And with thy plaintive voice relieved me.

And as the time ere long must come
When I lie silent in the tomb,
   Thou wilt preserve these mournful pages;
For gentle minds will love my verse,
And pity shall my strains rehearse,
   And tell my name to distant ages.

1807

Beachy Head

On thy stupendous summit, rock sublime!
That o'er the channel reared, halfway at sea
The mariner at early morning hails,[1]
I would recline; while fancy should go forth,
And represent the strange and awful hour
Of vast concussion[2] when the Omnipotent
Stretched forth his arm and rent the solid hills,
Bidding the impetuous main flood rush between
The rifted shores, and from the continent
Eternally divided this green isle.   10
Imperial lord of the high southern coast!
From thy projecting headland I would mark
Far in the east the shades of night disperse,
Melting and thinned, as from the dark blue wave
Emerging, brilliant rays of arrowy light
Dart from the horizon; when the glorious sun
Just lifts above it his resplendent orb.
Advances now, with feathery silver touched,
The rippling tide of flood; glisten the sands,
While, inmates of the chalky clefts that scar   20
Thy sides precipitous, with shrill harsh cry,

1. In crossing the Channel from the coast of France, Beachy Head is the first land made.
2. Alluding to an idea that this island was once joined to the continent of Europe, and torn from it by some convulsion of nature. I confess I never could trace the resemblance between the two countries. Yet the cliffs about Dieppe resemble the chalk cliffs on the southern coast. But Normandy has no likeness whatever to the part of England opposite to it.

Their white wings glancing in the level beam,
The terns, and gulls, and tarrocks, seek their food,[3]
And thy rough hollows echo to the voice
Of the gray choughs,[4] and ever restless daws,
With clamor not unlike the chiding hounds,
While the lone shepherd and his baying dog
Drive to thy turfy crest his bleating flock.

The high meridian of the day is past,
And ocean now, reflecting the calm heaven,   30
Is of cerulean hue, and murmurs low
The tide of ebb upon the level sands.
The sloop, her angular canvas shifting still,
Catches the light and variable airs
That but a little crisp the summer sea,
Dimpling its tranquil surface.

                        Afar off,
And just emerging from the arch immense
Where seem to part the elements, a fleet
Of fishing vessels stretch their lesser sails;
While more remote, and like a dubious spot   40
Just hanging in the horizon, laden deep,
The ship of commerce richly freighted makes
Her slower progress on her distant voyage,
Bound to the orient climates, where the sun
Matures the spice within its odorous shell,
And, rivaling the gray worm's filmy toil,
Bursts from its pod the vegetable down,[5]
Which, in long turbaned wreaths, from torrid heat
Defends the brows of Asia's countless castes.
There the earth hides within her glowing breast   50
The beamy adamant,[6] and the round pearl
Enchased in rugged covering, which the slave,
With perilous and breathless toil, tears off
From the rough sea-rock, deep beneath the waves.
These are the toys of nature and her sport
Of little estimate in reason's eye:
And they who reason, with abhorrence see

---

3. Terns: *Sterna hirundo*, or sea swallow; gulls: *Larus canus*; tarrocks: *Larus tridactylus*.

4. *Corvus Graculus*, Cornish choughs, or, as these birds are called by the Sussex people, saddle-backed crows, build in great numbers on this coast.

5. *Gossypium herbaceum*.

6. Diamonds, the hardest and most valuable of precious stones. For the extraordinary exertions of the Indians in diving for the pearl oysters, see the account of the pearl fisheries in Percival's *View of Ceylon*.

Man for such gauds and baubles violate
The sacred freedom of his fellow man—
Erroneous estimate! As Heaven's pure air,   60
Fresh as it blows on this aerial height,
Or sound of seas upon the stony strand,
Or inland, the gay harmony of birds,
And winds that wander in the leafy woods
Are to the unadulterate taste more worth
Than the elaborate harmony, brought out
From fretted stop, or modulated airs
Of vocal science. So the brightest gems,
Glancing resplendent on the regal crown,
Or trembling in the highborn beauty's ear,   70
Are poor and paltry to the lovely light
Of the fair star that as the day declines
Attendent on her queen, the crescent moon,
Bathes her bright tresses in the eastern wave.
For now the sun is verging to the sea,
And as he westward sinks, the floating clouds
Suspended move upon the evening gale,
And gathering round his orb, as if to shade
The insufferable brightness, they resign
Their gauzy whiteness; and more warmed, assume   80
All hues of purple. There, transparent gold
Mingles with ruby tints, and sapphire gleams,
And colors, such as nature through her works
Shows only in the ethereal canopy.
Thither aspiring fancy fondly soars,
Wandering sublime through visionary vales,
Where bright pavilions rise, and trophies, fanned
By airs celestial; and adorned with wreaths
Of flowers that bloom amid elysian bowers.
Now bright, and brighter still the colors glow,   90
Till half the lustrous orb within the flood
Seems to retire: the flood reflecting still
Its splendor, and in mimic glory dressed,
Till the last ray shot upward fires the clouds
With blazing crimson; then in paler light,
Long lines of tenderer radiance, lingering yield
To partial darkness; and on the opposing side
The early moon distinctly rising, throws
Her pearly brilliance on the trembling tide.

The fishermen, who at set seasons pass   100
Many a league off at sea their toiling night,
Now hail their comrades, from their daily task

Returning; and make ready for their own,
With the night tide commencing. The night tide
Bears a dark vessel on, whose hull and sails
Mark her a coaster from the north. Her keel
Now plows the sand; and sidelong now she leans,
While with loud clamors her athletic crew
Unload her; and resounds the busy hum
Along the wave-worn rocks. Yet more remote   110
Where the rough cliff hangs beetling o'er its base,
All breathes repose, the water's rippling sound
Scarce heard; but now and then the sea-snipe's[7] cry
Just tells that something living is abroad;
And sometimes crossing on the moonbright line,
Glimmers the skiff, faintly discerned awhile,
Then lost in shadow.

          Contemplation here,
High on her throne of rock, aloof may sit,
And bid recording Memory unfold
Her scroll voluminous—bid her retrace   120
The period, when from Neustria's hostile shore
The Norman launched his galleys, and the bay
O'er which that mass of ruin[8] frowns even now
In vain and sullen menace, then received
The new invaders, a proud martial race,
Of Scandinavia[9] the undaunted sons,

7. In crossing the channel this bird is heard at night, uttering a short cry and flitting along near the surface of the waves. The sailors call it the sea snipe, but I can find no species of sea bird of which this is the vulgar name. A bird so called inhabits the Lake of Geneva.

8. Pevensey Castle.

9. The Scandinavians [modern Norway, Sweden, Denmark, Lapland, etc.] and other inhabitants of the north began towards the end of the 8th century to leave their inhospitable climate in search of the produce of more fortunate countries.

The North-men made inroads on the coasts of France, and carrying back immense booty, excited their compatriots to engage in the same piratical voyages; and they were afterwards joined by numbers of necessitous and daring adventurers from the coasts of Provence and Sicily.

In 844, these wandering innovators had a great number of vessels at sea, and again visiting the coasts of France, Spain, and England, the following year they penetrated even to Paris, and the unfortunate Charles the Bald, king of France, purchased at a high price the retreat of the banditti he had no other means of repelling.

These successful expeditions continued for some time, till Rollo, otherwise Raoul, assembled a number of followers, and after a descent on England, crossed the channel and made himself master of Rouen, which he fortified. Charles the Simple, unable to contend

Whom Drogon, Fier-a-bras, and Humfroi led
To conquest; while Trinacria to their power
Yielded her wheaten garland; and when thou,
Parthenope! within thy fertile bay   130
Received the victors—

           In the mailed ranks
Of Normans landing on the British coast
Rode Taillefer; and with astounding voice
Thundered the war song daring Roland sang
First in the fierce contention: vainly brave,
One not inglorious struggle England made—
But failing, saw the Saxon heptarchy

---

with Rollo, offered to resign to him some of the northern provinces, and to give him his daughter in marriage. Neustria, since called Normandy, was granted to him and afterwards Brittany. He added the more solid virtues of the legislator to the fierce valor of the conqueror—converted to Christianity, he established justice and repressed the excesses of his Danish subjects, till then accustomed to live only by plunder. His name became the signal for pursuing those who violated the laws; as well as the cry of Haro, still so usual in Normandy. The Danes and Francs produced a race of men celebrated for their valor, and it was a small party of these that in 983, having been on a pilgrimage to Jerusalem, arrived on their return at Salerno and found the town surrounded by Mahometans, whom the Salernians were bribing to leave their coast. The Normans represented to them the baseness and cowardice of such submission, and notwithstanding the inequality of their numbers, they boldly attacked the Saracen camp and drove the infidels to their ships. The prince of Salerno, astonished at their successful audacity, would have loaded them with the marks of his gratitude, but refusing every reward, they returned to their own country, from whence, however, other bodies of Normans passed into Sicily [anciently called Trinacria]; and many of them entered into the service of the emperor of the East, others of the Pope, and the duke of Naples was happy to engage a small party of them in defense of his newly founded duchy. Soon afterwards three brothers of Coutance, the sons of Tancred de Hauteville, Guillaume Fier-a-bras, Drogon, and Humfroi, joining the Normans established at Aversa, became masters of the fertile island of Sicily; and Robert Guiscard joining them, the Normans became sovereigns both of Sicily and Naples [Parthenope]. How William, the natural son of Robert, duke of Normandy, possessed himself of England is too well known to be repeated here. William, sailing from St. Valori, landed in the bay of Pevensey and, at the place now called Battle, met the English forces under Harold; an esquire (*écuyer*) called Taillefer, mounted on an armed horse, led on the Normans, singing in a thundering tone the war song of Rollo. He threw himself among the English and was killed on the first onset. In a marsh not far from Hastings the skeletons of an armed man and horse were found a few years since, which are believed to have belonged to the Normans, as a party of their horse, deceived in the nature of the ground, perished in the morass.

Finish for ever. Then the holy pile,[10]
Yet seen upon the field of conquest, rose
Where, to appease heaven's wrath for so much blood,　　　　140
The conqueror bade unceasing prayers ascend,
And requiems for the slayers and the slain.
But let not modern Gallia form from hence
Presumptuous hopes, that ever thou again,
Queen of the isles! shalt crouch to foreign arms.
The enervate sons of Italy may yield;
And the Iberian, all his trophies torn
And wrapped in superstition's monkish weed,
May shelter his abasement, and put on
Degrading fetters. Never, never thou!　　　　150
Imperial mistress of the obedient sea;
But thou, in thy integrity secure,
Shalt now undaunted meet a world in arms.

England! 'twas where this promontory rears
Its rugged brow above the channel wave,
Parting the hostile nations, that thy fame,
Thy naval fame was tarnished, at what time
Thou, leagued with the Batavian, gavest to France[11]
One day of triumph—triumph the more loud
Because even then so rare. Oh! well redeemed　　　　160
Since, by a series of illustrious men
Such as no other country ever reared
To vindicate her cause. It is a list
Which, as fame echoes it, blanches the cheek
Of bold Ambition; while the despot feels
The extorted scepter tremble in his grasp.

10. Battle Abbey was raised by the Conqueror and endowed with an ample revenue, that masses might be said night and day for the souls of those who perished in battle.

11. In 1690, King William being then in Ireland, Tourville, the French admiral, arrived on the coast of England. His fleet consisted of seventy-eight large ships and twenty-two fire-ships. Lord Torrington, The English admiral, lay at St. Helens, with only forty English and a few Dutch ships, and conscious of the disadvantage under which he should give battle, he ran up between the enemy's fleet and the coast to protect it. The queen's council, dictated to by Russel, persuaded her to order Torrington to venture a battle. The orders Torrington appears to have obeyed reluctantly: his fleet now consisted of twenty-two Dutch and thirty-four English ships. Evertson, the Dutch admiral, was eager to obtain glory; Torrington, more cautious, reflected on the importance of the stake. The consequence was that the Dutch rashly sailing on were surrounded, and Torrington, solicitous to recover this false step, placed himself with difficulty between the Dutch and French—but three Dutch ships were burned, two of their admirals killed, and almost all their ships disabled. The English and Dutch, declining a second engagement, retired towards the mouth of the Thames. The French, from ignorance of the coast, and misunderstanding among each other, failed to take all the advantage they might have done of this victory.

From even the proudest roll by glory filled,
How gladly the reflecting mind returns
To simple scenes of peace and industry,
Where, bosomed in some valley of the hills,   170
Stands the lone farm; its gate with tawny ricks
Surrounded, and with granaries and sheds,
Roofed with green mosses, and by elms and ash
Partially shaded; and not far removed
The hut of sea-flints built; the humble home
Of one, who sometimes watches on the heights,[12]
When, hid in the cold mist of passing clouds,
The flock, with dripping fleeces, are dispersed
O'er the wide down; then from some ridged point
That overlooks the sea, his eager eye   180
Watches the bark that for his signal waits
To land its merchandise. Quitting for this
Clandestine traffic his more honest toil,
The crook abandoning, he braves himself
The heaviest snowstorm of December's night,
When with conflicting winds the ocean raves,
And on the tossing boat unfearing mounts
To meet the partners of the perilous trade,
And share their hazard. Well it were for him,
If no such commerce of destruction known,   190
He were content with what the earth affords
To human labor; even where she seems
Reluctant most. More happy is the hind
Who with his own hands rears on some black moor,
Or turbary, his independent hut
Covered with heather, whence the slow white smoke
Of smoldering peat arises. A few sheep,
His best possession, with his children share
The rugged shed when wintry tempests blow;
But when with spring's return the green blades rise   200
Amid the russet heath, the household live
Joint tenants of the waste throughout the day,
And often, from her nest, among the swamps,
Where the gemmed sun-dew[13] grows, or fringed buck-bean,
They scare the plover[14] that with plaintive cries

12. The shepherds and laborers of this tract of country, a hardy and athletic race of men, are almost universally engaged in the contraband trade, carried on for the coarsest and most destructive spirits, with the opposite coast. When no other vessel will venture to sea, these men hazard their lives to elude the watchfulness of the revenue officers, and to secure their cargoes.

13. Sun-dew: *Drosera rotundifolia*; buck-bean: *Menyanthes trifoliatum*.

14. *Tringa vanellus.*

Flutters, as sorely wounded, down the wind.
Rude and but just removed from savage life
Is the rough dweller among scenes like these
(Scenes all unlike the poet's fabling dreams
Describing Arcady)—but he is free;   210
The dread that follows on illegal acts
He never feels: and his industrious mate
Shares in his labor. Where the brook is traced
By crowding osiers, and the black coot[15] hides
Among the plashy reeds her diving brood,
The matron wades; gathering the long green rush
That well prepared hereafter lends its light
To her poor cottage, dark and cheerless else
Through the drear hours of winter. Otherwhile
She leads her infant group where charlock grows   220
"Unprofitably gay,"[16] or to the fields,
Where congregate the linnet and the finch
That on the thistle, so profusely spread,
Feast in the desert; the poor family
Early resort, extirpating with care
These, and the gaudier mischief of the ground;
Then flames the high raised heap; seen afar off
Like hostile war-fires flashing to the sky.[17]
Another task is theirs: On fields that show
As angry Heaven had rained sterility,   230
Stony and cold, and hostile to the plow;
Where, clamoring loud, the evening curlew[18] runs
And drops her spotted eggs among the flints;
The mother and the children pile the stones
In rugged pyramids—and all this toil
They patiently encounter, well content
On their flock bed to slumber undisturbed
Beneath the smoky roof they call their own.

Oh! little knows the sturdy hind, who stands
Gazing, with looks where envy and contempt   240
Are often strangely mingled, on the car
Where prosperous Fortune sits; what secret care
Or sick satiety is often hid

15. *Fulica aterrima.*
16. "With blossom'd furze, unprofitably gay"—Goldsmith.
17. The beacons formerly lighted up on the hills to give notice of the approach of an enemy. These signals would still be used in case of alarm, if the telegraph [semaphore] now substituted could not be distinguished on account of fog or darkness.
18. *Charadrius oedicnemus.*

Beneath the splendid outside. *He* knows not
How frequently the child of luxury,
Enjoying nothing, flies from place to place
In chase of pleasure that eludes his grasp;
And that content is e'en less found by him
Than by the laborer, whose pick-axe smoothes
The road before his chariot; and who doffs   250
What *was* a hat; and as the train pass on
Thinks how one day's expenditure like this
Would cheer him for long months, when to his toil
The frozen earth closes her marble breast.

Ah! who *is* happy? Happiness! a word
That like false fire from marsh effluvia born
Misleads the wanderer, destined to contend
In the world's wilderness with want or woe—
Yet *they* are happy, who have never asked
What good or evil means. The boy   260
That on the river's margin gaily plays,
Has heard that Death is there.—He knows not Death,
And therefore fears it not; and venturing in
He gains a bullrush, or a minnow—then,
At certain peril, for a worthless prize,
A crow's or raven's nest, he climbs the bole
Of some tall pine; and of his prowess proud,
Is for a moment happy. Are *your* cares,
Ye who despise him, never worse applied?
The village girl is happy, who sets forth   270
To distant fair gay in her Sunday suit
With cherry colored knots, and flourished shawl,
And bonnet newly purchased. So is he
Her little brother, who his mimic drum
Beats till he drowns her rural lovers' oaths
Of constant faith and still increasing love;
Ah! yet a while, and half those oaths believed,
Her happiness is vanished; and the boy
While yet a stripling, finds the sound he loved
Has led him on, till he has given up   280
His freedom and his happiness together.

I once was happy when, while yet a child,
I learned to love these upland solitudes,
And when, elastic as the mountain air,
To my light spirit care was yet unknown
And evil unforseen. Early it came
And, childhood scarcely passed, I was condemned,
A guiltless exile, silently to sigh,

While memory with faithful pencil drew
The contrast; and regretting, I compared   290
With the polluted smoky atmosphere
And dark and stifling streets, the southern hills
That to the setting sun, their graceful heads
Rearing, o'erlook the firth, where Vecta[19] breaks
With her white rocks the strong impetuous tide,
When western winds the vast Atlantic urge
To thunder on the coast. Haunts of my youth!
Scenes of fond day dreams, I behold ye yet!
Where 'twas so pleasant by thy northern slopes
To climb the winding sheep-path, aided oft   300
By scattered thorns, whose spiny branches bore
Small woolly tufts, spoils of the vagrant lamb
There seeking shelter from the noonday sun;
And pleasant, seated on the short soft turf,
To look beneath upon the hollow way,
While heavily upward moved the laboring wain,
And stalking slowly by, the sturdy hind,
To ease his panting team, stopped with a stone
The grating wheel.

           Advancing higher still,
The prospect widens, and the village church,   310
But little o'er the lowly roofs around,
Rears its gray belfry and its simple vane;
Those lowly roofs of thatch are half concealed
By the rude arms of trees, lovely in spring,[20]
When on each bough the rosy-tinctured bloom
Sits thick and promises autumnal plenty.
For even those orchards round the Norman farms,
Which, as their owners mark the promised fruit,
Console them for the vineyards of the south,
Surpass not these.

              Where woods of ash, and beech,   320
And partial copses fringe the green hill foot,
The upland shepherd rears his modest home;
There wanders by a little nameless stream

19. The Isle of Wight, which breaks the force of the waves when they are driven by southwest winds against this long and open coast. It is somewhere described as "Vecta shouldering the Western Waves."

20. Every cottage in this country has its orchard; and I imagine that not even those of Herefordshire or Worcestershire exhibit a more beautiful prospect, when the trees are in bloom, and the "Primavera candida e vermiglia" ["pure and rosy Spring," Petrarch] is everywhere so enchanting.

That from the hill wells forth, bright now and clear,
Or after rain with chalky mixture gray,
But still refreshing in its shallow course
The cottage garden, most for use designed,
Yet not of beauty destitute. The vine
Mantles the little casement; yet the briar
Drops fragrant dew among the July flowers;   330
And pansies rayed and freaked and mottled pinks
Grow among balm; and rosemary and rue
There honeysuckles flaunt; and roses blow
Almost uncultured: some with dark green leaves
Contrast their flowers of pure unsullied white;
Others, like velvet robes of regal state,
Of richest crimson; while in thorny moss
Enshrined and cradled, the most lovely wear
The hues of youthful beauty's glowing cheek.
With fond regret I recollect e'en now   340
In spring and summer, what delight I felt
Among these cottage gardens, and how much
Such artless nosegays, knotted with a rush
By village housewife or her ruddy maid,
Were welcome to me, soon and simply pleased.

An early worshipper at nature's shrine,
I loved her rudest scenes—warrens, and heaths,
And yellow commons, and birch-shaded hollows,
And hedge rows bordering unfrequented lanes
Bowered with wild roses, and the clasping woodbine   350
Where purple tassels of the tangling vetch[21]
With bittersweet and bryony inweave,[22]
And the dew fills the silver bindweed's[23] cups.
I loved to trace the brooks whose humid banks
Nourish the harebell and the freckled pagil;[24]
And stroll among o'ershadowing woods of beech,
Lending in summer from the heats of noon
A whispering shade; while haply there reclines
Some pensive lover of uncultured flowers,
Who, from the trumps with bright green mosses clad,   360
Plucks the wood sorrel,[25] with its light thin leaves
Heart-shaped and triply folded, and its root
Creeping like beaded coral; or who there

21. *Vicia sylvatica.*
22. Bittersweet: *Solanum dulcamara*; bryony: *Bryonia alba.*
23. *Convolvulus sepium.*
24. Harebell: *Hyacinthus non scriptus*; pagil: *Primula veris.*
25. *Oxalis acetosella.*

Gathers the copse's pride, anemones,[26]
With rays like golden studs on ivory laid,
Most delicate: but touched with purple clouds,
Fit crown for April's fair but changeful brow.

Ah! hills so early loved, in fancy still
I breathe your pure keen air, and still behold
Those widely spreading views, mocking alike   370
The poet and the painter's utmost art;
And still, observing objects more minute,
Wondering remark the strange and foreign forms
Of seashells with the pale calcareous soil
Mingled, and seeming of resembling substance.[27]
Though surely the blue ocean (from the heights
Where the downs westward trend but dimly seen)
Here never rolled its surge. Does nature then
Mimic, in wanton mood, fantastic shapes
Of bivalves and inwreathed volutes that cling   380
To the dark sea-rock of the watery world?
Or did this range of chalky mountains once[28]
Form a vast basin, where the ocean waves
Swelled fathomless? What time these fossil shells,
Buoyed on their native element, were thrown
Among the imbedding calx: when the huge hill
Its giant bulk heaved and in strange ferment
Grew up a guardian barrier 'twixt the sea
And the green level of the sylvan weald.

Ah! very vain is science' proudest boast,   390
And but a little light its flame yet lends
To its most ardent votaries; since from whence
These fossil forms are seen is but conjecture,
Food for vague theories or vain dispute,

26. *Anemone nemorosa.* It appears to be settled, on late and excellent authorities, that this word should not be accented on the second syllable, but on the penultima. I have however ventured the more known accentuation, as more generally used and suiting better the nature of my verse.

27. Among the crumbling chalk I have often found shells, some quite in a fossil state and hardly distinguishable from chalk. Others appeared more recent; cockles, mussels, and periwinkles, I well remember, were among the number, and some whose names I do not know. A great number were like those of small land snails. It is now many years since I made these observations. The appearance of seashells so far from the sea excited my surprise, though I then knew nothing of natural history. I have never read any of the late theories of the earth, nor was I ever satisfied with the attempts to explain many of the phenomena which call forth conjecture in those books I happened to have had access to on this subject.

28. The theory here slightly hinted at, is taken from an idea started by Mr. White.

While to his daily task the peasant goes,
Unheeding such inquiry, with no care
But that the kindly change of sun and shower
Fit for his toil the earth he cultivates.
As little recks the herdsman of the hill,
Who on some turfy knoll idly reclined   400
Watches his wether flock, that deep beneath
Rest the remains of men, of whom is left[29]
No traces in the records of mankind
Save what these half obliterated mounds
And half filled trenches doubtfully impart
To some lone antiquary, who on times remote,
Since which two thousand years have rolled away,
Loves to contemplate. He perhaps may trace,
Or fancy he can trace, the oblong square
Where the mailed legions under Claudius[30] reared   410
The rampire or excavated fossé delved;
What time the huge unwieldy elephant[31]

29. These downs are not only marked with traces of encampments, which from their forms are called Roman or Danish, but there are numerous tumuli among them, some of which, having been opened a few years ago, were supposed by a learned antiquary to contain the remains of the original natives of the country.

30. That the legions of Claudius were in this part of Britain appears certain. Since this emperor received the submission of Cantii, Atrebates, Irenobates, and Regni, in which latter denomination were included the people of Sussex.

31. In the year 1740, some workmen digging in the park at Burton in Sussex discovered, nine feet below the surface, the teeth and bones of an elephant; two of the former were seven feet eight inches in length. There were, besides these, tusks, one of which broke in removing it, a grinder not at all decayed, and a part of the jawbone, with bones of the knee and thigh, and several others. Some of them remained very lately at Burton House, the seat of John Biddulph, Esq. Others were in possession of the Rev. Dr. Langrish, minister of Petworth at that period, who was present when some of these bones were taken up and gave it as his opinion that they had remained there since the universal deluge. The Romans under the Emperor Claudius probably brought elephants into Britain. Milton, in the Second Book of his History, in speaking of the expedition, says that "he, like a great eastern king, with armed elephants, marched through Gallia." This is given on the authority of Dion Cassius, in his Life of the Emperor Claudius. It has therefore been conjectured that the bones found at Burton might have been those of one of these elephants, who perished there soon after its landing; or dying on the high downs, one of which, called Duncton Hill, rises immediately above Burton Park, the bones might have been washed down by the torrents of rain and buried deep in the soil. They were not found together but scattered at some distance from each other. The two tusks were twenty feet apart. I had often heard of the elephant's bones at Burton but never saw them, and I have no books to refer to. I think I saw, in what is now called the National Museum at Paris, the very large bones of an elephant, which were found in North America: though it is certain that this enormous animal is never seen in its natural state but in the countries under the torrid zone of the old world. I have, since making this note, been told that the bones of the rhinoceros and hippopotamus have been found in America.

Auxiliary reluctant, hither led
From Afric's forest glooms and tawny sands,
First felt the northern blast and his vast frame
Sunk useless; whence in after ages found,
The wondering hinds, on those enormous bones
Gazed and in giants[32] dwelling on the hills
Believed and marvelled. . . .

                    Hither, Ambition come!
Come and behold the nothingness of all   420
for which you carry through the oppressed earth
War and its train of horrors—see where tread
The innumerous hoofs of flocks above the works
By which the warrior sought to register
His glory and immortalize his name.
The pirate Dane,[33] who from his circular camp
Bore in destructive robbery, fire and sword
Down through the vale, sleeps unremembered here;
And here, beneath the green sward, rests alike
The savage native,[34] who his acorn meal   430
Shared with the herds that ranged the pathless woods;
And the centurion, who on these wide hills
Encamping, planted the Imperial Eagle.
All with the lapse of time have passed away,
Even as the clouds, with dark and dragon shapes,
Or like vast promontories crowned with towers,
Cast their broad shadows on the downs, then sail
Far to the northward, and their transient gloom
Is soon forgotten.

                But from thoughts like these,
By human crimes suggested, let us turn   440
To where a more attractive study courts
The wanderer of the hills, while shepherd girls
Will from among the fescue[35] bring him flowers
Of wonderous mockery, some resembling bees

32. The peasants believe that the large bones sometimes found belonged to giants who formerly lived on the hills. The devil also has a great deal to do with the remarkable forms of hill and vale: the Devil's Punch Bowl, the Devil's Leaps, and the Devil's Dyke are names given to deep hollows, or high and abrupt ridges, in this and the neighboring county.

33. The incursions of the Danes were for many ages the scourge of this island.

34. The aborigines of this country lived in woods, unsheltered but by trees and caves, and were probably as truly savage as any of those who are now termed so.

35. The grass called sheep's fescue (*Festuca ovina*) clothes these downs with the softest turf.

In velvet vest, intent on their sweet toil,[36]
While others mimic flies[37] that lightly sport
In the green shade or float along the pool,
But here seen perched upon the slender stalk
And gathering honey dew. While in the breeze
That wafts the thistle's plumed seed along,   450
Bluebells wave tremulous. The mountain thyme[38]
Purples the hassock of the heaving mole,
And the short turf is gay with tormentil,[39]
And bird's-foot trefoil, and the lesser tribes
Of hawkweed,[40] spangling it with fringed stars,
Near where a richer tract of cultured land
Slopes to the south; and burnished by the sun,
Bend in the gale of August, floods of corn.
The guardian of the flock with watchful care[41]
Repels by voice and dog the encroaching sheep—   460
While his boy visits every wired trap[42]
That scars the turf, and from the pitfalls takes
The timid migrants,[43] who from distant wilds,
Warrens, and stone quarries, are destined thus
To lose their short existence. But unsought
By luxury yet, the shepherd still protects

36. *Ophrys apifera*, bee ophrys, or orchis, found plentifully on the hills, as well as the next.

37. *Ophrys muscifera*, fly orchis. Linnæus, misled by the variations to which some of this tribe are really subject, has perhaps too rashly esteemed all those which resemble insects as forming only one species, which he terms *Ophrys insectifera*. See *English Botany*.

38. Bluebells: *Campanula rotundifolia*; mountain thyme: *Thymus serpyllum*. "It is a common notion, that the flesh of sheep which feed upon aromatic plants, particularly wild thyme, is superior in flavor to other mutton. The truth is that sheep do not crop these aromatic plants, unless now and then by accident, or when they are first turned on hungry to downs, heaths, or commons; but the soil and situations favorable to aromatic plants produce a short sweet pasturage, best adapted to feeding sheep, whom nature designed for mountains and not for turnip grounds and rich meadows. The attachment of bees to this, and other aromatic plants, is well known." Martyn's *Miller*.

39. *Tormentilla reptans*.

40. Bird's-foot trefoil: *Trifolium ornithopoides*; hawkweed: *Hieracium*, many sorts.

41. The downs, especially to the south, where they are less abrupt, are in many places under the plow, and the attention of the shepherds is there particularly required to keep the flocks from trespassing.

42. Square holes cut in the turf, into which a wire noose is fixed, to catch wheatears. Mr. White says, that these birds (*Motacilla oenanthe*) are never taken beyond the river Adur and Beding Hill, but this is certainly a mistake.

43. These birds are extremely fearful and on the slightest appearance of a cloud run for shelter to the first rut or heap of stone that they see.

The social bird,[44] who from his native haunts
Of willowy current or the rushy pool
Follows the fleecy crowd and flirts and skims
In fellowship among them.

                               Where the knoll   470
More elevated takes the changeful winds,
The windmill rears its vanes; and thitherward
With his white load, the master traveling
Scares the rooks rising slow on whispering wings,
While o'er his head, before the summer sun
Lights up the blue expanse, heard more than seen,
The lark sings matins and, above the clouds
Floating, embathes his spotted breast in dew.
Beneath the shadow of a gnarled thorn
Bent by the sea blast,[45] from a seat of turf   480
With fairy nosegays strewn, how wide the view![46]
Till in the distant north it melts away
And mingles indiscriminate with clouds.
But if the eye could reach so far, the mart
Of England's capital, its domes and spires
Might be perceived. Yet hence the distant range
Of Kentish hills[47] appear in purple haze;
And nearer undulate the wooded heights
And airy summits[48] that above the mole
Rise in green beauty; and the beaconed ridge   490
Of Black-down[49] shagged with heath, and swelling rude
Like a dark island from the vale; its brow
Catching the last rays of the evening sun
That gleam between the nearer park's old oaks,
Then lighten up the river, and make prominent

44. *Motacilla flava.* It frequents the banks of rivulets in winter, making its nest in meadows and cornfields. But after the breeding season is over, it haunts downs and sheep-walks and is seen constantly among the flocks, probably for the sake of the insects it picks up. In France the shepherds call it *La Bergeronette* and say it often gives them, by its cry, notice of approaching danger.

45. The strong winds from the southwest occasion almost all the trees, which on these hills are exposed to it, to grow the other way.

46. So extensive are some of the views from these hills that only the want of power in the human eye to travel so far prevents London itself being discerned. Description falls so infinitely short of the reality that only here and there distinct features can be given.

47. A scar of chalk in a hill beyond Sevenoaks in Kent is very distinctly seen of a clear day.

48. The hills about Dorking in Surrey, over almost the whole extent of which county the prospect extends.

49. This is a high ridge, extending between Sussex and Surrey. It is covered with heath and has almost always a dark appearance. On it is a telegraph.

The portal, and the ruined battlements[50]
Of that dismantled fortress; raised what time
The Conqueror's successors fiercely fought,
Tearing with civil feuds the desolate land.
But now a tiller of the soil dwells there,
And of the turret's looped and raftered halls   500
Has made a humbler homestead—where he sees,
Instead of armed foemen, herds that gaze
Along his yellow meadows, or his flocks
At evening from the upland driven to fold.

In such a castellated mansion once
A stranger chose his home; and where hard by,
In rude disorder fallen, and hid with brushwood,
Lay fragments gray of towers and buttresses,
Among the ruins often he would muse—   510
His rustic meal soon ended, he was wont
To wander forth, listening the evening sounds
Of rushing milldam, or the distant team,
Or night-jar, chasing fern-flies.[51] The tired hind
Passed him at nightfall, wondering he should sit
On the hilltop so late; they from the coast
Who sought bypaths with their clandestine load,
Saw with suspicious doubt the lonely man
Cross on their way; but village maidens thought
His senses injured, and with pity say   520
That he, poor youth! must have been crossed in love—
For often, stretched upon the mountain turf

50. In this country there are several of the fortresses or castles built by Stephen of Blois in his contention for the kingdom with the daughter of Henry the First, the empress Matilda. Some of these are now converted into farmhouses.

51. Dr. Aikin remarks, I believe, in his essay "On the Application of Natural History to the Purpose of Poetry," how many of our best poets have noticed the same circumstance, the hum of the dor beetle (*Scaraboeus stercorarius*) among the sounds heard by the evening wanderer. I remember only one instance in which the more remarkable, though by no means uncommon noise of the fern owl, or goatsucker, is mentioned. It is called the night hawk, the jar bird, the churn owl, and the fern owl, from its feeding on the *Scaraboeus solstitialis*, or fern chafer, which it catches while on the wing with its claws, the middle toe of which is long and curiously serrated, on purpose to hold them. It was this bird that was intended to be described in the Forty-second Sonnet. I was mistaken in supposing it as visible in November; it is a migrant, and leaves this country in August. I had often seen and heard it, but I did not then know its name or history. It is called goatsucker (*Caprimulgus*), from a strange prejudice taken against it by the Italians, who assert that it sucks their goats; and the peasants of England still believe that a disease in the backs of their cattle—occasioned by a fly, which deposits its egg under the skin and raises a boil, sometimes fatal to calves—is the work of this bird, which they call a puckeridge. Nothing can convince them that their beasts are not injured by this bird, which they therefore hold in abhorrence.

With folded arms, and eyes intently fixed
Where ancient elms and firs obscured a grange
Some little space within the vale below,
They heard him as complaining of his fate,
And to the murmuring wind, of cold neglect
And baffled hope he told. The peasant girls
These plaintive sounds remember, and even now
Among them may be heard the stranger's songs.   530

Were I a shepherd on the hill
    And ever as the mists withdrew
Could see the willows of the rill
Shading the footway to the mill
    Where once I walked with you—

And as away night's shadows sail,
    And sounds of birds and brooks arise,
Believe, that from the woody vale
I hear your voice upon the gale
    In soothing melodies;   540

And viewing from the alpine height,
    The prospect dressed in hues of air,
Could say, while transient colors bright
Touched the fair scene with dewy light,
    'Tis that *her* eyes are there!

I think, I could endure my lot
    And linger on a few short years,
And then, by all but you forgot,
Sleep, where the turf that clothes the spot
    May claim some pitying tears.   550

For 'tis not easy to forget
    One, who through life has loved you still.
And you, however late, might yet
With sighs to memory given, regret
    The shepherd of the hill.

Yet otherwhile it seemed as if young hope
Her flattering pencil gave to fancy's hand
And, in his wanderings, reared to soothe his soul
Ideal bowers of pleasure. Then, of solitude
And of his hermit life still more enamored,   560
His home was in the forest; and wild fruits

And bread sustained him. There in early spring
The barkmen[52] found him, ere the sun arose;
There at their daily toil, the wedgecutters[53]
Beheld him through the distant thicket move.
The shaggy dog following the truffle hunter[54]
Barked at the loiterer; and perchance at night
Belated villagers from fair or wake,
While the fresh night-wind let the moonbeams in
Between the swaying boughs, just saw him pass,   570
And then in silence, gliding like a ghost
He vanished! lost among the deepening gloom.
But near one ancient tree, whose wreathed roots
Formed a rude couch, love-songs and scattered rhymes,
Unfinished sentences, or half erased,
And rhapsodies like this were sometimes found:

Let us to woodland wilds repair
    While yet the glittering night-dews seem
To wait the freshly breathing air,
    Precursive of the morning beam   580
That rising with advancing day
Scatters the silver drops away.

An elm, uprooted by the storm,
    The trunk with mosses gray and green,
Shall make for us a rustic form
    Where lighter grows the forest scene;
And far among the bowery shades,
Are ferny lawns and grassy glades.

Retiring May to lovely June
    Her latest garland now resigns;   590
The banks with cuckoo-flowers[55] are strewn,
    The woodwalks blue with columbines,[56]

52. As soon as the sap begins to rise, the trees intended for felling are cut and barked, at which time the men who are employed in that business pass whole days in the woods.

53. The wedges used in shipbuilding are made of beech wood, and great numbers are cut every year in the woods near the downs.

54. Truffles are found under the beech woods by means of small dogs trained to hunt them by the scent.

55. *Lychnis dioica*. Shakespeare describes the cuckoo buds as being yellow. He probably meant the numerous Ranunculi, or March marigolds (*Caltha palustris*), which so gild the meadows in spring; but poets have never been botanists. The cuckoo flower is the *Lychnis floscuculi*.

56. *Aquilegia vulgaris.*

And with its reeds the wandering stream
Reflects the flag-flower's[57] golden gleam.

There, feathering down the turf to meet,
   Their shadowy arms the beeches spread,
While high above our sylvan seat
   Lifts the light ash its airy head;
And later leaved, the oaks between
Extend their boughs of vernal green.   600

The slender birch its paper rind
   Seems offering to divided love,
And shuddering even without a wind
   Aspens their paler foliage move,
As if some spirit of the air
Breathed a low sigh in passing there.

The squirrel in his frolic mood
   Will fearless bound among the boughs;
Yaffils[58] laugh loudly through the wood,
   And murmuring ring-doves tell their vows;   610
While we, as sweetest woodscents rise,
Listen to woodland melodies.

And I'll contrive a sylvan room
   Against the time of summer heat,
Where leaves, inwoven in Nature's loom,
   Shall canopy our green retreat;
And gales that "close the eye of day"[59]
Shall linger, ere they die away.

And when a sear and sallow hue
   From early frost the bower receives,   620
I'll dress the sand rock cave for you
   And strew the floor with heath and leaves,
That you, against the autumnal air,
May find securer shelter there.

The nightingale will then have ceased
   To sing her moonlight serenade;

---

57. *Iris pseudacorus.*

58. Woodpeckers *(Picus)*; three or four species in Britain.

59. "And liquid notes that close the eye of day"—Milton. The idea here meant to be conveyed is of the evening wind, so welcome after a hot day of summer, and which appears to soothe and lull all nature into tranquility.

But the gay bird with blushing breast[60]
   And woodlarks[61] still will haunt the shade,
And by the borders of the spring
Reed-wrens[62] will yet be caroling.   630

The forest hermit's lonely cave
   None but such soothing sounds shall reach;
Or hardly heard, the distant wave
   Slow breaking on the stony beach;
Or winds, that now sigh soft and low,
Now make wild music as they blow.

And then, before the chilling North,
   The tawny foliage falling light
Seems as it flits along the earth
   The footfall of the busy sprite,   640
Who, wrapt in pale autumnal gloom,
Calls up the mist-born mushroom.

Oh! could I hear your soft voice there
   And see you in the forest green
All beauteous as you are, more fair
   You'd look, amid the sylvan scene,
And in a wood-girl's simple guise
Be still more lovely in mine eyes.

Ye phantoms of unreal delight,
   Visions of fond delirium born!   650
Rise not on my deluded sight,
   Then leave me drooping and forlorn
To know such bliss can never be,
Unless Amanda loved like me.

The visionary, nursing dreams like these,
Is not indeed unhappy. Summer woods
Wave over him and whisper as they wave
Some future blessings he may yet enjoy.
And as above him sail the silver clouds,
He follows them in thought to distant climes,   660
Where, far from the cold policy of this,
Dividing him from her he fondly loves,

---

60. The robin (*Motacilla rubecula*), which is always heard after other songsters have ceased to sing.

61. The woodlark (*Alauda nemorosa*) sings very late.

62. Reed-wrens (*Motacilla arundinacea*) sing all the summer and autumn and are often heard during the night.

He, in some island of the southern sea,[63]
May haply build his cane-constructed bower
Beneath the bread-fruit or aspiring palm,
With long green foliage rippling in the gale.
Oh! let him cherish his ideal bliss—
For what is life when hope has ceased to strew
Her fragile flowers along its thorny way?
And sad and gloomy are his days who lives   670
Of hope abandoned!

               Just beneath the rock
Where Beachy overpeers the channel wave,
Within a cavern mined by wintry tides,
Dwelt one,[64] who long disgusted with the world
And all its ways, appeared to suffer life
Rather than live; the soul-reviving gale,
Fanning the beanfield or the thymy heath,
Had not for many summers breathed on him;
And nothing marked to him the season's change,
Save that more gently rose the placid sea,   680
And that the birds which winter on the coast
Gave place to other migrants; save that the fog,
Hovering no more above the beetling cliffs,
Betrayed not then the little careless sheep[65]
On the brink grazing, while their headlong fall
Near the lone hermit's flint-surrounded home
Claimed unavailing pity; for his heart
Was feelingly alive to all that breathed;
And outraged as he was in sanguine youth
By human crimes, he still acutely felt   690
For human misery.

63. An allusion to the visionary delights of the newly discovered islands, where it was at first believed men lived in a state of simplicity and happiness, but where, as later enquiries have ascertained, that exemption from toil which the fertility of their country gives them produces the grossest vices and a degree of corruption that late navigators think will end in the extirpation of the whole people in a few years.

64. In a cavern almost immediately under the cliff called Beachy Head, there lived, as the people of the country believed, a man of the name of Darby, who for many years had no other abode than this cave and subsisted almost entirely on shellfish. He had often administered assistance to shipwrecked mariners, but venturing into the sea on this charitable mission during a violent equinoctial storm, he himself perished. As it is above thirty years since I heard this tradition of Parson Darby (for so I think he was called), it may now perhaps be forgotten.

65. Sometimes in thick weather the sheep feeding on the summit of the cliff miss their footing and are killed by the fall.

Wandering on the beach,
He learned to augur from the clouds of heaven,
And from the changing colors of the sea,
And sullen murmurs of the hollow cliffs,
Or the dark porpoises[66] that near the shore
Gamboled and sported on the level brine
When tempests were approaching. Then at night
He listened to the wind; and as it drove
The billows with o'erwhelming vehemence
He, starting from his rugged couch, went forth;   700
And hazarding a life too valueless,
He waded through the waves with plank or pole
Towards where the mariner in conflict dread
Was buffeting for life the roaring surge;
And now just seen, now lost in foaming gulfs,
The dismal gleaming of the clouded moon
Showed the dire peril. Often he had snatched
From the wild billows some unhappy man
Who lived to bless the hermit of the rocks.
But if his generous cares were all in vain,   710
And with slow swell the tide of morning bore
Some blue swollen corpse to land, the pale recluse
Dug in the chalk a sepulchre—above
Where the dank sea-wrack marked the utmost tide—
And with his prayers performed the obsequies
For the poor helpless stranger.

One dark night
The equinoctial wind blew south by west,
Fierce on the shore; the bellowing cliffs were shook
Even to their stony base, and fragments fell
Flashing and thundering on the angry flood.   720
At daybreak, anxious for the lonely man,
His cave the mountain shepherds visited,
Though sand and banks of weeds had choked their way—
He was not in it; but his drowned corpse,
By the waves wafted near his former home,
Received the rites of burial. Those who read,
Chiseled within the rock, these mournful lines,
Memorials of his sufferings, did not grieve,
That dying in the cause of charity,
His spirit, from its earthly bondage freed,   730
Had to some better region fled forever.

1807

66. *Delphinus phocæna.*

ANN YEARSLEY

née Cromartie; pseud., Lactilla (1752–1806)

❧

A milkwoman like her mother, Yearsley described her rural work in "Clifton Hill" (1785). *Married in 1774 to John Yearsley, a laborer, she had six children. When close to starvation, she read "to allay her hunger"; her favorite authors were Virgil, Milton, and Young. Yearsley bought slops from the cook of Hannah More, who on learning of "Lactilla's" gifts arranged for publication of* Poems on Several Occasions (1785), *with the support of a thousand subscribers. More found that Yearsley's verses, "though incorrect, breathed the genuine spirit of poetry." The volume went through four editions, to glowing reviews of its "captivating power," and eventually earned more than £600. Like More, Yearsley published a* Poem on the Inhumanity of the Slave Trade (1788). *The two quarreled: More and her circle felt "parish Sapphos" should be kept in their station. After recovering the moneys that More was husbanding for an annuity (but not her manuscripts), Yearsley invested in a circulating library in 1793. Her novel* The Royal Captives (1795) *earned £200. Her son, whom she had educated as an engraver, illustrated one of her works.*

Poems on Various Subjects (1787) proved Yearsley's growing sophistication and declared her independence of More; "On Jephtha's Vow," renarrates the Biblical account of the daughter sacrificed to guarantee victory in battle, and "To Ignorance" subversively locates Virgil and Ovid shivering in Charing Cross. Political observations are woven into many of her works: English peasant uprisings and the French Revolution figure in Yearsley's tragedy Earl Goodwin (1789); Stanzas of Woe (1790), addressed to the former mayor of Bristol, accuses him and his groom of an unprovoked attack that caused her to miscarry. The Royal Lyre (1796) contains neoclassical experiments, such as an epic "fragment" on Brutus, epistolary poems that aim at a dignified simplicity, and an elegy on the Bristol massacre of 1793, which was triggered by demonstrations against bridge tolls. The bookseller Joseph Cottle admired her "unequivocal mark of Genius," and the poet laureate, Robert Southey, included her in his overview of "the uneducated poets."

To Mira

On the Care of Her Infant

Whilst war, destruction, crimes that fiends delight,
Burst on the globe, and millions sink in night;
Whilst here a monarch, there a subject dies,
Equally dear to him who rules the skies;
Whilst man to man opposed would shake the world,
And see vast systems into chaos hurled,
Rather than turn his face from yon dread field,
Or, by forgiving, teach his foe to yield:
Let us, whose sweet employ the gods admire,
Serenely blest, to softer joys retire!   10
Spite of those wars, we will mild pleasure know—
Pleasure that, long as woman lives, shall flow!
We are not made for Mars; we ne'er could bear
His ponderous helmet and his burning spear;
Nor in fierce combat prostrate lay that form
That breathes affection whilst the heart is warm:—
No: whilst our heroes from our home retire,
We'll nurse the infant, and lament the sire.
    I am no Amazon; nor would I give
One silver groat by iron laws to live.   20
Nay, if, like hers, my heart were iron-bound
My warmth would melt the fetters to the ground.
    Ah, weep not, Mira! In this cradle view
Thy lovely charge—Amyntor's copy true;
Think, by this pledge the absent fire ensures
Thy constant memory and thy heart secures.
And, whilst we read, reflect, by turns converse,
Comment on wars in prose or mimic verse,
Permit me, pensive friend, who long have known
A mother's duty, pleasing cares to own,   30
Teach thee to gently nurse thy beauteous boy—
Lest custom gentle nature's power destroy:
So young an infant should reposing lie,
Unswathed and loose, that the fair limbs may ply
To every motion happy nature tries,
Whilst life seems fluid, and from pressure flies.
Clothe him with easy warmth. Of ills the worst
Are cruel swathes, of infant griefs the first.
Think what the stomach feels when hardly pressed!—
The breath confined swells high the snowy chest: 40
The pulses throb, the heart with fluttering beats;
The eyes roll ghastly; wind the nurture meets;

And ere the new-born appetite hath dined,
The food's rejected and the head reclined.
  Be tender, Mira!—Downy beds prepare;
To thy own bosom clasp Amyntor's heir!
See not thy babe pining with speechless grief,
His thirsty lip craving thy kind relief:
Relief that Nature bids the infant claim;
Withheld by healthy mothers, to their shame.   50
  Behold gay Circe in her gig!—Old Night
Hath from one moon received her valued light,
Since Circe's heir was with his grandsire laid;
And all her grief on yon rich tomb displayed.
  Her child was lovely, strong, and promised fair;
His looks transporting, his complexion clear;
Ardent to seek her bosom, and recline
Where dear affection makes the gift divine!
But no: could Circe dress renounce, the ball—
For a child's humor suffer TASTE to fall?   60
"Immensely monstrous! singular!" she cried—
A boisterous nurse her wished-for love supplied.
And soon her babe's wan look proclaimed the cheat:
He loathed the bosom he was forced to meet;
Refused in silence, starved in robes of lace,
And oft imploring viewed his mother's face.
Too proud to nurse, maternal fevers came—
Her burdened bosom caught the invited flame;
Too late she wooed her infant to her breast,
He only sighed and sunk to lasting rest.   70
  Do thou not, Mira, follow Circe's line—
In thee, let soft maternal pleasure shine;
Pleasure that virtuous mothers highly taste,
When generous Hymen makes them more than chaste.
Benign and social, new affections grow;
Their minds enlarged, their noblest spirits flow;
Friendship, compassion, sympathy, and love,
Such as the self-corrected mind may prove,
Stamp every act. These generous joys are thine—
Wouldst thou exchange them for Golconda's mine?   80
  I own such is the force of social law,
The unmarried *** loves her babe with awe:
Nursed far from public view in yon lone wild,
She sometimes strays to tremble o'er her child.
There coarse rusticity, vice, vulgar sound—
All that can sentiment or wisdom wound—
Breaks on the eye and ear. Unhappy fair!

Yet not condemned, if thy sweet pledge be dear,
Leave thy fond soul with him, to him return:
O let his FUTURE on thy fancy burn!   90
Quick bear him thence! Instruct him, point to fame—
Neglected, he will mourn; ay, seal thy shame!
   Mira, as thy dear Edward's senses grow,
Be sure they all will seek this point—TO KNOW:
Woo to enquiry; strictures long avoid—
By force the thirst of weakly sense is cloyed;
Silent attend the frown, the gaze, the smile,
To grasp far objects the incessant toil;
So play life's springs with energy, and try
The unceasing thirst of knowledge to supply.   100
   I saw the beauteous Caleb the other day
Stretch forth his little hand to touch a spray,
Whilst on the grass his drowsy nurse inhaled
The sweets of Nature as her sweets exhaled:
But ere the infant reached the playful leaf,
She pulled him back—his eyes o'erflowed with grief;
He checked his tears; her fiercer passions strove—
She looked a vulture cowering o'er a dove!
"I'll teach you, brat!" The pretty trembler sighed,
When, with a cruel shake, she hoarsely cried,   110
"Your mother spoils you—everything you see
You covet. It shall ne'er be so with me!
Here, eat this cake, sit still, and don't you rise—
Why don't you pluck the sun down from the skies?
I'll spoil your sport— Come, laugh me in the face—
And henceforth learn to keep your proper place.
You rule me in the house!—to hush your noise
I, like a spaniel, must run for toys:
But here, Sir, let the trees alone, nor cry—
Pluck, if you dare— Who's master? you, or I?"   120
   O brutal force, to check the inquiring mind,
When it would pleasure in a rosebud find!
Whose wondrous strength was never yet discerned
By millions gone, by all we yet have learned.
   True to the senses, systematic man
Conceives himself a mighty, finished plan;
To see, to touch, to taste, and smell and hear,
He strives to prove, make full existence here:
These to the brain exquisite forms convey;
On these she works, these keep her life in play.   130
   And is this all, Mira, we boast below?
Does not the soul spring forward still TO KNOW;

Pant for the future as her powers expand,
And pine for more than sense can understand?
Does she not, when the senses weary lie,
Paint brighter visions on some unknown sky;
Again forego her visionary joy,
To guide the senses in their strong employ;
With life's affections share their gentle flow,
But still, unsated, onward rove TO KNOW?
In infancy, when all her force is young,
She patient waits behind the useless tongue;
Silent attunes her senses, silent sees
Objects through mists, plainer by swift degrees.
SOUND strikes at first on her new-organed ear
As if far off; monotonous comes near.
Her taste yet sleeps, no melody she owns,
Nor wakes to joyous or to thrilling tones:
Dull indiscrimination blinds her views;
But still, the sound, once caught, the ear pursues;   150
Till cadence whispers o'er the eager thought,
And human accents strike, with MEANING fraught;
Then gentle breathings in the babe inspire
Joy, pleasure, sympathy, newborn desire;
He feels instinctive happiness and tries
To grasp her fully as she onward flies.
Hence Mira's soft endearments shall excite
In her dear Edward exquisite delight.

  Wouldst thou Amyntor should adore his child,
Nurse him thyself, for thou canst make him mild;   160
Grant him the toy that suits his young desire
Nor, when he pensive moans, his temper tire;
Keep forward passions from his tranquil breast—
By irritation, who were ever blest?—
Distorting frowns delirious fear create;
And blows, a sense of injury and hate.
Long—very long—should surly chiding sleep;
Nay, it were best thy babe should never weep.
No cure, no medicine fills the tear—the eye
Whose owner ne'er offended should be dry.   170

  I grant, when he the distant toy would reach,
Stern self-denial maiden aunts would preach:
But, contrary to this cold maxim tried,
Bestow the gift, indulgence be thy guide;
Ay, give unasked; example has its kind,
Pouring its image on the ductile mind.
Hence nobler spirits shall their likeness breed,

And ONE great virtue take the mental lead;
Hence vice and ignorance (What ills are worse?)
Arise contagious in the artful nurse;   180
For virtue's self she ne'er could virtue prize,
O'er THOUGHT deformed she throws the fair disguise;
Coarse in idea, furious in her ire,
Her passions grow amid their smothered fire.
O trust not Edward to so warm a breast,
Lest she infuse the evils you detest.
    Early instruction does the infant need—
On pictured lessons we are prone to feed:
Through every stage, what strikes the eye bestrides
Attention; judgment follows and decides.   190
With mental vision deck the instructive show.
Say what we will, we wish ourselves to know;
For this the child of seventy eager tries—
Explores his inward world, exploring dies!
However, early teach him mind to scan:
And when he's weary, tell him, "SUCH IS MAN."
    Next, try thy soothing skill—a challenge make—
An apple, orange, or some gewgaw stake.
Which shall read best the alphabetic line,
Be his the wished reward—the sorrow thine.   200
This rule perhaps is contrary to those
Who on the failing babe some talk impose:
Ah, too severe! they chill the struggling mind.
'Tis hard to learn—the tutor should be kind.
When Edward fails, console him—let him see
Thou mourn'st his loss and he will mourn with thee:
Not long he will thy mimic sorrow view;
Thy point once seen, he will that point pursue.
A rival for perfection, generous shame
Will touch the soul's best spark and blaze it into fame.   210
    Thus far I've lightly tripped the infant stage:
Truths bold and strong await the second age.
To ancient fathers be thy boy consigned,
But plant thyself true virtue in his mind.
Watch his belief, his doubts, his fruitless fears;
Convince him, the frail babe of seventy years
Will unresisting slumber on the sod,
The sole undoubted property of God!

                                    1795 / 1796

Familiar Poem

From Nisa to Fulvia of the Vale

Argument

Nisa of the Sabine race, having been informed by Marl, a goatherd, that old Fulvia, who lived harmlessly by selling poultry, was a sybil, or witch, writes to the dame on a subject that seems to have interested her. Fearing, however, to reveal too much, she merely inquires if Fulvia can cure the mind, and artfully breaks off.

Fulvia, our Consul bids me thank thee; why
My thanks to thee are due, I know not. Dawn
Had scarcely borrowed from the wakeful sun
One hour of light when hooting to our door
The camel-drivers came. Their crookèd horns
They blew, to waken Tellus. Gentle sleep
Had on our lowly pillow laid his head;
His breath, sweet as the newmown herbage, flew
In fragrant gales auspicious to the east.
Down his fair bosom drooped his golden hair   10
In heavy ringlets; these I softly moved,
To steal one parting kiss, ere the rude horn
Should from my wish abash me. Blest is he
Who drives no camels! Hapless lot! Ah! when
Will Ceres[1] come and bid the swain repose
Some minutes after sunrise? The loud laugh,
From men who tarried with their market-ware,
Came high to shame him. He arose, unclasped
Our latticed casement, breathed one soft adieu,
Descended, and renewed his daily toil,   20
Befriended by my prayer. I slept too long.
My duty, soon as Tellus went, had been
Fulfilled had I arose and took my reel.
    Fulvia, old churlish Marl, who sometimes milks
His goats beside the Tarpeian mount, that night
When thunder shook the Capital[2] and woods
In one sad murmur hailed that scathing fire
Which Jove sends down to warn us, cried aloud,
"Hey! Fulvia! midnight hag!" We marveled much.
The hind went on: "My cabin will come down,   30
Flat, smooth to the turf! She has already scathed
My beechen bower. Ah me! what safer chance
Waits my she-goat, behind the fatal rock

---

1. Supposed here to be the Goddess of Plenty.
2. A temple on the same mount. The whole has since been named Capitolium.

Whence we plunge quick the guilty?—Yes, my kids,
Bad omen! both this morn mistook their dams.
My chickens, too, lingered around their grain,
Nor did their bills rebound. All Fulvia's work!
Fulvia, sweet Nisa, murks the blessèd sun
With mists, that many swear rise from the sea.
Aye, aye! I know!—Nisa, I ween mischance   40
Will come to thee and me; yea, all who dwell
Within a stone's-throw of the beldam's cell."
    We chided surly Marl for this. "Away!"
He cried—"Dolts feel no lack of wisdom. Now,
The hag is somewhere circling round her spell,
Pinching our trembling blades; or, on the turf,
Sprinkling her juice of aconite. Dark yews
She clips, o'erhanging sacred dust; collects
Night dew; draws mimic mandrakes from their sleep;
And dries the forehead of the early foal,   50
To strew against the north wind, as it blows
Directly to my cabin. I ne'er met
That woman first at morn, when to the hills
I hied with my young kids, but foul mischance
Struck me or mine. Nisa, do thou beware,
Nor meet her; or, if meeting, ne'er offend."
    Art thou thus wise, dear Fulvia? Darest thou coop
The furies in a ring? unclose their lips
On the dread secrets of Tartarean realms?
What! teach the sun to woo the waves on high?
To shape centaurs and gorgon-headed men
Around the horizon, whilst the shepherd strains
Fancy to their wild measurement? I guess,
If Phoebus, at thy bidding, dress his skies
With exhalations in the evening hour,
Thou wilt, when I implore, arrest the moon;
When brazen in her belt she draws up woe
From the deep breast to o'erwhelm the gentle thought
And tremulate the wise and virtuous mind.
Should this dread power be thine, if thou art grown   70
A favorite with the gods, O Fulvia, try
In mercy to compose the troubled soul
Of one brave Roman . . .
               Here I purposed much;
Yet have I not, in this epistle, penned
Great information. Tellus is arrived
Weary and faint; his aged camel fell
Near the hillside. He looks so pensive!—well,
I am so apt to check myself—in haste

I wrote; am grown uncheerful. When
We pay our holy rites to Juno, come:
Thou shalt our priestess be; all who lack wealth
Should not lack piety. To Fulvia, health.

1796

FRANCES O'NEILL

née Carroll (fl. 1785)

꤮

*O'Neill, about whom we know little, came to London from Dublin sometime after 1789;
to a possible patron she explained, "I us'd my needle and employ'd my pen" to survive,
but she found the task increasingly difficult in later years. Her* Poetical Essays: Being
a Collection of Satirical Poems, Songs, and Acrostics *appeared in 1802. Her
poems tell us that she "works at Mrs. Robins's," an upholsterer in Warwick Street,
as a seamstress. Her satiric poems, she says, are "drawn from real life," apparently
about a fellow servant. Her acrostic verse compliments to patrons failed to win her a pen-
sion—possibly because her lively scatological pen needled those who disappointed or dis-
pleased her.*

To Mr. Kelly

Who Lives in a Respectable Family in Berkeley Square

Canto I

Kelly's Birth and Education in Ireland

In vain, dull critic, would you spurn me down,
And reprobate your countrymen in town;
In vain you strive, for lo! I'll write again,
And silence Irish grinders with my pen:
For one who touched me, sure, had better far
Go fight with tigers, or with lions war.
What, though repulsed, the Muse returns again,
Well armed with satire in his pregnant pen;
Whoe'er resists his glory lasts not long,
Who braves the power of keen satiric song,
With which, well armed my pen severely bang,
An eagle's talons, or a lion's fangs;

Thus shall my satire war with old and young,
Nor let an Irish grinder live unsung.
Satire's my theme, my theme without remorse,
For I, like Toby, I've a hobbyhorse;
How vain, proud fool, how vain, if I begin
Thy filthy language, and thy stupid grin.
The modest Muse such horrid vice detests,
At once despising both thy grins and jests;   20
'Tis mine to curb, thou vain censorious fool,
To curb thy fictious tongue of ridicule;
Thou Irish blockhead still to envy prone,
And skilled to expose all frailties but thy own;
Read, read my satire, and endure the scourge
To probe thy soul, thy rank offense to purge;
'Tis meet and just for such a growling rogue,
Who swears so loud, and talks the Irish brogue.
Come then, O Muse, we'll jointly burlesque him,
His gauldy optics, and his visage grim;   30
Kelly has sense, for sure that sense was seen
While yet a silly stripling of sixteen;
For oft at twilight, through an evening's fog,
He found his way o'er Tipperary's bog,
And oft at night he dashed through thick and thin,
By many a ditch, but seldom tumbled in.
Gods! with what ease he trampled o'er the clod,
His hands ungloved, and both his feet unshod,
Or hung half-naked o'er the standing pool,
Intent to study without book or school.   40
   Once, as I heard, as rumor tells for truth,
He robbed an orchard in the prime of youth,
And passed the fence high-bounding like a frog,
Without the fear of spring-trap, gun, or dog;
Now in the tree, his bold companions round,
He shook a shower of apples o'er the ground;
Scarce from the turf an apron full they'd got
When lo! from far, the keeper fired a shot!
He heard the noise and, filled with dire surprise,
Beheld the fire with his red gauldy eyes;   50
Below his partners heard the dire alarm,
And fled for safety o'er the well-stocked farm;
Now past the meadows, now they take the bog,
Pursued at distance by the man and dog;
But soon they baffled their pursuers' sight,
Sheltered beneath the friendly wings of night;
Our hero still remained alone, and now,
Sat all haphazard, on the waving bough.

And now, returning from the vain pursuit,
The dog was barking, but the man was mute,   60
Sagacious, least he scented in the wind,
The hapless wretch whom these had left behind;
The man alarmed, now stood beneath the tree,
With his long gun, to see what he could see.
The night was warm, the stars now fade away,
Yet faintly shining at the approach of day;
Through the dim shade each object stood confessed,
Before the doubtful gleam had streaked the east;
Kelly beheld the gun, alarmed him more
Than all the dangers he had met before.   70
The tree was low, the loaded branches rocked,
The man was near him, and the gun was cocked,
This Kelly saw, and gave a horrid glare,
With starting eyeballs and with upright hair;
He could not move, and instant, with affright,
Through his old breeches dropped his rousing sh——e;
From leaf to leaf, the substance tumbling down,
Full on the man, it fairly topped his crown;
But scattered in the fall; and here and there,
It clogged his eyes, and plastered all his hair.   80
He dropped his gun, and roared in sad surprise,
O murder! murder! while he wiped his eyes.
Kelly rejoiced, and with a furious bound,
He slipped his hold, and leaped upon the ground;
In vain the dog might bark, the man might call;
He passed the fences, and o'er-leaped the wall;
Then o'er the field with nimble feet he passed,
Which none could trace because he ran so fast.
Thus for an hour or more, nor ever lagged,
And as he ran his loaded pockets wagged;   90
These every now and then he stopped and d——d,
Long, large, and strong with heaps of apples crammed.
And now he reached his home at break of day,
Where his old mother snored the night away;
Nor could he tell, alas! nor could he guess
What happened all his partners in distress;
Whither they fled for safety, what they did,
Or took some apples, or those apples hid;
For in his fright descending from the tree,
He lost all thoughts, nor could he hear or see,   100
But yet at first, and sure 'twas nothing loath,
He shook the tree, and crammed his pockets both;
For then, as now, well practiced he to grind,
Took every mean advantage he could find.

Now tired with running o'er the twilight lawn,
He spied his cottage at the peep of dawn.
'Twas thatched with straw, the door of woven twigs,
That safely guards the matron and her pigs;
And ducks and hens all jointly slept together,
That kept them warm as wool in coldest weather.   110
Now breathless, pale, he entered at the door,
And cast his body on the clay-cold floor,
To rest his limbs; his mother raised his head,
From the long straw, that formed his rural bed;
No, 'twas not straw, 'twas rushes scattered round,
Or fragrant lougher¹ thrown upon the ground.
She raised her head, and still the dame kept staring,
With eyes like his, all gauldy, red and blaring;
He d——d her wrinkled face, she d——d at him,
His gauldy optics and his visage grim;   120
Irish and English he made use of both,
And in each language muttered out an oath,
Then seized her by the heels, devoid of feeling,
While hens were cackling, and while pigs were squealing;
She without clothes, yet void of every stitch,
To seek for shelter in a neighboring ditch;
He kicked her out; she roared, nor did he mind her,
But d——d her limbs, and smacked the door behind her.
This Kelly once performed, and this expressed,
The evil genius ripening in his breast,   130
Which now matured, even to the worst excess,
He sports with pain, and wantons with distress;
Still, still more cruel, more the tyrant now,
Raised to a skip, than when he drove the plow.

Canto II

The Contention of Kelly and Sangster

Kelly, Butler, and Sangster, housekeeper to a certain great family, No. 39,
Great Charles Street, Berkeley Square—Description of Kelly—His employment
in the morning—His evil disposition, and how he exerts his power over whom
he has authority—His contention with Mrs. Sangster—His unlucky breaking
the cup—A Sylph interposes

Kelly, at nine just broke from sound repose,
Opes his red eyes, and picks his Irish nose;
Now in his shoes his stinking feet he crammed,
Unforced he swore, and unprovoked he d——d;
Just rising from his bed, no creature near,

---

1. A kind of rushes or long grass, of which they make beds in summer.

Now breakfast waits, the bell salutes his ear;
Shuffling he enters, like an awkward clown,
And hauls a chair, and instant pops him down;
Now grins at Sangster, whom his words provoke,
Now sips his tea, and cracks his filthy joke,   10
Studious in all fair virtue to despise,
To slander merit, and defame the wise:
Well skilled in bawdy jest and filthy jeers,
He dwells on both to wound the modest ears;
He grins contempt, and faults her every word;
That term is nonsense, this is most absurd,
Zounds! d——n the trollop; now the gabey calf
Distorts his face to make the servants laugh;
Now sips and crunches, now distends his jaws,
Shuts his red eyes, and grins his own applause;   20
Then reprobates the King, abuses Pitt;
Heaven keep me dull if this be Irish wit.
And now good Sangster, grumbling side by side,
Pours out the tea, and thus begins to chide:
"O, Mr. Kelly, cease, we've heard enough
Of filthy love, of d——d confounded stuff;
Say to what purpose shall your tongue get loose,
And on the world discharge such rank abuse;
What's Pitt to us, or what affairs of state
Disturbs your brain? Come drink your tea, and eat,"   30
And while she spoke, she now presents the plate.
Thus she, while Kelly's inmost passions rise,
He gnashed his teeth, and rolled his gauldy eyes,
Resembling more a satyr than a man;
In this rough tone he at length began:
"D——n your Scotch tongue, d——n your impertinence;
You've neither manners, wit, or common sense;
Go to the kitchen, sawney, that's your place;
There squeeze your dishclout, there collect your grease,
And wash your scurvied hands and barrackbeaten face;
It best becomes you there to hold your clack,
To clean your coppers, and wind up your jack,
To sieve the cinders in your mean attire,
To sweep the dust, and poke the kitchen fire;
Go skim your broth, your stew-pans scrape and drain,
Collect your fat, and all your fragments glean;
You're called the grinder, in that song of songs;
To you, not me, the foul reproach belongs.
You grind your master, and your bills enlarge,
Given up with double interest in the charge;   50
You cringe and bend where grinding is your guide

But treat the wretched with contempt and pride.
Go scold and roar, and drink, and lean and lollop;
Crack the foul jest and play the common trollop,
Studious whate'er is lovely to defame;
And jeer the envied blush of modest shame:
All these are yours, but know foul plague 'tis mine,
To wait, to change the plates, and pour the wine,
Far, far from me be that unworthy task,
To lie and slander under friendship's mask,   60
This is thy task, and never-ending theme,
To lie, to swear, to slander and defame."
     Sangster, at this, with just resentment burns,
And her flushed face grew red and pale by turns;
Anger and hatred, in her bosom pent,
Raged in conjunction but could find no vent;
Then thus, at last, she made her fury known,
In half formed accents, and a stammering tone:
"D——n your red eyes, you noisy grinding rogue,
Your clownish manners, and your Irish brogue,   70
A vain conceited block, a stupid fool,
An Irish blundering butt of ridicule,
Born, as we hear, on Tipperary's bog;
Go cringe to Pocock, go, you Irish dog;
Search England round, could we your equal find!
So prone to practice, and skilled, to grind,
'Tis meet and just your cankered heart to bear,
And well the song has termed you what you are."
She spoke, and Kelly's Irish blood was up,
Fierce from the board he snatched a smoking cup;   80
This from his hand, with wrath descending full,
Leaped on the floor rebounding from her skull.
Wide o'er the dame the scalding deluge spread,
Down her fair breast, and o'er her dowd-capped head,
And reached her hair, which, studious here to shroud,
Sangster concealed beneath this flannel dowd
Because 'twas grey; she wished not to be seen
Where time had ravaged o'er her hair or skin;
For she, like all her sex, whom God forgive,
Despised old age, and yet still she wished to live: 90
This now uncovering, all her head was bare.
And showed the honors of her hoary hair;
She screamed, he swore, and adding blows to blows,
Dragged her Scotch arms, she pulled his Irish nose;
Struggling and hauling both continued long,
Both in a rage, both hardy, rough, and strong;
Now to the table where they first had place,

Kelly dragged Sangster, Sangster scratched his face;
Kelly was mad, his heart was filled with ire,
He spit, he spurned, his red eyes flashed like fire,   100
And just o'erturned the teaboard in his rage,
And all the teaboard's shining equipage;
Now cups and saucers both had felt his power,
Swept to destruction in a shining shower,
Had not some Sylph, unseen by mortal eyes,
To view the conflict, stooping from the skies,
Beheld the impending danger from afar,
Perched on the summit of a gilded jar,
High in a rich buffet, whose ample space,
Contained full many a jar and many a vase   110
Of curious figures, and crystalian frames,
That from the light reflects a thousand gleams;
From this the Sylph with anxious thought repairs,
For Sylphs, like Ladies, love such pleasing cares;
To guard the board she stretched her airy length,
Now spreads her pinions, now exerts her strength;
To shove grim Kelly from the board she tries,
And slapped his cheeks, and pecked his gauldy eyes;
Now with her wings she raised a mighty wind,
Blew back his hair, and fanned his neck behind;   120
Now in his nose her needle upright stood,
She jammed his cheek, and showed his Irish blood;
This needle, pilfered from a lady's case,
She now exerts, and maimed his ugly face;
Meantime, in many a fragment on the floor,
Lay the bright basin he had broke before,
A curious vase, indeed, of finest mold,
From distant China, edged with circling gold;
This broke the set that old Sir George had chosen,
Completely full, in one unblemished dozen.   130
A silver teapot, too, of shining frame,
With stand and spoons, and ewer to hold the cream;
Plates, knives, and egg-cups, tea-urn and whatnot,
And all the rest whom I have now forgot;
Whate'er a teaboard or buffet could grace,
Each bright material, and each shining vase,
All these were purchased by his master's Sire,
And formed the shining equipage entire,
At vast expense, but not too dearly bought,
Which Kelly used as if not worth a groat.   140
He d——d the basin, swore 'twas brittle ware,
And kicked the shining splinters here and there.
At Sangster now, by turns, he swears and grins,

Now grips her shoulders, and now kicks her shins;
Here points his malice, here exerts his spite,
And shows his grinders where he dare not bite;
Shuffling and wrestling both continued yet,
While neither conquered, neither could submit;
Yet see Miss Sangster, tiring out at length,
No longer now resists the tyrant's strength;   150
She lost her center with a sudden smack,
And hides the floor beneath her brawny back;
All this he saw, rejoiced at what was done;
He roared for sport, and clapped his hands for fun;
Then raised her up, and with a mighty shout,
Wide opes the door, and fairly banged her out:
Thus, freed triumphant from the dire attack,
He banged the sounding portal at her back;
Returned to breakfast, now he crunched his prog,
Now closed his gauldy eyes, and snored like any hog.

1802

JANE WEST

née Iliffe; pseud., Prudentia Homespun (1758–1852)

Although self-educated, West began to write at thirteen, versifying Biblical and classical themes; in later years her work was coached by one Christopher Smyth. She married a yeoman farmer in Leicestershire, "made pies and puddings," and raised three children; "engrossed by the essential duties of domestic life," she assured readers that her pen was not indulged at the expense of her "needle." Despite her modest background, she secured the patronage of a number of aristocrats, clerics, and members of the military, who subscribed to her volumes. Miscellaneous Poetry *(1786) was followed by* Miscellaneous Poems, and a Tragedy *(1791), and several volumes of fiction. Her politics were conservative: she published an elegy on Edmund Burke (1797), an anti-Jacobin* Tale of the Time *(1799), and poems on "The British Mother," and the king and queen of France.*

Her formulaic poems in praise of Elizabeth Carter, Charlotte Smith, Sarah Trimmer, and Anna Seward express her commitment to "pure morality"; her elegies, odes, pastorals, and "characters" are conventional. Her lighter occasional verse, written for friends or for a child's school performance, retains greater interest. She filled four volumes of her works in Poems and Plays *(1799–1805).* The Mother, *a poem in five books, appeared in 1809. Critics praised her language as "elegant, spirited, and correct," her doctrine as "orthodox, temperate, uniform, and liberal."*

To a Friend on Her Marriage, 1784

Accept the verse, sincere and free,
Which flows, unstudied flows, to thee;
And though the critic's searching eye
Might many a latent error spy,
Let not thy kinder taste condemn

The failings of thy sister's pen;
Some send a message, some a card,
Verse is the tribute of the bard;
Congratulate's a word so long,
I scarce can weave it in my song,   10
And fear I must again employ
The ancient phrase of "wish you joy!"
I'm forced to write without the muses;
I asked them, but they sent excuses;
They fancied that I meant to flout 'em,
But I can scribble on without 'em.

So, Lady Juno, Queen of Marriage,
Ordered the peacocks to her carriage;
Miss Iris had a hasty summons
To fetch a license from the Commons;   20
Venus and all the little loves
A-shopping went for ring and gloves;
Apollo brought his chariot down,
In hopes to drive you up to town;
Minerva wove new-fashioned satins;
Vulcan perhaps might make your pattens;
Bacchus (this rather strains belief)
Turned cook, and spitted the roast beef;
Hebe, like Hannah, dressed so fine,
With curtsies carried round the wine;   30
The Love his torch to Hymen carried,
And, in plain English, you were married.

Married, poor soul! your empire's over;
Adieu the duteous kneeling lover;
Farewell, eternally farewell,
The glory of the stately belle;
The plumed head, the trailing gown,
The crowded ball, the busy town,
For one short month are yours, and then
Must never be resumed again;   40
No more attentive Strephon flies,
Awed by the lightning of your eyes;
No longer "Madam, hear my vows,"
But "Mend this ragged wristband, spouse;
I mean to call upon a friend—
Do you your household cares attend."
"Mayn't I go too, my dear?"—"Oh, Lord!
What, married women go abroad!
Your horse is lame, the roads are rough;
Besides, at home you've work enough."   50

Off goes the husband, brisk and airy;
The wife in a profound quandary,
Whilst he of wit or scandal chatters,
Remains mumchance, and darns old tatters.
   I almost think the nuptial hour
Possessed of talismanic power;
For in a little time, how strange,
We grow enamored of the change,
Our tables and our chairs, in fact,
Possess perfections which attract,   60
Till, like the snail, we gladly bear
The constant weight of household care;
The things are trifles which we leave,
For trifles none but triflers grieve.
Like insects of the summer sky,
Were we but born to sport and die,
Then might we spread our gilded plumes
And court the flower that sweetest blooms.
But heaven, which gave us nobler powers,
With ample duties filled our hours.   70
These shrink from solitary life
To grace the faithful active wife.
Her breast each social virtue warms,
Her mind each useful science charms;
Pleased when she walks abroad to hear
The orphan's thanks, the poor man's prayer.
Whene'er she makes the social call,
Her neighbor meets her in the hall
And cries, "I'm glad to see you come,
You really grow too fond of home";   80
That home, well ordered, proves her merit,
She is its animating spirit.
Each servant at the task assigned
Proclaims a regulating mind.
Pleased she surveys her infant charge,
Beholds the mental powers enlarge,
And as the young ideas rise,
Directs their issues to the skies.
Thus whilst performing Martha's part
To serve the master of her heart,   90
How sweet the thought that he approves,
Silent esteems, and deeply loves!
   Joy then, my Sally, since I see
The path of wedlock trod by thee;
Thy virtues shall secure the palm,
Hymeneal friendship's placid calm,

And show to a too polished nation
Example worthy imitation.

1784 / 1799

On the Sonnets of Mrs. Charlotte Smith

The widowed turtle, mourning for her love,
  Breathes the soft plaintive melody of woe:
And streams that gently steal along the grove,
  In murmurs dear to melancholy, flow.

Yet to thy strains, sweet nymph of Arun's vale,
  Harsh is the turtle's note, and harsh the stream,
Even when their echoes die upon the gale,
  Or catch attention by the lunar beam.

Thy strains soul-harrowing melting pity hears,
  Yet fears to break thy privacy of pain;   10
She blots thy page with sympathetic tears,
  And while she mourns thy wrongs enjoys thy strain.

Hast thou indeed no solace? does the earth
  Afford no balm thy anguish to relieve?
Still must thou feel the pang of suffering worth,
  Taught by refinement but to charm and grieve.

Oh! if despair directs thy pensive eyes
  To where death terminates terrestrial woes,
May faith from thence exalt them to the skies,
  Where glory's palm for suffering virtue grows.   20

There may thy lyre, whose sweetly magic powers
  From pained attention forced applauding tears,
With hallelujahs fill the eternal bowers,
  The theme prolonging through eternal years.

1791

Ode IV
For the Year 1789

WRITTEN ON NEW YEAR'S DAY, 1790

I.

Cold, distant far, the sun scarce seems
  To give his salutary ray;
Moist vapors chill his struggling beams

And cloud the transitory day.
Soon to his glowing South he flies,
And evening, deepening all her dyes,
    Calls full-orbed Cynthia and her train:
To me yon starry choir appear
To sing the requiem of the year,
And hail the newborn babe, predestined now to reign.   10

II.

That newborn babe is hailed by man,
    Shortsighted man, who soon shall mourn
That of his life's allotted span,
    No portion shall again return:
Though time, now silent, steals away,
Roused by perceptible decay,
    He shall the eagle's flight arraign,
Hang on the pinions of the year,
And beg, with agonizing fear,
The months, the days, the hours, so oft misspent, in vain.   20

III.

But go, departed year! and join
    The numerous synod of thy sires;
Bid them produce their actions: Thine
    A noble eulogy requires.
Hear some of martial exploits tell;
Others on plagues and famines dwell;
    A few of gentler aspect boast
Of seas explored, of truths explained,
Of provinces from ocean gained,
Of many a well-formed state, or new discovered coast.   30

IV.

Yet envy not the garland Fame
    Grateful around their memory twines;
Go, for thyself the laurel claim,
    Which high in Freedom's temple shines:
For lo! in thy auspicious reign
The awakened nations heard the strain
    Her energetic voice impressed,
When, with divine Astrea joined,
The goddess visited mankind,
Blew her inspiring trump, and bade the world be blest.   40

V.

Before her, in effulgent light,
    With dove-like aspect Science came;
She dared false sophistry to fight,
    And triumphed in her rival's shame.
She first disclosed the liberal plan,
Which ascertains the rights of man,
    Not built on variable laws,
But at his first creation given;
The privilege bestowed by heaven,
Whence he his generous love of independence draws.   50

VI.

She told why rulers were assigned,
    And salutary laws ordained;
What fit restrictions these confined;
    How those wild anarchy restrained.
She spoke with ecstasy impelled:
Along the banks of foaming Scheld,
    The peaceful Fleming, armed for fight,
Bade a capricious prince, with shame,
His inconsistent schemes disclaim,
Nor hope the brave will yield their well-attested right.   60

VII.

Sprung from a race of tyrants, see
    The monarch of the Gallic shores
A captive, and his people free!
    He now the policy deplores,
Which hailed him unrestricted Lord,
And bade him with despotic sword
    To spread proud empire's purple pall,
Regardless of the nobler art,
Which, while it subjugates the heart,
Deals with benignant hand felicity to all.   70

VIII.

Thy present aims, fair France! pursue,
    With glory's palm thy brows enwreath;
No more let luxury subdue;
    No more let levity deceive.
Will not the luster of thy reign
Revive the wonted worth of Spain?
    She awed the Roman and the Moor.

Let godlike Africanus tell,
Speak ye who at Grenada fell,
If the Iberian mind should slavery endure.   80

IX.

Lo! Prejudice, who vainly strove
    By time to fortify her lies,
From all her dark recesses drove,
    Before the sun of Freedom flies:
Bright in the Western world it beams,
And shall the orient lack its gleams?
    There did its ancient luster shine
Where sleeps the manly Spartan soul;
    See haughty Athens brook control;
See enterprising Thebes her dear-bought rights resign.   90

X.

In vain, luxuriant Asia boasts
    Of nature's gifts on her conferred:
Alas, along her beauteous coasts
    Are slavery's clanking fetters heard.
In silent pomp, in barbarous state,
There Desolation stalks elate
    O'er regions wasted by his spear;
The abject mind, with servile awe,
Submits to each new master's law,
And pays with cringing dread the rites of heartless fear.   100

XI.

Yet here ingenious labor reigns:
    For whom, poor artist, dost thou toil?
Reapest thou the profit of thy pains?
    Is thine this richly cultured soil?
A tear suffuses his meek eye;
He faints for want; I see him die!
    My breast with indignation heaves.
Stern Tyranny, is this thy joy?
Seekest thou to blast, oppress, destroy?
Are dying groans the sounds thy idol pleased receives?   110

XII.

Oh! cast thy eyes on Afric's sons,
    Who blacken in the solar beam;
Where Niger or where Gambia runs,

Resounds the agonizing scream
Of slaves condemned to ceaseless toil,
To perish in a distant soil,
    Far from their country, kindred, sires.
Roused by reiterated groans,
Their cause indignant Justice owns,
And man's inherent right from brother man requires.   120

XIII.

Her voice, let British wisdom hear;
    Let British freedom give redress:
Britain, whose name oppressors fear,
    Whose aid the injured ever bless;
When mighty nations all around,
Sunk in servility profound,
    Or armed but in a despot's cause,
Impelled by Freedom's magic charm,
She bade her couchant lion arm,
And taught her kings to fear the spirit of her laws.   130

XIV.

Whence was this recent tide of woe?
    Can sighs from thee, stern nation, spring?
From gratitude thy sorrows flow,
    And weep the Father and the King:
Trembling she sees that mighty mind
To fever's burning rage resigned,
    Where late each tempered virtue shone.
If human hopes of succour fail,
Oh! let her prayers with heaven prevail—
The patriot king restored, fills his paternal throne.   140

XV.

To thee, fair realm, at heaven's award,
    A year profuse in blessings came;
For when it healed thy wounded lord,
    It fixed thy greatness and thy fame.
Luxuriant plenty decks thy shores;
And see, where sound yon dashing oars,
    On peace enamored commerce smiles;
His loved society she craves,
And shows her dowry, which the waves
From every region bear to these, her favorite isles.   150

XVI.

Perfect, thou youngest child of time!
   Thy predecessors' noble care:
Let virtue, in each peopled clime,
   Freedom's unsullied standard rear;
The sanguine sword of discord sheath,
And o'er the harassed nations breathe
   The renovating gales of peace;
Bid thy mild suns to Britain's king
Arise with healing on their wing:
Then will his country's joys admit no more increase!   160

1790 / 1791

To the Hon. Mrs. C——e

C——e, whom providence hath placed
In the rich realms of polished taste,
Where judgment penetrates to find
The treasures of the unwrought mind,
Where conversation's ardent spirit
Refines from dross the ore of merit,
Where emulation aids the flame
And stamps the sterling bust of fame,
Can you, accustomed to behold
The purest intellectual gold,   10
Where genius sheds its living rays,
Bright as the sunny diamond's blaze,
Like idle virtuoso deign
To pick up pebbles from the plain?
Pleased, if the worthless flints pretend
Fantastic characters to blend,
These in your cabinet insert,
And real excellence desert?
   Just the comparison will be,
If you suppose the pebble me,   20
My verse, inelegant and crude,
Confused in sense, in diction rude.
You, not content with praising, spout
To friends of fashion at a rout.
You said the author was a charmer,
Self-taught, and married to a farmer,
Who wrote all kind of verse with ease,
Made pies and puddings, frocks and cheese;

Her situation, though obscure,
Was not contemptible or poor;   30
Her conversation spoke a mind
Studious to please, but unrefined.
So warm an interest you expressed,
It was not possible to jest.
The company, amazed, perplexed,
Wondering what whim would seize you next,
Perhaps expecting you would praise
The muse of Quarles, or Sternhold's lays,
Stammered, as due to complaisance,
The civil speech of nonchalance.   40
But at the instant you withdrew,
The conversation turned on you.
The sonnet might perhaps have merit.
You had recited it with spirit.
Your manner was so full of grace,
They could not judge in such a case.
But give each character its due,
You seemed a little partial too.
All, to commend your taste, agreed—
But friendship would the best mislead.   50
A warm enthusiastic heart
Would soon be wrought upon by art.
The poem—though, indeed, no wonder
The uneducated muse should blunder—
Had here and there a small defect,
But 'twere invidious to object.
One thought alliteration fine,
And liked it every other line.
Another, might she be so free,
Would substitute a *that* for *the*.   60
A third said, "Judges will perceive
Crown has a harsher sound than *wreath*."
A witty beau observed, the nation
Had verse enough for exportation;
Wished ladies would such arts despise,
And trust their conquests to their eyes.
For, on his honor, if the whim
Should spread, they'd be too wise for him.
A man of rank grew warm, and swore
The times were bad enough before.   70
He offered to bet ten to one
The nation would be soon undone:
For honour, spirit, courage, worth,

Were all appendages on birth;
And if the rustics grew refined,
Who would the humble duties mind?
They might, from scribbling odes and letters,
Proceed to dictate to their betters.
A fellow of a college said
He studied nothing but the dead; 80
For men of sense have ne'er denied
That learning with the ancients died.
A lady of distinguished taste
Much stress on well-bred authors placed.
Though she could never time bestow
On trash inelegant and low;
Yet science was her darling passion,
And she read everything in fashion.
With her a lovely nymph agreed
That people should with caution read: 90
And really, if she must confess,
That what with visiting and dress,
Music, her ever dear delight,
And cards, the business of the night,
Her leisure was so very small,
She could not say she read at all.
  Oh! that the great ones would confine
Such treatment to such verse as mine,
Adapted but to entertain
A partial friend or simple swain. 100
Yet, with a votary's ardent zeal,
The sorrows of the muse I feel.
While Painting for her sons can claim
At once emolument and fame;
While Music, when she strikes the chord,
Confers distinction and reward;
Contemptuous scorn, or cold regard,
Awaits the heaven-illumined bard.
No more shall wealth, with fostering care,
Fair Poesy's frail blossoms rear. 110
No more shall favor's influence bland
Bid the luxuriant growth expand.
No more shall candid judgment deign
That wild luxuriance to restrain.
No more shall chiefs, in arms renowned,
Sue by the muses to be crowned.
Neglected, while the wintry storm
Tears the fine fibers of its form,
As if disdaining to complain

Of patronage, implored in vain,
It withering droops its lovely head,
And sinks upon its native bed;
Mourned only by the liberal few—
I mean the counterparts of YOU.

120

1791

MARY ROBINSON

*née Darby; pseud., Anne Frances Randall, Sappho, Laura Maria,
Tabitha Bramble, Oberon, Lesbia, etc. (1758–1800)*

*In her memoir, Robinson wrote, "through life the tempest has followed my footsteps." Her
father, an American merchant (later a captain in the Russian navy) and nephew of
Benjamin Franklin, was often absent; he abandoned the family when Robinson was in
her teens. As a child she attended the school run by Hannah More's sisters in Bristol; she
read Barbauld "with rapture." Married at fifteen to a wastrel, she soon found herself
burdened by debts and the tasks of a mother, attempting to write in "the mixed confusion
of a study and a nursery." After several months in debtor's prison with her husband, she
published her first volume,* Poems *(1775), followed by* Captivity *(1777), drawn
from her own experience. Under the sponsorship of Garrick she turned in 1777 to the
stage, where she played tragic and comic roles. As Perdita in Shakespeare's* Winter
Tale, *she caught the eye of the young Prince of Wales, whose official mistress she became
for a year; but the annuity he contracted to pay her came irregularly, causing her to fall
repeatedly into debt. Reluctant to return to the stage at the end of this affair, she had
several others, the longest one (lasting sixteen years) with Colonel Banastre Tarleton,
whom she helped compose his parliamentary speeches and a history of his campaign in
North America.*

*Struck by paralysis of her legs in her twenties, she nonetheless maintained lively con-
tact with the literary circle of the Della Cruscans, publishing* Ainsi va le monde
*(1790) and several other volumes of poems in the next two decades. Her eight novels,
partly autobiographical, fed on popular curiosity and scandal about her life, while ad-
dressing political issues.* The Widow *(1794) provoked popular debate by its "Spirit of
Democracy";* Walsingham *(1797) attacked gender conventions by depicting a cross-
dressed heroine educated as a man. In the 1790s the "English Sappho" entertained
friends by reciting spontaneous verses, anticipating the fashion for improvisation inspired
by Mme. de Staël's* Corinne *(1807); her sonnet sequence* Sappho and Phaon *(1796)
ventriloquizes the plight of the Greek poet when abandoned by her lover, as described by
Ovid. Although she wrote an ode to the "Progress of Liberty," she also dedicated a*

monody to "the beauteous martyr" Marie Antoinette. Her memoir, completed after her death by her daughter, offered another occasion for theatrical self-fashioning.

With the encouragement of Mary Wollstonecraft and William Godwin, she addressed A Letter to the Women of England on the Injustice of Mental Subordination *(1799), first under the pseudonym Anne Frances Randall, then a few months later under her own name, as* Thoughts on the Condition of Women. *The* Thoughts *argue that women "are not the mere appendages of domestic life, but the partners, the equal associates of man." Because the system of women's "mental subordination" blights universal knowledge and retards social happiness, Robinson proposes a "university for women; where they should be politely, and at the same time classically educated." She energetically attacks the double standard, arguing that weak men are wrongly preferred to strong women, and mocking those thinkers who assign the "weaker sex" all forms of poorly paid "laborious avocations" and the "supreme honor" of "unbrutifying man." Among the many women whose "literary splendor" and "genius" she praises are Sappho, Mme. de Sévigné, Mary Wollstonecraft, Catherine Macaulay, Charlotte Smith, and Helen Maria Williams.*

From 1798 to 1800 she contributed dozens of poems to the Morning Post *as M.R., or under such pen names as Laura, Oberon, Julia, Lesbia, and Tabitha Bramble; among them are ballads and satiric collages of contemporary urban life as well as poems from her novels* Walsingham *and* The Natural Daughter. *S. T. Coleridge, another contributor to the* Post, *showed her "Kubla Khan" in manuscript and called her "a woman of undoubted Genius." In response to Wordsworth's* Lyrical Ballads, *her* Lyrical Tales *(1800) address everyday figures and political subjects in both comic rhymes and serious blank verse; it was praised for its "rich and lively coloring" and its range of pathos and humor. In the last year of her life, she was arrested again for debt. Her daughter Maria, herself a novelist, collected a few late poems in the posthumous* Memoirs *(1801); she edited most of the poetry in the three-volume* Poetical Works *(1806).*

London's Summer Morning

Who has not waked to list the busy sounds
Of summer's morning, in the sultry smoke
Of noisy London? On the pavement hot
The sooty chimney-boy, with dingy face
And tattered covering, shrilly bawls his trade,
Rousing the sleepy housemaid. At the door
The milk-pail rattles, and the tinkling bell
Proclaims the dustman's office, while the street
Is lost in clouds impervious. Now begins
The din of hackney-coaches, wagons, carts;   10
While tinmen's shops, and noisy trunk-makers,
Knife-grinders, coopers, squeaking cork-cutters,
Fruit-barrows, and the hunger-giving cries
Of vegetable venders, fill the air.

Now every shop displays its varied trade,
And the fresh-sprinkled pavement cools the feet
Of early walkers. At the private door
The ruddy housemaid twirls the busy mop,
Annoying the smart 'prentice, or neat girl,
Tripping with band-box lightly. Now the sun   20
Darts burning splendor on the glittering pane,
Save where the canvas awning throws a shade
On the gay merchandise. Now, spruce and trim,
In shops (where beauty smiles with industry)
Sits the smart damsel, while the passenger
Peeps through the window, watching every charm.
Now pastry dainties catch the eye minute
Of humming insects, while the limy snare
Waits to enthral them. Now the lamplighter
Mounts the tall ladder, nimbly venturous   30
To trim the half-filled lamp, while at his feet
The pot-boy yells discordant! All along
The sultry pavement, the old-clothes-man cries
In tone monotonous, and sidelong views
The area for his traffic: now the bag
Is slyly opened, and the half-worn suit
(Sometimes the pilfered treasure of the base
Domestic spoiler), for one half its worth,
Sinks in the green abyss. The porter now
Bears his huge load along the burning way;   40
And the poor poet wakes from busy dreams
To paint the summer morning.

                                      1794 / 1804

A Fragment

I love the labyrinth, the silent glade,
For soft repose and conscious rapture made;
The melancholy murmurs of the rill,
The moaning zephyrs, and the breezy hill;
The torrent, roaring from the flinty steep,
The morning gales that o'er the landscape sweep,
The shade that dusky twilight meekly draws
O'er the calm interval of nature's pause!
Till the chaste moon, slow stealing o'er the plain,
Wraps the dark mountain in her silvery train!   10
Soothing, with sympathetic tears, the breast
That seeks for solitude and sighs for rest!

                                      1806

January 1795

Pavement slippery, people sneezing,
Lords in ermine, beggars freezing;
Titled gluttons dainties carving,
Genius in a garret starving.

Lofty mansions, warm and spacious;
Courtiers cringing and voracious;
Misers scarce the wretched heeding;
Gallant soldiers fighting, bleeding.

Wives who laugh at passive spouses;
Theaters, and meeting-houses;   10
Balls, where simpering misses languish;
Hospitals, and groans of anguish.

Arts and sciences bewailing;
Commerce drooping, credit failing;
Placemen mocking subjects loyal;
Separations, weddings royal.

Authors who can't earn a dinner;
Many a subtle rogue a winner;
Fugitives for shelter seeking;
Misers hoarding, tradesmen breaking.   20

Taste and talents quite deserted;
All the laws of truth perverted;
Arrogance o'er merit soaring;
Merit silently deploring.

Ladies gambling night and morning;
Fools the works of genius scorning;
Ancient dames for girls mistaken,
Youthful damsels quite forsaken.

Some in luxury delighting;
More in talking than in fighting;   30
Lovers old, and beaux decrepit;
Lordlings empty and insipid.

Poets, painters, and musicians,
Lawyers, doctors, politicians:
Pamphlets, newspapers, and odes,
Seeking fame by different roads.

Gallant souls with empty purses;
Generals only fit for nurses;
Schoolboys, smit with martial spirit,
Taking place of veteran merit.   40

Honest men who can't get places,
Knaves who show unblushing faces;
Ruin hastened, peace retarded;
Candor spurned, and art rewarded.

1795 / 1806

Sonnet 4

From Sappho and Phaon

WHY, when I gaze on Phaon's beauteous eyes,
   Why does each thought in wild disorder stray?
   Why does each fainting faculty decay,
And my chilled breast in throbbing tumults rise?
Mute on the ground my lyre neglected lies,
   The muse forgot, and lost the melting lay;
   My downcast looks, my faltering lips betray
That stung by hopeless passion—Sappho dies!
   Now on a bank of cypress let me rest;
Come, tuneful maids, ye pupils of my care,   10
Come, with your dulcet numbers soothe my breast
And, as the soft vibrations float on air,
   Let pity waft my spirit to the blest,
To mock the barbarous triumphs of despair!

1796

Modern Female Fashions

A form, as lank as taper, fine;
   A head like half-pint basin;
Where golden cords and bands entwine,
   As rich as fleece of Jason.

A pair of shoulders strong and wide,
   Breastworks of size resisting;
Bare arms long dangling by the side
   And shoes of ragged listing!

Cravats like towels, thick and broad,
   Long tippets made of bearskin,   10
Muffs that a Russian might applaud,
   And rouge to tint a fair skin.

Long petticoats to hide the feet,
   Silk hose with clocks of scarlet;
A load of perfumes, sickening sweet,
   Made by Parisian varlet.

A bowl of straw to deck the head,
  Like porringer unmeaning;
A bunch of poppies flaming red,
  With tawdry ribbons streaming.   20

A bush of hair, the brow to shade,
  Sometimes the eyes to cover;
A necklace such as is displayed
  By Otaheitean lover!

Long chains of gold about the neck,
  Like a sultana shining;
Bracelets, the snowy arms to deck,
  And cords the body twining.

Bare ears on either side the head,
  Like wood-wild savage satyr;   30
Tinted with deep vermilion red,
  To mock the flush of nature.

Red elbows, gauzy gloves that add
  An icy covering merely;
A wadded coat, the shape to pad,
  Like Dutch women—or nearly.

Such is caprice! but, lovely kind!
  Oh! let each mental feature
Proclaim the labor of the mind,
  And leave your charms to nature.   40

1799

Modern Male Fashions

Crops like hedgehogs, high-crowned hats,
  Whiskers like Jew Moses;
Collars padded, thick cravats,
  And cheeks as red as roses.

Faces painted deepest brown,
  Waistcoats striped and gaudy;
Sleeves thrice doubled, thick with down,
  And straps to brace the body.

Short greatcoats that reach the knees,
  Boots like French postillion;
Meant the lofty race to please,   10
  But laughed at by the million.

Square-toed shoes, with silken strings,
  Pantaloons tight fitting;

Finger decked with golden rings,
   And small-clothes made of knitting.

Bludgeons, like a pilgrim's staff,
   Or canes as slight as osiers;
Doubled hose, to show the calf,
   And swell the bills of hosiers!   20

Curricles so low that they
   Along the earth are dragging;
Hacks that weary half the day
   In Rotten-row are fagging.

Bulldogs fierce and boxers bold
   In their train attending;
Beauty which is bought with gold,
   And flatterers vice commending.

Married women, who have seen
   The fiat of the Commons;   30
Tradesmen, with terrific mien,
   And bailiffs, with a summons!

Tailors, with their bills unpaid;
   Parasites, high-feeding;
Letters, from a chambermaid,
   And billets not worth reading!

Perfumes, wedding rings to show
   Many a lady's favor,
Bought by every vaunting *beau*,
   With mischievous endeavor.   40

Such is giddy fashion's son!
   Such a modern lover!
Oh! would their reign had ne'er begun!
   And may it soon be over!

           1800

The Poet's Garret

Come, sportive fancy! come with me, and trace
The poet's attic home! the lofty seat
Of the heaven-tutored nine! the airy throne
Of bold imagination, rapture fraught
Above the herds of mortals. All around
A solemn stillness seems to guard the scene,
Nursing the brood of thought—a thriving brood

In the rich mazes of the cultured brain.
Upon thy altar, an old worm-eat board,
The panel of a broken door, or lid   10
Of a strong coffer, placed on three-legged stool,
Stand quires of paper, white and beautiful!
Paper, by destiny ordained to be
Scrawled o'er and blotted; dashed, and scratched, and torn;
Or marked with lines severe, or scattered wide
In rage impetuous! Sonnet, song, and ode,
Satire, and epigram, and smart charade;
Neat paragraph, or legendary tale,
Of short and simple meter, each by turns
Will there delight the reader.
                       On the bed   20
Lies an old rusty suit of "solemn black"—
Brushed threadbare, and, with brown, unglossy hue,
Grown somewhat ancient. On the floor is seen
A pair of silken hose, whose footing bad
Shows they are travelers, but who still bear
Marks somewhat holy. At the scanty fire
A chop turns round, by packthread strongly held;
And on the blackened bar a vessel shines
Of battered pewter, just half filled, and warm,
With Whitbread's beverage pure. The kitten purrs,   30
Anticipating dinner; while the wind
Whistles through broken panes, and drifted snow
Carpets the parapet with spotless garb
Of vestal coldness. Now the sullen hour
(The fifth hour after noon) with dusky hand
Closes the lids of day. The farthing light
Gleams through the cobwebbed chamber, and the bard
Concludes his pen's hard labor. Now he eats
With appetite voracious! nothing sad
That he with costly plate, and napkins fine,   40
Nor china rich, nor fork of silver, greets
His eye or palate. On his lyric board
A sheet of paper serves for tablecloth;
A heap of salt is served—oh! heavenly treat—
On ode Pindaric! while his tuneful puss
Scratches his slipper for her fragment sweet
And sings her love song soft, yet mournfully.
Mocking the pillar Doric, or the roof
Of architecture Gothic, all around
The well-known ballads flit, of Grub Street fame!   50
The casement, broke, gives breath celestial
To the long dying-speech; or gently fans

The love-inflaming sonnet. All around
Small scraps of paper lie, torn vestiges
Of an unquiet fancy. Here a page
Of flights poetic—there a dedication—
A list of dramatis personæ, bold,
Of heroes yet unborn, and lofty dames
Of perishable compound, light as fair,
But sentenced to oblivion!
                On a shelf,   60
(Yclept a mantlepiece) a phial stands,
Half filled with potent spirits!—spirits strong,
Which sometimes haunt the poet's restless brain,
And fill his mind with fancies whimsical.
Poor poet! happy art thou, thus removed
From pride and folly! for in thy domain
Thou can'st command thy subjects; fill thy lines;
Wield the all-conquering weapon heaven bestows
On the gray goose's wing! which, towering high,
Bears thy sick fancy to immortal fame!   70

                  1800

Ode

Inscribed to the Infant Son of S. T. Coleridge, Esq.

BORN SEPTEMBER 14, 1800, AT KESWICK, IN CUMBERLAND

Spirit of Light! whose eye unfolds
    The vast expanse of Nature's plan!
And from thy eastern throne beholds
    The mazy paths of the lorn traveler—Man!
To thee I sing! Spirit of Light, to thee
Attune the varying strain of wood-wild minstrelsy!

O Power creative!—but for thee
    Eternal chaos all things would enfold,
And black as Erebus this system be,
    In its ethereal space—benighted—rolled;   10
But for thy influence, e'en this day
Would slowly, sadly, pass away,
Nor proudly mark the mother's tear of joy,
The smile seraphic of the baby boy,
The father's eyes, in fondest transport taught
To beam with tender hope—to speak the enraptured thought.

To thee I sing, Spirit of Light! to thee
Attune the strain of wood-wild minstrelsy.

Thou sailest o'er Skiddaw's heights sublime,
Swift borne upon the wings of joyous time!   20
The sunny train, with widening sweep,
Rolls blazing down the misty-mantled steep,
And far and wide its rosy ray
Flushes the dewy-silvered breast of day!
Hope-fostering day! which Nature bade impart
Heaven's proudest rapture to the parent's heart.
Day! first ordained to see the baby pressed
Close to its beauteous mother's throbbing breast;
While instinct, in its laughing eyes, foretold
The mind susceptible—the spirit bold—   30
The lofty soul—the virtues prompt to trace
The wrongs that haunt mankind o'er life's tempestuous space.

Romantic mountains! from whose brows sublime
    Imagination might to frenzy turn!
Or to the starry worlds in fancy climb,
    Scorning this low earth's solitary bourn—
Bold cataracts! on whose headlong tide
The midnight whirlwinds howling ride—
Calm-bosomed lakes! that trembling hail
The cold breath of the morning gale,   40
And on your lucid mirrors wide display,
In colors rich, in dewy luster gay,
Mountains and woodlands, as the dappled dawn
Flings its soft pearl-drops on the summer lawn,
Or paly moonlight, rising slow,
While o'er the hills the evening zephyrs blow—
Ye all shall lend your wonders—all combine
To bless the baby boy with harmonies divine.

O baby! when thy unchained tongue
    Shall, lisping, speak thy fond surprise,   50
When the rich strain thy father sung
    Shall from thy imitative accents rise,
When through thy soul rapt Fancy shall diffuse
The mightier magic of his loftier muse,
Thy wakened spirit, wondering, shall behold
Thy native mountains, capped with streamy gold!
Thy native lakes, their cloud-topped hills among—
O hills! made sacred by thy parent's song!
Then shall thy soul, legitimate, expand,
And the proud lyre quick throb at thy command!   60
And Wisdom, ever watchful, o'er thee smile,
His white locks waving to the blast the while;

And pensive Reason, pointing to the sky,
Bright as the morning star her clear broad eye,
Unfold the page of Nature's book sublime,
The lore of every age—the boast of every clime!

Sweet baby boy! accept a stranger's song;
   An untaught minstrel joys to sing of thee!
And, all alone, her forest haunts among,
   Courts the wild tone of mazy harmony!   70
A stranger's song! babe of the mountain wild,
Greets thee as inspiration's darling child!
O! may the fine-wrought spirit of thy sire
Awake thy soul and breathe upon thy lyre!
And blest, amid thy mountain haunts sublime,
   Be all thy days, thy rosy infant days,
And may the never-tiring steps of time
   Press lightly on with thee o'er life's disastrous maze.

Ye hills, coeval with the birth of time!
   Bleak summits, linked in chains of rosy light!   80
   O may your wonders many a year invite
Your native son the breezy path to climb,
Where, in majestic pride of solitude,
   Silent and grand, the hermit thought shall trace,
   Far o'er the wild infinity of space,
The somber horrors of the waving wood,
The misty glen, the river's winding way,
The last deep blush of summer's lingering day,
The winter storm that, roaming unconfined,
Sails on the broad wings of the impetuous wind.   90

O! whether on the breezy height
Where Skiddaw greets the dawn of light,
Ere the rude sons of labor homage pay
To Summer's flaming eye or Winter's banner gray;
Whether Lodore its silver torrent flings—
The mingling wonders of a thousand springs!
Whether smooth Basenthwaite, at eve's still hour,
   Reflects the young moon's crescent pale;
Or meditation seeks her silent bower,
   Amid the rocks of lonely Borrowdale.   100
Still may thy name survive, sweet boy! till time
Shall bend to Keswick's vale thy Skiddaw's brow sublime!

               1800, rev. 1806

To the Poet Coleridge

Rapt in the visionary theme!
  Spirit divine! with thee I'll wander,
Where the blue, wavy, lucid stream,
  'Mid forest glooms, shall slow meander!
With thee I'll trace the circling bounds
  Of thy new paradise extended,
And listen to the varying sounds
  Of winds and foamy torrents blended.

Now by the source which laboring heaves
  The mystic fountain, bubbling, panting,   10
While gossamer its network weaves,
  Adown the blue lawn slanting!
I'll mark thy *sunny dome*, and view
Thy *caves of ice*, thy fields of dew!
Thy ever-blooming mead, whose flower
Waves to the cold breath of the moonlight hour!
Or when the day-star, peering bright
On the gray wing of parting night;
While more than vegetating power
Throbs grateful to the burning hour,   20
As summer's whispered sighs unfold
Her million, million buds of gold;
Then will I climb the breezy bounds
  Of thy new paradise extended
And listen to the distant sounds
  Of winds and foamy torrents blended!

Spirit divine! with thee I'll trace
Imagination's boundless space!
With thee, beneath thy *sunny dome*,
  I'll listen to the minstrel's lay,   30
  Hymning the gradual close of day;
In *caves of ice* enchanted roam,
Where on the glittering entrance plays
The moon's beam with its silvery rays;
  Or, when glassy stream
    That through the deep dell flows
Flashes the noon's hot beam,
    The noon's hot beam, that midway shows
Thy flaming temple, studded o'er
With all Peruvia's lustrous store!   40
  There will I trace the circling bounds
    Of thy new paradise extended!

And listen to the awful sounds
   Of winds and foamy torrents blended!

And now I'll pause to catch the moan
   Of distant breezes, cavern-pent;
Now, ere the twilight tints are flown,
Purpling the landscape, far and wide,
On the dark promontory's side
I'll gather wild flowers, dew besprent,   50
And weave a crown for thee,
Genius of heaven-taught poesy!
While, opening to my wondering eyes,
Thou bidst a new creation rise,
I'll raptured trace the circling bounds
   Of thy rich paradise extended
And listen to the varying sounds
   Of winds and foaming torrents blended.

And now, with lofty tones inviting,
Thy nymph, her dulcimer swift smiting,   60
Shall wake me in ecstatic measures!
Far, far removed from mortal pleasures!
In cadence rich, in cadence strong,
Proving the wondrous witcheries of song!
   I hear her voice! thy *sunny dome*,
Thy *caves of ice*, loud repeat,
Vibrations, maddening sweet,
   Calling the visionary wanderer home.
She sings of thee, O favored child
Of minstrelsy, sublimely wild!   70
Of thee, whose soul can feel the tone
Which gives to airy dreams a *magic* all thy own!

               1800

The Fugitive

Oft have I seen yon solitary man
Pacing the upland meadow. On his brow
Sits melancholy, marked with decent pride,
As it would fly the busy, taunting world,
And feed upon reflection. Sometimes, near
The foot of an old tree, he takes his seat
And with the page of legendary lore
Cheats the dull hour, while evening's sober eye
Looks tearful as it closes. In the dell,

By the swift brook he loiters, sad and mute,   10
Save when a struggling sigh, half murmured, steals
From his wrung bosom. To the rising moon,
His eye raised wistfully, expression fraught,
He pours the cherished anguish of his soul,
Silent yet eloquent: for not a sound
That might alarm the night's lone sentinel,
The dull-eyed owl, escapes his trembling lip,
Unapt in supplication. He is young,
And yet the stamp of thought so tempers youth
That all its fires are faded. What is he?   20
And why, when morning sails upon the breeze,
Fanning the blue hill's summit, does he stay
Loitering and sullen, like a truant boy,
Beside the woodland glen; or stretched along
On the green slope, watch his slow wasting form
Reflected, trembling, on the river's breast?

His garb is coarse and threadbare, and his cheek
Is prematurely faded. The checked tear,
Dimming his dark eye's luster, seems to say,
"This world is now, to me, a barren waste,   30
A desert, full of weeds and wounding thorns,
And I am weary: for my journey here
Has been, though short, but cheerless." Is it so?
Poor traveler! Oh tell me, tell me all—
For I, like thee, am but a fugitive,
An alien from delight, in this dark scene!

And, now I mark thy features, I behold
The cause of thy complaining. Thou art here
A persecuted exile! one, whose soul
Unbowed by guilt, demands no patronage   40
From blunted feeling, or the frozen hand
Of gilded ostentation. Thou, poor priest!
Art here a stranger, from thy kindred torn—
Thy kindred massacred! thy quiet home,
The rural palace of some village scant,
Sheltered by vineyards, skirted by fair meads,
And by the music of a shallow rill
Made ever cheerful, now thou hast exchanged
For stranger woods and valleys.

                                        What of that?
Here, or on torrid deserts; o'er the world   50
Of trackless waves, or on the frozen cliffs
Of black Siberia, thou art not alone!

For there, on each, on all, the Deity
Is thy companion still! Then, exiled man!
Be cheerful as the lark that o'er yon hill,
In nature's language, wild, yet musical,
Hails the Creator! nor thus sullenly
Repine that through the day the sunny beam
Of lustrous fortune gilds the palace roof,
While thy short path, in this wild labyrinth,   60
Is lost in transient shadow.
                              Who that lives
Hath not his portion of calamity?
Who that feels can boast a tranquil bosom?
The fever throbbing in the tyrant's veins
In quick strong language tells the daring wretch
That he is mortal, like the poorest slave
Who wears his chain yet healthfully suspires.
The sweetest rose will wither, while the storm
Passes the mountain thistle. The bold bird,
Whose strong eye braves the ever burning orb,   70
Falls like the summer fly and has at most
But his allotted sojourn. Exiled man!
Be cheerful! Thou art not a fugitive!
All are thy kindred—all thy brothers, here—
The hoping—trembling creatures—of *one* God!

                                        1800

The Camp

Tents, *marquees*, and baggage wagons;
Suttling houses, beer in flagons;
Drums and trumpets, singing, firing;
Girls seducing, *beaux* admiring;
Country lasses gay and smiling,
City lads their hearts beguiling;
Dusty roads and horses frisky,
Many an *Eton boy* in whisky;
Taxed carts full of farmers' daughters;
Brutes condemned, and man—who slaughters!   10
Public houses, booths, and castles;
Belles of fashion, serving vassals;
Lordly generals fiercely staring,
Weary soldiers, sighing, swearing;
Petit maîtres always dressing—
In the glass themselves caressing;
Perfumed, painted, patched, and blooming

Ladies—manly airs assuming!
Dowagers of fifty, simpering
Misses, for a lover whimpering;   20
Husbands drilled to household tameness,
Dames heartsick of wedded sameness.
Princes setting girls a-madding;
Wives forever fond of gadding;
Princesses with lovely faces,
Beauteous children of the Graces!
Britain's pride and virtue's treasure,
Fair and gracious beyond measure!
Aides-de-camp and youthful pages;
Prudes and vestals of all ages!   30
Old coquettes, and matrons surly;
Sounds of distant *hurly-burly*!
Mingled voices, uncouth singing;
Carts full laden, forage bringing;
Sociables and horses weary;
Houses warm and dresses airy;
Loads of fattened poultry; pleasure
Served (to nobles) without measure;
Doxies, who the wagons follow;
Beer, for thirsty hinds to swallow;   40
Washerwomen, fruit-girls cheerful,
Ancient ladies—*chaste* and *fearful*!
Tradesmen leaving shops and seeming
More of *war* than profit dreaming;
Martial sounds and braying asses,
Noise that every noise surpasses!
All confusion, din, and riot,
Nothing clean—and nothing quiet.

1800

ELIZABETH HANDS

pseud., Daphne (fl. 1789)

As recounted in the dedication to her only published volume, Hands faced the obstacles of one "born in obscurity, and never emerging beyond the lower stations in life." She worked as a maidservant, then lived near Rugby as wife of a blacksmith with whom she had a daughter in 1785. Under the name "Daphne" she published verse in Jopson's Coventry Mercury. *Her epic on an Old Testament incident of incestuous rape and fratricide,* The Death of Amnon *(1789), collected with pastoral and occasional verse, drew the attention and support of masters at Rugby School, who organized a subscription for its publication that was supported by Anna Seward as well as other local patrons. The volume, which includes witty and conversational pieces, received a favorable review in the* Gentleman's Magazine *(June 1790).*

On an Unsociable Family

O what a strange parcel of creatures are we,
Scarce ever to quarrel, or ever agree;
We all are alone, though at home all together,
Except to the fire constrained by the weather;
Then one says, " 'Tis cold," which we all of us know,
And with unanimity answer, " 'Tis so."
With shrugs and with shivers all look at the fire,
And shuffle ourselves and our chairs a bit nigher;
Then quickly, preceded by silence profound,
A yawn epidemical catches around: 10
Like social companions we never fall out,
Nor ever care what one another's about;
To comfort each other is never our plan,
For to please ourselves, truly, is more than we can.

1789

[A Poem]

*Written, Originally Extempore, on Seeing a Mad Heifer Run
Through the Village Where the Author Lives*

When summer smiled, and birds on every spray
In joyous warblings tuned their vocal lay,
Nature on all sides showed a lovely scene,
And people's minds were, like the air, serene;
Sudden from the herd we saw an heifer stray
And to our peaceful village bend her way.
She spurns the ground with madness as she flies,
And clouds of dust, like autumn mists, arise;
Then bellows loud. The villagers, alarmed,
Come rushing forth with various weapons armed: 10
Some run with pieces of old broken rakes,
And some from hedges pluck the rotten stakes;
Here one in haste with hand-staff of his flail,
And there another comes with half a rail;
Whips, without lashes, sturdy plowboys bring,
While clods of dirt and pebbles others fling;
Voices tumultuous rend the listening ear:
"Stop her"—one cries; another—"Turn her there,"
But furiously she rushes by them all,
And some huzza and some to cursing fall;   20
A mother snatched her infant off the road,
Close to the spot of ground where next she trod;
Camilla, walking, trembled and turned pale:
See o'er her gentle heart what fears prevail!
At last the beast, unable to withstand
Such force united, leapt into a pond;
The water quickly cooled her maddened rage;
No more she'll fright our village, I presage.

1789

A Poem

*On the Supposition of an Advertisement Appearing in a Morning Paper,
of the Publication of a Volume of Poems by a Servant Maid*

The teakettle bubbled, the tea things were set,
The candles were lighted, the ladies were met;
The how-d'ye's were over and entering bustle,
The company seated, and silks ceased to rustle:
The great Mrs. Consequence opened her fan;
And thus the discourse in an instant began:
(All affected reserve and formality scorning)

"I suppose you all saw in the paper this morning,
A *volume of poems* advertised—'tis said
They're produced by the pen of a poor *servant maid*."   10
"A servant write verses!" says Madam Du Bloom;
"Pray what is the subject?—a *mop*, or a *broom*?"
"He, he, he," says Miss Flounce; "I suppose we shall see
An *ode on a dishclout*—what else can it be?"
Says Miss Coquettella, "Why, ladies, so tart?
Perhaps Tom the footman has fired her heart;
And she'll tell us how charming he looks in new clothes,
And how nimble his hand moves in brushing the shoes;
Or how the last time that he went to Mayfair,
He bought her some sweethearts of gingerbread ware."   20
"For my part I think," says old Lady Mar-Joy,
"A servant might find herself other employ:
Was she mine I'd employ her as long as 'twas light,
And send her to bed without candle at night."
"Why so?" says Miss Rhymer, displeased; "I protest
'Tis pity a genius should be so depressed!"
"What ideas can such low-bred creatures conceive,"
Says Mrs. Noworthy, and laughed in her sleeve.
Says old Miss Prudella, "If servants can tell
How to write to their mothers, to say they are well,   30
And read of a Sunday *The Duty of Man*—
Which is more I believe than one half of them can—
I think 'tis much *properer* they should rest there,
Than be reaching at things so much out of their sphere."
Says old Mrs. Candor, "I've now got a maid
That's the plague of my life—a young gossipping jade;
There's no end of the people that after her come,
And whenever I'm out, she is never at home;
I'd rather ten times she would sit down and write,
Than gossip all over the town every night."   40
"Some whimsical trollop, most like," says Miss Prim,
"Has been scribbling of nonsense, just out of a whim,
And conscious it neither is witty or pretty,
Conceals her true name, and ascribes it to Betty."
"I once had a servant myself," says Miss Pines,
"That wrote on a *wedding*, some very good lines."
Says Mrs. Domestic, "and when they were done,
I can't see for my part, what use they were *on*;
Had she wrote a receipt, to've instructed you how
To warm a cold breast of veal, like a ragout,   50
Or to make cowslip wine, that would pass for champagne,
It might have been useful, again and again."
On the sofa was old Lady Pedigree placed.

She owned that for poetry she had no taste,
That the study of heraldry was more in fashion,
And boasted she knew all the crests in the nation.
Says Mrs. Routella, "Tom, take out the urn,
And stir up the fire, you see it don't burn."
The tea things removed, and the tea table gone,
The card tables brought, and the cards laid thereon,　　60
The ladies ambitious for each other's crown,
Like courtiers contending for honors sat down.

1789

A Poem

On the Supposition of the Book Having Been Published and Read

The dinner was over, the tablecloth gone,
The bottles of wine and the glasses brought on;
The gentlemen filled up the sparkling glasses
To drink to their king, to their country and lasses;
The ladies a glass or two only required,
To the drawing room then in due order retired;
The gentlemen likewise that chose to drink tea;
And after discussing the news of the day—
What wife was suspected; what daughter eloped;
What thief was detected; that 'twas to be hoped　　10
The rascals would all be convicted and roped;
What chambermaid kissed when her lady was out;
Who won, and who lost, the last night at the rout;
What lord gone to France; and what tradesman unpaid;
And who and who danced at the last masquerade;
What banker stopped payment with evil intention—
And twenty more things much too tedious to mention,
Miss Rhymer says, "Mrs. Routella, ma'am, pray
Have you seen the new book (that we talked of that day,
At your house, you remember) of *poems*, 'twas said　　20
Produced by the pen of a poor *servant maid*?"
The company silent, the answer expected;
Says Mrs. Routella, when she'd recollected,
"Why, ma'am, I have bought it for Charlotte; the child
Is so fond of a book, I'm afraid it is spoiled.
I thought to have read it myself, but forgat it;
In short, I have never had time to look at it.
Perhaps I may look it o'er some other day;
Is there anything in it worth reading, I pray?
For your nice attention there's nothing can 'scape."　　30
She answered, "There's one piece, whose subject's a rape—"

"A *rape*!" interrupted the Captain Bonair,
"A delicate theme for a female, I swear";
Then smirked at the ladies, they simpered all round,
Touched their lips with their fans—Mrs. Consequence frowned.
The simper subsided, for she with her nods,
Awes these lower assemblies as Jove awes the gods.
She smiled on Miss Rhymer, and bade her proceed—
Says she, "There are various subjects indeed:
With some little pleasure I read all the rest,   40
But the *Murder of Amnon*'s the longest and best."
"Of Amnon, of Amnon, Miss Rhymer, who's he?
His name," says Miss Gaiety, "is quite new to me."
" 'Tis a Scripture tale, ma'am—he's the son of King David,"
Says a reverend old rector. Quoth madam, "I have it;
A Scripture tale?—ay—I remember it—true;
Pray is it i'th' old Testament or the new?
If I thought I could readily find it, I'd borrow
My housekeeper's Bible, and read it tomorrow."
" 'Tis in Samuel, ma'am," says the Rector—Miss Gaiety   50
Bowed, and the Reverend blushed for the laity.
"You've read it, I find," says Miss Harriot Anderson;
"Pray, sir, is it anything like *Sir Charles Grandison*?"
"How you talk," says Miss Belle. "How should such a girl write
A novel or anything else that's polite?
You'll know better in time, miss"—she was but fifteen;
Her mamma was confused—with a little chagrin,
Says, "Where's your attention, child? Did not you hear
Miss Rhymer say that it was poems, my dear?"
Says Sir Timothy Turtle, "My daughters ne'er look   60
In anything else but a cookery book,
The properest study for women designed."
Says Mrs. Domestic, "I'm quite of your mind."
"Your haricots, ma'am, are the best I e'er eat,"
Says the Knight. "May I venture to beg a receipt?"
" 'Tis much at your service," says madam, and bowed,
Then fluttered her fan, of the compliment proud.
Says Lady Jane Rational, "The bill of fare
Is the utmost extent of my cookery care:
Most servants can cook for the palate I find,   70
But very few of them can cook for the mind."
"Who," says Lady Pedigree, "can this girl be?
Perhaps she's descended of some family—"
"Of family, doubtless," says Captain Bonair,
"She's descended from Adam, I'd venture to swear."
Her Ladyship drew herself up in her chair,
And twitching her fan-sticks, affected a sneer.

"I know something of her," says Mrs. Devoir,
"She lived with my friend, Jacky Faddle, Esq.
'Tis sometime ago, though; her mistress said then,   80
The girl was excessively fond of a pen;
I saw her, but never conversed with her—*though*
One can't make acquaintance with servants, you know."
" 'Tis pity the girl was not bred in high life—"
Says Mr. Fribbello; "Yes—then," says his wife,
"She doubtless might have wrote something worth notice."
" 'Tis pity," says one; says another, "And so 'tis."
"O law!" says young Seagram, "I've seen the book, now
I remember, there's something about a mad cow."
"A mad cow!—ha, ha, ha, ha," returned half the room;   90
"What can ye expect better?" says Madam Du Bloom.
They look at each other—a general pause—
And Miss Coquettella adjusted her gauze.
The Rector reclined himself back in his chair
And opened his snuffbox with indolent air;
"This book," says he—*snift, snift*—"has in the beginning"
(The ladies give audience to hear his opinion)
"Some pieces, I think, that are pretty correct;
A style elevated you cannot expect:
To some of her equals they may be a treasure,   100
And country lasses may read 'em with pleasure.
That *Amnon*, you can't call it poetry neither,
There's no flights of fancy, or imagery either;
You may style it prosaic, blank verse at the best;
Some pointed reflections, indeed, are expressed;
The narrative lines are exceedingly poor:
Her Jonadab is a—" the drawing room door
Was opened; the gentlemen came from below
And gave the discourse a definitive blow.

                                                          1789

The Death of Amnon

Canto I

The royal youth I sing, whose sister's charms
Inspired his heart with love; a latent love
That preyed upon his health; he drooped; so droops
A beauteous flower, when in the stalk some vile
Opprobrious insect 'bides. In conscious pain
He passed the hapless hours, while in his breast
The aspiring passion, yet by virtue swayed,

Its proper limits knew. "I love," said he.
"Whom do I love? My sister—ah, my sister;
Can I my misplaced passion gratify,   10
And bring disgrace on her? No, sweetest maid,
I am thy brother; 'tis a brother's part
Thy honor to protect and not destroy.
When Shechem burning with untamed desire
Dishonored Dinah, how her brethren raged!
Each took his sword: the princely ravisher
And every citizen a victim fell
To their just fury. I'm an Israelite;
Shall I forgo this high prerogative,
And plunge myself and sister into ruin?   20
An act that even a heathen would degrade.
No; sooner shall my passion unrevealed
Lie cankering in my bosom, till it taints
My very blood, and stops my panting breath.
Better my loved companions pass my grave
And shed a tear to think I died so young
Than shun me living as a vile reproach
To nature, royalty, and Israel.
Already I perceive my strength to fail,
The ruddy bloom of health forsakes my cheeks;   30
Perhaps death's not far off— O welcome guest,
Hasten thy tardy steps; why lingerest thou,
Or waitest on those who wish thee far away?
O thou, that hast the powers of life and death,
Take hence my life and end my wretchedness.
A spacious land I see on every side
Blest with fertility; the cultured vales
Yield plenteous crops; the rising hills are rich,
With verdant pasture mantled, crowned with trees;
My father's kingdom this. What is it to me?   40
It fires not my ambition; all I ask
Is one small spot of earth to lay me down
Beneath the turf, forgetting and forgot:
A small request and yet, though small, denied.
Methinks I feel my strength renewed; 'tis so;
Struggling with life I sigh for death in vain.
Again my passions rise, again rebel;
I still must live and live in misery.
But I've a thought, that stings me yet more deep:
Doubtless some happy rival will be crowned   50
With Tamar's love; O torturing thought, must I
Behold her decked in bridal robes to bless
A rival? 'tis too much—I cannot bear

E'en to suppose it; I'll from court retire:
My gay companions now are irksome grown,
And all my pleasures are transformed to pains.
My sister's cheering smiles, that once conveyed
Soft raptures to my heart, awake such pangs,
As I can scarce endure. Again I feel
My spirits sink—Oh! welcome, fading sickness!   60
I'll cherish thee and aid thee with my sighs
To still this heart, that now rebellious beats
Against my reason's strongest argument.
Though Tamar's beauty prompts my warmest wish,
Her fairer virtues keep me still in awe,
Forbidding my aspiring love to soar.
With sweet simplicity she smiles, secure
In innocence, commanding my respect,
And this command I must— I will obey;
But fly her presence, lest some hapless smile   70
Inflame my soul, and I in passion's frenzy
Should act against my final resolution
To bear my griefs untold and secret pine
Till saddening sorrow sinks me to the grave."
Thus, to himself complaining, he resolved,
Nor sought a confidant to share his grief.

A friend he had, the son of Shimeah,
Named Jonadab; a man by nature subtle,
Proud, and ambitious; yet would meanly stoop
To the most base and most ignoble acts   80
To serve his private ends. The artless youth
Oft to his plausibilities gave ear,
Not e'en suspecting that beneath the cloak
Of formal flatteries self-interest hides
Its serpent head. Yet still the youth from him
His wayward passion labored to conceal
By forcing smiles to veil his grief; nor knew,
How little they resemble those that spring
From gentle impulses of hearts at ease.
For Jonadab, with penetrating eye,   90
Quickly discerned the grief he strove to hide.
"What cause," said he, "can Amnon have to mourn?
A king's son now—a king in time may be.
Was it in probability that I
Should be a king, the very contemplation
Would shut my soul to sorrow. Oh! the thought
Swells my imagination. Did but Amnon
Aspire as much to greatness, I could plot

Surprising stratagems. But he, poor prince,
Has long imbibed such close contracted notions,   100
As bar his path to honor. Like a maid
He talks of virtue, weeps at others' woes,
Yet talks of greatness too; 'tis in the soul,
He says, all greatness dwells; 'tis not the crown
That makes his father great, but 'tis his virtues;
And those alone he wishes to inherit,
Thereby to gain dominion o'er himself,
And reign unenvied; but perchance there now
Springs in his soul some change of sentiment;
And he his principles, so long retained,   110
Loath to renounce, may want a friend to prompt
And urge him to the attainment of his will.
Then who so fit for such a task as I?
I'm great in his esteem, have free access
To him at all times; but if now I'm slack,
Perhaps I may be rivaled in his favor
By some more forward to promote his wish.
I'll to him straight; in these cool evening hours
Into his private garden he retires,
Sighs to the winds, and to the moon complains.   120
But I must him approach with seeming awe,
As fearful to disturb his solitude,
And with a gentle flow of soothing words
Insinuate myself into his soul,
Then guide him as I please."
                                    The love-sick youth
Beneath the thickest solitary shade
Was wandering, lost in melancholy mood,
So deep in thought, he ne'er perceived the approach
Of Jonadab till startled by his voice;
Then smiled, as usual, as his friend drew near,   130
Who thus the royal youth addressed: "Oh! why
Dost thou, a king's son, pine in discontent?
Can there be ought that's unattainable
To crown thy soul with peace? Thy father's kind,
Too fond and too indulgent to refuse
A son's request, be what it will methinks.
But why from me conceal thy griefs? Am I,
A friend, unworthy of thy confidence?
Have I e'er been unfaithful to my trust?
Or has some jealous whisperer imposed   140
Upon my royal friend's credulity,
To vilify his faithful Jonadab?"
Half lost in thought, the prince made no reply,

And Jonadab awhile suspended stood;
But, recollecting, took his hand and said,
"Why weeps my prince? what sorrow wounds thy heart?"
"I love," says Amnon; and his hand withdrew
To wipe his tears, and turned from Jonadab;
Then seems returning, then he onward goes
In pensive sadness. Jonadab pursues,   150
Resolved to urge his full confession, lest
Some other should be made his confidant,
And he, discarded, lose the prince's favor.

Amnon returned, as ready to confess
As he to hear, and thus his speech began:
"O friend, I love—I love thee as my friend,
And such thou art, the sharer of my joys;
All my delights were doubled, shared with thee.
But now a strange dilemma has befallen me;
I would not speak it to an ear but thine;   160
I love my sister, Tamar; tell it not,
My reason almost fails to be my guide.
This passion—oh! this wild rebellious passion—
If cherished, fast it grows as noisome weeds,
And, if suppressed, still strengthens in the stalk.
So let it strengthen, till, too strong for me,
I sink beneath its weight. But Jonadab,
Ne'er let the secret pass thy lips, for I
So much respect and honor her I love
That for the richest diadem on earth   170
I would not give her pain; her heart's so prone
To pity, it would burst in grief for me,
Did she but know the half I feel for her."
Then Jonadab, with seeming kind affection,
And tears of sympathy replied: "Kind Prince,
Distrust me not, thy confidence I claim;
Thou knowest the feelings of my friendly heart
Admit no rest if Amnon is unhappy;
Shall David's meanest subjects smile secure
Beneath his prudent equitable sway,   180
Their least complaints regarded and his son
Repine without redress? It must not be."
Amnon replied, "I cannot thee distrust,
And if thou knowest a way to ease my heart,
Discover it, my friend, for I despair."
"Dispel those useless tears," says Jonadab.
"Think not to drown it in those briny floods:
Love is a flame those waters cannot quench;

Nor is there any cure short of enjoyment."
"Then there's no hope for me," the prince replied,   190
"Till the kind earth receive me; for can I—?
I cannot—oh! I cannot injure her."
"Droop not, my gentle friend," says Jonadab;
"This timorous tenderness but ill becomes
A royal prince, the hope of Israel,
The son of David; think but who thou art,
The eldest son of Israel's mighty king,
Whose dreaded name through all the nations round
Strikes terror to his enemies and fills
The grateful hearts of all his friends with joy;   200
Whose tongues with pleasure tell his mighty deeds,
And virgins celebrate his fame in songs,
While Amnon thus effeminately weeps
Like some fair captive maid, snatched from the arms
Of her fond lover. O my royal friend,
Better ten thousand injured virgins mourn
Than David's son thus live inglorious.
There is a sort of viand she prepares,
Unparalleled, of which none other knows
The just proportion of ingredients used.   210
A sickness feigned might veil the deep design
And put her in thy power, by this excuse:
That thou canst take nought else. Nor fear but she
Will keep the secret to preserve her fame."
After a little pause the youth replied,
"It shall be so; but yet I doubt—I fear—
If I— I'll think no more of consequences,
I am determined—yes, it shall be so."
"Tomorrow be it done," said Jonadab.
Amnon replied, "Tomorrow is the day."   220

So parted they that night; and Jonadab
In conscious pride of self-sufficiency,
Thus to himself his royal friend derides.
"Poor thing, how easily he's wrought upon!
In time the kingdom will be his, and I,
In fact, shall reign, though he the title bears.
That time might be anticipated, but
Amnon wants courage for so bold a stroke.
He's unambitious, nor has resolution
To seize a tempting crown within his reach;   230
But should it gently fall upon his head,
Perhaps he'll wear it, if some bolder hand
Don't snatch it off. But this amour may prove

A clue to guide to greater enterprises.
When these precise ones once extend beyond
The bounds their narrow minds have circumscribed,
From step to step insensibly they go,
Till so familiarized by custom, they
With calmness will transact the very things,
Which but to mention, ere they launched so far,   240
They'd shudder at. But I must wait the event."
So saying, he retired to take repose,
The common blessing graciously diffused
Through nature, to refresh her wearied sons,
That with new strength and vigor they may hail
The rising day, rejoicing in the light.

Canto II

From Ammon's wasted cities, with the crown
Of Hanun, their proud contumacious king,
Whose insolence had caused his overthrow,
The conquering king of Israel returned
In glorious triumph to Jerusalem;
There from exhausting toils of bloody war
In safety to repose his wearied soul
And taste the sweets of calm domestic bliss.
But ere the tumults of triumphal joy
Subsided, and the sacred rites performed   10
Of general praises with the harp and song,
The king's long-wished tranquility's disturbed
By the sad news that Amnon, his dear son,
A captive now to dangerous sickness lies,
While life and death dispute their doubtful right.
The pious king laid down his harp, the song
Unfinished, and with anxious haste repaired
To Amnon, whose dissimulation passed
Quite unsuspected. How could he suspect
A fraud of such sort in a virtuous son?   20
Full oft a partial parent overlooks
An obvious fault, or by affection blind
Discerns it not; but here no cause appeared
To awake suspicion, for his languid eyes
And pallid cheeks gave signals of disease.
While thus the son in feeble tone complained,
The tender father stooping low to hear,
"I'm very sick, and whatsoever food
My servants here prepare gives me disgust.
My sister, Tamar, with superior skill,   30

Prepares a cake delicious to my taste;
This I could eat methinks from her kind hand,
Was she permitted to attend me here."
The king with fond solicitude retired
And speedily dispatched a messenger
To Tamar, saying 'twas his royal will
That she should go direct to Amnon's house
And there administer with friendly aid
Whate'er his sickly appetite demands.

The hour had passed, at which the royal maid   40
Came from her closet, splendidly attired;
Her hair with precious sparkling gems beset,
Faint mimics of her more illustrious eyes.
About her neck a shining golden chain,
And o'er her loosely thrown, in careless folds,
A various colored robe, which, as she moved,
Trailed on the ground or fluttered in the wind.
Thus all the virgin daughters of the king
In splendid raiment shone; but none so bright
In beauty as the daughter of Maacah.   50
Soon as the sun had drank the morning dew,
Into her garden walked the lovely fair:
Not like a proud imperious haughty queen,
With tossing head and scornful eyes that glared
Malignant, scattering discontent around,
And vain in fancied greatness; greater she
In inoffensive modesty and bright
In virtue as the rays that gild the morn,
Warming the flowers to ripeness, and exhaling
Their various sweets to fill the garden air.   60
Pleased with the grateful smell, she skips about
From flower to flower and cautiously selects
The sweetest in a wreath, to deck that breast,
Which never yet inflamed by vicious thought,
Or by unreasonable rebukes depressed,
Had felt a secret pang or learned to sigh.
But oh! how happy for the mortal race
That from their eyes the future is obscured;
Did we but know the secret ills that wait
In darkness to surprise us, what would be   70
Our life but one sad scene of misery?
All present pleasures would be bitter made
By aggravating thoughts of ills to come.
But blind to future things the present bless.
When peace and plenty smile auspiciously,

The heart with sense of Providence impressed
O'erflows with gratitude and conscious joy.
Such joy now filled the royal fair one's breast,
Intent on the formation of her wreath;
When lo! her handmaid came to her in haste   80
With tidings that a message had arrived
Straight from the king, declaring his desire
That she to Amnon's house immediately
Would go and dress him cakes, for he is sick.
The king's command she instantly obeyed;
Down dropped the unfinished wreath; she skimmed along
O'er the parterres, nor stayed to find the path.
Her sweeping garments gently brushed the flowers;
The ripest, shedding, strewed the way she went
With variegated fragments. So the breeze   90
Whisks o'er the forest, and some shattering leaves
Fall gently rustling through the shrubs beneath.
Then, gathering up her robe, she onward sprang,
And sisterly affection urged her haste.

Amnon in highest expectation lies,
Counting the slow-paced moments as they passed;
Now thinks his scheme's discovered—he's betrayed—
Or some cursed intervening accident
Delays, perhaps prevents, her coming. Thus
Doubts, fears, and wild impatience in his breast   100
Tumultuously contended till she came,
With all the feelings of a tender sister;
But not a thought of vile licentious love
Profaned her breast; to see him thus she wept,
But turning, wiped her tears, suppressed her grief,
And with officious haste the cakes prepared.
Wisdom has power, like the meridian sun,
To hide all other brightness in its glare;
But virgin modesty, with winning smiles,
Shines a perpetual morning. So she shone   110
Serenely mild, nor knew her power to please.
But oh! the graceful dignity of virtue
Unthinking captivates the worthy soul,
The feebly good with emulation fires,
And strikes the very libertines with awe.
So Amnon, awed to see her lovely form,
Became irresolute; and recantation
Staggered his purpose. First he paused; then, thus
Expostulating with himself, he lay:
"Oh! how can I despoil this lovely maid,   120

This fairest of the fair? I cannot—no—
I'll let her go untouched. But then must I
Still pine in languishment, as heretofore;
And Jonadab will at my weakness laugh."
At last some wine he snatched, and eager drank
To drown his scruples and to fire his soul.
Such aid the most abandoned oft require,
When unsuspecting innocence at once
Tempts and forbids—more powerfully forbids
Than the persuasive eloquence of speech.   130
But the defense, which innocence can boast
With tears and mild entreaties, is but weak
When love and wine unite their frantic powers,
And leaving virtue fainting in the rear,
Rush on impetuous. Hapless Tamar thus
To lawless outrage falls the unwilling prey.

Canto III

Heaven gave to man superior strength, that he
The weaker sex might succor and defend;
But he that dares pervert this given blessing,
To ruin and destroy their innocence,
Shall feel pursuing vengeance, nor escape
Her rod uplifted, nor avert the stroke.
Conviction's sword shall pierce him, and remorse
With all the tortures of the mind assail,
Till he a victim falls to grim despair,
Except repentance timely to his aid   10
Come with her tears to soothe, to mitigate,
While her attendant hope extends a ray
To point where mercy spreads her healing wings.
Nor e'en with this is vengeance satisfied,
She'll still pursue with some external ills,
Exhausted health and spirits; drooping—drear,
An outcast of society he roams,
Alike discarded by his friends and foes;
Perhaps assassination proves his end.
    The hapless Amnon from his couch arose,   20
Inflamed with hatred more than once with love.
Frantic with keen remorse and conscious guilt,
He raved—he stamped—when to him Jonadab
Came to congratulate him; but the prince
Shot from his eyes a keen malignant glance,
That spoke displeasure, and with threatening hand
Upheld, thus in an angry tone began:

"Hence from my sight, thou basest, worst of fiends,
Nor ever dare approach my presence more."
Struck with this strange reception, Jonadab   30
Stepped back, and bowing with respectful awe,
Said, "O my prince, why am I thus discarded?
I still remain thy well-affected friend,
Ready to—" "Prompt me" (interrupts the prince)
"To do some greater crime than I have done.
Curse on thy instigations; to my heart,
My inexperienced heart thou drilledst a way
To infuse licentiousness; and thou a friend?
Ere thou presumest to take that sacred name,
Abandon thy base principles and learn   40
'Tis virtue only constitutes a friend."
He paused—the astonished Jonadab approached
Nearer to Amnon; begged him to resume
His wonted calmness, but to hear him speak.
"I'll hear no more of thee," replied the prince;
"I'm lost; I'm irrecoverably lost:
What were the pains I felt to those I feel?
An hell within me burns, and deep remorse,
That never dying worm, now gnaws my soul;
And thou, my instigator. Villain, flee,   50
Lest this my crime I complicate with murder."
Then Jonadab withdrew chagrined, and full
Of rancorous malice, muttering as he went,
"Shall murder crown thy crime, young man?—it shall;
But thou the murdered, not the murderer.
I'll hence to Absalom, the brother kind
Of this fair injured maid; he doubtless will
Avenge her wrongs, and show himself a brother.
He has a noble, calm, undaunted spirit,
Deliberately resolute and fit   60
For such an enterprise; and Jonadab
Shall not be slack to aggravate the crime
And urge him on or aid him, if required.
But I must veil my real sentiments
With counterfeited sorrow, and observe
Each secret movement of his varying soul,
And sympathize with him."

                        Young Absalom,
Returning from the fields, where he had been
To view his teeming flocks, jocund and gay,
In all the sprightliness of youth and beauty,   70
Upon his slow-paced mule rode gently on

In careless attitude and smiled to see
All nature smile around, when Jonadab,
With solitary gait, approached, then turned
Aside, as if to shun the royal youth,
Which Absalom, perceiving, stopped his mule
And, leaning on his neck, with courteous air
Thus Jonadab in gentlest tone addressed:
"What mean those solemn looks, that downcast eye?
Now peace and plenty bless our happy land: 80
Joy should methinks extend its cheering ray
To every individual, but thou
Lookest half dejected, wandering in the fields
At this late hour. The day is in decline;
The shepherds to their folds have led their flocks,
And to their peaceful homes are hastening. Come,
Return with me, my friend, nor farther go;
If ought distress thee, hide it not from me:
I have an heart to feel for the distressed;
An hand too ever ready to revenge   90
The wrongs imposed by violence and injustice.
Smile and be happy," said the royal youth,
And rising from his leaning posture, looked
So gracefully endearing and so kind
That Jonadab thus ventured to begin:
" 'Tis not for me to smile, most noble prince,
While inconsolable and unredressed,
Dishonored Tamar weeps in bitter woe."
"Dishonored, and by whom?" says Absalom,
"Name but the villain; vengeance on his head   100
Shall instant fall; this hand shall strike the blow.
Earth, canst thou bear the wretch's feet to touch
Thy surface, and not groan? Whoe'er he be,
The miscreant shall not see tomorrow's sun."
"Too hasty, prince," says Jonadab; "be calm;
Recall the fatal sentence; 'tis too much
To raise thine hand against a brother's life,
Thine elder brother—" "Brother?" said the prince.
"And is it possible my brother thus
Should be depraved? my brother Amnon too?   110
O virtue, where dost thou reside, if not
In Amnon? but if he's thus lost to shame,
It cancels all the duty that I owe him;
Henceforth shall intercourse between us cease,
Till I have formed a scheme to be revenged;
Amnon shall die, and die by Absalom.
Go Jonadab, go home, and secret keep

This purpose of my soul—I'll be thy friend,"
Said Absalom.

    Then, onward as he passed,
Thus Jonadab congratulates himself: 120
"Oh! happy I, no sooner have I lost
The favor of one prince, but I have gained
Another; Absalom is more aspiring;
Not cool and passive, like the silly Amnon,
But pants to rule; he has a kingly spirit.
Once in his garden, as I lay concealed,
I heard him in soliloquy, 'Oh! to reign—
To wield a scepter and establish laws;
Oh! did the people seek to me for judgment,
And princes wait for my decisive voice,   130
Ere they the cause determined; could I hear
The loud applauding multitude exclaim,
"Long live King Absalom." '—He's fit to rule.
When Amnon is dispatched, perhaps he may
Assume the kingdom—be it so, and I
Will be his ready agent, if he please,
To aid his plots, or form them. Oh! how sweet
The counsel that is framed to please our wills,
How readily adopted; how despised
That which is adverse, be it e'er so good.   140
But dear, dear self stands first in the account
Of friends, and that's the friend I'll ever serve:
Whether to Amnon or to Absalom
I pay external homage. If to me
This Absalom proves too imperious,
I'll aid the king, and keep myself secure.
Ay—that's the center to which I must point
All schemes and plots." Then smiling as he went,
With eager pace he hastened to his home.

Grief and revenge now labored in the breast   150
Of Absalom; but artfully he hides
The struggling passions; a composure feigned
Sits on his countenance with placid ease;
And he in seeming gaiety rode home.
His servants there in readiness attend,
Each anxious to receive the first command;
Nor fear unjust reproofs, nor angry frowns,
The unwelcome greetings of imperious lords.
Too oft do masters, void of judgment, check,
By forward peevishness and discontent,   160
The many little assiduities,

Which otherwise a servant's zeal would mark,
Nor make distinction between good and bad;
But Absalom, with nicest judgment, scans
Their merits and defects; he in reproof
Is slowly cautious and exactly just;
No clamorous oaths re-echo through his hall,
Nor muttering servants whisper imprecations;
Though affable and courteous, yet he ne'er
To low familiarity descends;   170
But with great dignity is nobly kind,
Reigns in their hearts, and by enlivening smiles
Encouraged, they spontaneously attend;
And love completes their servitude with joy.
So now, as always at their lord's approach,
A secret transport thrilled through every heart.
The gate one opened; one received the mule,
Whilst he dismounting with a sprightly bound,
Tripped lightly o'er the pavement; and those eyes
Which ever spread serenity around,   180
Sparkled with seeming pleasure till he came,
Entering his mansion, to where Tamar sat
In the most striking attitude of woe;
Her head, bestrewed with ashes and reclined,
One trembling hand supported; the other hid
Among the fragments of her robe, which she
In the first agonies of her grief had torn.
He stopped, turned pale; then in his changing face
Resentment flushed, and sorrow swelled his heart,
Which laboring to suppress, he trembling stood;   190
But like a torrent which breaks down a bank
New raised to stop its course, so burst his grief
Through all his feigned composure. In his arms
He clasped the grieving fair, and mutual tears
Proclaimed the anguish of their burdened hearts.
But though his sorrow thus had burst its bounds,
Revenge in ambush lurked, while thus the prince
With soothing words his sister thus addressed:
"I know the sad occasion of thy woe;
But he's thy brother: silent bear thy wrongs,   200
Nor by immoderate grief enhance the ill
Which cannot be redressed. No blame is thine;
My sister still in heart is undefiled."

Tamar attempts reply; but from their springs
In swifter currents flowed the briny pearls;
At length the power of speech returned, the fair

Heaved a deep sigh, and thus her moan began:
"O injury unparalleled! O deed
More cruel than the murderer's deadly blow!
He takes our life, 'twas lent but for a time: 210
Perhaps some years—perhaps a day—an hour;
But he that robs a woman of her honor,
Robs her of more than life; a brother too
Still aggravates the guilt. O purity,
Thou first of female charms, to thee we owe
Our dignity, which, if in meekness clad,
Gives us insuperable power; but if
Of this deprived, our most presumptuous claim
Is cool compassion. O dejected state!
That humble homage we receive from men,   220
In such proportion as our virtue fails,
Diminishes. The inestimable gem—
More precious than fine gold or rubies—far
Outvies the dazzling rays of beauteous forms,
Which like gay meteors but excite our gaze
Then fade away. But this preeminence
No more I boast; now stamped with infamy,
That due respect, that deference ever paid
To my exalted state shall hence be changed
To scorn: though by the dignity of birth   230
Protected from low insult, can I escape
The meaning leer, the vain contemptuous smile,
Or the more humbling pity of the proud?"
Such moving strains in Absalom called forth
All the fond raptures of fraternal love;
Who thus consoled her grief: "Thou ne'er shalt be
Abandoned to the scorn of taunting dames,
Who triumph in the downfall of the fair.
My home be ever thine; in me behold
Thy guardian, brother, friend, companion kind.   240
It shall be my earliest and my latest care,
With cheerful converse to enliven thy hours;
All thou canst wish which I have power to grant
Expect from me." His sister gave her hand,
An earnest of conformity—he pressed
The given pledge; her grateful heart replied,
"O brother, always kind, now doubly so,
To ope thy friendly arms in this distress
And take me to protection: I accept
Thy offered boon. Farewell, ye courtly scenes;   250
No more shall Tamar shine in your resorts;
But here recluse and tranquil ever 'bide,

Regaling in that never-cloying feast,
The internal calm of an untainted mind.
This none can ravish from me; this is life.
That God which raised my father to the throne
And still protects him with his powerful arm
Shall be my all in all. To him I'll pray
Incessant, and the great Jehovah's name
Shall fire my theme and fill my heavenly song."　　　260

Canto IV

Now solemn evening drew her silent veil
O'er smiling nature, and the pious king
In supplication spent the sacred hour
With special fervor, making intercession
To the great sole dispenser of all good
To bless his son and soon restore his health.
He scarce had ended prayer, when tidings came
That Jonadab begged audience. The king
Eager to learn, thus instantly replied,
"Go send him hither; welcome to my soul　　　　　10
Is Jonadab, my Amnon's social friend;
He doubtless comes to bring me news of him."
He enters. Thus the king: "O Jonadab,
How does thy friend, my son, my Amnon now?"
"Amnon is well, O King," says Jonadab.
"Is well!" returned the astonished king. "Is well!
'Tis but few hours since I myself him saw,
And saw him sick—and sayest thou now he's well;
Thou knowest it not, which much I wonder at,
Because I know he loves thee; go now to him,　　　20
Go act a friendly part, go comfort him,
I tell thee he is sick." Says Jonadab,
"I can inform thee of the whole device
Of his pretended sickness." Then the king,
"Sayest thou 'pretended sickness'? If there is
Dissimulation in my son, declare it;
I'll hear thee; but take heed thou slander not,
Nor censure him unjustly, on thy life."
"Amnon has not been sick," says Jonadab;
" 'Twas but a feint to lure his sister there　　　　30
To his embraces, and he has succeeded."
"What do I hear?" replied the king; "my son
Defiled my daughter!"
　　　　　　　　Rising as he spoke,
With indignation flashing from his eyes,

Forth from his house he rushed with hasty steps
To Amnon, who was unprepared to see
This unexpected visitant. The youth
Already self-convicted, now abashed,
Ne'er ventured once to raise his downcast eyes,
But speechless and confounded stood to hear   40
His sharp rebuke; when thus the king began:
"O son, thou shameful troubler of my house,
What hast thou done? Where are thy princely virtues,
Inculcated so long? Now blasted all.
My elder-born, my first, my greatest joy,
Thus to debase thyself, thou that shouldst be
The first in virtue, as the first in birth.
How can a prince, himself debased with crimes,
Aspire to judge and punish wicked men?
In which of all my sons can I confide   50
Now Amnon fails, whom I have faultless deemed?
Thou bitter herb, thou blemish of my honor;
How can I brook this foul disgrace? Must I
Forever bear confusion in my face,
And blush for thee, thou worse than enemy?"
Amnon, no longer able to support
Such just reproof, in silence turned away
And bursting into tears withdrew. The king
Returned with anger burning in his breast
Mingled with sorrow for his daughter's wrongs.   60
"My daughter! Oh! my daughter!" he exclaimed,
"I would avenge thy wrongs; but oh! if I
Avenge my daughter, I destroy my son."
Then all a father's tenderness prevailed:
He wept—his wrath subsided and he paused,
His own past failings rising in his mind:
His guilty love for Bathsheba—he sighed
Her murdered husband; shuddering at the thought,
He saw no way to soothe the present ills
But suffering and forbearance. Then the king,   70
As if the stroke came from the hand of Heaven,
Fell prostrate to the earth, submitting thus:
"Righteous art thou, O Lord, and all thy judgments just."

Amnon meanwhile, with piercing grief oppressed,
Doubled by the sore displeasure of the king,
Sat down and wept, while tears supplied their streams.
Then rising, walked about with restless steps
And thus in bitter agonies complained:
"What am I now, and where? Of late I pined

In hopeless love, yet then I had some stay,   80
An heartfelt innocence that could support
And cheer the drooping spirits. But alas!
Virtue has left me now, and I'm exposed;
Exposed to what? to what, alas! I know not;
'Tis Hell itself bursts in upon my soul,
And pours forth all its torments. Terrors! Death!
O irrecoverable innocence!
Where art thou gone? forever banished hence.
Arise, ye thickest mists, ye darkest clouds,
O'ercast those twinkling stars. O sable night,   90
Wrap me in deepest shades, nor let a beam
Of penetrating light expose me more:
Darkness is fitted to the guilty mind
That shrinks and starts at every glimmering ray.
But oh! it is not in the power of darkness
To hide the hated self from self; within,
A sacred light perpetually shines,
Exposing every failure to the sense
That vainly struggles to compose the mind
And hush her sad inquietudes to peace.   100
But peace, the guest of innocence alone,
Takes an eternal leave when guilt intrudes,
And now has took eternal leave of me.
Ah! wretched me! Oh! curse on vicious friends!
Had Jonadab advised me virtuously,
I'd still been innocent, and Tamar pure;
My father still had smiled on me with joy,
Nor had I trembled at his chiding frowns;
Absalom would have called me brother still,
But now he'll own me not—this slight is just,   110
And this the least part of my punishment:
For inward guilt has yet severer pangs."
So wandered he, complaining half the night,
Then sought for rest in sleep but sought in vain:
Terrific dreams invade his wished repose;
He sleeps, starts, wakes; then sleeps and starts again;
And rises soon, but not to meet the morn
With joy as heretofore, but to bewail
The loss of that sweet calm that ever dwells
Within the guiltless breast; and in the world   120
Dwells no one more entitled to the bliss
That waits on virtue, than was Amnon once.
He therefore more severely feels the loss
For having tasted in its first degree

Its sovereign blessedness. Who'd then forsake
The peaceful path of virtue to pursue
Alluring vice through folly's labyrinth,
Grasping at shadows of felicity,
Till overtaken by her evil train
Of shame, remorse, confusion, and despair?   130
Such evils now the hapless Amnon haunt,
While in the avenging hand of Absalom
Death lurking lies.

               The ambitious prince, resolved
At once to avenge his sister and remove
An obstacle betwixt him and the crown,
With unremitting vigilance attends
The silent shades and unfrequented paths
Where Amnon used to walk and meditate,
Hoping to meet defenseless and alone
The destined youth and steal away his life.   140
But Amnon now as cautiously avoids
His dreaded presence; not with dread of death—
Such fear ne'er filled his unsuspicious breast—
But conscious guilt, that daunter of the soul
That few can brave, deterred the timid youth.
Two years within the breast of Absalom
Revenge in ambush lurked, while in his face
The mildest gentleness and sweetness played:
Thus secret burns the subterraneous fire
While on earth's teeming surface gaily smiles   150
The verdant herbage strewed with various flowers
Till, bursting from beneath, the sulphurous fumes
O'erturn the mountains, and the crumbling mold
Buries the blooming beauties that it bore.
So he unable longer to contain
The hidden rancor burning in his breast
Determined by some bold and desperate stroke
To effect his purpose; and with Jonadab
Consulted, who thus readily advised:
"Assume the friend—entice him to thine house;   160
The credulous youth will ne'er suspect a fraud.
Now is the time: now comes the yearly feast
When shepherds fleece their flocks. Make him thy guest
With all thy brothers; when with mirth and wine
His heart's elate, how easy will it be
To give the final blow." With lowering brow
Revengeful Absalom the rash advice
Adopted, and a sullen gloom o'ercast

His lively features. Stern as that grim lord
That through the forest takes his fearless way,   170
With high deportment Absalom retired.

Canto V

Returning summer now came smiling on,
Exciting every peaceful breast to mirth;
But Amnon meets with tears the fatal season:
This sad remembrancer of his past crime
Awoke his grief, and from his couch he rose
Ere yet the approaching day began to dawn,
While the full moon reigned mistress of the night.
"Sleep on ye sons of innocence and ease"
(The restless Amnon with a sigh exclaimed,
As from his window high he cast a look   10
Over the silent streets, for not a voice
Disturbed the solemn hour) "sleep on—sleep on:
So was I wont to sleep away the night,
Rise with the morn, and in the day rejoice;
But now in morn or night, or sleep or 'wake,
I feel no joy. Oh that I could forget
I once was happy! Oh that this one step—
One erring step—should kill my peace forever.
O moon, I blush beneath thy silver beams;
I've oft beheld thee with exulting heart,   20
But now I shrink at everything that's pure:
A modest virgin, innocent and fair,
Strikes terror to my soul: to me she seems
Exalted high above my fallen state.
If such a one I venture to approach,
I instantly recoil and justly pay
A secret adoration to the breast
Of innocence; for Oh! what parity
Can there subsist 'twixt innocence and guilt?
The world's reproaches and censorious sneers   30
Harrow the heart and aggravate the sense;
But yet that aggravation poised against
The pangs of guilt is of but little weight:
The world offended may again be won,
Or all its vain reproaches set at nought,
When the heart, firmly steeled with innocence,
Shrinks not, but rises with true nobleness,
Superior to the groveling sons of vice,
And smiles at powerless envy— But alas!

To me, returns, whether of day or night,   40
Aid sharp reflection and new-point its spears."

Now waking birds in cheerful concert join
Their every note proclaims them innocent.
The sun arises and the world awakes;
The prince retires with melancholy steps
Into his garden, where recluse and still
Beneath the arching boughs of shady trees,
With head declined and arms locked round his breast,
He sighed the heavy slow-paced hours away
Till interrupted by a messenger,   50
Who, with due deference approaching near,
Thus spake: "O Prince, I come from Absalom,
His sheep he shears tomorrow and entreats
Thee with thy royal brothers to partake
The feast and spend with him the day in mirth."
Surprise and pleasure rushed into his heart
At such an unexpected invitation,
Which he accepted, nor did hesitate
One moment to resolve; for Amnon still
Was unsuspicious as an infant child   60
That fearless trusts itself to every arm
That opens to receive it. With quick step
He paces to and fro; his bosom glows,
And thus anticipates the expected bliss:
"O joyful day when I again shall meet
My dear offended brother, whom so long
I've cautiously avoided: his goodwill
Greatly exceeds my most adventurous hope:
Forgetful of my faults, he kindly now
Invites me to his house without reproach   70
Or intimation of my late misdeeds.
Yes, my good brother, I will be thy guest—
My grateful heart o'erflows; I now could fall
Down at thy feet and from thy hand receive
The death I do deserve." Thus Amnon still,
In humble strain and true repentant heart,
Poured forth his soul in such soliloquies
All day and night till, in the morning fair,
The foremost of the princely cavalcade,
He gladly hasted to the fatal feast.   80

Now Absalom with secret pleasure sees
The long-wished day arrive, and in the morn
Assiduously in comely dress arrayed
His lovely person, lovely in extreme:

Not in all Israel's numerous tribes was found
His peer in beauty; for from head to foot
No blemish, no deformity was seen,
But well-proportioned limbs and features fair,
With every natural, every borrowed grace
That gives to beauty power. The conscious prince   90
Omitted no external ornament
That might, if possible, such gifts improve;
But looking at his spotless hands, he said,
"Must these be dyed in blood? a brother's blood?
No, I have servants, they shall give the blow."
Then to and fro he through his chamber stalked,
Revolving in his mind the consequence
Of opening his design. He paused; he thought
His servants might refuse—or worse, betray.
At length he says, "I'm wrong to censure them;   100
Great proofs I've had of their fidelity;
I'll trust them now." Then called he those he loved;
They came. He says, "You have done all things well
According to my order for this feast,
But on your cares I can so well depend
That whatsoever is given to your charge
I think no more of, for I've always found
You true and faithful; therefore I make choice
Of you for my accomplices this day:
'Tis not intended for a day of mirth,   110
As it appears and must as yet appear
Till I've fulfilled the purpose of my soul.
Our guests must sumptuously be entertained,
But when they have partook the rich repast
And wine exhilarates and mirth prevails,
Be you prepared, and when I give the word,
Pierce Amnon to the heart, for he must die."
His servants tremble at the dire command.
"Why tremble ye?" said Absalom. "Fear not,
'Tis I command you—all the deed is mine;   120
Ye are but instruments within my grasp
And of his blood are spotless: if there's guilt
In taking vengeance for the atrocious crime,
Let all that guilt be mine: since justice sleeps
In his fond father's hand, 'tis right that I
Assume the power and on his impious head
Hurl vengeance. But observe, it next behooves
Us to evade the storm that will ensue;
In Geshur we shall find a safe retreat.
My fleetest horses for the flight prepare;   130

Soon as the wound is given, we'll mount and flee;
Swift as the sweeping winds we'll o'er the hills
And leave the king to bury him and mourn."
His servants, more by love than duty bound,
All bowed obedient to his sovereign will.

Now came the royal guests, and Amnon, first
Dismounting from his mule, with conscious blush
And faltering voice, thus ventured to address
The offended brother: "O my Absalom,
Forgive," he said—and interrupting tears   140
Pleading more powerfully than eloquence,
Staggered the purpose of Maacah's son,
And in his feeling soul a conflict raised
Betwixt his brother's life and sister's fame.
He silent paused; but in his breast revenge
Was too deep rooted by a two-year's growth
For one soft moment to eradicate.
He therefore wiped away a piteous tear
And made to Amnon this composed reply:
"I did not send for thee to weep and mourn;   150
Today I have a feast; this prosperous year
Increasing flocks increase the shepherd's joy;
Rejoice with me, my brother, and be glad."
Then did he warmly press his hand and point
The chiefest place. The prince shed tears of joy,
Then sat him down, forgot his grief, and smiled.
Wine in profusion sparkled in the bowls,
Inspiring social mirth; they freely quaffed;
But Absalom the emolient draught evades,
Lest it relax his stern determination;   160
But quick replenishes the sinking bowls,
Pressing on all the intoxicating cup
Till mirth predominates and every heart
Expands with social freedom. Absalom
Then gives the fatal word; his servants plunge
The destined dart, and from the prince's side
Gushed forth life's reeking stream—he fell—up rose
In consternation those whom vengeance spared,
Each trembling for his life; confused, they fled.
Mingling with gore, the wine in currents flowed;   170
While, rolling in the flood, the murdered prince
Alone, in all the agonies of woe,
Groaned out his soul and closed his eyes in death.

1789

HELEN MARIA WILLIAMS

(1762–1827)

After the death of her father, an army officer, Williams was raised by her mother in Scotland. A family friend helped her publish her first book, Edwin and Eltruda *(1782), a verse legend. In London, to which she moved in 1781, she was introduced to Samuel Johnson, Elizabeth Montagu, Anna Seward, and Fanny Burney; she joined radical circles, meeting Priestley, Godwin, and Charlotte Smith. Most of her writing was explicitly political:* Ode to Peace *(1783) depicts scenes of familial grief and suffering caused by war;* Peru *(1784), which attacked European imperialism, was admired by Burns; like Hannah More and Ann Yearsley she published an abolitionist work,* Poem on the Bill Lately Passed for Regulating the Slave Trade *(1788). Her writing was fashionable:* Poems *(1786, expanded in 1791) had 1500 subscribers.*

A visit to Paris in 1790, on the anniversary of the taking of the Bastille, made her an enthusiastic supporter of the Girondins. Julia *(1790), a novel, and the essays in* Letters Written from France *(1790) celebrated the fall of the Bastille as "the most sublime spectacle." In Paris, she met Thomas Paine, Mary Wollstonecraft, and the Girondin Mme. Roland; Wordsworth, when he visited her, repeated her sonnet "On Hope" to her from memory. Her Paris salon drew Henry Crabb Robinson, Lady Morgan, and the American poet Joel Barlow. Wordsworth borrowed her story of friends' exile in his "Vaudracour and Julia" fragment.*

During the revolutionary period further volumes of Letters from France *(1792–96) recorded eyewitness accounts, anecdotes about street scenes, and cases of pathetic suffering. Her Girondist sympathies led to her arrest by Robespierre in October 1793. While under arrest, she translated Bernardin de Saint Pierre's* Paul and Virginia, *adding a series of her own sonnets. She went into exile in Switzerland in 1794 for four months, an experience she would exploit in* A Tour in Switzerland *(1798). Despite her own difficulties, her* Letters *suggest that the struggle to overcome tyranny requires violence: "I do not pretend to justify the French, but I do not see much right that we at least have to condemn them." Her democratic sentiments and her arguments for the equal education of women, exacerbated by her long liaison with John Hurford Stone, a radical, caused English gossip and slander about her as a "scribbling trollop." She was* dedicated to her family, however; when her sister died in 1798 she adopted her two nephews, who became Protestant leaders in Paris and Amsterdam.

Under Napoleon, her political opinions again provoked difficulties: He imprisoned her for a day in 1802, then confiscated one of her works in 1803. To earn an income, she translated six volumes of Humboldt's and Bonpland's Travels in America (1814–21) and continued her series of letters with "Sketches" of the French republic, a history of the Napoleonic years, and a report on the first years of the Restoration. Poems on Various Subjects (1823) was her last volume.

To Dr. Moore

In Answer to a Poetical Epistle Written by Him in Wales

While in long exile far from you I roam,
To soothe my heart with images of home,
For me, my friend, with rich poetic grace
The landscapes of my native isle you trace;
Her cultured meadows and her lavish shades,
Her winding rivers and her verdant glades;
Far as where, frowning on the flood below,
The rough Welsh mountain lifts its craggy brow;
Where nature throws aside her softer charms
And with sublimer views the bosom warms.   10

Meanwhile my steps have strayed where autumn yields
A purple harvest on the sunny fields;
Where, bending with their luscious weight, recline
The loaded branches of the clustering vine;
There, on the Loire's sweet banks, a joyful band
Culled the rich produce of the fruitful land;
The youthful peasant and the village maid
And feeble age and childhood lent their aid.
The labors of the morning done, they haste
Where the light dinner in the field is placed;   20
Around the soup of herbs a circle make,
And all from one vast dish at once partake:
The vintage-baskets serve, reversed, for chairs,
And the gay meal is crowned with tuneless airs;
For each in turn must sing with all his might,
And some their carols pour in nature's spite.

Delightful land! ah, now with general voice
The village sons and daughters may rejoice.
Thy happy peasant, now no more—a slave
Forbade to taste one good that nature gave—   30
Views with the anguish of indignant pain
The bounteous harvest spread for him in vain.

Oppression's cruel hand shall dare no more
To seize with iron grip his scanty store
And from his famished infants wring those spoils,
The hard-earned produce of his useful toils;
For now on Gallia's plains the peasant knows
Those equal rights impartial heaven bestows.
He now, by freedom's ray illumined, taught
Some self-respect, some energy of thought,   40
Discerns the blessings that to all belong
And lives to guard his humble shed from wrong.

   Auspicious Liberty! in vain thy foes
Deride thy ardor, and thy force oppose;
In vain refuse to mark thy spreading light,
While, like the mole, they hide their heads in night,
Or hope their eloquence with taper-ray
Can dim the blaze of philosophic day;
Those reasoners who pretend that each abuse,
Sanctioned by precedent, has some blest use!   50
Does then some chemic power to time belong,
Extracting by some process right from wrong?
Must feudal governments forever last,
Those gothic piles, the works of ages past?
Nor may obtrusive reason boldly scan,
Far less reform, the rude, misshapen plan?
The winding labyrinths, the hostile towers,
Whence danger threatens, and where horror lowers;
The jealous drawbridge, and the moat profound,
The lonely dungeon in the caverned ground;   60
The sullen dome above those central caves,
Where lives one despot and a host of slaves?
Ah, Freedom, on this renovated shore
That fabric frights the mortal world no more!
Shook to its basis by thy powerful spell,
Its triple walls in massy fragments fell;
While, rising from the hideous wreck, appears
The temple thy firm arm sublimely rears;
Of fair proportions, and of simple grace,
A mansion worthy of the human race.   70
For me, the witness of those scenes, whose birth
Forms a new era in the storied earth,
Oft, while with glowing breast those scenes I view,
They lead, ah friend beloved, my thoughts to you!
Ah, still each fine emotion they impart
With your idea mingles in my own heart;
You, whose warm bosom, whose expanded mind,

Have shared this glorious triumph of mankind;
You, whom I oft have heard, with generous zeal,
With all that truth can urge or pity feel,   80
Refute the pompous argument that tried
The common cause of millions to deride;
With reason's force the plausive sophist hit,
Or dart on folly the bright flash of wit;
Too swift, my friend, the moments winged their flight
That gave at once instruction and delight;
That ever from your ample stores of thought
To my small stock some new accession brought.
How oft remembrance, while this bosom bleeds,
My pensive fancy to your dwelling leads;   90
Where, round your cheerful hearth, I weeping trace
The social circle and my vacant place!
When, to that dwelling friendship's tie endears,
When shall I hasten with the "joy of tears"?
That joy whose keen sensation swells to pain
And strives to utter what it feels, in vain.

1792

To the Curlew

Soothed by the murmurs on the sea-beat shore,
His dun-gray plumage floating to the gale,
The curlew blends his melancholy wail
With those hoarse sounds the rushing waters pour.
Like thee, congenial bird! my steps explore
The bleak lone sea-beach or the rocky dale,
And shun the orange bower, the myrtle vale,
Whose gay luxuriance suits my soul no more.
I love the ocean's broad expanse, when dressed
In limpid clearness, or when tempests blow;   10
When the smooth currents on its placid breast
Flow calm as my past moments used to flow;
Or, when its troubled waters refuse to rest,
And seem the symbol of my present woe.

1796

JOANNA BAILLIE

(1762–1851)

*Baillie was sent by her father, a professor of divinity at Glasgow University, to be edu-
cated at a Glasgow boarding school. After his death in 1784 she moved with her mother
and sister to London, where her aunt, the poet Anne Hunter, introduced her to Henry
Mackenzie (author of* A Man of Feeling*) and the circle of Bluestockings. Her friends
included Anna Barbauld and Maria Edgeworth, who recalled that "an innocent
maiden grace hovered over her to the end of old age." Wordsworth also considered her "a
model of an English gentlewoman."*

Her early, anonymous Poems, Wherein It Is Attempted to Describe Certain
Views of Nature and of Rustic Manners *(1790), were extensively revised and
tamed for inclusion in* Fugitive Verses *(1840). Her poetic range includes earthy
monologue, descriptive pastoral, ballads, and songs in dialect; a reviewer praised her
"minute and circumstantial descriptions of natural objects, scenes, and characters . . . in
easy though peculiar language." Agnes Mary Robinson admired the grace, vigor, and
shrewd observation of her country sketches, as well as the enduring simplicity and fresh
humor of her Scottish ballads. She herself aimed to be "a poet of a simple and homely
character."*

Baillie's reputation was built on the three volumes of her Series of Plays in
Which It Is Attempted to Delineate the Stronger Passions of the Mind, *known
as* Plays on the Passions *(1798, 1802, 1812), which juxtaposed tragic and comic
treatments of a passion; the preface is an important romantic manifesto in defense of "the
plain order of things in this everyday world." Sir Walter Scott called her "the tenth
Muse," and his* Marmion *suggested that "the bold enchantress" had brought Shake-
speare back to life. Byron considered her the only exception to the rule that women could
not write tragedy. Her plays were produced at Drury Lane, the English Opera House,
and theaters in Edinburgh, Dublin, and Liverpool; two volumes were translated into
German in 1806. Alice Meynell says of her comic writing, "she deviated delightfully."*

A Winter's Day

The cock, warm roosting 'mid his feathered mates,
Now lifts his beak and snuffs the morning air,
Stretches his neck and claps his heavy wings,
Gives three hoarse crows and, glad his task is done,
Low chuckling turns himself upon the roost,
Then nestles down again into his place.
The laboring hind,[1] who on his bed of straw
Beneath his home-made coverings, coarse but warm,
Locked in the kindly arms of her who spun them,
Dreams of the gain that next year's crop should bring;   10
Or at some fair, disposing of his wool,
Or by some lucky and unlooked-for bargain,
Fills his skin purse with store of tempting gold,
Now wakes from sleep at the unwelcome call,
And finds himself but just the same poor man
As when he went to rest.
He hears the blast against his window beat
And wishes to himself he were a laird,
That he might lie a-bed. It may not be:
He rubs his eyes and stretches out his arms;   20
Heigh ho! heigh ho! he drawls with gaping mouth,
Then most unwillingly creeps from his lair,
And without looking-glass puts on his clothes.

   With rueful face he blows the smothered fire
And lights his candle at the reddening coal;
First sees that all be right among his cattle,
Then hies him to the barn with heavy tread,
Printing his footsteps on the new-fallen snow.
From out the heaped-up mow he draws his sheaves,
Dislodging the poor red-breast from his shelter,   30
Where all the livelong night he slept secure,
But now, affrighted, with uncertain flight,
Flutters round walls and roof to find some hole
Through which he may escape.
Then whirling o'er his head, the heavy flail
Descends with force upon the jumping sheaves,
While every rugged wall and neighboring cot
The noise re-echoes of his sturdy strokes.

---

1. *Hind* does not perfectly express the condition of the person here intended, who is somewhat above a common laborer—the tenant of a very small farm, which he cultivates with his own hands; a few cows, perhaps a horse, and some six or seven sheep being all the wealth he possessed. A class of men very common in the west of Scotland, ere political economy was thought of.

The family cares call next upon the wife
To quit her mean but comfortable bed.   40
And first she stirs the fire and fans the flame,
Then from her heap of sticks for winter stored
An armful brings; loud crackling as they burn,
Thick fly the red sparks upward to the roof,
While slowly mounts the smoke in wreathy clouds.
On goes the seething pot with morning cheer,
For which some little wistful folk await,
Who, peeping from the bedclothes, spy, well pleased,
The cheery light that blazes on the wall
And bawl for leave to rise.   50
Their busy mother knows not where to turn,
Her morning's work comes now so thick upon her.
One she must help to tie his little coat,
Unpin another's cap, or seek his shoe
Or hosen lost, confusion soon o'ermastered!
When all is o'er, out to the door they run
With new-combed sleeky hair and glistening faces,
Each with some little project in his head.
His new-soled shoes one on the ice must try;
To view his well-set trap another hies,   60
In hopes to find some poor unwary bird
(No worthless prize) entangled in his snare;
While one, less active, with round rosy cheeks,
Spreads out his purple fingers to the fire
And peeps most wishfully into the pot.

But let us leave the warm and cheerful house
To view the bleak and dreary scene without,
And mark the dawning of a Winter day.
The morning vapor rests upon the heights
Lurid and red, while growing gradual shades   70
Of pale and sickly light spread o'er the sky.
Then slowly from behind the southern hills,
Enlarged and ruddy comes the rising sun,
Shooting askance the hoary waste his beams
That gild the brow of every ridgy bank,
And deepen every valley with a shade.
The crusted window of each scattered cot,
The icicles that fringe the thatched roof,
The new-swept slide upon the frozen pool,
All keenly glance, new kindled with his rays;   80
And even the rugged face of scowling Winter
Looks somewhat gay. But only for a time

He shows his glory to the brightening earth,
Then hides his face behind a sullen cloud.

   The birds now quit their holes and lurking sheds,
Most mute and melancholy, where through night,
All nestling close to keep each other warm,
In downy sleep they had forgot their hardships;
But not to chant and carol in the air,
Or lightly swing upon some waving bough,   90
And merrily return each other's notes;
No, silently they hop from bush to bush,
Can find no seeds to stop their craving want,
Then bend their flight to the low smoking cot,
Chirp on the roof or at the window peck
To tell their wants to those who lodge within.
The poor lank hare flies homeward to his den
But little burthened with his nightly meal
Of withered colworts from the farmer's garden,
A wretched scanty portion, snatched in fear;   100
And fearful creatures, forced abroad by hunger,
Are now to every enemy a prey.

   The husbandman lays by his heavy flail
And to the house returns, where for him wait
His smoking breakfast and impatient children,
Who, spoon in hand and ready to begin,
Toward the door cast many an eager look
To see their dad come in.
Then round they sit, a cheerful company;
All quickly set to work and with heaped spoons   110
From ear to ear besmear their rosy cheeks.
The faithful dog stands by his master's side,
Wagging his tail and looking in his face,
While humble puss pays court to all around
And purrs and rubs them with her furry sides;
Nor goes this little flattery unrewarded.
But the laborious sit not long at table:
The grateful father lifts his eyes to heaven
To bless his God, whose ever bounteous hand
Him and his little ones doth daily feed,   120
Then rises satisfied to work again.

   The varied rousing sounds of industry
Are heard through all the village.
The humming wheel, the thrifty housewife's tongue,
Who scolds to keep her maidens to their work,
The wool-card's grating—most unmusical!—

Issue from every house.
But hark! the sportsman from the neighboring hedge
His thunder sends! loud bark the village curs;
Up from her cards or wheel the maiden starts   130
And hastens to the door; the housewife chides,
Yet runs herself to look, in spite of thrift,
And all the little town is in a stir.

   Strutting before, the cock leads forth his train
And, chuckling near the barn door 'mid the straw,
Reminds the farmer of his morning's service.
His grateful master throws a liberal handful;
They flock about it, while the hungry sparrows,
Perched on the roof, look down with envious eye,
Then, aiming well, amidst the feeders light   140
And seize upon the feast with greedy bill,
Till angry partlets peck them off the field.
But at a distance, on the leafless tree,
All woebegone, the lonely blackbird sits;
The cold north wind ruffles his glossy feathers;
Full oft he looks but dare not make approach,
Then turns his yellow beak to peck his side
And claps his wings close to his sharpened breast.
The wandering fowler from behind the hedge,
Fastens his eye upon him, points his gun,   150
And firing wantonly, as at a mark,
Of life bereaves him in the cheerful spot
That oft hath echoed to his summer's song.

   The midday hour is near; the pent-up kine
Are driven from their stalls to take the air.
How stupidly they stare! and feel how strange!
They open wide their smoking mouths to low—
But scarcely can their feeble sound be heard—
Then turn and lick themselves and, step-by-step,
Move, dull and heavy, to their stalls again.   160

   In scattered groups the little idle boys,
With purple fingers molding in the snow
Their icy ammunition, pant for war;
And drawing up in opposite array,
Send forth a mighty shower of well-aimed balls.
Each tiny hero tries his growing strength
And burns to beat the foe-men off the field.
Or on the well-worn ice in eager throngs,
After short race, shoot rapidly along,
Trip up each other's heels, and on the surface   170

With studded shoes draw many a chalky line.
Untired and glowing with the healthful sport,
They cease not till the sun hath run his course
And threatening clouds, slow rising from the north,
Spread leaden darkness o'er the face of heaven;
Then by degrees they scatter to their homes,
Some with a broken head or bloody nose,
To claim their mother's pity, who—most skillful!—
Cures all their troubles with a bit of bread.

    The night comes on apace—   180
Chill blows the blast and drives the snow in wreaths;
Now every creature looks around for shelter,
And whether man or beast, all move alike
Towards their homes; and happy they who have
A house to screen them from the piercing cold!
Lo, o'er the frost a reverend form advances!
His hair white as the snow on which he treads,
His forehead marked with many a careworn furrow;
Whose feeble body bending o'er a staff,
Shows still that once it was the seat of strength,   190
Though now it shakes like some old ruined tower.
Clothed indeed, but not disgraced with rags,
He still maintains that decent dignity
Which well becomes those who have served their country.
With tottering steps he gains the cottage door;
The wife within, who hears his hollow cough
And pattering of his stick upon the threshold,
Sends out her little boy to see who's there.
The child looks up to mark the stranger's face
And, seeing it enlightened with a smile,   200
Holds out his tiny hand to lead him in.
Round from her work, the mother turns her head,
And views them, not ill pleased.
The stranger whines not with a piteous tale
But only asks a little to relieve
A poor old soldier's wants.
The gentle matron brings the ready chair
And bids him sit to rest his weary limbs
And warm himself before her blazing fire.
The children, full of curiosity,   210
Flock round and, with their fingers in their mouths,
Stand staring at him, while the stranger, pleased,
Takes up the youngest urchin on his knee.
Proud of its seat, it wags its little feet
And prates and laughs and plays with his white locks.

But soon a change comes o'er the soldier's face:
His thoughtful mind is turned on other days,
When his own boys were wont to play around him,
Who now lie distant from their native land
In honorable but untimely graves;   220
He feels how helpless and forlorn he is,
And big round tears course down his withered cheeks.
His toilsome daily labor at an end,
In comes the wearied master of the house
And marks with satisfaction his old guest
In the chief seat, with all the children round him.
His honest heart is filled with manly kindness;
He bids him stay and share their homely meal
And take with them his quarters for the night.
The aged wanderer thankfully accepts,   230
And by the simple hospitable board,
Forgets the bypast hardships of the day.

When all are satisfied, about the fire
They draw their seats and form a cheerful ring.
The thrifty housewife turns her spinning wheel;
The husband, useful even in his hour
Of ease and rest, a stocking knits, belike,
Or plaits stored rushes, which with after skill
Into a basket formed may do good service,
With eggs or butter filled at fair or market.   240

Some idle neighbors now come dropping in;
Draw round their chairs and widen out the circle;
And every one in his own native way
Does what he can to cheer the social group.
Each tells some little story of himself,
That constant subject upon which mankind,
Whether in court or country, love to dwell.
How, at a fair, he saved a simple clown
From being tricked in buying of a cow;
Or laid a bet on his own horse's head   250
Against his neighbor's bought at twice his price,
Which failed not to repay his better skill;
Or on a harvest day bound in an hour
More sheaves of corn than any of his fellows,
Though e'er so stark, could do in twice the time;
Or won the bridal race with savory bruise
And first kiss of the bonny bride, though all
The fleetest youngsters of the parish strove
In rivalry against him.
But chiefly the good man, by his own fire,   260

Hath privilege of being listened to;
Nor dare a little prattling tongue presume,
Though but in play, to break upon his story.
The children sit and listen with the rest;
And should the youngest raise its lisping voice,
The careful mother, ever on the watch
And ever pleased with what her husband says,
Gives it a gentle tap upon the fingers
Or stops its ill-timed prattle with a kiss.
The soldier next, but not unasked, begins   270
His tale of war and blood. They gaze upon him
And almost weep to see the man so poor,
So bent and feeble, helpless and forlorn,
Who has undaunted stood the battle's brunt,
While roaring cannons shook the quaking earth
And bullets hissed round his defenseless head.
Thus passes quickly on the evening hour,
Till sober folks must needs retire to rest;
Then all break up, and by their several paths
Hie homeward, with the evening pastime cheered   280
Far more, belike, than those who issue forth
From city theater's gay scenic show
Or crowded ballroom's splendid moving maze.
But where the song and story, joke and gibe
So lately circled, what a solemn change
In little time takes place!
The sound of psalms, by mingled voices raised
Of young and old, upon the night air borne,
Haply to some benighted traveller,
Or the late-parted neighbors on their way,   290
A pleasing notice gives that those whose sires
In former days on the bare mountain's side,
In deserts, heaths, and caverns, praise and prayer,
At peril of their lives, in their own form
Of covenanted worship offered up,
In peace and safety in their own quiet home
Are—(as in quaint and modest phrase is termed)
Are now engaged in *evening exercise*.[2]

But long accustomed to observe the weather,
The farmer cannot lay him down in peace   300
Till he has looked to mark what bodes the night.

---

2. In the first edition of the *Winter Day*, nothing regarding family worship was mentioned: a great omission, for which I justly take shame to myself. "The evening exercise," as it was called, prevailed in every house over the simple country parts of the West of Scotland, and I have often heard the sound of it passing through the twilight air, in returning from a late walk.

He lifts the latch, and moves the heavy door,
Sees wreaths of snow heaped up on every side
And black and dismal all above his head.
Anon the northern blast begins to rise;
He hears its hollow growling from afar,
Which, gathering strength, rolls on with doubled might
And raves and bellows o'er his head. The trees
Like pithless saplings bend. He shuts his door
And, thankful for the roof that covers him,   310
Hies him to bed.

                              1790, rev. 1840

A Summer's Day

The dark blue clouds of night, in dusky lines
Drawn wide and streaky o'er the purer sky,
Wear faintly morning purple on their skirts.
The stars that full and bright shone in the west
But dimly twinkle to the steadfast eye
And, seen and vanishing and seen again,
Like dying tapers winking in the socket,
Are by degrees shut from the face of heaven;
The fitful lightning of the summer cloud,
And every lesser flame that shone by night;   10
The wandering fire that seems, across the marsh,
A beaming candle in a lonely cot,
Cheering the hopes of the benighted hind,
Till, swifter than the very change of thought,
It shifts from place to place, eludes his sight,
And makes him wondering rub his faithless eyes;
The humble glowworm and the silver moth,
That cast a doubtful glimmering o'er the green—
All die away.
For now the sun, slow moving in his glory,   20
Above the eastern mountains lifts his head;
The webs of dew spread o'er the hoary lawn,
The smooth, clear bosom of the settled pool,
The polished plowshare on the distant field,
Catch fire from him and dart their new-got beams
Upon the gazing rustic's dazzled sight.

    The wakened birds upon the branches hop,
Peck their soft down, and bristle out their feathers,
Then stretch their throats and trill their morning song,
While dusky crows, high swinging overhead,   30

Upon the topmost boughs, in lordly pride,
Mix their hoarse croaking with the linnet's note,
Till in a gathered band of close array,
They take their flight to seek their daily food.
The villager wakes with the early light
That through the window of his cot appears
And quits his easy bed, then o'er the fields
With lengthened active strides betakes his way,
Bearing his spade or hoe across his shoulder,
Seen glancing as he moves, and with goodwill   40
His daily work begins.
The sturdy sunburnt boy drives forth the cattle
And, pleased with power, bawls to the lagging kine
With stern authority, who fain would stop
To crop the tempting bushes as they pass.
At every open door in lawn or lane
Half-naked children, half awake, are seen
Scratching their heads and blinking to the light,
Till, rousing by degrees, they run about,
Roll on the sward, and in some sandy nook   50
Dig caves and houses build, full oft defaced
And oft begun again, a daily pastime.
The housewife, up betimes, her morning cares
Tends busily; from tubs of curdled milk
With skillful patience draws the clear green whey
From the pressed bosom of the snowy curd,
While her brown comely maid, with tucked-up sleeves
And swelling arm, assists her. Work proceeds,
Pots smoke, pails rattle, and the warm confusion
Still more confused becomes, till in the mold   60
With heavy hands the well-squeezed curd is placed.

So goes the morning till the powerful sun,
High in the heavens, sends down his strengthened beams,
And all the freshness of the morn is fled.
The idle horse upon the grassy field
Rolls on his back; the swain leaves off his toil
And to his house with heavy steps returns,
Where on the board his ready breakfast placed
Looks most invitingly, and his good mate
Serves him with cheerful kindness.   70
Upon the grass no longer hangs the dew;
Forth hies the mower with his glittering scythe,
In snowy shirt bedight and all unbraced.
He moves athwart the mead with sidling bend
And lays the grass in many a swathey line;

In every field in every lawn and meadow
The rousing voice of industry is heard;
The haycock rises and the frequent rake
Sweeps on the fragrant hay in heavy wreaths.
The old and young, the weak and strong are there   80
And, as they can, help on the cheerful work.
The father jeers his awkward half-grown lad,
Who trails his tawdry armful o'er the field,
Nor does he fear the jeering to repay.
The village oracle and simple maid
Jest in their turns and raise the ready laugh;
All are companions in the general glee;
Authority, hard favored, frowns not there.
Some, more advanced, raise up the lofty rick,
Whilst on its top doth stand the parish toast   90
In loose attire and swelling ruddy cheek.
With taunts and harmless mockery she receives
The tossed-up heaps from fork of simple youth,
Who, staring on her, takes his aim awry,
While half the load falls back upon himself.
Loud is her laugh, her voice is heard afar:
The mower busied on the distant lawn,
The carter trudging on his dusty way
The shrill sound know, their bonnets toss in the air
And roar across the field to catch her notice;   100
She waves her arm to them, and shakes her head,
And then renews her work with double spirit.
Thus do they jest and laugh away their toil
Till the bright sun, now past his middle course,
Shoots down his fiercest beams which none may brave.
The stoutest arm feels listless, and the swart
And brawny-shouldered clown begins to fail.
But to the weary, lo—there comes relief!
A troop of welcome children o'er the lawn
With slow and wary steps approach; some bear   110
In baskets oaten cakes or barley scones,
And gusty cheese and stoups of milk or whey.
Beneath the branches of a spreading tree,
Or by the shady side of the tall rick,
They spread their homely fare and, seated round,
Taste every pleasure that a feast can give.

   A drowsy indolence now hangs on all;
Each creature seeks some place of rest, some shelter
From the oppressive heat; silence prevails;
Nor low nor bark nor chirping bird are heard.   120

In shady nooks the sheep and kine convene;
Within the narrow shadow of the cot
The sleepy dog lies stretched upon his side,
Nor heeds the footsteps of the passerby,
Or at the sound but raises half an eyelid,
Then gives a feeble growl and sleeps again;
While puss composed and grave on threshold stone
Sits winking in the light.
No sound is heard but humming of the bee,
For she alone retires not from her labor,   130
Nor leaves a meadow flower unsought for gain.

    Heavy and slow, so pass the sultry hours,
Till gently bending on the ridge's top
The drooping seedy grass begins to wave,
And the high branches of the aspen tree
Shiver the leaves and gentle rustling make.
Cool breathes the rising breeze, and with it wakes
The languid spirit from its state of stupor.
The lazy boy springs from his mossy lair
To chase the gaudy butterfly, who oft   140
Lights at his feet as if within his reach,
Spreading upon the ground its mealy wings,
Yet still eludes his grasp and high in air
Takes many a circling flight, tempting his eye
And tiring his young limbs.
The drowsy dog, who feels the kindly air
That passing o'er him, lifts his shaggy ear,
Begins to stretch him, on his legs half-raised,
Till fully waked with bristling cocked-up tail,
He makes the village echo to his bark.   150

    But let us not forget the busy maid
Who by the side of the clear pebbly stream
Spreads out her snowy linens to the sun
And sheds with liberal hand the crystal shower
O'er many a favorite piece of fair attire,
Revolving in her mind her gay appearance,
So nicely tricked, at some approaching fair.
The dimpling, half-checked smile and muttering lip
Her secret thoughts betray. With shiny feet,
There, little active bands of truant boys   160
Sport in the stream and dash the water round,
Or try with wily art to catch the trout,
Or with their fingers grasp the slippery eel.
The shepherd lad sits singing on the bank
To while away the weary lonely hours,

Weaving with art his pointed crown of rushes,
A guiltless easy crown, which, having made,
He places on his head and skips about,
A chanted rhyme repeats, or calls full loud
To some companion lonely as himself,   170
Far on the distant bank; or else, delighted
To hear the echoed sound of his own voice
Returning answer from some neighboring rock
Or roofless barn, holds converse with himself.

   Now weary laborers perceive, well pleased,
The shadows lengthen and the oppressive day
With all its toil fast wearing to an end.
The sun, far in the west, with level beam
Gleams on the cocks of hay, on bush or ridge,
And fields are checkered with fantastic shapes,   180
Or tree or shrub or gate or human form,
All lengthened out in antic disproportion
Upon the darkened ground. Their task is finished,
Their rakes and scattered garments gathered up,
And all right gladly to their homes return.

   The village, lone and silent through the day,
Receiving from the fields its merry bands,
Sends forth its evening sound, confused but cheerful:
Yelping of curs, and voices stern and shrill,
And true-love ballads in no plaintive strain,   190
By household maid at open window sung;
And lowing of the home-returning kine,
And herd's dull, droning trump and tinkling bell,
Tied to the collar of the master-sheep,
Make no contemptible variety
To ears not over nice.
With careless lounging gait the favored youth
Upon his sweetheart's open window leans,
Diverting her with joke and harmless taunt.
Close by the cottage door with placid mien,   200
The old man sits upon his seat of turf.
His staff with crooked head laid by his side,
Which oft some tricky youngling steals away,
And straddling o'er it, shows his horsemanship
By raising clouds of sand; he smiles thereat,
But *seems* to chide him sharply;
His silver locks upon his shoulders fall,
And not ungraceful is his stoop of age.
No stranger passes him without regard,

And neighbors stop to wish him a good e'en   210
And ask him his opinion of the weather.
They fret not at the length of his remarks
Upon the various seasons he remembers,
For well he knows the many diverse signs
That do foretell high winds, or rain, or drought,
Or aught that may affect the rising crops.
The silken-clad, who courtly breeding boast,
Their own discourse still sweetest to their ear,
May at the old man's lengthened story fret
Impatiently, but here it is not so.   220

   From every chimney mounts the curling smoke,
Muddy and gray, of the new evening fire;
On every window smokes the family supper,
Set out to cool by the attentive housewife,
While cheerful groups, at every door convened,
Bawl 'cross the narrow lane the parish news,
And oft the bursting laugh disturbs the air.
But see who comes to set them all agape:
The weary-footed peddler with his pack;
Stiffly he bends beneath his bulky load,   230
Covered with dust, slipshod and out at elbows;
His greasy hat set backwards on his head;
His thin straight hair, divided on his brow,
Hangs lank on either side his glistening cheeks,
And woebegone yet vacant is his face.
His box he opens and displays his ware.
Full many a varied row of precious stones
Cast forth their dazzling luster to the light,
And ruby rings and china buttons, stamped
With love devices, the desiring maid   240
And simple youth attract; while streaming garters
Of many colors, fastened to a pole,
Aloft in air their gaudy stripes display
And from afar the distant stragglers lure.
The children leave their play and round him flock;
Even sober, aged granddame quits her seat
Where by the door she twines her lengthened threads,
Her spindle stops, and lays her distaff by,
Then joins with step sedate the curious throng.
She praises much the fashions of her youth   250
And scorns each useless nonsense of the day,
Yet not ill pleased the glossy ribbon views,
Unrolled and changing hues with every fold,
Just measured out to deck her grandchild's head.

Now red but languid the last beams appear
Of the departed sun across the lawn,
Gilding each sweepy ridge on many a field,
And from the openings of the distant hills
A level brightness pouring, sad though bright;
Like farewell smiles from some dear friend they seem,   260
And only serve to deepen the low vale
And make the shadows of the night more gloomy.
The varied noises of the cheerful village
By slow degrees now faintly die away,
And more distinctly distant sounds are heard
That gently steal adown the river's bed,
Or through the wood come on the ruffling breeze.
The white mist rises from the meads, and from
The dappled skirting of the sober sky
Looks out with steady gleam the evening star.   270
The lover, skulking in some neighboring copse
(Whose half-seen form, shown through the dusky air
Large and majestic, makes the traveler start
And spreads the story of a haunted grove),
Curses the owl, whose loud, ill-omened hoot
With ceaseless spite takes from his listening ear
The well-known footsteps of his darling maid,
And fretful chases from his face the nightfly
That, buzzing round his head, doth often skim
With fluttering wings across his glowing cheek;   280
For all but him in quiet balmy sleep
Forget the toils of the oppressive day;
Shut is the door of every scattered cot,
And silence dwells within.

1790, rev. 1840

A Reverie

Beside a spreading elm, from whose high boughs
Like knotted tufts the crow's light dwelling shows,
Where, screened from northern blasts and winter proof,
Snug stands the parson's barn with thatched roof;
At chaff-strewed door where in the morning ray
The gilded motes in mazy circles play
And sleepy Comrade in the sun is laid,
More grateful to the cur than neighboring shade;
In snowy shirt unbraced, brown Robin stood
And leaned upon his flail in thoughtful mood: 10
His full round cheek where deeper flushes glow,

The dewy drops which glisten on his brow;
His dark cropped pate that erst at church or fair,
So smooth and silky showed his morning's care,
Which, all uncouth in matted locks combined,
Now, ends erect, defies the ruffling wind;
His neckband loose and hosen rumpled low,
A careful lad, nor slack at labor show.
Nor scraping chickens chirping 'mongst the straw,
Nor croaking rook o'erhead, nor chattering daw;   20
Loud-breathing cow amongst the rampy weeds,
Nor grunting sow that in the furrow feeds;
Nor sudden breeze that shakes the quaking leaves,
And lightly rustles through the scattered sheaves;
Nor floating straw that skims athwart his nose,
The deeply musing youth may discompose.
For Nelly fair, and blithest village maid,
Whose tuneful voice beneath the hedgerow shade
At early milking o'er the meadows born
E'er cheered the plowman's toil at rising morn: 30
The neatest maid that e'er in linen gown
Bore cream and butter to the market town;
The tightest lass that with untutored air
E'er footed alehouse floor at wake or fair,
Since Easter last had Robin's heart possessed,
And many a time disturbed his nightly rest.
Full oft, returning from the loosened plow,
He slacked his pace and knit his thoughtful brow;
And oft, ere half his thresher's task was o'er,
Would muse with arms across at cooling door.   40
His mind thus bent, with downcast eyes he stood,
And leaned upon his flail in thoughtful mood.
His soul o'er many a soft remembrance ran,
And muttering to himself, the youth began:

"Ah! happy is the man whose early lot
Hath made him master of a furnished cot;
Who trains the vine that round his window grows,
And after setting sun his garden hoes;
Whose wattled pales his own enclosure shield,
Who toils not daily in another's field.   50
Where'er he goes, to church or market town,
With more respect he and his dog are known;
A brisker face he wears at wake or fair,
Nor views with longing eyes the peddler's ware,
But buys at will, or ribbons, gloves, or beads,
And willing maidens to the alehouse leads.

And, oh! secure from toils which cumber life,
He makes the maid he loves an easy wife.
Ah, Nelly! canst thou with contented mind,
Become the helpmate of a laboring hind,   60
And share his lot, whate'er the chances be,
Who hath no dower but love to fix on thee?
Yes, gayest maid may meekest matron prove,
And things of little note may 'token love.
When from the church thou camest at eventide
And I and red-haired Susan by thy side,
I pulled the blossoms from the bending tree
And some to Susan gave and some to thee;
Thine were the best, and well thy smiling eye
The difference marked and guessed the reason why.   70
When on a holiday we rambling strayed,
And passed old Hodge's cottage in the glade;
Neat was the garden dressed, sweet hummed the bee,
I wished both cot and Nelly made for me;
And well methought thy very eyes revealed
The selfsame wish within thy breast concealed.
When artful, once, I sought my love to tell,
And spoke to thee of one who loved thee well,
You saw the cheat and, jeering, homeward hied,
Yet secret pleasure in thy looks I spied.   80
Ay, gayest maid may meekest matron prove,
And smaller signs than these have 'tokened love."

Now, at a distance on the neighboring plain,
With creaking wheels slow comes the heavy wain:
High on its towering load a maid appears,
And Nelly's voice sounds shrill in Robin's ears.
Quick from his hand he throws the cumbrous flail
And leaps with lightsome limbs the enclosing pale.
O'er field and fence he scours, and furrow wide,
With wakened Comrade barking by his side,   90
Whilst tracks of trodden grain, and sidelong hay,
And broken hedgeflowers sweet mark his impetuous way.

                                                    1790

A Mother to Her Waking Infant

Now in thy dazzling half-oped eye,
Thy curled nose, and lip awry,
Thy up-hoist arms, and noddling head,
And little chin with crystal spread,

Poor helpless thing! what do I see,
  That I should sing of thee?

From thy poor tongue no accents come,
Which can but rub thy toothless gum:
Small understanding boasts thy face;
Thy shapeless limbs nor step, nor grace;   10
A few short words thy feats may tell,
  And yet I love thee well.

When sudden wakes the bitter shriek,
And redder swells thy little cheek;
When rattled keys thy woe beguile,
And through the wet eye gleams the smile;
Still for thy weakly self is spent
  Thy little silly plaint.

But when thy friends are in distress,
Thou wilt laugh and chuckle ne'ertheless;   20
Nor e'en with sympathy be smitten,
Though all are sad but thee and kitten;
Yet little varlet that thou art,
  Thou twitchest at the heart.

Thy rosy cheek so soft and warm;
Thy pinky hand, and dimpled arm;
Thy silken locks that scantly peep,
With gold-tipped ends, where circle deep
Around thy neck in harmless grace
So soft and sleekly hold their place,   30
Might harder hearts with kindness fill,
  And gain our right goodwill.

Each passing clown bestows his blessing,
Thy mouth is worn with old wives' kissing;
E'en lighter looks the gloomy eye
Of surly sense when thou art by;
And yet I think, whoe'er they be,
  They love thee not like me.

Perhaps when time shall add a few
Short years to thee, thou wilt love me too.   40
Then wilt thou through life's weary way
Become my sure and cheering stay:
Wilt care for me and be my hold
  When I am weak and old.

Thou wilt listen to my lengthened tale
And pity me when I am frail—

But see, the sweepy spinning fly
Upon the window takes thine eye.
Go to thy little senseless play—
    Thou dost not heed my lay.   50

1790

Address to the Muses

Ye tuneful sisters of the lyre,
Who dreams and fantasies inspire,
Who over poesy preside,
And on a lofty hill abide
Above the ken of mortal sight,
Fain would I sing of you, could I address ye right.

Thus known, your power of old was sung,
And temples with your praises rung;
And when the song of battle rose,
Or kindling wine, or lovers' woes,   10
The poet's spirit inly burned,
And still to you his upcast eyes were turned.

The youth, all wrapped in vision bright,
Beheld your robes of flowing white;
And knew your forms benignly grand—
An awful but a lovely band;
And felt your inspiration strong
And warmly poured his rapid lay along.

The aged bard all heavenward glowed
And hailed you daughters of a god.   20
Though to his dimmer eyes were seen
Nor graceful form nor heavenly mien,
Full well he felt that ye were near
And heard you in the breeze that raised his hoary hair.

Ye lightened up the valley's bloom
And gave the forest deeper gloom;
The mountain peak sublimer stood,
And grander rose the mighty flood;
For then religion lent her aid,
And o'er the mind of man your sacred empire spread.   30

Though rolling ages now are past,
And altars low and temples waste;
Though rites and oracles are o'er,
And gods and heroes rule no more,

Your fading honors still remain,
And still your votaries call, a long and motley train.

They seek you not on hill or plain,
Nor court you in the sacred fane;
Nor meet you in the midday dream,
Upon the bank of hallowed stream;   40
Yet still for inspiration sue,
And still each lifts his fervent prayer to you.

He woos ye not in woodland gloom,
But in the close and shelfed room
And seeks ye in the dusty nook,
And meets ye in the lettered book:
Full well he knows ye by your names
And still with poet's faith your presence claims.

Now youthful poet, pen in hand,
All by the side of blotted stand,   50
In reverie deep which none may break,
Sits rubbing of his beardless cheek
And well his inspiration knows,
E'en by the dewy drops that trickle o'er his nose.

The tuneful sage of riper fame
Perceives you not in heated frame,
But at conclusion of his verse,
Which still his muttering lips rehearse,
Oft waves his hand in grateful pride
And owns the heavenly power that did his fancy guide.   60

O lovely Sisters! is it true
That they are all inspired by you,
And write by inward magic charmed
And high enthusiasm warmed?
We dare not question heavenly lays,
And well, I wot, they give you all the praise.

O lovely Sisters! well it shows
How wide and far your bounty flows.
Then why from me withhold your beams?
Unvisited of visioned dreams,   70
Whene'er I aim at heights sublime
Still downward am I called to seek some stubborn rhyme.

No hasty lightning breaks my gloom,
Nor flashing thoughts unsought for come,
Nor fancies wake in time of need:
I labor much with little speed,

And when my studied task is done,
Too well—alas!—I mark it for my own.

Yet, should you never smile on me,
And rugged still my verses be,   80
Unpleasing to the tuneful train
Who only prize a flowing strain,
And still the learned scorn my lays,
I'll lift my heart to you and sing your praise.

Your varied ministry of grace,
Your honored names and godlike race,
Your sacred caves where fountains flow
They will rehearse, who better know;
I praise ye not with Grecian lyre,
Nor hail ye daughters of a heathen sire.   90

Ye are the spirits who preside
In earth and air and ocean wide;
In rushing flood and crackling fire,
In horror dread and tumult dire;
In stilly calm and stormy wind,
And rule the answering changes in the human mind.

High on the tempest-beaten hill,
Your misty shapes ye shift at will;
The wild fantastic clouds ye form;
Your voice is in the midnight storm,   100
While in the dark and lonely hour
Oft starts the boldest heart, and owns your secret power.

When lightning ceases on the waste,
And when the battle's broil is past,
When scenes of strife and blood are o'er,
And groans of death are heard no more,
Ye then renew each sound and form,
Like afterechoing of the overpassed storm.

The shining day and nightly shade,
The cheerful plain and sunny glade,   110
The homeward kine, the children's play,
The busy hamlet's closing day,
Give pleasure to the peasant's heart,
Who lacks the gift his feelings to impart.

Oft when the moon looks from on high,
And black around the shadows lie,
And bright the sparkling waters gleam,
And rushes rustle by the stream,

Voices and fairy forms are known
By simple folk who wander late alone.   120

Ye kindle up the inward glow,
Ye strengthen every outward show;
Ye overleap the strongest bar,
And join what nature sunders far,
And visit oft in fancies wild
The breast of learned sage and simple child.

From him who wears a monarch's crown
To the unlettered simple clown,
All in some fitful, lonely hour
Have felt, unsought, your secret power   130
And loved your inward visions well;
You add but to the bard the art to tell.

Ye mighty spirits of the song,
To whom the poet's prayers belong,
My lowly bosom to inspire
And kindle with your sacred fire,
Your wild and dizzy heights to brave,
Is boon—alas!—too great for me to crave.

But O, such sense of nature bring!
As they who feel and never sing   140
Wear on their hearts; it will avail
With simple words to tell my tale;
And still contented will I be,
Though greater inspiration never fall to me.

                                          1790

London

It is a goodly sight through the clear air
From Hampstead's heathy height to see at once
England's vast capital in fair expanse:
Towers, belfries, lengthened streets, and structures fair.
St. Paul's high dome, amidst the vassal bands
Of neighboring spires, a regal chieftain stands,
And over fields of ridgy roofs appear,
With distance softly tinted, side-by-side
In kindred grace, like twain of sisters dear,
The towers of Westminster, her Abbey's pride;   10
While far beyond, the hills of Surrey shine
Through thin soft haze and show their wavy line.
Viewed thus, a goodly sight! but when surveyed

Through denser air, when moistened winds prevail,
In her grand panoply of smoke arrayed,
While clouds aloft in heavy volumes sail,
She is sublime. She seems a curtained gloom
Connecting heaven and earth—a threatening sign of doom.
With more than natural height reared in the sky,
'Tis then St. Paul's arrests the wondering eye;   20
The lower parts in swathing mist concealed,
The higher through some half-spent shower revealed,
So far from earth removed that well, I trow,
Did not its form man's artful structure show,
It might some lofty alpine peak be deemed,
The eagle's haunt, with cave and crevice seamed.
Stretched wide on either hand, a rugged screen
In lurid dimness, nearer streets are seen
Like shoreward billows of a troubled main
Arrested in their rage. Through drizzly rain,   30
Cataracts of tawny sheen pour from the skies,
Black furnace-smoke in curling columns rise,
And many-tinted vapors slowly pass
O'er the wide draping of that pictured mass.

So shows by day this grand imperial town,
And when o'er all the night's black stole is thrown,
The distant traveler doth with wonder mark
Her luminous canopy athwart the dark,
Cast up from myriads of lamps that shine
Along her streets in many a starry line: 40
He wondering looks from his yet distant road
And thinks the northern streamers are abroad.
"What hollow sound is that?"—approaching near,
The roar of many wheels breaks on his ear.
It is the flood of human life in motion!
It is the voice of a tempestuous ocean!
With sad but pleasing awe his soul is filled;
Scarce heaves his breast and all within is stilled,
As many thoughts and feelings cross his mind—
Thoughts, mingled, melancholy, undefined,   50
Of restless, reckless man, and years gone by,
And time fast wending to eternity.

1800 / 1840

Verses Written in February 1827

Like gleam of sunshine on the mountain's side,
Fair, bright, and beautiful, while all beside,
Slope, cliff, and pinnacle in shadow lie
Beneath the awning of a wintry sky,
Through loophole in its cloudy texture beaming
A cataract of light, so softly streaming,
Shines one blest deed of ruth when war's grim form
O'er a scourged nation guides his passing storm.

    Like verdant islet spots that softly peer
Through the dull mist as morning breezes clear   10
The brooding vapor from the wide-stretched vale,
So in a land where Mammon's cares prevail
Do frequent deeds of gentle charity
Refresh the moral gazer's mental eye.

    Britain, thou art in arms and commerce graced
With many generous acts that, fairly traced
On thy long annals, give a luster far
Exceeding those of wealth or trophied war;
And may we not say truthfully of thee,
Thou art a land of mercy?—May it be!   20

    What forms are those with lean, galled sides? In vain
Their laxed and ropy sinews sorely strain
Heaped loads to draw, with lash and goad urged on.
They were in other days but lately gone
The useful servants, dearly prized, of those
Who to their failing age give no repose—
Of thankless, heartless owners. Then, full oft
Their arched graceful necks so sleek and soft
Beneath a master's stroking hand would rear
Right proudly, as they neighed his well-known voice to hear.   30
But now how changed!— And what marred things are these,
Starved, hooted, scarred, denied or food or ease,
Whose humbled looks their bitter thralldom show,
Familiar with the kick, the pinch, the blow?
Alas! in this sad fellowship are found
The playful kitten and the faithful hound,
The gallant cock that hailed the morning light,
All now hard-fated mates in woeful plight.

    Ah no! a land of mercy is a name
Which thou in all thy glory mayest not claim!   40

    But yet there dwell in thee the good, the bold,
Who in thy streets, courts, senates bravely hold

Contention with thy wayward cruelty
And shall subdue it ere this age glide by.
Meantime as they their manly power exert,
"God speed ye well!" bursts from each kindly heart.
And they *will* speed; for this foul blot of shame
Must be washed out from Britain's honored name,
And she among enlightened nations stand,
A brave, a merciful, and generous land.   50

                              1827 / 1840

CAROLINA, BARONESS NAIRNE

née Oliphant; pseud., Mrs. Bogan of Bogan (1766–1845)

Carolina Oliphant was named in honor of Prince Charles Stuart and raised a Jacobite in a family with powerful clan ties. She made a late marriage in 1806 to a cousin, Major William Nairne, with whom she had one child. Burns's songs influenced those she wrote for her brother and friends. After her marriage, she concealed her verse from her family under a pseudonym. Between 1821 and 1824 she contributed to R. A. Smith's The Scottish Minstrel, *a collection of Scottish songs. After her husband's death in 1829, she traveled with her invalid son on the Continent.*

Nairne set her ballads in Scots dialect to traditional tunes; some, like "The Laird o' Cockpen," are narrative; others belong to the tradition of market cries. After she died her ballads were gathered in Lays from Strathearn *(1846); those like "Charlie Is My Darling" and "Caller Herrin" were popular long afterward.*

The Laird o' Cockpen

AIR—"WHEN SHE CAM' BEN, SHE BOBBIT."

The laird o' Cockpen, he's proud an' he's great;
His mind is ta'en up wi' things o' the State;
He wanted a wife, his braw house to keep,
But favor wi' wooin' was fashious to seek.

Down by the dykeside a lady did dwell,
At his table head he thought she'd look well:
McClish's ae daughter o' Claverse-ha' Lee,
A penniless lass wi' a lang pedigree.

His wig was weel pouther'd and as gude as new;
His waistcoat was white, his coat it was blue;
He put on a ring, a sword and cock'd hat,
And wha could refuse the laird wi' a' that?

He took the gray mare and rade cannily,
An' rapp'd at the yett o' Claverse-ha' Lee;
"Gae tell Mistress Jean to come speedily ben:
She's wanted to speak to the laird o' Cockpen."

Mistress Jean was makin' the elder-flower wine.
"An' what brings the laird at sic a like time?"
She put aff her apron, and on her silk gown,
Her mutch wi' red ribbons, and gaed awa' down.   20

An' when she cam' ben he bowed fu' low,
An' what was his errand he soon let her know;
Amazed was the laird when the lady said, "Na,"
And wi' a laigh curtsie she turned awa.'

Dumbfoundered he was, nae sigh did he gie;
He mounted his mare—he rade cannily;
And aften he thought, as he gaed thro' the glen,
She's daft to refuse the laird o' Cockpen.

1822

CHARLOTTE NOOTH

(fl. 1800)

Daughter of the Duke of Kent's personal physician, Nooth moved in comfortable London circles, dedicating verses to friends and writing on topical matters such as a painting exhibit or a debate over the waltz. After a stay in Northern Ireland she published a collection, the lighthearted Irish Ballads *(1807). In addition she composed a melodrama,* Clara, or the Nuns of Charity, *and a satiric novel,* Eglantine, or The Family of Fortescue *(1808). Her buoyant* Original Poems, and a Play *(1815) included the ballads,* Clara, *and translations from Italian, French, and Spanish.*

Irregular Lines

ADDRESSED TO THE BARONNE DE STAËL-HOLSTEIN

Lady, though rival France may boast thy birth,
    Yet not to France alone confined
    The treasure of thy mighty mind,
A glorious gift from nature to the world.
    'Tis not a country nor an age
Which claims alone thy precious page;
For genius, when he deigns to visit Earth,
    Beams upon every clime his ray
    And pours the intellectual day
More wide than faction's brand was ever hurled.   10

Lady, thy Tuscan lyre has caused the tear
    For woman's sorrows oft to flow
    In all the luxury of woe;
All see Corinne as Nelvil saw her first,
Ere by inconstancy's foul demon cursed,
    The slave to habit, prejudice, and pride;

Too late he wept upon her sable bier,
　　Whence from her car triumphal he had brought
　　Her, who to him resigning every thought,
For him alone had lived and loved—and died!　　　　20
Lady, thy magic pen has loved to trace
　　In many a rich and glowing line
　　The land where, still in fitful shine,
The embers of a sinking state are strewed,
　　Where marble ruins scattered wide
　　The vines in purple clusters hide;
And silence and oblivion rule the place
　　Where once the voice of Tully spoke;
　　Now crushed beneath a tyrant yoke,
Art dies on nature's lap, and all again is rude.　　　30

Lady, to thee Germania's sons shall owe
　　The moral history of their state:
　　By thee they live—by thee are great,
And *De l'Allemagne* shall rouse full many a sage
　　Their brilliant fictions to explore
　　And revel in Teutonic lore,
To soar with Klopstock, melt o'er Goethe's page,
　　But wilt thou not *another wreath* bestow?
　　Lives there not yet a nation which may claim
Thy pen to trace the records of its fame?　　　　40
　　To bid its glories live at thy command
　　And veil its errors with indulgent hand?
Is there not yet a people bold and free,
　　Worthy of immortality and thee!
　　A people prompt to every generous deed
At home to cherish, and abroad, to bleed!
　　Oh! let this favored land thy notice share,
And give the expecting world *De l'Angleterre*.

　　　　　　　　　1815

Love and Chemistry

　　Ah! not to those who, *light* and vain,
　　Dare love's *phenomena* to feign,
　　My Ellen, turn thy listening ear,
　　But read its rationale here;
　　My heart, of metal *pure* and true,
　　Was *fused* by one bright glance from you,
　　And by your lineaments impressed,

On the *reverse* your name expressed:
While hope *amalgamates* the mass,
For Cupid's coin may current pass.   10
   Alternate *strata* fill my mind,
Of tender words and words unkind,
Yet oft a *vein* of true delight
Pervades with love's *effulgence* bright.
Thou brilliant as the diamond art,
But *not inflammable* thy heart.
Yet still I breathe in hope to see
Thy pride *evaporate* from thee,
Sublimed to *ether* every thought
Which so much woe to me has wrought.   20
Thy breath as *vital air* I own,
Azote is in thy killing frown—
Galvanic combinations rise
Whene'er I meet thy beaming eyes.
To thee *connected*, all my days
Would pass in happiness and praise,
Oh! mayest thou *insulated* be
From every other one but me;
To none beside *attraction* give,
And I thy sole *conductor* live!   30

                —Phosphor
                1815

A Dish of Tea!

Of all the ills that Fate can hurl at me,
This most I dread: *a friendly dish of tea*.
Think not a meeting of true friends is meant;
To those they hate, the selfsame words are sent,
And Friendship (heavenly goddess) never yet
Was found among the gossip-making set;
Sinks my sad heart when I prepare to dress,
And murmurs at my fate I scarce suppress;
The early hour enjoined, augments the wrong,
The penance is not only sharp but long;   10
For ere the rites of dinner are complete
The formal trains of ancient madams meet,
Their choice of seats the first half-hour employs,
The window here, and there the door annoys,
Then frequent repetitions tire the ear
Of meanless speeches, dull and insincere.
Inquiries made by those who little heed

And, in the tedious answer, *judged indeed*;
Though for their neighbor's health none care a pin,
They ask, not knowing else how to begin.   20
In all the pride of idleness, sedate,
They sit erect—in stiff and stupid state;
Her company demeanor each assumes,
Folds down her lace, and smoothes her gauzy plumes.

   Then each her stock of public news details;
Woe to the absent when the topic fails!
Yet I remain in philosophic doubt
If those can suffer less who *hear them out*:
Then, dull ill-nature deals the leaden death,
And slander kills with pestilential breath;   30
No sportive satire glances bright and keen,
Amusive fancy shuns the courts of spleen,
Insulted truth the room indignant flies,
Faint with repeated wounds, poor grammar dies.
E'en common sense, of firm and sturdy frame,
Is chased by cunning, who assumes his name;
Dullness with flagging wing the group o'ershades,
And the fair form of social pleasure fades.

   At length arrives the equipage of tea;
Oh! welcome sound of clattering cups to me!   40
All interruption I must deem a treat,
And for employment merely sip and eat.
I care not if *imperial* or *souchong*;
It serves to help the weary hours along,
For time on crutches seems to move while I
Am doomed in noisy solitude to sigh,
While oft the wordy torrent sweeps away
The fairy fabric fancy formed so gay.

   The tea withdrawn, a solemn pause ensues,
Portentous silence reigns. . . . I sit and muse   50
What great event the hand of time prepares,
When lo! the mighty power of frauds and cares,
Important whist, with furrowed brow stalks in!
His eager worshippers their rites begin:
The hostess brings the talismanic card,
By chance the willing votaries are paired.

   Now every passion, sense of joy or pain
Is lost in one, the anxious hope of gain.
Hence the shrill voice in eager scolding sounds,
And hence the rude retort or sneer abounds.   60
Oh! sad the fate of those who listening sit

Where vulgar pertness holds the place of wit!
Sad, when so short our date of life assigned,
To prove so dire a waste of genius, heart, and mind.

1815

DOROTHY WORDSWORTH

(1771–1855)

For a century Wordsworth has been remembered primarily as the echo and muse of her brother William, who addressed some of his most celebrated poems to her and who drew on her journals for the materials of his art. When her mother died, the child Dorothy was separated from her four brothers, to be raised by relatives. Only when she was twenty-four could she rejoin William, after he received a small legacy from a friend. They lived at Racedown, then Alfoxden in Dorsetshire, near Coleridge, and finally in the Lake country at Grasmere. Her journals, begun to "give William pleasure," not only record the demands of domesticity on a slender budget but capture a vision of individual nodes of beauty within the disorder of the natural panorama, as well as the rhythms of rural life. Later journals of a walking tour in Scotland and a family tour on the Continent were more prosaic. She apparently suffered from arteriosclerosis from 1829 onward and was an invalid for the last twenty-five years of her life.

The amanuensis of her brother, Dorothy also served William as housekeeper, then as nursemaid for his children after he married Mary Hutchinson. She did not think of herself as a poet. In an epistolary poem to her goddaughter, Julia Marshall, she explained her "bashfulness" as a poet: "I reverenced the poet's skill / and might have nursed a mounting will / to imitate the tender lays / of them who sang in Nature's praise." She was held back, however, by fear of ridicule or shame. The poetry she did compose, she persistently rewrote. She excerpted pieces or built composite versions, transcribed into different notebooks over the decades. Thus the observations in "A Sketch" (c.1805) and "After-recollection" (c.1807), as well as "A Winter's Ramble" (c.1834), are folded into "Grasmere—a Fragment," which celebrates her arrival with her brother in December 1799 at Grasmere. At her best, she captures the autonomous workings and mysterious aura of the natural world. William published several of her poems with his own in 1815, replacing them with "Floating Island" in a collection of 1842.

A Sketch

There is one cottage in our dale,
In naught distinguished from the rest,
Save by a tuft of flourishing trees,
The shelter of that little nest.

The public road through Grasmere Vale
Winds close beside that cottage small,
And there 'tis hidden by the trees
That overhang the orchard wall.

You lose it there—its serpent line
Is lost in that close household grove—   10
A moment lost—and then it mounts
The craggy hills above.

c. 1805 / 1987

Grasmere—a Fragment

Peaceful our valley, fair and green;
    And beautiful the cottages,
Each in its nook, its sheltered hold,
    Or underneath its tuft of trees.

Many and beautiful they are;
    But there is one that I love best.
A lowly roof in truth it is,
    A brother of the rest.

Yet when I sit on rock or hill
    Down-looking on the valley fair,   10
That cottage with its grove of trees
    Summons my heart; it settles there.

Others there are whose small domain
    Of fertile fields with hedgerows green
Might more seduce the traveler's mind
    To wish that there his home had been.

Such wish be his! I blame him not;
    My fancies they, perchance, are wild:
I love that house because it is
    The very mountain's child.   20

Fields hath it of its own, green fields,
    But they are craggy, steep, and bare;
Their fence is of the mountain stone,
    And moss and lichen flourish there.

And when the storm comes from the north,
   It lingers near that pastoral spot,
And piping through the mossy walls,
   It seems delighted with its lot.

And let it take its own delight,
   And let it range the pastures bare   30
Until it reach that grove of trees
   —It may not enter there!

A green unfading grove it is,
   Skirted with many a lesser tree,
Hazel and holly, beech and oak,
   A fair and flourishing company!

Precious the shelter of those trees!
   They screen the cottage that I love;
The sunshine pierces to the roof
   And the tall pine trees tower above.   40

When first I saw that dear abode
   It was a lovely winter's day:
After a night of perilous storm
   The west wind ruled with gentle sway;

A day so mild, it might have been
   The first day of the gladsome spring;
The robins warbled; and I heard
   One solitary throstle sing.

A stranger in the neighborhood,
   All faces then to me unknown,   50
I left my sole companion-friend
   To wander out alone.

Lured by a little winding path,
   I quitted soon the public road;
A smooth and tempting path it was
   By sheep and shepherds trod.

Eastward, toward the mighty hills,
   This pathway led me on,
Until I reached a lofty rock
   With velvet moss o'ergrown.   60

With russet oak and tufts of fern
   Its top was richly garlanded;
Its sides adorned with eglantine
   Bedropped with hips of glossy red.

There too in many a sheltered chink
    The foxglove's broad leaves flourished fair,
And silver birch, whose purple twigs
    Bend to the softest breathing air.

Beneath that rock my course I stayed
    And, looking to its summit high,   70
"Thou wear'st," said I, "a splendid garb,
    Here winter keeps his revelry.

"I've been a dweller on the plains,
    Have sighed when summer days were gone;
No more I'll sigh; for winter here
    Hath gladsome gardens of his own.

"What need of flowers? The splendid moss
    Is gayer than an April mead;
More rich its hues of various green,
    Orange and gold and glowing red."   80

—Beside that gay and lovely rock
    There came with merry voice:
A foaming streamlet glancing by;
    It seemed to say "Rejoice!"

My youthful wishes all fulfilled
    Wishes matured by thoughtful choice,
I stood an inmate of this vale—
    How could I but rejoice?

                    *c.*1805 / 1892

After-recollection at Sight of the Same Cottage

When first I saw that dear abode
It was a lovely winter's day;
After a night of perilous storm
The west wind ruled with gentle sway—

A day so mild it might have been
The first day of the gladsome spring;
The robins warbled, and I heard
One solitary throstle sing.

        *c.*1807–1826 / 1987

Floating Island

Harmonious powers with nature work
On sky, earth, river, lake and sea;
Sunshine and cloud, whirlwind and breeze,
All in one duteous task agree.

Once did I see a slip of earth
By throbbing waves long undermined,
Loosed from its hold—how, no one knew,
But all might see it float, obedient to the wind,

Might see it from the mossy shore
Dissevered, float upon the lake,   10
Float with its crest of trees adorned,
On which the warbling birds their pastime take.

Food, shelter, safety, there they find;
There berries ripen, flowerets bloom;
There insects live their lives—and die:
A peopled world it is, in size a tiny room.

And thus through many seasons' space
This little island may survive,
But nature (though we mark her not)
Will take away, may cease to give.   20

Perchance when you are wandering forth
Upon some vacant sunny day
Without an object, hope, or fear,
Thither your eyes may turn—the isle is passed away,

Buried beneath the glittering lake,
Its place no longer to be found.
Yet the lost fragments shall remain
To fertilize some other ground.

1828–29 / 1842

Christian Milne

née Ross (b. 1773; d. after 1816)

Child of a carpenter, Milne was "without external aid from birth or education"; her mother died soon after her birth, and her stepmother tried to prevent her learning to read and write. She contracted tuberculosis at eighteen, and was frequently bedridden. The only one of ten siblings surviving by the time she reached thirty, she helped her unemployed father by working in Aberdeen as a servant. When she started writing poetry at the age of fourteen her fellow servants called her idle, but she later found a middle-class audience sympathetic to "the simple annals of the poor," as she states in her "Preface." At twenty-four, she married a journeyman ship's carpenter, with whom she had eight children. Her only volume of poems, Simple Poems on Simple Subjects *(1805), includes occasional verse ("Written on my Little Girl's Introduction to Reading" and "Address to a New-Weaned Child") and topical narratives, such as "The Wounded Soldier" and "The Captive Sailor." The £100 from the subscription she invested in a sixteenth share of a ship.*

Written at Fourteen Years of Age
On an Elderly Lady Whom I Then Served

Why am I destined here to stay,
Excluded from the world that's gay;
Confinement and a brawling tongue,
My spirits curbed and I so young!
I thought them pious who were old;
I thought they were nor proud nor bold:
But sure her equals are but rare
Or who would hoary age revere?
To find such trifles stir to rage
A blasted form, quite spent with age;
I'm shocked her lifted crutch to see
Stretched out to strike a child like me.

10

"You're inexperienced, vain, and young,"
Flows oft in vollies from her tongue!
Yet this she knew before I came;
Why is it now a cause of blame?
When she engaged me for her maid,
She valued not my work, she said;
If I could novels read, and plays,
And printed news on paper days.   20
Nay, I must knit the stocking too,
The book above, my hands below
The table, where I worked and read,
Till twelve o'clock I went to bed!

    She cannot move without my aid,
Nor turn without her little maid;
Yet she must show her pride and spleen,
She cries, "I'm great, and you are mean!"
She boasts she's sister to a lord,
But can he health or heaven afford?   30
Her peevish, proud, and fretful mind
Makes him and all her friends unkind.
Though death looks ghastly in her face,
None comes to claim her last embrace—
To close her eyes, or catch her breath,
Or do what's friendly at her death!
I tend her with unwearied care;
For months I have not tasted air!
I sleepless watch her every night!
I oft extinguish, too, the light: 40
That she may sleep I sit in gloom;
Nor sees the sun the darkened room!

    At times she calls me very kind,
And says, in heaven reward I'll find;
She'll mark me in her latter will,
To pay my care of her when ill.
I tend her not from selfish art,
But conscience and a feeling heart
Still rule me with respect to her;
Nor influenced by love nor fear.   50
If fate would send a blackened barge,
To rid me of my fretful charge,
And she embarked in it, I'd pray
Then e'en to bliss she'd find her way:
For her I'd mourn with outward show,
Equipped in black from top to toe.

1805

Preface

Since yet no author e'er did introduce
His works to notice without some excuse,
And "books had better want a title page,
Than want a preface," cries each learned sage,
Be it known mid all who pant for public fame
That one more modest ne'er put in a claim
To be enrolled an author than the mean,
Unlettered, female bard of Aberdeen!
In Burns and Bloomfield, poets fondly prized,   10
'Tis only wondrous that, when criticized,
Their works should nature's brightest charms display,
In verse correct as Milton, Pope, or Gay;
For though to "poortith cauld" both doomed to yield,
Though "Giles"[1] did harrow, while "Rab" plowed the field,
Those cares[2] they felt not which distract the mind,
And not a "wreck of genius" leave behind.
But "menial maid," with no release from toil,
And quite estranged from nature's 'witching smile,
Through lanes and dirty streets sent out to roam,
Or sit, like "bottle in the smoke," at home;   20
Sure, state more adverse to poetic skill
(With apathy more apt the mind to fill)
The world knows not, save its counterpart,
That state, more irksome to the feeling heart,
When menial maid becomes a wedded wife,
Her term of slavery then the term of life!

Yet, mid these frowns of fortune here detailed,
Without her having e'er in duty failed
To parent, master, child, or husband dear,
The following compositions now appear.   30
Let no stern critic "mark them for his own,"
And talk of rules, when rules are all unknown,
That rule except, which fails not to suppress
Whate'er might virtue's sacred bound transgress.
A classic stream, the Dee, still flows along,
Its banks the birthplace still of tuneful song;
Yet, faint the praise to which the bard lays claim,
She dwells at Foot-Dee—reader, mark the name!

1805

1. The name given by [Robert] Bloomfield to his farmer's boy, as descriptive of his own early occupation.
2. "Though our poet gave the powers of his body to the labors of the farm, he refused to bestow on them his thoughts or his cares." Currie's *Life of Burns*, vol. I, p. 100.

On a Lady

*Who Spoke with Some Ill-Nature of the Advertisement of
My Little Work in the* Aberdeen Journal

Says pert Miss Prue,
"There's something new
In Chalmers' weekly papers—
A shipwright's wife,
In humble life,
Writes *rhyme* by nightly tapers!

"That folks of taste
Their time should waste
To read them, makes me wonder!
A lowborn fool   10
Ne'er bred at school,
What can *she* do but blunder?

"Write rhyme, forsooth!
Upon my truth,
'Twill put it out of fashion;
She can but paint
In colors faint
Rude nature's lowest passion.

"A wife so mean
Should nurse and clean   20
And mend her husband's jacket,
Not spend her time
In writing rhyme
And raising such a racket!"

1805

MARY MATILDA BETHAM

(1776–1852)

One of fifteen children of a village rector who had penned a history of the baronetage, Betham was educated informally. She struggled to make a living from her poetry and miniature painting in London, where she knew the Lambs, Coleridge, and Southey, for whom she painted several family portraits. Southey reported that she had suffered a breakdown at least once, around 1818. She described herself as "delighted and rapt" by the eloquence of Madame de Staël on the savante's visit to London. Over two decades Betham published three collections: Elegies and Other Small Poems (1797), Poems (1808), and Vignettes in Verse (1818). Charles Lamb volunteered to correct the spelling and slant rhymes of her romance, the Lay of Marie (1816). Her Biographical Dictionary of the Celebrated Women of Every Age and Country (1804), which includes Mary Wollstonecraft, testifies to her interest in tracing a female tradition.

[Ye men, we willingly yield these to you]

"Since 'tis superior skill in arts refined
That ranks the male above the female kind,
Ye fair, each meaner vanity control
And study how to ornament the soul!
By learning's polish let it be your plan,
In dignity of mind to equal man!
For selfish men monopolize the parts,
In arms, in trade, in government, in arts!
In arms, as strongest, doubtless 'tis their due;
Perhaps in trade, as ablest to pursue," etc.

Ye men, we willingly yield these to you.
We wish not the mechanic arts to scan,
But leave the slavish work to selfish man!
He claims alone the privilege to war,

But 'tis our smiles that must reward the scar!
We need not these heroic dangers brave,
Who hold the laureled conqueror a slave.
We need not search the world for sordid gain,
While we its proud possessors can enchain.
When their pursuit is only meant to prove   10
How much they'd venture to deserve our love;
For wealth and honors they can only prize
As making them more worthy in our eyes.
Their insufficiency they would supply,
And to these glittering resources fly!
Let the poor boasters then indulge their pride,
And think they o'er the universe preside;
Let them recount their numerous triumphs o'er,
And tell the tales, so often told before,
Their own much-doubted merit to enhance   20
And gain the great reward—a favoring glance!
Let them, in bondage, fancy themselves free;
And while fast fettered, vaunt their liberty!
Because they do not massy chains behold
Suppose that they are monarchs uncontrolled.
How vain to hope 'twould be to them revealed!
The flame burns strongest that is most concealed!
Then with what potent, what resistless art,
Those hidden bonds are twined about the heart
So that the captive wanders unconfined   30
And has no sovereign but o'er his mind!
The prize is mutual, either power or fame;
We have the substance, *they* may keep the name!

*c.*1798 / 1905

JANE TAYLOR

pseud., Q.Q. (1783–1824)

The Taylor family were successful engravers: Jane's grandfather illustrated Goldsmith and taught Thomas Bewick, and her father busied himself not only engraving but also writing about twenty books. He also became a Dissenting minister after their move from London to Lavenham, when the children were still small. Jane and her sister Ann (1782–1866), the oldest of eleven children, composed couplets and narratives together; as the "saucy" one, Jane "used to be placed on the kneading-board, in order to recite, preach, narrate, etc." to the baker's customers. Later Jane and Ann worked as engravers in their father's workshop, snatching moments to jot down bits of verse. In response to a submission of juvenilia by Jane, the publishers Darton and Harvey invited the girls to contribute more poetry; Mr. Taylor remarked, "I do not want my girls to be authors," but allowed them to print Original Poems for Infant Minds (1804) for that "interesting little race"—children. Jane won immortality with "Twinkle, twinkle, little Star"; Ann's best known children's poem is "Dance, little baby."

After the family moved to Ongar, Jane fitted up an unoccupied attic as a study with a view over the countryside and gave up engraving. Translations and adaptations from French figure among the sisters' prose work; they received £10 for their first book, £20 for their second. Rhymes for the Nursery (1806) introduced them to Mrs. Barbauld and other writers. Original Poems went through thirty editions by 1834, and Hymns for Infant Minds (1807) through forty-five editions before 1860. After 1811, to retain more of their profits, the sisters published their own work. Jane published didactic prose sketches in Display in 1815, followed by the satirical Essays in Rhyme on Morals and Manners (1816). Also in 1816, Jane began to contribute as "Q.Q." to the Youth's Magazine, work collected in 1824. After she died of cancer at the age of forty, her Memoirs and Poetical Remains appeared in two volumes.

Charles and Mary Lamb were among the first to imitate the work of the Taylor sisters, who offered a model of playful musicality to writers throughout the nineteenth century. Charlotte Yonge praised their "astonishing simplicity without puerility." Sir Walter Scott, Robert Southey, and Maria Edgeworth all reported that children in their family had learned the Taylors' poems by heart.

Recreation

We took our work and went, you see,
To take an early cup of tea.
We did so, now and then, to pay
The friendly debt—and so did they.
Not that our friendship burned so bright
That all the world could see the light;
'Twas of the ordinary *genus*,
And little love was lost between us.
We loved, I think, about as true
As such near neighbors mostly do.   10

At first, we all were somewhat dry;
Mamma felt cold, and so did I.
Indeed, that room, sit where you will,
Has draft enough to turn a mill.
"I hope you're warm," says Mrs. G.
"Oh, quite so," says mamma, says she;
"I'll take my shawl off by and by."
"This room is always warm," says I.

At last the tea came up, and so
With that our tongues began to go.   20
Now in that house you're sure of knowing
The smallest scrap of news that's going.
We find it there the wisest way
To take some care of what we say.

Says she, "There's dreadful doings still
In that affair about the will;
For now the folks in Brewer's Street
Don't speak to James's, when they meet.
Poor Mrs. Sam sits all alone
And frets herself to skin and bone.   30
For months she managed, she declares,
All the old gentleman's affairs;
And always let him have his way,
And never left him night nor day;
Waited and watched his every look
And gave him every drop he took.
Dear Mrs. Sam, it was too bad!
He might have left her all he had."

"Pray, ma'am," says I, "has poor Miss A.
Been left as handsome as they say?"   40
"My dear," says she, " 'tis no such thing;
She'd nothing but a mourning ring.

But is it not *uncommon* mean
To wear that rusty bombazine!"
"She had," says I, "the very same
Three years ago, for—what's his name?"
"The Duke of Brunswick; very true,
And has not bought a thread of new,
I'm positive," said Mrs. G.
So then we laughed and drank our tea.   50

   "So," says mamma, "I find it's true
What Captain P. intends to do—
To hire that house, or else to buy—"
"Close to the tanyard, ma'am," says I.
"Upon my word it's very strange;
I wish they mayn't repent the change!"
"My dear," says she, " 'tis very well
You know, if they can bear the smell."

   "Miss F.," says I, "is said to be
A sweet young woman, Mrs. G."   60
"Oh, excellent! I hear," she cried;
"Oh, truly so!" mamma replied.
"How old should you suppose her, pray?
She's older than she looks, they say."
"Really," says I, "she seems to me
Not more than twenty-two or three."
"Oh, then you're wrong," says Mrs. G.
"Their upper servant told our Jane
She'll not see twenty-nine again."
"Indeed, so old? I wonder why   70
She does not marry, then," says I;
"So many thousands to bestow,
And such a beauty, too, you know."
"A beauty! Oh, my dear Miss B.,
You must be joking now," says she.
"Her figure's rather pretty—" "Ah!
That's what I say," replied mamma.

   "Miss F.," says I, "I've understood,
Spends all her time in doing good.
The people say her coming down   80
Is quite a blessing to the town."
At that our hostess fetched a sigh,
And shook her head; and so says I,
"It's very kind of her, I'm sure,
To be so generous to the poor."
"No doubt," says she, " 'tis very true;

Perhaps here may be reasons too—
You know some people like to pass
For patrons with the lower class."

And here I break my story's thread,   90
Just to remark that what she said,
Although I took the other part,
Went like a cordial to my heart.

Some innuendos more had passed,
Till out the scandal came at last.
"Come, then, I'll tell you something more,"
Says she, "—Eliza, shut the door.
I would not trust a creature here,
For all the world, but you, my dear.
Perhaps it's false—I wish it may—   100
But let it go no further, pray!"
"Oh," says mamma, "you need not fear;
We never mention what we hear."
"Indeed we shall not, Mrs. G.,"
Says I, again, impatiently.
And so we drew our chairs the nearer,
  And whispering, lest the child should hear her,
She told a tale at least too long
To be repeated in a song—
We, panting every breath between,   110
With curiosity and spleen.
And how we did enjoy the sport,
And echo every faint report,
And answer every candid doubt,
And turn her motives inside out,
And holes in all her virtues pick
Till we were sated, almost sick.

Thus having brought it to a close,
In great good humor we arose.
Indeed, 'twas more than time to go;   120
Our boy had been an hour below.
So, warmly pressing Mrs. G.
To fix a day to come to tea,
We muffled up in cloak and plaid
And trotted home behind the lad.

1816

A Pair

There was a youth—but woe is me!
I quite forget his name, and he,
Without some label round his neck,
Is like one pea among a peck.
Go search the country up and down—
Port, city, village, parish, town—
And saving just the face and name,
You shall behold the very same
Wherever pleasure's train resorts,
From the Land's-End to Johnny Groats';   10
And thousands such have swelled the herd,
From William down to George the Third.

   To life he started, thanks to fate,
In contact with a good estate:
Provided thus, and quite at ease,
He takes for granted all he sees;
Ne'er sends a thought nor lifts an eye
To ask what am I? where? and why?—
All that is no affair of his;
Somehow he came—and there he is!   20
Without such prosing, stupid stuff,
Alive and well, and that's enough.

   Thoughts! why, if all that crawl like trains
Of caterpillars through his brains,
With every syllable let fall,
Bon mot, and compliment, and all,
Were melted down in furnace fire,
I doubt if shred of golden wire
To make, amongst it all would linger,
A ring for Tom Thumb's little finger.   30
Yet, think not that he comes below
The modern average ratio—
The current coin of fashion's mint—
The common, ballroom-going stint.
Of trifling cost his stock in trade is,
Whose business is to please the ladies;
Or who to honors may aspire
Of a town beau or country squire.
The cant of fashion and of vice
To learn, slight effort will suffice;   40
And he was furnished with that knowledge
Even before he went to college.
And thus, without the toil of thought,

Favor and flattery may be bought.
No need to win the laurel now
For lady's smile or vassal's bow;
To lie exposed in patriot camp,
Or study by the midnight lamp.

Nature and art might vainly strive
To keep his intellect alive.   50
—'Twould not have forced an exclamation,
Worthy a note of admiration,
If he had been on Gibeon's hill
And seen the sun and moon stand still.
What prodigy was ever known
To raise the pitch of fashion's tone!
Or make it yield, by any chance,
That studied air of nonchalance,
Which, after all, however graced,
Is apathy and want of taste.   60

The vulgar every station fill—
St. Giles' or James's, which you will;
Spruce drapers in their masters' shops
Rank with right honorable fops;
No real distinction marks the kinds—
The raw material of their minds.
But *mind* claims rank that cannot yield
To blazoned arms and crested shield:
Above the need and reach it stands
Of diamond stars from royal hands;   70
Nor waits the nod of courtly state
To bid it be or not be great.
The regions where it wings its way
Are set with brighter stars than they:
With calm contempt it thence looks down
On fortune's favor or its frown;
Looks down on those who vainly try,
By strange inversion of the eye,
From that poor molehill where they sit,
To cast a downward look on it: 80
As robin, from his pear tree height,
Looks *down* upon the eagle's flight.

Before our youth had learned his letters,
They taught him to despise his betters;
And if some things have been forgot,
That lesson certainly has not.
The haunts his genius chiefly graces

Are tables, stables, taverns, races;
The things of which he most afraid is
Are tradesmen's bills and learned ladies: 90
He deems the first a grievous bore
But loathes the latter even more
Than solitude or rainy weather,
Unless they happen both together.

Soft his existence rolls away,
Tomorrow plenteous as today:
He lives, enjoys, and lives anew,
And when he dies—what shall we do!

❧

Down a close street, whose darksome shops display
Old clothes and iron on both sides the way;   100
Loathsome and wretched, whence the eye in pain
Averted turns nor seeks to view again;
Where lowest dregs of human nature dwell,
More loathsome than the rags and rust they sell—
A pale mechanic rents an attic floor.
By many a shattered stair you gain the door:
'Tis one poor room, whose blackened walls are hung
With dust that settled there when he was young.
The rusty grate two massy bricks displays,
To fill the sides and make a frugal blaze.   110
The door unhinged, the window patched and broke,
The panes obscured by half a century's smoke:
There stands the bench at which his life is spent,
Worn, grooved, and bored, and worm-devoured, and bent,
Where daily, undisturbed by foes or friends,
In one unvaried attitude he bends.
His tools, long practiced, seem to understand
Scarce less their functions than his own right hand.
With these he drives his craft with patient skill;
Year after year would find him at it still.   120
The noisy world around is changing all:
War follows peace, and kingdoms rise and fall;
France rages now, and Spain, and now the Turk;
Now victory sounds—but there he sits at work!
A man might see him so, then bid adieu;
Make a long voyage to China or Peru;
There traffic, settle, build; at length might come,
Altered, and old, and weather-beaten home,
And find him on the same square foot of floor

On which he left him twenty years before   130
—The selfsame bench, and attitude, and stool,
The same quick movement of his cunning tool;
The very distance 'twixt his knees and chin—
As though he had but stepped just out and in.

Such is his fate—and yet you might descry
A latent spark of meaning in his eye.
—That crowded shelf beside his bench contains
One old worn volume that employs his brains:
With algebraic lore its page is spread,
Where *a* and *b* contend with *x* and *zed*—   140
Sold by some student from an Oxford hall;
Bought by the pound upon a broker's stall.
On this it is his sole delight to pore,
Early and late, when working time is o'er;
But oft he stops, bewildered and perplexed,
At some hard problem in the learned text;
Pressing his hand upon his puzzled brain
At what the dullest schoolboy could explain.

From needful sleep the precious hour he saves,
To give his thirsty mind the stream it craves: 150
There, with his slender rush beside him placed,
He drinks the knowledge in with greedy haste.
At early morning, when the frosty air
Brightens Orion and the northern Bear,
His distant window mid the dusky row
Shows a dim light to passenger below
—A light more dim is flashing on his mind,
That shows its darkness, and its views confined.
Had science shone around his early days,
How had his soul expanded in the blaze!   160
But penury bound him, and his mind in vain
Struggles and writhes beneath her iron chain.

—At length the taper fades, and distant cry
Of early sweep bespeaks the morning nigh:
Slowly it breaks—and that rejoicing ray
That wakes the healthful country into day,
Tips the green hills, slants o'er the level plain,
Reddens the pool, and stream, and cottage pane,
And field, and garden, park, and stately hall,
Now darts obliquely on his wretched wall.   170
He knows the wonted signal; shuts his book,
Slowly consigns it to its dusty nook;
Looks out awhile with fixed and absent stare

On crowded roofs, seen through the foggy air;
Stirs up the embers, takes his sickly draft,
Sighs at his fortunes, and resumes his craft.

1816

Accomplishment

How is it that masters and science and art
One spark of intelligence fail to impart
Unless in that chemical union combined
Of which the result, in one word, is a *mind*?

A youth may have studied and traveled abroad,
May sing like Apollo and paint like a Claude,
And speak all the languages under the pole,
And have every gift in the world but a soul.

That drapery, wrought by the leisurely fair,
Called *patchwork* may well to such genius compare,   10
Wherein every tint of the rainbow appears,
And stars to adorn it are forced from their spheres.

There glows a bright pattern (a sprig or a spot)
'Twixt clusters of roses full-blown and red-hot;
Here magnified tulips divided in three,
Alternately shaded with sections of tree.

But when all is finished, this labor of years,
A mass unharmonious, unmeaning appears;
'Tis showy but void of intelligent grace;
It is not a landscape, it is not a face.   20

'Tis thus Education (so called in our schools),
With costly materials and capital tools,
Sits down to her work, and at last she produces
Exactly the job that her customer chooses.

See French and Italian spread out on her lap;
Then Dancing springs up and skips into a gap;
Next Drawing and all its varieties come,
Sewed down in their place by her finger and thumb.

And then, for completing her fanciful robes,
Geography, Music, the use of the Globes,   30
&c. &c., which, match as they will,
Are sewn into shape and set down in the bill.

Thus Science distorted and torn into bits,
Art tortured and frightened half out of her wits,

In portions and patches, some light and some shady,
Are stitched up together and make a young lady.

1816

The Toad's Journal

It is related by Mr. Belzoni in the interesting narrative of his late discoveries in Egypt that having succeeded in clearing a passage to the entrance of an ancient temple, which had been for ages buried in the sand, the first object that presented itself, upon entering, was a toad of enormous size; and (if we may credit the assertions of some naturalists respecting the extraordinary longevity of these creatures when in a state of solitary confinement) we may believe that it was well stricken in years.

Whether the subjoined document was entrusted to our traveler by the venerable reptile as a present to the British Museum, or with the more mercantile view of getting it printed in London in preference to Alexandria, on condition of receiving one percent on the profits after the sale of the 500th edition (provided the publisher should by that time be at all remunerated for his risk and trouble), we pretend not to say. Quite as much as can be vouched for is, the Mss. being faithfully rendered from the original hieroglyphic character.

(The dates are omitted.)

—"Crawled forth from some rubbish and winked with
    one eye;
Half opened the other but could not tell why:
Stretched out my left leg, as it felt rather queer,
Then drew all together and slept for a year.
Awakened, felt chilly—crept under a stone;
Was vastly contented with living alone.
One toe became wedged in the stone like a peg,
Could not get it away—had the cramp in my leg:
Began half to wish for a neighbor at hand
To loosen the stone, which was fast in the sand;   10
Pulled harder—then dozed, as I found 'twas no use;
Awoke the next summer, and lo! it was loose.
Crawled forth from the stone, when completely awake
Crept into a corner and grinned at a snake.
Retreated and found that I needed repose;
Curled up my damp limbs and prepared for a doze:
Fell sounder to sleep than was usual before,
And did not awake for a century or more;
But had a sweet dream, as I rather believe—
Methought it was light, and a fine summer's eve;   20
And I, in some garden, deliciously fed
In the pleasant moist shade of a strawberry bed.

There fine speckled creatures claimed kindred with me,
And others that hopped, most enchanting to see.
Here long I regaled with emotion extreme—
Awoke—disconcerted to find it a dream;
Grew pensive; discovered that life is a load;
Began to be weary of being a toad:
Was fretful at first, and then shed a few tears."—
Here ends the account of the first thousand years.   30

Moral

To find a moral where there's none
Is hard indeed yet must be done.
Since only morals sound and sage
May grace this consecrated page,
Then give us leave to search a minute
Perhaps for one that is not in it.
    How strange a waste of life appears
This wondrous reptile's length of years!
Age after age afforded him
To wink an eye or move a limb,   40
To doze and dream—and then to think
Of noting this with pen and ink;
Or hieroglyphic shapes to draw,
More likely, with his hideous claw;
Sure length of days might be bestowed
On something better than a toad!
Had his existence been eternal,
What better could have filled his journal?
    True, we reply, our ancient friend
Seems to have lived to little end;   50
This must be granted—nay the elf
Seems to suspect as much himself.
Refuse not then to find a teacher
In this extraordinary creature:
And learn at least, whoe'er you be,
To moralize as well as he.
It seems that life is all a void,
On selfish thoughts alone employed;
That length of days is not a good
Unless their use be understood;   60
While if good deeds one year engage,
That may be longer than an age;
But if a year in trifles go,
Perhaps you'd spend a thousand so.
Time cannot stay to make us wise;

We must improve it as it flies.
The work is ours, and they shall rue it
Who think that time will stop to do it.
   And then, again, he lets us know
That length of days is length of woe.   70
His long experience taught him this,
That life affords no solid bliss;
Or if of bliss on earth you scheme,
Soon you shall find it but a dream.
The visions fade, the slumbers break,
And then you suffer wide awake.
What is it but a vale of tears,
Though we should live a thousand years?

                              1824

To Madame de Staël
Written After Reading Corinne, ou l'Italie

   O woman, greatly gifted! why
Wert thou not gifted from on high?
What had that noble genius done,
That knew all hearts—all things but *one*—
Had that been known? Oh, would it might
Be whispered, Here she took her flight!
Where, where is that fine spirit hurled,
That seemed unmeet for either world?

   While o'er thy magic page I bend,
I know thee, claim thee for my friend;   10
With thee a secret converse hold
And see my inmost thoughts unfold.
Each notion crude, defined, expressed;
And certain, what I vaguely guessed.
And hast thou taught, with cruel skill,
The art to suffer better still;
Grief's finest secret to explore,
Though understood too well before?
Ah, well! I'd thank thee if I might;
Although so wrong, thou art so right!   20
While I condemn, my heart replies,
And deeper feelings sympathize.

   Thy view of life, that painful view,
How false it is! and yet how true!
"Life without love—a cheerless strife;
Yet love so rarely given to life."

And why must truth and virtue, why,
This mighty claim of love deny?
What was this earth, so full, so fair?
A cheerless desert, bleak and bare—   30
God knew it was—till love was there.
Say, has the heart a glance at bliss—
One—till it glance or gaze at this?
Ah, no! unblessed, unsoothed the lot,
Fair though it seem, that knows it not!
'Tis true! and to the truth replies
A thousand joyless hearts and eyes—
Eyes beamless, hearts that do not break—
They cannot—but that always ache;
And slowly wither, day by day,   40
Till life at last is dried away.

   "Love, or Religion"; yes, she knew
Life has no choice but 'twixt the two.
But when she sought *that* balm to find,
She guessed and groped but still was blind.
Aloft she flew yet failed to see
Aught but an earthly deity.
The humble Christian's holy love,
Oh, how it calmly soars above
These storms of passion! Yes, too much   50
I've felt her talent's magic touch.
Return, my soul, to that retreat
From sin and woe—thy Savior's feet!
There learn an art she never knew:
The heart's own empire to subdue.
A large, but willing sacrifice,
All to resign that He denies;
To him in meek submission bend,
Own Him an all-sufficient friend;
Here, and in holy worlds above,   60
My portion—and my only love!

1822 / 1825

LADY CAROLINE LAMB

née Ponsonby (1785–1828)

❧❦☙

Caroline Ponsonby suffered from the neglect peculiar to aristocratic privilege. Because she was thought frail, the third Earl of Bessborough sent his child to spend six years in Italy with a governess, then had her educated with her cousins. She married William Lamb, future Lord Melbourne, in 1805; their only surviving child was mentally retarded. For a few months in 1812 she had an affair with Lord Byron, whom she described as "mad, bad, and dangerous to know." Although he was repelled by her indiscretions—which included an attempted elopement, threatened suicide, and scenes in the street—he responded to her passion: "Then your heart, my poor Caro—what a little volcano! that pours lava through your veins!" To conciliate her, he wrote, "I have always thought you the cleverest most agreeable absurd amiable perplexing dangerous fascinating little being that lives now." Another letter assured her, "You are the only woman I know who never bored me."

Contemporaries commented on the "kaleidoscope" of her emotions; Lady Morgan praised her instinctive generosity. Her "open frankness" was delightful, but invited "mis-construction." Dependent on alcohol and laudanum, she had later affairs, including one with the young writer Bulwer-Lytton. Virginia Woolf observed that she was "insane but generous," and would have made Byron a better wife than the mathematical Miss Milbanke.

Lamb's mini-epic, "A New Canto" (1819), written in the stanza of Don Juan, *pretends to be Byron's vision of a fiery apocalypse that will melt down Arctic snows, church, bank, courts, poets, and their creditors. Her scandalous first novel,* Glenarvon *(1816), places her lover in the world of Gothic passion. Two more novels,* Graham Hamilton *(1822) and* Ada Reis *(1823), followed. After Byron's death in 1824 she had a mental breakdown and retired to the country until her death.*

A New Canto

I.

I'm sick of fame—I'm gorged with it, so full
  I almost could regret the happier hour
When northern oracles proclaimed me dull,
  Grieving my Lord should so mistake his power—
E'en they who now my consequence would lull
  And vaunt they hailed and nursed the opening flower.
Vile cheats! He knew not, impudent reviewer,
Clear spring of Helicon from common sewer.

II.

'Tis said they killed the gentle-souled Montgomery;
  I'll swear they did not shed for him a tear!   10
He had not spirit to revenge their mummery,
  Nor lordly purse to print and persevere.
I measured stings with 'em—a method summary—
  Not that I doubt their penitence sincere;
And I've a fancy running in my head
They'll like—or so by some it will be said.

III.

When doomsday comes, St. Paul's will be on fire
  (I should not wonder if we live to see it);
Of us, proof pickles, Heaven must rather tire
  And want a reckoning—if so, so be it: 20
Only about the cupola, or higher,
  If there's a place unoccupied, give me it—
To catch, before I touch my sinner's salary,
The first grand crackle in the whispering gallery.

IV.

The ball comes tumbling with a lively crash,
  And splits the pavement up, and shakes the shops,
Teeth chatter, china dances, spreads the flash,
  The omnium falls, the Bank of England stops;
Loyal and radical, discreet and rash,
  Each on his knees in tribulation flops;   30
The Regent raves (Moore chuckling at his pain)
And sends about for ministers in vain.

V.

The roaring streamers flap, red flakes are shot
   This way and that, the town is a volcano—
And yells are heard like those provoked by Lot,
   Some of the Smithfield sort and some *soprano*;
Some holy water seek, the font is hot,
   And fizzing in a teakettle *piano.*
"Now bring your magistrates, with yeomen backed,"
Bawls Belial, "and read the riot act!"   40

VI.

The Peak of Derbyshire goes to and fro;
   Like drunken sot the Monument is reeling;
Now fierce and fiercer comes the furious glow—
   The planets, like a juggler's ball, are wheeling!
I am a graceless poet, as you know,
   Yet would not wish to wound a proper feeling,
Nor hint you'd hear, from saints in agitation,
The *lapsus linguae* of an execration.

VII.

Mark yon bright beauty in her tragic airs,
   How her clear white the mighty smother tinges!   50
Delicious chaos, that such beauty bares!
   And now those eyes outstretch their silken fringes,
Staring bewildered—and anon she tears
   Her raven tresses ere the wide flame singes—
Oh would she feel as I could do and cherish
One wild forgetful rapture ere all perish!

VIII.

Who would be vain? Fair maids and ugly men
   Together rush, the dainty and the shabby
(No gallantry will soothe ye, ladies, then),
   High dames, the wandering beggar and her *babby*,   60
In motley agony, a desperate train,
   Flocking to holy places like the Abbey,
Till the black volumes, closing o'er them, scowl,
Muffling forever curse and shriek and howl.

IX.

A woman then may rail, nor would I stint her;
   Her griefs, poor soul, are past redress in law—

And if this matter happen in the winter,
　　There'll be at Petersburg a sudden thaw,
And Alexander's palace, every splinter,
　　Burn Christmas-like and merry, though the jaw　　70
Of its imperial master take to trembling,
As when the French were quartered in the Kremlin.

X.

Rare doings in the north! as trickle down
　　Primeval snows, and white bears swash and caper,
And Bernadotte, that swaggerer of renown,
　　To Bonaparte again might hold a taper—
Aye, truckle to him, cap in hand or crown,
　　To save his distance from the sturdy vapor.
Napoleon, too, will he look blank and paly?
He hung the citizens of Moscow gaily;　　80

XI.

He made a gallant youth his darkling prey,
　　Nor e'er would massacre or murder mince;
And yet I fear, on this important day,
　　To see the hero pitifully wince!
Go yield him up to Beelzebub, and say,
　　"Pray treat him like a gentleman and prince."
I doubt him thoroughbred, he's not a true one,
A bloodhound spaniel-crossed, and no Don Juan.

XII.

Death-watches now, in every baking wall, tick
　　Faster and faster, till they tick no more,　　90
And Norway's copper mines about the Baltic
　　Swell, heave, and rumble with their boiling ore,
Like some griped giant's motion peristaltic,
　　Then burst and to the sea vast gutters pour;
And as the waters with the fire-stream curl,
Zooks! what a whizzing, roaring, sweltering whirl!

XIII.

Lo! the great deep laid bare, tremendous yawning,
　　Its scalding waves retiring from the shore,
Affrighted whales on dry land sudden spawning,
　　And small fish fry where fish ne'er fried before.　　100
No Christian eye shall see another dawning—
　　The Turkish infidel may now restore

His wives to liberty and, ere to hell he go,
Roll to the bottom of the Archipelago!

XIV.

And now, ye coward sinners (I'm a bold one,
   Scorning all here, nor caring for hereafter,
A radical, a stubborn, and an old one),
   Behold! each riding on a burning rafter,
The devils (in my arms I long to fold one),
   Splitting their blue and brazen sides with laughter,   110
Play at snapdragon in their merry fits
O'er some conventicle for hypocrites.

XV.

Aye, serve the skulkers, with their looks so meek,
   As they've, no doubt, served lobsters in their time
(Poor *blacks*! No Wilberforce for them can speak,
   Pleading their color is their only crime);
Trundle them all to bubble and to squeak—
   No doubt they shut their ears against my rhyme,
Yet sneak, rank elders, fearful of denials,
To pick Susannahs up in Seven Dials.   120

XVI.

Brave fiends! for usurers and misers melt
   And make a hell-broth of their cursed gold!
On all who mock at want they never felt,
   On all whose consciences are bought and sold,
E'en as on me, be stern damnation dealt—
   And lawyers, damn them all! The blood runs cold
That man should deal with misery to mock it
And filch an only shilling from its pocket.

XVII.

Aye, damn them all, a deep damnation wait
   On all such callous, crooked, hopeless souls!   130
Ne'er mince the matter to discriminate,
   But let the devil strike them from the rolls:
'Twill cheer their clients to behold their fate
   And round their bonfires dance in merry shoals!
Some poor men's tales I've heard upon my journeys
Would make a bishop long to roast attorneys!

XVIII.

Perhaps the thing may take another turn,
    And one smart shock may split the world in two,
And I in Italy, you soon may learn,
    On t'other half am reeling far from you.   140
No doubt 'twould split where first it ought to burn—
    Across some city that its sins should rue,
Some wicked capital, for instance, Paris,
And stop the melodrames from Mr. Harris.

XIX.

Save London, none is wickeder or bigger,
    An odious place, too, in these modern times;
Small incomes, runaways, and swindlers eager
    To fleece and dash; and then their quacks and mimes,
Their morals lax, and literary rigor,
    Their prim caesuras, and their gendered rhymes—   150
Mine never could abide their statutes critical;
They'd call them neutral or hermaphroditical.

XX.

True, their poor playwrights (truth, I speak with pain)
    Yield ours a picking, and I beg their pardon;
'Tis needless—down must come poor Drury Lane,
    And scarcely less poor, down come Covent Garden!
If we must blaze, no squabbles will remain
    That actor's hearts against each other harden—
Committees, creditors, all wrapped in flames
That leave no joke for Horace Smith or James.   160

XXI.

In rebus modus est: whene'er I write
    I mean to rhapsodize and nothing more;
If some poor nervous souls my muse affright,
    I might a strain of consolation pour,
Talk of the spotless spirits, snowy white,
    Which, newly clad, refreshing graves restore
And, silvery wreaths of glory round them curled,
Serenely rise above the blazing world.

XXII.

Free, bursting from his mound of lively green,
    Winged light as zephyr of the rosy morn,   170

The poor man smiling on the proud is seen
    With something of a mild, forgiving scorn—
The marbled proud one, haply with the mean,
    Sole on his prayer of intercession borne:
Upward in peal harmonious they move,
Soft as the midnight tide of hallowed love.

XXIII.

The rich humane, who with their common clay
    Divided graciously, distinguished few;
Good Christians who had slept their wrongs away,
    In peace with this life, and the next in view;   180
Strugglers with tyrant passion and its prey,
    Love's single-hearted victims, sacred, true,
Who, when dishonor's path alone could save,
Bore a pure pang to an untimely grave—

XXIV.

Blest they, who wear the vital spirit out
    Even thus, degrading not the holy fire,
Nor bear a prostituted sense about—
    The misery of never-quenched desire
(Still quenched, still kindling, every thought devout
    Lost in the changeful torment—portion dire!).   190
Return we to our heaven, our fire and smoke,
Though now you may begin to take the joke!

XXV.

What joke? My verses—mine, and all beside,
    Wild, foolish tales of Italy and Spain,
The gushing shrieks, the bubbling squeaks, the bride
    Of nature, blue-eyed, black-eyed, and her swain,
Kissing in grottos near the moonlit tide,
    Though to all men of commonsense 'tis plain,
Except for rampant and amphibious brute,
Such damp and drizzly places would not suit.   200

XXVI.

Mad world! For fame we rant, call names, and fight—
    I scorn it heartily yet love to dazzle it,
Dark intellects by day, as shops by night,
    All with a bright, new, speculative gas lit,
Wars the blue vapor with the oil-fed light,
    Hot sputter Blackwood, Jeffrey, Gifford, Hazlitt—

The muse runs madder and, as mine may tell,
Like a loose comet, mingles heaven and hell.

XXVII.

You shall have more of her another time,
   Since gulled you will be with our flights poetic,   210
Our eight, and ten, and twenty feet sublime,
   Our maudlin, hey-down-derrified pathetic;
For my part, though I'm doomed to write in rhyme,
   To read it would be worse than an emetic—
But something must be done to cure the spleen
And keep my name in capitals, like Kean.

                                                    1819

[Would I had seen thee dead and cold]

Would I had seen thee dead and cold,
   In thy lone grave asleep,
Than live, thy falsehood to behold,
   And penitent to weep:
For better I thy grave could see
Than know that thou art false to me!

Or rather, would that I had died,
   When happy on thy breast—
My love had then been satisfied
   And life's last moments blest,   10
For they taste bliss without alloy,
Who die in the sweet dream of joy!

But no! I feel the fault was mine,
   To think affection's chain
Could thy proud wayward heart confine,
   When honor's claim was vain:
Who robs the shrine where virtue lies
Will not the stolen relic prize!

                                                    1829

Lines to Harriet Wilson

Harriet Wilson, shall I tell thee where,
Beside my being *cleverer*,
We differ?—thou wert hired to hold thy tongue;
Thou hast no right to do thy lovers wrong:
But I, whom none could buy or gain,

Who am as proud, girl, as thyself art vain,
And like thyself, or sooner like the wind,
Blow raging ever free and unconfined.
What should withhold my tongue with pen of steel
The faults of those who have wronged me to reveal?   10
Why should I hide men's follies whilst my own
Blaze like the gas along this talking town?
Is it being bitter to be too sincere?
Must we adulterate truth as they do beer?
I'll tell thee why then! as each has his price,
I have been bought at last—I am not ice:
Kindness and gratitude have chained my tongue;
From henceforth I will do no mortal wrong.
Prate those who please—laugh—censure who that will;
My mouth is sealed—my thoughts—my pen—are still.   20
In the meantime (we Lambs are seldom civil),
I wish thy book—*not thee*—at the Devil.

1829

CAROLINE BOWLES

later Southey (1786–1854)

The comfortable leisure of Bowles' wealthy family evaporated after the death of Caroline's parents, when a dishonest guardian absconded with her property. She turned to writing as a means of support, eventually finding a publisher for her verse narrative Ellen Fitzarthur *(1820), which was followed by* The Widow's Tale and Other Poems *(1822). Later collections included* Solitary Hours *(1826) and* Tales of the Factories *(1833). The autobiographical narrative* The Birthday *(1836) drew comparisons to Cowper. Early in her career she corresponded with Robert Southey, who introduced her to Wordsworth and invited her to collaborate on a poem about Robin Hood, never completed. After the death of Southey's wife, Bowles married the aged poet, but his mental illness blighted their marriage. She received a crown pension in 1854.*

The Birthday

(excerpts)

Part the First

Dark gloomy day of winter's darkest month!
Scarce through the lowering sky your dawning light
In one pale watery streak breaks feebly forth.
No sunbeam through that congregated mass
Of heavy rolling clouds will pierce today.
Beams of the cheering sun! I court ye not:
Best with the saddened temper of my soul
Accords the pensive stillness nature wears;
For memory, with a serious reckoning, now
Is busy with the past—with other years,
When the return of this, my natal day,
Brought gladness to warm hearts that loved me well.
As way-worn pilgrim on the last hilltop

10

Lingers awhile and, leaning on his staff,
Looks back upon the pleasant plain o'erpassed,
Retracing far with retrospective eye
The course of every little glancing stream
And winding valley path, late hurried o'er
Perchance with careless unobservant eye,
Fixed on some distant point of fairer promise;   20
As with long pause the highest summit gained
(Dividing, like the Tyrolean ridge,
Summer from winter) that wayfaring man
Leans on his staff and looks a long farewell
To all the lovely land, so linger I
(Life's lonely pilgrim!) on the last hilltop,
With thoughtful, tender, retrospective gaze,
Ere turning, down the deep descent I go,
Of the cold shadowy side.

. . . .

How vivid still, how deep the hues, the imprint
Left by those childish pastimes! Later joys,
Less puerile, more exciting, have I known
(Ah! purer none; from earth's alloy so free),
But memory hoards no picture so distinct
In freshness as of yesterday as those
Life's first impressions, exquisite and strong—
Their stamp, compared to that of later days,
Like a proof print from the engraver's plate
The first struck off—most forcibly impressed.   490
Lo! what a train like Bluebeard's wives appear,
So many headless! half dismembered some,
With battered faces—eyeless—noseless—grim—
With cracked enamel and unsightly scars—
Some with bald pates or hempen wigs unfrizzed,
And ghastly stumps, like Greenwich pensioners;
Others mere torsos—arms, legs, heads, all gone!—
But precious all. And chief that veteran doll,
She, from whose venerable face is worn
All prominence of feature: shining brown   500
(Like chestnut from its prickly coating freed)
With equal polish as the wigless skull—
Well I remember, with what bribery won
Of a fair rival—one of waxen mold
(Long coveted possession!) I was brought
The mutilated favorite to resign.
The blue-eyed fair one came—perfection's self!
With eager joy I clasped her waxen charms;

But then—the stipulated sacrifice!
"And must we part?" my piteous looks expressed—   510
(Mute eloquence!) "And *must* we part, dear Stump!
Oh! might I keep ye both!"—and both I kept.

Unwelcome hour I ween, that tied me down,
Restless, reluctant, to the seamstress' task!
Sight horrible to me, the allotted seam
Of stubborn Irish, or more hateful length
Of handkerchief, with folded edge tacked down,
All to be hemmed—ay, *selvidge sides* and all.
And so they were in tedious course of time,
With stitches long and short, "cat's teeth" yclept;   520
Or jumbled thick and thin, oblique, transverse,
At last, in sable line imprinted grim.
But less distasteful was the sampler's task;
There green and scarlet vied, and fancy claimed
Her privilege to crowd the canvass field
With hearts and zigzags, strawberries and leaves,
And many a quaint device; some moral verse
Or Scripture text enwrought; and last of all,
Last, though not least, the self-pleased artist's name.

And yet, with more alacrity of will,   530
I fashioned various raiment—caps, cloaks, gowns—
Gay garments for the family of dolls;
No matter how they fitted—they were made;
Ay, and applauded, and rewarded, too,
With silver thimble. Precious gift! bestowed
By a kind aunt, one ever kind and good,
Mine early benefactress! since approved
By time and trial mine unchanging friend;
Yet most endeared by the affecting bond
Of mutual sorrows, mutual sympathies.   540

Part the Second

How I hate
Those London Sparrows! Vile, pert, noisy things!   250
Whose ceaseless clamor at the windowsill
(The back-room window, opening on some mews)
Reminds one of the country just so far
As to bemock its wild and blithesome sounds,
And press upon the heart our pent-up state
In the great Babylon;—oppressed, engulfed
By crowds and smoke and vapor: Where one sees,
For laughing vales fair winding in the sun

And hilltops gleaming in his golden light,
The dingy red of roofs and chimneys tall   260
On which a leaden orb looks dimly down!
For limpid rills, the kennel's stream impure;
For primrose banks, the rifled scentless things
Tied up for sale, held out by venal hands;
For lowing herds and bleating flocks, the cries
Of noisy venders threading every key,
From base to treble, of discordant sound;
For trees, unnatural stinted mockeries
At windows and, on balconies, stuck up
Fir trees in vases!—picturesque conceit!   270
Whereon, to represent the woodland choir,
Perch those sweet songsters of the sooty wing.

*   *   *   *   *

Yet as I write, the light and flippant mood
Changes to one of serious saddened thought,
And my heart smites me for the sorry jest,
Calling to mind a sight that filled me once
With tenderest sympathy.

     In a great city,
Blackened and deafening with the smoke and din
Of forge and engine—traffic's thriving mart,
Chartered by Mammon—underneath a range   280
Of gorgeous showrooms where all precious metals,
In forms innumerous, exquisitely wrought,
Dazzled the gazer's eye, I visited
The secret places of the "Prison House."
From den to den of a long file I passed
Of dingy workshops—each affording space
But for the sallow inmate and his tools:
His table, the broad, timeworn, blackened slab
Of a deep sunken window, whose dim panes
Tinged with a sickly hue the blessed beams   290
Of the bright noonday sun. I tarried long
In one of those sad cells, conversing free
With its pale occupant, a dark-browed man
Of hard repellant aspect—hard and stern.
But having watched awhile the curious sleight
Of his fine handicraft, when I expressed
Pleased admiration—in few words, but frank,
And toned by kindly feeling, for my heart
Yearned with deep sympathy—the moody man
Looked up into my face, and in that look   300

Flashed out an intellectual soul-fraught gleam
Of pleased surprise, that changed to mild and good
The harsh expression of that care-marred face.
There lay beside him on the window slab
A dirty ragged book turned downwards open
Where he had last been reading, from his toil
Snatching a hurried moment. Anxiously
I glanced towards it, but forbore to question,
Restrained by scrupulous feeling, shunning most
Shadow of disrespect to low estate—   310
But from the book my wandering gaze passed on
To where, beyond it, close to the dim panes,
A broken flowerpot, with a string secured,
Contained a living treasure—a green clump
(Just bursting into bloom) of the field orchis.
"You care for flowers," I said, "and that fair thing,
The beautiful orchis, seems to flourish well
With little light and air."

              "It won't for long,"
The man made answer, with a mournful smile
Eying the plant. "I took it up, poor thing!   320
But Sunday evening last from the rich meadow
Where thousands bloom so gay, and brought it here
To smell of the green fields for a few days
Till Sunday comes again—and rest mine eyes on,
When I look up fatigued from these dead gems
And yellow glittering gold."
                     With patient courtesy,
Well spoken, clear (no ignorant churl was he),
That poor artificer explained the process
Of his ingenious art—I looked and listened,   330
But with an aching heart that loathed the sight
Of those bright pebbles and that glittering ore;
And when I turned to go—not unexpressed
My feelings of good will and thankfulness—
He put into my hand a small square packet
Containing powder that would quite restore
(He told me) to dull gems and clouded pearls
Their pristine luster. I received, well pleased,
Proffering payment; but he shook his head,
Motioning back my hand; and stooping down,   340
Resumed his task, in a low deep-toned voice
Saying, "You're kindly welcome."

   . . . .

Say with a friend we contemplate some scene
Of natural loveliness, from which the heart
Drinks in its fill of deep admiring joy,
Some landscape scene, all glorious with the glow
Of summer evening, when the recent shower
(Transient and sudden) all the dry white road
Has moistened to red firmness, every leaf
(Washed from the dust) restored to glossy green—
In such an evening, oft the setting sun,
Flaming in gold and purple clouds, comes forth   900
To take his farewell of our hemisphere;
Sudden the face of nature brightens o'er
With such effulgence, as no painter's art
May imitate with faint similitude.
The raindrops dripping fast from every spray
Are liquid topazes; bright emeralds those
Set on the green foil of the glistening leaves,
And every little hollow, concave stone
And pebbly wheeltrack holds its sparkling pool
Brimming with molten amber. Of those drops   910
The blackbird lights to drink, then, scattering thick
A diamond shower among his dusty plumes,
Flies up rejoicing to some neighboring elm
And pours forth such a strain as wakens up
The music of unnumbered choristers.
Thus nature to her great creator hymns
An hallelujah of ecstatic praise.
And are *our* voices mute? Oh, no! we turn
(Perhaps with glistening eyes), and our full heart
Pour out, in rapturous accents, broken words   920
Such as require no answer but by speech
As little measured, or that best reply,
Feeling's true eloquence, a speaking look.
But other answer waits us; for the *friend*
(Oh! heaven! that there are such) with a calm smile
Of sweet *no-meaning* gently answers, "Yes,
Indeed it's very pretty— Don't you think
It's getting late though—time to go to tea?"

1836

FELICIA DOROTHEA HEMANS

née Browne (1793–1835)

Few poets were more popular in her day than Felicia Hemans, who was admired as an icon of female domesticity and representative of "the dignity of her sex." Educated at home under the guidance of a trilingual mother, Felicia Browne showed a gift for languages and had a photographic memory, which permitted her to recall a large body of poetry. Her first volume appeared in 1808, when she was fourteen. By 1818, when she published Translations from Camoëns and Other Poets, *she had mastered Portuguese and Spanish. Her ability to draw permitted her to illustrate her own work; musically accomplished, she preferred national airs. Much of her poetry has a nationalist message, celebrating not only the English motherland, but heroic moments in the histories of other nations, as in* England and Spain; or Valour and Patriotism *(1808),* Modern Greece *(1817), and* National Lyrics and Songs for Music *(1834). Her marriage in 1812 to Captain Alfred Hemans, who (like her brothers) had served in the Peninsular War, produced five sons. When he abandoned her, she was forced to support the family by writing, and published over fifty thousand lines in two dozen volumes. She continued to live with her mother, to whom she was devoted.*

Hemans focused on such "feminine" topics as emotions and domesticity in volumes from The Domestic Affections *(1812) to* Songs of the Affections *(1830). Her poems are replete with subtly ironic images of home, suicidal maternal love, and martyrdom to a meaningless system. Her* Records of Women *(1828) were dedicated to Joanna Baillie. Modern readers have noted the tensions and pessimism embedded within her cult of domesticity and patriotism; typical of her titles are "Grave of a Poetess," "Songs of Captivity," "The Ruined House," and "Song of Emigration." While she may have been unconscious of the ironies in her poetry, she skillfully cultivated a sweet and holy attitude appropriate to contemporary notions of femininity and modeled her writing to meet the demands of the annuals and their publishers.*

Much of Hemans' poetry was celebrated in her day; Wallace's Invocation to Bruce *(1819) won a literary prize, as did* Dartmoor *(1821). The* Forest Sanctuary *(1825), her favorite work, contained the best known of her poems, "Casabianca" ("The boy stood on the burning deck"). Her moralizing strand runs through* The Sceptic *(1820)*, Superstition and Error *(1822)*, Hymns on the Works of Nature *(1833)*, Hymns for Childhood *(1834)*, *and* Scenes and Hymns of Life *(1834)*. *Also a dramatist, Hemans saw her* Vespers of Palermo *staged in 1823.*

In their youth, poets such as Percy Shelley, Charlotte Brontë, and George Eliot avowedly enjoyed her. Byron, as her rival for popular favor, mocked "Mrs. Hewoman" and condemned "that false stilted trashy style which is a mixture of all the styles of the day." While Elizabeth Barrett Browning respected Hemans' piety, she found her always "a lady rather than a woman" or poet, and compared her refinement to "the prisoner's iron." Though he was a friend of Hemans, Sir Walter Scott summed up his view as "too many flowers and too little fruit." William Rossetti, who edited her work, regretted the "cloying flow" of her verse. Agnes Mary Robinson found in Hemans' poetry on high topics "the warmth of painted fire," settling into greater Wordsworthian simplicity after 1828.

Properzia Rossi

Properzia Rossi, a celebrated female sculptor of Bologna, possessed also of talents for poetry and music, died in consequence of an unrequited attachment. A painting by Ducis, represents her showing her last work, a basso-relievo of Ariadne, to a Roman Knight, the object of her affection, who regards it with indifference.

> Tell me no more, no more
> Of my soul's lofty gifts! Are they not vain
> To quench its haunting thirst for happiness?
> Have I not loved, and striven, and failed to bind
> One true heart unto me, whereon my own
> Might find a resting place, a home for all
> Its burden of affections? I depart,
> Unknown, though Fame goes with me; I must leave
> The earth unknown. Yet it may be that death
> Shall give my name a power to win such tears
> As would have made life precious.

I.

> One dream of passion and of beauty more!
> And in its bright fulfilment let me pour
> My soul away! Let earth retain a trace
> Of that which lit my being, though its race
> Might have been loftier far— Yet one more dream!
> From my deep spirit one victorious gleam
> Ere I depart! For thee alone, for thee!
> May this last work, this farewell triumph be,
> Thou, loved so vainly! I would leave enshrined
> Something immortal of my heart and mind,   10
> That yet may speak to thee when I am gone,

Shaking thine inmost bosom with a tone
Of lost affection—something that may prove
What she hath been, whose melancholy love
On thee was lavished; silent pang and tear,
And fervent song that gushed when none were near,
And dream by night, and weary thought by day,
Stealing the brightness from her life away,
While thou— Awake! not yet within me die
Under the burden and the agony   20
Of this vain tenderness—my spirit, wake!
Even for thy sorrowful affection's sake,
Live! in thy work breathe out!—that he may yet,
Feeling sad mastery there, perchance regret
Thine unrequited gift.

II.

It comes—the power
Within me born, flows back; my fruitless dower,
That could not win me love. Yet once again
I greet it proudly, with its rushing train
Of glorious images—they throng—they press—
A sudden joy lights up my loneliness—   30
I shall not perish all!

The bright work grows
Beneath my hand, unfolding, as a rose,
Leaf after leaf, to beauty; line by line,
I fix my thought, heart, soul, to burn, to shine,
Through the pale marble's veins. It grows—and now
I give my own life's history to thy brow,
Forsaken Ariadne! Thou shalt wear
My form, my lineaments; but oh! more fair,
Touched into lovelier being by the glow
Which in me dwells, as by the summer light   40
All things are glorified. From thee my woe
Shall yet look beautiful to meet his sight,
When I am passed away. Thou art the mold
Wherein I pour the fervent thoughts, the untold,
The self-consuming! Speak to him of me,
Thou, the deserted by the lonely sea;
With the soft sadness of thine earnest eye,
Speak to him, lorn one! deeply, mournfully,
Of all my love and grief! Oh! could I throw
Into thy frame a voice, a sweet, and low,   50
And thrilling voice of song! when he came nigh,
To send the passion of its melody

Through his pierced bosom—on its tones to bear
My life's deep feeling, as the southern air
Wafts the faint myrtle's breath—to rise, to swell,
To sink away in accents of farewell,
Winning but one, *one* gush of tears, whose flow
Surely my parted spirit yet might know,
If love be strong as death!

III.

Now fair thou art,

Thou form, whose life is of my burning heart!   60
Yet all the vision that within me wrought,
　　It cannot make thee! Oh! I might have given
Birth to creations of far nobler thought;
　　I might have kindled, with the fire of heaven,
Things not of such as die! But I have been
Too much alone; a heart whereon to lean,
With all these deep affections that o'erflow
My aching soul and find no shore below,
An eye to be my star, a voice to bring
Hope o'er my path, like sounds that breathe of spring,   70
These are denied me—dreamt of still in vain—
Therefore my brief aspirings from the chain
Are ever but as some wild fitful song,
Rising triumphantly, to die ere long
In dirgelike echoes.

IV.

Yet the world will see

Little of this, my parting work, in thee.
　　Thou shalt have fame! Oh, mockery! give the reed
From storms a shelter—give the drooping vine
Something round which its tendrils may entwine—
　　Give the parched flower a raindrop, and the meed   80
Of love's kind words to woman! Worthless fame!
That in *his* bosom wins not for my name
The abiding-place it asked! Yet how my heart,
In its own fairy world of song and art,
Once beat for praise!—Are those high longings o'er?
That which I have been can I be no more?—
Never, oh! nevermore; though still thy sky
Be blue as then, my glorious Italy!
And though the music, whose rich breathings fill
Thine air with soul, be wandering past me still,   90
And though the mantle of thy sunlight streams,

Unchanged on forms, instinct with poet dreams,
Never, oh! nevermore! where'er I move,
The shadow of this brokenhearted love
Is on me and around! Too well *they* know,
   Whose life is all within, too soon and well,
When there the blight hath settled—but I go
   Under the silent wings of peace to dwell;
From the slow wasting, from the lonely pain,
The inward burning of those words—*"in vain,"*   100
   Seared on the heart—I go. 'Twill soon be past.
Sunshine, and song, and bright Italian heaven,
   And thou, oh! thou, on whom my spirit cast
Unvalued wealth—who knowest not what was given
In that devotedness—the sad, and deep,
And unrepaid—farewell! If I could weep
Once, only once, beloved one! on thy breast,
Pouring my heart forth ere I sink to rest!
But that were happiness, and unto me
Earth's gift is *fame.* Yet I was formed to be   110
So richly blest! With thee to watch the sky,
Speaking not, feeling but that thou wert nigh;
With thee to listen, while the tones of song
Swept even as part of our sweet air along,
To listen silently; with thee to gaze
On forms, the deified of olden days,
This had been joy enough; and hour by hour,
From its glad wellsprings drinking life and power,
How had my spirit soared, and made its fame
   A glory for thy brow!—Dreams, dreams!—the fire   120
Burns faint within me. Yet I leave my name—
   As a deep thrill may linger on the lyre
When its full chords are hushed—awhile to live,
And one day haply in thy heart revive
Sad thoughts of me. I leave it, with a sound,
A spell o'er memory, mournfully profound,
I leave it, on my country's air to dwell—
Say proudly yet, " *'Twas hers who loved me well!"*

1828

Corinne at the Capitol

Les femmes doivent penser qu'il est dans cette carrière bien peu de sorte qui puissent valoir la plus obscure vie d'une femme aimée et d'une mère heureuse.

—Madame de Staël

Daughter of the Italian heaven!
Thou, to whom its fires are given,
Joyously thy car hath rolled
Where the conqueror's passed of old;
And the festal sun that shone
O'er three hundred triumphs gone[1]
Makes thy day of glory bright
With a shower of golden light.

Now thou treadest the ascending road   10
Freedom's foot so proudly trode;
While from tombs of heroes borne,
From the dust of empire shorn,
Flowers upon thy graceful head,
Chaplets of all hues, are shed
In a soft and rosy train,
Touched with many a gemlike stain.

Thou hast gained the summit now!
Music hails thee from below—
Music, whose rich notes might stir   20
Ashes of the sepulcher—
Shaking with victorious notes
All the bright air as it floats.
Well may woman's heart beat high
Unto that proud harmony!

Now afar it rolls—it dies—
And thy voice is heard to rise
With a low and lovely tone
In its thrilling power alone;
And thy lyre's deep silvery string,
Touched as by a breeze's wing,   30
Murmurs tremblingly at first,
Ere the tide of rapture burst.

All the spirit of thy sky
Now hath lit thy large dark eye,
And thy cheek a flush hath caught
From the joy of kindled thought;

1. "The trebly hundred triumphs."—Byron

And the burning words of song
From thy lip flow fast and strong,
With a rushing stream's delight
In the freedom of its might.   40

Radiant daughter of the sun!
Now thy living wreath is won.
Crowned of Rome!—Oh! art thou not
Happy in that glorious lot?—
Happier, happier far than thou
With the laurel on thy brow,
She that makes the humblest hearth
Lovely but to one on earth!

1830

JANET HAMILTON

(1795–1873)

The child of a Scottish laborer, Hamilton was set early to labor at a spinning wheel and embroidery frame but read the Bible daily. At age eight she found Paradise Lost *and Allan Ramsay's ballads "on the loom of an intellectual weaver" and carried the books off to the kitchen "to devour the contents." Her father subscribed to the village library, where she discovered Rollin's history of the ancients, Plutarch's* Lives, The Spectator, *and* The Rambler. *"Shakespeare was my teacher," she remembered. When she became the wife of a shoemaker and mother of ten children, she would read "holding the book in one hand and nursing an infant on my lap with the other."*

Reviewers of her first volume of poetry worried she might be a second "Chatterton," or fraud, but friends testified that she had learned to write in laborious print at the age of fifty, and by seventy was nearly blind. In a second edition of her Poems and Essays of a Miscellaneous Character on Subjects of General Interest *(1863), she thanked patrons for their "kind indulgence" and explained her "power of language" by her long course of reading, adding that "God has given me a good tack of natural grammar." Two other volumes followed:* Poems of Purpose and Sketches in Prose of Scottish Peasant Life and Character *(1865) and* Poems and Ballads *(1868). Her verse ranges in style from political satire in dialect to elevated tributes to political figures she admired and commentaries on contemporary events. Her prose sketches address Scottish life and the dangers of alcohol.*

Leddy Mary—a Ballad

O! mirk[1] was the nicht, an' the hour it was late,
Whan a bonnie young leddy gaed up the gate;
Sae slow was her stap—sae sair was the mane[2]
That fell frae her lips aye noo an' again.

1. dark
2. sore was the moan

She was row'd in a mantle baith rich an' wide,
But page nor maiden were there by her side.
She stude at a door, an' she tirl'd the sneck;[3]
An aul' wife cam' but, wi' a boo an' a beck;[4]
She thocht the rich mantle an' white-jewel'd haun
Belang'd to some leddy o' rank in the lan'.   10
"O! ha'e ye a room ye can pit me intill?
Can ye gi'e me a bed, an' gi'e me yer skill?
For here I maun bide till my bairnie is born—
For I maun be deid, or hame on the morn—
An' ye s'all ha'e gowd, an' bountith,[5] an' fee;
But whaur I ha'e come frae, or what I may be,
Ye never maun speer;[6] for nae livin' on yirth
Maun ken what I'm here for, my name, or my birth."
She gied her a room, an' she gied her a bed;
She gied her her skill; whan twa hours were sped,   20
The leddy was lichter—but she cou'dna bruck[7]
On the face o' her wee greetin' laddie to leuk:
"My heart it wad saften, an' that maunna be
Till I ha'e revenge on his faither," said she.
O! rich were the pearlin's an' costly the lace
That lay on the bosom and roun' the sweet face
That was droukit[8] wi' tears like a lily wi' dew,
An' her e'e it was stern, tho' her words were few.
She drew frae her bosom a lang purse o' gowd—
"Tak' that for propine,[9] fu' weel it's bestow'd;   30
Ye did what ye cou'd for helpin' o' me;
Twa hours an nae mair I'll tarry wi' thee."
An' true to the time, she gat up on her feet
An' said—"Noo, ye maunna leuk oot on the street;
My gate I maun gang, my weird I maun dree;[10]
In my faither's at hame this day I maun be."
An' sae she gaed oot as she cam' in the dark,
But to whaur she wad gang the wife had nae mark.
She tended the bairn, an' warm'd his wee feet,
Laid him intill the bed, an' sat doun to greet;   40
She fear'd the sweet leddy wad come by her deid,
An' naebody near her that kenn'd o' her need.

3. rapped on the latch
4. came out with a bow and a curtsy
5. gold and bounty
6. ask
7. bear
8. drenched
9. tip
10. my fate I must suffer

Neist day thro' the city word gaed like a bell
That a nobleman's dochter had deet by hersel';
On the flure o' her room she was lyin' cauld deid,
Her mantle rowt roun'[11] her, the hood on her heid.
Whan the wife heard the news it stoun'd her oot thro'—[12]
"My sweet Leddy Mary! my bonnie young doo![13]
It maun ha'e been thee that was wi' me yestreen;
In the pride o' thy beauty hoo aft I ha'e seen   50
Thee trippin' the street on thy gay gallant's arm!
My malison[14] on him that wrocht thee sic harm!"

1868

A Lay of the Tambour Frame

Bending with straining eyes
   Over the tambour frame,
Never a change in her weary routine—
   Slave in all but the name.
Tambour, ever tambour,
   Tambour the wreathing lines
Of 'broidered silk, till beauty's robe
   In rainbow luster shines.

There, with colorless cheek;
   There, with her tangling hair;   10
Still bending low o'er the rickety frame,
   Seek, ye will find her there.
Tambour, ever tambour,
   With fingers cramped and chill—
The panes are shattered, and cold the wind
   Blows over the eastern hill.

Why quail, my sisters, why,
   As ye were abjects vile,
When begging some haughty brother of earth
   "To give you leave to toil"?   20
It is tambour you must;
   Naught else you have to do,
Though paupers' dole be of higher amount
   Than pay oft earned by you.

11. rolled around
12. surprised her thoroughly
13. dove
14. malediction

No union strikes for you;
   Unshielded and alone,
In the battle of life—a battle it is
   Where virtue is oft o'erthrown.
O working men! O why
   Pass ye thus careless by,   30
Nor give to the working woman's complaint
   One word of kind reply?

Selfish, unfeeling men!
   Have ye not had your will?
High pay, short hours; yet your cry, like the leech,
   Is "Give us, give us" still.
She who tambours—tambours
   For fifteen hours a day—
Would have shoes on her feet, and dress for church
   Had she a third of your pay.   40

Sisters, cousins, and aunts
   Are they; yet, if not so,
Say, are they not sisters by human ties,
   And sympathy's kindly flow?
To them how dear the boon
   From brother's hand that came!
It would warm the heart and brighten the eyes
   While bending o'er the frame.

Raise ye a fund to aid
   In times of deep distress;   50
While man helps man, to their sisters in need
   Brothers can do no less.
Still the tambourer bends
   Wearily o'er the frame.
Patterns oft vary, for fashions will change—
   She is ever the same.

1868

LETITIA ELIZABETH LANDON

pseud., L.E.L. (1802–1838)

Landon supported her widowed mother by publishing novels, poems, and essays, after starting her career at thirteen; she claimed to write verse more rapidly than prose. She was called "the female Byron" because of her youthful fame and the social scandal provoked after gossip about her male friendships led to a broken engagement. Her precipitous marriage in 1838 to George Maclean, governor of a British outpost at Cape Coast, Ghana, was apparently not happy; after a few months in exile she died of a dose of prussic acid, sparking new rumors both of suicide and murder.

With Felicia Hemans, Landon was one of the first women to earn a sizable income from poetry alone. For the English version of Mme. de Staël's novel Corinne, she translated the improvised odes of the heroine. Among her many volumes were The Fate of Adelaide (1821), The Improvisatrice (1824), The Troubadour (1825), Poetical Works (1827), The Golden Violet, with Its Tales of Romance and Chivalry (1827), Miscellaneous Poetical Works (1835), and The Vow of the Peacock, and Other Poems (1835). Contemporaries praised the touching melancholy of her works and the melody of the later lyrics. Elizabeth Barrett Browning felt "she had the gift, though in certain respects she dishonored the art."

Landon successfully addressed the middle-class audience of literary magazines, gift books, and annuals; she edited Fisher's Drawing-Room Scrap Book (1832–39), Heath's Book of Beauty (1833), and New Juvenile Keepsake (1838). She also wrote several novels: Romance and Reality (1831), Francesca Carrara (1834), Ethel Churchill (1837), Duty and Inclination (1838), and Lady Anne Granard (1842). Her poetry helped market journals such as The Literary Gazette, and they in turn helped market her image, transposed into popular stereotypes of forlorn love and self-sacrifice. Though she was witty in society, as the preface to The Venetian Bracelet (1829) states, "I have ever endeavored to bring forward grief, disappointment, the fallen leaf, the faded flower, the broken heart, and the early grave."

Revenge

Aye, gaze upon her rose-wreathed hair,
    And gaze upon her smile;
Seem as you drank the very air
    Her breath perfumed the while:

And wake for her the gifted line,
    That wild and witching lay,
And swear your heart is as a shrine
    That only owns her sway.

'Tis well: I am revenged at last—
    Mark you that scornful cheek—   10
The eye averted as you passed
    Spoke more than words could speak.

Aye, now by all the bitter tears
    That I have shed for thee—
The racking doubts, the burning fears—
    Avenged they well may be

By the nights passed in sleepless care,
    The days of endless woe;
All that you taught my heart to bear,
    All that yourself will know.   20

I would not wish to see you laid
    Within an early tomb;
I should forget how you betrayed
    And only weep your doom:

But this is fitting punishment,
    To live and love in vain—
Oh my wrung heart, be thou content,
    And feed upon his pain.

Go thou and watch her lightest sigh—
    Thine own it will not be;   30
And bask beneath her sunny eye—
    It will not turn on thee.

'Tis well: the rack, the chain, the wheel,
    Far better hadst thou proved;
Even I could almost pity feel,
    For thou art not beloved.

1825

Lines of Life

Orphan in my first years, I early learned
To make my heart suffice itself, and seek
Support and sympathy in its own depths.

Well, read my cheek and watch my eye—
    Too strictly schooled are they
One secret of my soul to show,
    One hidden thought betray.

I never knew the time my heart
    Looked freely from my brow:
It once was checked by timidness;
    'Tis taught by caution now.

I live among the cold, the false,
    And I must seem like them;   10
And such I am, for I am false
    As those I most condemn.

I teach my lip its sweetest smile,
    My tongue its softest tone;
I borrow others' likeness, till
    Almost I lose my own.

I pass through flattery's gilded sieve,
    Whatever I would say;
In social life, all, like the blind,
    Must learn to feel their way.   20

I check my thoughts like curbed steeds
    That struggle with the rein;
I bid my feelings sleep like wrecks
    In the unfathomed main.

I hear them speak of love, the deep,
    The true, and mock the name;
Mock at all high and early truth,
    And I too do the same.

I hear them tell some touching tale,
    I swallow down the tear;   30
I hear them name some generous deed,
    And I have learned to sneer.

I hear the spiritual, the kind,
    The pure, but named in mirth,
Till all of good, aye, even hope,
    Seems exiled from our earth.

And one fear, withering ridicule,
    Is all that I can dread;
A sword hung by a single hair
    For ever o'er the head.   40

We bow to a most servile faith,
    In a most servile fear,
While none among us dares to say
    What none will choose to hear.

And if we dream of loftier thoughts,
    In weakness they are gone;
And indolence and vanity
    Rivet our fetters on.

Surely I was not born for this!
    I feel a loftier mood   50
Of generous impulse, high resolve,
    Steal o'er my solitude!

I gaze upon the thousand stars
    That fill the midnight sky
And wish, so passionately wish,
    A light like theirs on high.

I have such eagerness of hope
    To benefit my kind;
And feel as if immortal power
    Were given to my mind.   60

I think on that eternal fame,
    The sun of earthly gloom,
Which makes the gloriousness of death,
    The future of the tomb—

That earthly future, the faint sign
    Of a more heavenly one—
A step, a word, a voice, a look—
    Alas! my dream is done.

And earth, and earth's debasing stain,
    Again is on my soul;   70
And I am but a nameless part
    Of a most worthless whole.

Why write I this? because my heart
    Towards the future springs,
That future where it loves to soar
    On more than eagle wings.

The present, it is but a speck
 In that eternal time
In which my lost hopes find a home;
 My spirit knows its clime. 80

Oh! not myself—for what am I?—
 The worthless and the weak,
Whose every thought of self should raise
 A blush to burn my cheek.

But song has touched my lips with fire
 And made my heart a shrine;
For what, although alloyed, debased,
 Is in itself divine.

I am myself but a vile link
 Amid life's weary chain, 90
But I have spoken hallowed words,
 Oh do not say in vain!

My first, my last, my only wish,
 Say, will my charmed chords
Wake to the morning light of fame
 And breathe again my words?

Will the young maiden, when her tears
 Alone in moonlight shine—
Tears for the absent and the loved—
 Murmur some song of mine? 100

Will the pale youth by his dim lamp,
 Himself a dying flame,
From many an antique scroll beside
 Choose that which bears my name?

Let music make less terrible
 The silence of the dead;
I care not, so my spirit last
 Long after life has fled.

1825

Stanzas on the Death of Mrs. Hemans

> *The rose—the glorious rose is gone.*
> —FELICIA HEMANS, *Lays of Many Lands*

Bring flowers to crown the cup and lute,
 Bring flowers, the bride is near;

Bring flowers to soothe the captive's cell,
  Bring flowers to strew the bier!
Bring flowers!—thus said the lovely song;
  And shall they not be brought
To her who linked the offering
  With feeling and with thought?

Bring flowers, the perfumed and the pure,
  Those with the morning dew,   10
A sigh in every fragrant leaf,
  A tear on every hue.
So pure, so sweet thy life has been,
  So filling earth and air
With odors and with loveliness
  Till common scenes grew fair.

Thy song around our daily path
  Flung beauty born of dreams,
That shadows on the actual world
  The spirit's sunny gleams.   20
Mysterious influence, that to earth
  Brings down the heaven above,
And fills the universal heart
  With universal love.

Such gifts were thine—as from the block,
  The unformed and the cold,
The sculptor calls to breathing life
  Some shape of perfect mold;
So thou from common thoughts and things
  Didst call a charmed song,   30
Which on a sweet and swelling tide
  Bore the full soul along.

And thou from far and foreign lands
  Didst bring back many a tone,
And giving such new music still,
  A music of thine own.
A lofty strain of generous thoughts,
  And yet subdued and sweet—
An angel's song, who sings of earth,
  Whose cares are at his feet.   40

And yet thy song is sorrowful
  Its beauty is not bloom;
The hopes of which it breathes are hopes
  That look beyond the tomb.
Thy song is sorrowful as winds

That wander o'er the plain,
And ask for summer's vanished flowers,
And ask for them in vain.

Ah, dearly purchased is the gift,
The gift of song like thine;   50
A fated doom is hers who stands
The priestess of the shrine.
The crowd—they only see the crown,
They only hear the hymn—
They mark not that the cheek is pale
And that the eye is dim.

Wound to a pitch too exquisite,
The soul's fine chords are wrung;
With misery and melody
They are too highly strung.   60
The heart is made too sensitive
Life's daily pain to bear;
It beats in music, but it beats
Beneath a deep despair.

It never meets the love it paints,
The love for which it pines;
Too much of heaven is in the faith
That such a heart enshrines.
The meteor wreath the poet wears
Must make a lonely lot;   70
It dazzles only to divide
From those who wear it not.

Didst thou not tremble at thy fame
And loathe its bitter prize,
While what to others triumph seemed,
To thee was sacrifice?
Oh flower brought from paradise
To this cold world of ours,
Shadows of beauty such as thine
Recall thy native bowers.   80

Let others thank thee—'twas for them
Thy soft leaves thou didst wreathe;
The red rose wastes itself in sighs
Whose sweetness others breathe!
And they have thanked thee—many a lip
Has asked of thine for words,
When thoughts, life's finer thoughts, have touched
The spirit's inmost chords.

How many loved and honored thee
  Who only knew thy name,   90
Which o'er the weary working world
  Like starry music came!
With what still hours of calm delight
  Thy songs and image blend;
I cannot choose but think thou wert
  An old familiar friend.

The charm that dwelt in songs of thine
  My inmost spirit moved;
And yet I feel as thou hadst been
  Not half enough beloved.   100
They say that thou wert faint and worn
  With suffering and with care;
What music must have filled the soul
  That had so much to spare!

Oh weary one! since thou art laid
  Within thy mother's breast—
The green, the quiet mother earth—
  Thrice blessèd be thy rest!
Thy heart is left within our hearts
  Although life's pang is o'er;   110
But the quick tears are in my eyes,
  And I can write no more.

                        1835

Elizabeth Barrett Browning

(1806–1861)

The eldest of eleven children, Elizabeth Barrett studied classics with her brother's tutor and was the favorite of her father, who derived his wealth from plantations in Jamaica. He arranged for her Battle of Marathon (1820) to be printed when the "dear Sapho" of the family was only fourteen. She read Wollstonecraft's Vindication of the Rights of Women with enthusiasm and resolved to dress in men's clothes and seek her fortune. At fifteen, however, she became an invalid following a spinal injury, and over the next two decades apparently suffered from tuberculosis, which was medicated with morphine and ether. Secluded from the world, she was virtually imprisoned by her father, becoming, as she herself put it, a "blind poet." Unfamiliar with society and even with nature, she longed to exchange her book knowledge for "some experience of life and man." In that "prison," Byron and the French novelists George Sand and Honoré de Balzac provided a window to let in the colors of life.

Especially after her mother's death in 1828, Barrett was close to her father, who forbade his children to marry, perhaps fearing some taint of miscegenation might be revealed. In 1838, she suffered a lung hemorrhage and was sent from London to Torquay, in Cornwall. She then lost two brothers in close succession. The accidental drowning of her brother Edward in 1840, for which she felt indirectly responsible, caused her "hopeless grief." Despite her immurement in a darkened room, Barrett formed a number of close relationships, especially with the essayist Mary Russell Mitford and her cousin John Kenyon. He supported her decision to elope with the younger poet Robert Browning in 1846, when she was forty. Kenyon then handled their financial affairs, and at his death in 1856 made them secure by his bequest. With Robert she found a common "level" of intellect and feeling in a model companionate marriage; they immersed themselves in culture and politics under the Italian sun.

In her teens Barrett drafted an "Essay on Woman" in rhyming couplets that asserted, "She stands the equal of her Master, Man." Her early work also reflected her interest in classics and philosophy: She translated Prometheus Bound (1833), wrote a study of Greek Christian poets, and evoked idyllic motifs such as the figure of Pan. After her death, her husband proudly showed her annotated copies of the classics to

Michael Field, whose Sapphic volume Long Ago *shimmers with the images of Greek pastoral.*

Barrett's fame had been secured by the stylistic innovations of her Poems *(1844), which led Robert Browning to initiate their correspondence. Despite the apparent self-confidence of this volume, which met critical acclaim and went into an American edition introduced by Edgar Allan Poe, she looked at the past and asked: "Where were the poetesses? . . . I look everywhere for grandmothers and see none." G. K. Chesterton praised her wit and similes, but contemporaries criticized her colloquial meters and half rhymes. Dante Gabriel Rossetti was disturbed by what seemed to him "falsetto muscularity."*

After their marriage, the Brownings moved to Florence, where her friends included Harriet Beecher Stowe and Margaret Fuller; on visits to Paris she met George Sand, whose last volume she read with an eagerness that seemed to "burn" the page in front of her. Despite several miscarriages, she finally bore a son, Pen, in 1849.

Her famous "Sonnets from the Portuguese," love poems addressed to Robert, were published in Poems *(1850). She attacked the slavery on which her father's wealth had depended in "The Runaway Slave at Pilgrim's Point" and "A Curse for a Nation."* Casa Guidi Windows *(1851) and* Poems Before Congress *(1860) both reflect her growing interest in Italian politics. In her lifetime, Barrett Browning displaced Felicia Hemans, becoming the most popular woman poet of the nineteenth century.* Aurora Leigh *(1856), a nine-book narrative poem about the conflicts between profession and passion that face a woman poet, was praised by Ruskin as "the greatest poem which the century has produced in any language." To Ruskin she wrote, "My poetry, which you once called 'sickly,' " has the awkwardness that springs from "the desire speaking or spluttering the real truth out broadly." Virginia Woolf found* Aurora Leigh *to be "a masterpiece in embryo."* Last Poems *(1862) appeared after Barrett Browning's death.*

Felicia Hemans

TO L.E.L.,
REFERRING TO HER MONODY ON THE POETESS

I.

Thou bay-crowned living one that o'er the bay-crowned dead art bowing,
And o'er the shadeless moveless brow the vital shadow throwing,
And o'er the sighless songless lips the wail and music wedding,
And dropping o'er the tranquil eyes the tears not of their shedding!—

II.

Take music from the silent dead whose meaning is completer,
Reserve thy tears for living brows where all such tears are meeter,
And leave the violets in the grass to brighten where thou treadest,
No flowers for her! no need of flowers, albeit "bring flowers!" thou saidest.

III.

Yes, flowers, to crown the "cup and lute," since both may come to breaking,
Or flowers to greet the "bride"—the heart's own beating works its aching;   10
Or flowers to soothe the "captive's" sight, from earth's free bosom gathered,
Reminding of his earthly hope, then withering as it withered:

IV.

But bring not near the solemn corpse a type of human seeming;
Lay only dust's stern verity upon the dust undreaming;
And while the calm perpetual stars shall look upon it solely,
Her spherèd soul shall look on *them* with eyes more bright and holy.

V.

Nor mourn, O living one, because her part in life was mourning:
Would she have lost the poet's fire for anguish of the burning?
The minstrel harp, for the strained string? the tripod, for the afflated
Woe? or the vision, for those tears in which it shone dilated?   20

VI.

Perhaps she shuddered while the world's cold hand her brow was wreathing
But never wronged that mystic breath which breathed in all her breathing,
Which drew, from rocky earth and man, abstractions high and moving,
Beauty, if not the beautiful, and love, if not the loving.

VII.

Such visionings have paled in sight; the Savior she descrieth,
And little recks *who* wreathed the brow which on His bosom lieth:
The whiteness of His innocence, o'er all her garments, flowing,
There learneth she the sweet "new song" she will not mourn in knowing.

VIII.

Be happy, crowned and living one! and as thy dust decayeth,
May thine own England say for thee what now for her it sayeth—   30
"Albeit softly in our ears her silver song was ringing,
The footfall of her parting soul is softer than her singing."

1835

The Cry of the Children

"Φεῦ φεῦ, τί προσδέρκεσθέ μ' ὅμμασιν, τέκνα;" —*Medea*

I.

Do ye hear the children weeping, O my brothers,
  Ere the sorrow comes with years?
They are leaning their young heads against their mothers,
  And *that* cannot stop their tears.
The young lambs are bleating in the meadows,
  The young birds are chirping in the nest,
The young fawns are playing with the shadows,
  The young flowers are blowing toward the west—
But the young, young children, O my brothers,
   They are weeping bitterly!   10
They are weeping in the playtime of the others,
  In the country of the free.

II.

Do you question the young children in the sorrow
  Why their tears are falling so?
The old man may weep for his tomorrow
  Which is lost in long ago;
The old tree is leafless in the forest,
  The old year is ending in the frost,
The old wound, if stricken, is the sorest,
  The old hope is hardest to be lost;   20
But the young, young children, O my brothers,
  Do you ask them why they stand
Weeping sore before the bosoms of their mothers,
  In our happy Fatherland?

III.

They look up with their pale and sunken faces,
  And their looks are sad to see,
For the man's hoary anguish draws and presses
  Down the cheeks of infancy;
"Your old earth," they say, "is very dreary,
  Our young feet," they say, "are very weak;   30
Few paces have we taken, yet are weary—
  Our grave-rest is very far to seek:
Ask the agèd why they weep, and not the children,
  For the outside earth is cold,
And we young ones stand without, in our bewildering,
  And the graves are for the old.

IV.

"True," say the children, "it may happen
    That we die before our time:
Little Alice died last year, her grave is shapen
    Like a snowball, in the rime.   40
We looked into the pit prepared to take her:
    Was no room for any work in the close clay!
From the sleep wherein she lieth none will wake her,
    Crying, 'Get up, little Alice! it is day.'
If you listen by that grave, in sun and shower,
    With your ear down, little Alice never cries;
Could we see her face, be sure we should not know her,
    For the smile has time for growing in her eyes;
And merry go her moments, lulled and stilled in
    The shroud by the kirk chime.   50
It is good when it happens," say the children,
    "That we die before our time."

V.

Alas, alas, the children! they are seeking
    Death in life, as best to have;
They are binding up their hearts away from breaking
    With a cerement from the grave.
Go out, children, from the mine and from the city,
    Sing out, children, as the little thrushes do;
Pluck your handfuls of the meadow cowslips pretty,
    Laugh aloud, to feel your fingers let them through!   60
But they answer, "Are your cowslips of the meadows
    Like our weeds anear the mine?
Leave us quiet in the dark of the coal shadows,
    From your pleasures fair and fine!

VI.

"For oh," say the children, "we are weary,
    And we cannot run or leap;
If we cared for any meadows, it were merely
    To drop down in them and sleep.
Our knees tremble sorely in the stooping,
    We fall upon our faces, trying to go;   70
And underneath our heavy eyelids drooping,
    The reddest flower would look as pale as snow.
For all day we drag our burden tiring
    Through the coal-dark, underground,
Or all day we drive the wheels of iron
    In the factories round and round.

VII.

"For all day the wheels are droning, turning;
    Their wind comes in our faces
Till our hearts turn, our heads with pulses burning,
    And the walls turn in their places.   80
Turns the sky in the high window, blank and reeling,
   Turns the long light that drops adown the wall,
Turn the black flies that crawl along the ceiling:
   All are turning, all the day, and we with all.
And all day the iron wheels are droning,
    And sometimes we could pray,
'O ye wheels' (breaking out in a mad moaning),
    'Stop! be silent for today!' "

VIII.

Ay, be silent! Let them hear each other breathing
    For a moment, mouth to mouth!   90
Let them touch each other's hands, in a fresh wreathing
    Of their tender human youth!
Let them feel that this cold metallic motion
   Is not all the life God fashions or reveals;
Let them prove their living souls against the notion
   That they live in you, or under you, O wheels!
Still, all day, the iron wheels go onward,
    Grinding life down from its mark;
And the children's souls, which God is calling sunward,
    Spin on blindly in the dark.   100

IX.

Now tell the poor young children, O my brothers,
    To look up to Him and pray;
So the blessed One, who blesseth all the others,
    Will bless them another day.
They answer, "Who is God that He should hear us
   While the rushing of the iron wheels is stirred?
When we sob aloud, the human creatures near us
   Pass by, hearing not, or answer not a word.
And *we* hear not (for the wheels in their resounding)
    Strangers speaking at the door: 110
Is it likely God, with angels singing round Him,
    Hears our weeping any more?

X.

"Two words, indeed, of praying we remember,
        And at midnight's hour of harm
'Our Father,' looking upward in the chamber,
        We say softly for a charm.
We know no other words except 'Our Father,'
    And we think that in some pause of angels' song,
God may pluck them with the silence sweet to gather
    And hold both within His right hand which is strong.   120
'Our Father!'   If He heard us, He would surely
        (For they call Him good and mild)
Answer, smiling down the steep world very purely,
        'Come and rest with me, my child.'

XI.

"But, no!" say the children, weeping faster,
        "He is speechless as a stone;
And they tell us, of His image is the master
        Who commands us to work on.
Go to!" say the children, "—up in Heaven,
    Dark, wheel-like, turning clouds are all we find.   130
Do not mock us; grief has made us unbelieving:
    We look up for God, but tears have made us blind."
Do you hear the children weeping and disproving,
        O my brothers, what ye preach?
For God's possible is taught by His world's loving,
        And the children doubt of each.

XII.

And well may the children weep before you!
        They are weary ere they run;
They have never seen the sunshine, nor the glory
        Which is brighter than the sun.   140
They know the grief of man, without its wisdom;
    They sink in man's despair, without its calm;
Are slaves, without the liberty in Christdom,
    Are martyrs, by the pang without the palm;
Are worn as if with age, yet unretrievingly
        The harvest of its memories cannot reap—
Are orphans of the earthly love and heavenly.
        Let them weep! let them weep!

XIII.

They look up with their pale and sunken faces,
    And their look is dread to see,   150
For they mind you of their angels in high places,
    With eyes turned on Deity.
"How long," they say, "how long, O cruel nation,
   Will you stand, to move the world, on a child's heart—
Stifle down with a mailed heel its palpitation,
   And tread onward to your throne amid the mart?
Our blood splashes upward, O gold-heaper,
    And your purple shows your path!
But the child's sob in the silence curses deeper
    Than the strong man in his wrath."   160

                          1843

Grief

I tell you, hopeless grief is passionless;
That only men incredulous of despair,
Half-taught in anguish, through the midnight air
Beat upward to God's throne in loud access
Of shrieking and reproach. Full desertness,
In souls as countries, lieth silent-bare
Under the blanching, vertical eye-glare
Of the absolute Heavens. Deep-hearted man, express
Grief for thy dead in silence like to death—
Most like a monumental statue set   10
In everlasting watch and moveless woe
Till itself crumble to the dust beneath.
Touch it; the marble eyelids are not wet:
If it could weep, it could arise and go.

                          1844

To George Sand, A Desire

Thou large-brained woman and large-hearted man,
Self-called George Sand! whose soul, amid the lions
Of thy tumultuous senses, moans defiance
And answers roar for roar, as spirits can:
I would some mild miraculous thunder ran
Above the applauded circus, in appliance
Of thine own nobler nature's strength and science,
Drawing two pinions, white as wings of swan,
From thy strong shoulders, to amaze the place

With holier light! that thou to woman's claim   10
And man's, mightst join beside the angel's grace
Of a pure genius sanctified from blame,
Till child and maiden pressed to thine embrace
To kiss upon thy lips a stainless fame.

1844

To George Sand, A Recognition

True genius, but true woman! dost deny
The woman's nature with a manly scorn
And break away the gauds and armlets worn
By weaker women in captivity?
Ah, vain denial! that revolted cry
Is sobbed in by a woman's voice forlorn—
Thy woman's hair, my sister, all unshorn,
Floats back dishevelled strength in agony,
Disproving thy man's name; and while before
The world thou burnest in a poet-fire   10
We see thy woman-heart beat evermore
Through the large flame. Beat purer, heart, and higher,
Till God unsex thee on the heavenly shore
Where unincarnate spirits purely aspire!

1844

From *Sonnets from the Portuguese*
1

I thought once how Theocritus had sung
Of the sweet years, the dear and wished-for years,
Who each one in a gracious hand appears
To bear a gift for mortals, old or young:
And as I mused it in his antique tongue,
I saw, in gradual vision through my tears,
The sweet, sad years, the melancholy years,
Those of my own life, who by turns had flung
A shadow across me. Straightway I was 'ware,
So weeping, how a mystic Shape did move   10
Behind me, and drew me backward by the hair;
And a voice said in mastery, while I strove—
"Guess now who holds thee?"—"Death," I said. But there
The silver answer rang—"Not Death, but Love."

6

Go from me. Yet I feel that I shall stand
Henceforward in thy shadow. Nevermore
Alone upon the threshold of my door
Of individual life, I shall command
The uses of my soul, nor lift my hand
Serenely in the sunshine as before,
Without the sense of that which I forbore—
Thy touch upon the palm. The widest land
Doom takes to part us leaves thy heart in mine
With pulses that beat double. What I do   10
And what I dream include thee, as the wine
Must taste of its own grapes. And when I sue
God for myself, He hears that name of thine
And sees within my eyes the tears of two.

10

Yet, love, mere love, is beautiful indeed
And worthy of acceptation. Fire is bright,
Let temple burn, or flax; an equal light
Leaps in the flame from cedar-plank or weed:
And love is fire. And when I say at need
I love thee . . . mark! . . . *I love thee*—in thy sight
I stand transfigured, glorified aright,
With conscience of the new rays that proceed
Out of my face toward thine. There's nothing low
In love, when love the lowest: meanest creatures   10
Who love God, God accepts while loving so.
And what I *feel*, across the inferior features
Of what I *am*, doth flash itself and show
How that great work of Love enhances Nature's.

13

And wilt thou have me fashion into speech
The love I bear thee, finding words enough,
And hold the torch out, while the winds are rough,
Between our faces, to cast light on each?—
I drop it at thy feet. I cannot teach
My hand to hold my spirit so far off
From myself—me—that I should bring thee proof
In words of love hid in me out of reach.

Nay, let the silence of my womanhood
Commend my woman-love to thy belief—   10
Seeing that I stand unwon, however wooed,
And rend the garment of my life, in brief,
By a most dauntless, voiceless fortitude,
Lest one touch of this heart convey its grief.

22

When our two souls stand up erect and strong,
Face to face, silent, drawing nigh and nigher,
Until the lengthening wings break into fire
At either curvèd point—what bitter wrong
Can the earth do to us, that we should not long
Be here contented? Think. In mounting higher,
The angels would press on us and aspire
To drop some golden orb of perfect song
Into our deep, dear silence. Let us stay
Rather on earth, Belovèd—where the unfit   10
Contrarious moods of men recoil away
And isolate pure spirits, and permit
A place to stand and love in for a day,
With darkness and the death-hour rounding it.

43

How do I love thee? Let me count the ways.
I love thee to the depth and breadth and height
My soul can reach when feeling out of sight
For the ends of being and ideal grace.
I love thee to the level of everyday's
Most quiet need, by sun and candlelight.
I love thee freely, as men strive for right;
I love thee purely, as they turn from praise.
I love thee with the passion put to use
In my old griefs, and with my childhood's faith.   10
I love thee with a love I seemed to lose
With my lost saints—I love with the breath,
Smiles, tears of all my life!—and if God choose,
I shall but love thee better after death.

1850

The Runaway Slave at Pilgrim's Point

I.

I stand on the mark beside the shore
    Of the first white pilgrim's bended knee,
Where exile turned to ancestor,
    And God was thanked for liberty.
I have run through the night, my skin is as dark,
I bend my knee down on this mark:
    I look on the sky and the sea.

II.

O pilgrim-souls, I speak to you!
    I see you come proud and slow
From the land of the spirits pale as dew   10
    And round me and round me ye go.
O pilgrims, I have gasped and run
All night long from the whips of one
    Who in your names works sin and woe!

III.

And thus I thought that I would come
    And kneel here where ye knelt before,
And feel your souls around me hum
    In undertone to the ocean's roar;
And lift my black face, my black hand,
Here, in your names, to curse this land   20
    Ye blessed in freedom's, evermore.

IV.

I am black, I am black,
    And yet God made me, they say:
But if He did so, smiling back
    He must have cast His work away
Under the feet of His white creatures,
With a look of scorn, that the dusky features
    Might be trodden again to clay.

V.

And yet He has made dark things
    To be glad and merry as light: 30
There's a little dark bird sits and sings,
    There's a dark stream ripples out of sight,

And the dark frogs chant in the safe morass,
And the sweetest stars are made to pass
   O'er the face of the darkest night.

VI.

But *we* who are dark, we are dark!
   Ah God, we have no stars!
About our souls in care and cark
   Our blackness shuts like prison bars:
The poor souls crouch so far behind
That never a comfort can they find
   By reaching through the prison bars.

VII.

Indeed we live beneath the sky,
   That great smooth Hand of God stretched out
On all His children fatherly
   To save them from the dread and doubt
Which would be if, from this low place,
All opened straight up to His face
   Into the grand eternity.

VIII.

And still God's sunshine and His frost,
   They make us hot, they make us cold,
As if we were not black and lost;
   And the beasts and birds in wood and fold
Do fear and take us for very men:
Could the whippoorwill or the cat of the glen
   Look into my eyes and be bold?

IX.

I am black, I am black!
   But, once, I laughed in girlish glee,
For one of my color stood in the track
   Where the drivers drove and looked at me,
And tender and full was the look he gave—
Could a slave look *so* at another slave?—
   I look at the sky and the sea.

X.

And from that hour our spirits grew
   As free as if unsold, unbought:

Oh, strong enough, since we were two,
   To conquer the world, we thought.
The drivers drove us day by day;
We did not mind; we went one way
   And no better a freedom sought.   70

XI.

In the sunny ground between the canes,
   He said, "I love you," as he passed;
When the shingle roof rang sharp with the rains,
   I heard how he vowed it fast:
While others shook, he smiled in the hut
As he carved me a bowl of the coconut
   Through the roar of the hurricanes.

XII.

I sang his name instead of a song,
   Over and over I sang his name,
Upward and downward I drew it along   80
   My various notes—the same, the same!
I sang it low, that the slavegirls near
Might never guess, from aught they could hear,
   It was only a name—a name.

XIII.

I look on the sky and the sea.
   We were two to love and two to pray:
Yes, two, O God, who cried to Thee,
   Though nothing didst Thou say!
Coldly Thou satst behind the sun:
And now I cry who am but one,   90
   Thou wilt not speak today.

XIV.

We were black, we were black;
   We had no claim to love and bliss,
What marvel if each went to wrack?
   They wrung my cold hands out of his;
They dragged him—where? I crawled to touch
His blood's mark in the dust . . . not much,
   Ye pilgrim-souls, though plain as *this*!

XV.

Wrong, followed by a deeper wrong!
   Mere grief's too good for such as I,   100
So the white men brought the shame ere long
   To strangle the sob of my agony.
They would not leave me for my dull
Wet eyes!—it was too merciful
   To let me weep pure tears and die.

XVI.

I am black, I am black!
   I wore a child upon my breast,
An amulet that hung too slack
   And, in my unrest, could not rest:
Thus we went moaning, child and mother,   110
One to another, one to another,
   Until all ended for the best.

XVII.

For hark! I will tell you low, low,
   I am black, you see—
And the babe who lay on my bosom so
   Was far too white, too white for me;
As white as the ladies who scorned to pray
Beside me at church but yesterday,
   Though my tears had washed a place for my knee.

XVIII.

My own, own child! I could not bear   120
   To look in his face, it was so white;
I covered him up with a kerchief there,
   I covered his face in close and tight:
And he moaned and struggled, as well might be,
For the white child wanted his liberty—
   Ha, ha! he wanted the master-right.

XIX.

He moaned and beat with his head and feet,
   His little feet that never grew;
He struck them out, as it was meet,
   Against my heart to break it through;   130
I might have sung and made him mild,

But I dared not sing to the white-faced child
      The only song I knew.

XX.

I pulled the kerchief very close:
      He could not see the sun, I swear,
More, then, alive, than now he does
      From between the roots of the mango . . . where?
I know where. Close! A child and mother
Do wrong to look at one another
      When one is black and one is fair.   140

XXI.

Why, in that single glance I had
      Of my child's face, . . . I tell you all,
I saw a look that made me mad!
      The *master's* look, that used to fall
On my soul like his lash . . . or worse!
And so, to save it from my curse,
      I twisted it round in my shawl.

XXII.

And he moaned and trembled from foot to head,
      He shivered from head to foot;
Till after a time, he lay instead   150
      Too suddenly still and mute.
I felt, beside, a stiffening cold:
I dared to lift up just a fold,
      As in lifting a leaf of the mango fruit.

XXIII.

But *my* fruit . . . ha, ha!—there had been
      (I laugh to think on it at this hour!)
Your fine white angels (who have seen
      Nearest the secret of God's power)
And plucked my fruit to make them wine
And sucked the soul of that child of mine   160
      As the hummingbird sucks the soul of the flower.

XXIV.

Ha, ha, the trick of the angels white!
      They freed the white child's spirit so.
I said not a word, but day and night,

I carried the body to and fro,
And it lay on my heart like a stone—as chill
—The sun may shine out as much as he will:
I am cold, though it happened a month ago.

XXV.

From the white man's house, and the black man's hut,
I carried the little body on;   170
The forest's arms did round us shut,
And silence through the trees did run:
They asked no question as I went;
They stood too high for astonishment;
They could see God sit on His throne.

XXVI.

My little body, kerchiefed fast,
I bore it on through the forest, on;
And when I felt it was tired at last,
I scooped a hole beneath the moon:
Through the forest tops the angels far,   180
With a white sharp finger from every star,
Did point and mock at what was done.

XXVII.

Yet when it was all done aright—
Earth, 'twixt me and my baby, strewed—
All, changed to black earth—nothing white—
A dark child in the dark!—ensued
Some comfort, and my heart grew young;
I sat down smiling there and sung
The song I learned in my maidenhood.

XXVIII.

And thus we two were reconciled,   190
The white child and black mother, thus;
For as I sang it, soft and wild,
The same song, more melodious,
Rose from the grave whereon I sat:
It was the dead child singing that,
To join the souls of both of us.

XXIX.

I look on the sea and the sky.
  Where the pilgrims' ships first anchored lay
The free sun rideth gloriously,
  But the pilgrim ghosts have slid away   200
Through the earliest streaks of the morn:
My face is black, but it glares with a scorn
  Which they dare not meet by day.

XXX.

Ha!—in their stead, their hunter sons!
  Ha, ha! they are on me—they hunt in a ring!
Keep off! I brave you all at once;
  I throw off your eyes like snakes that sting!
You have killed the black eagle at nest, I think:
Did you ever stand still in your triumph and shrink
  From the stroke of her wounded wing?   210

XXXI.

(Man, drop that stone you dared to lift!—)
  I wish you who stand there five abreast,
Each, for his own wife's joy and gift,
  A little corpse as safely at rest
As mine in the mangoes! Yes, but *she*
May keep live babies on her knee
  And sing the song she likes the best.

XXXII.

I am not mad: I am black.
  I see you staring in my face—
I know you staring, shrinking back,
  Ye are born of the Washington race,   220
And this land is the free America,
And this mark on my wrist—(I prove what I say)
  Ropes tied me up here to the flogging-place.

XXXIII.

You think I shrieked then? Not a sound!
  I hung, as a gourd hangs in the sun;
I only cursed them all around
  As softly as I might have done
My very own child: from these sands
Up to the mountains, lift your hands,   230
  O slaves, and end what I begun!

XXXIV.

Whips, curses; these must answer those!
   For in this Union you have set
Two kinds of men in adverse rows,
   Each loathing each; and all forget
The seven wounds in Christ's body fair,
While He sees gaping everywhere
   Our countless wounds that pay no debt.

XXXV.

Our wounds are different. Your white men
   Are, after all, not gods indeed,   240
Nor able to make Christs again
   Do good with bleeding. *We* who bleed
(Stand off!) we help not in our loss!
We are too heavy for our cross,
   And fall and crush you and your seed.

XXXVI.

I fall, I swoon! I look at the sky.
   The clouds are breaking on my brain;
I am floated along, as if I should die
   Of liberty's exquisite pain.
In the name of the white child waiting for me   250
In the death-dark where we may kiss and agree,
White men, I leave you all curse-free
   In my broken heart's disdain!

1848

Aurora Leigh

(excerpts)

Book I

[Aurora Leigh begins her autobiography with the early deaths of her Italian mother and English father, which left her feeling "a mother-want about the world." At thirteen, she goes to live with her English aunt, who imposes Victorian concepts of femininity and moral education on her niece. Aurora will recover slowly from her grief under the healing influence of nature, the kindness of her cousin, Romney Leigh, and the stimulus of her father's books, which she finds in the attic.]

I think I see my father's sister stand   270
Upon the hall step of her country house

To give me welcome. She stood straight and calm,
Her somewhat narrow forehead braided tight
As if for taming accidental thoughts
From possible pulses; brown hair pricked with gray
By frigid use of life (she was not old,
Although my father's elder by a year);
A nose drawn sharply, yet in delicate lines;
A close mild mouth, a little soured about
The ends, through speaking unrequited loves   280
Or peradventure niggardly half-truths;
Eyes of no color—once they might have smiled,
But never, never have forgot themselves
In smiling; cheeks, in which was yet a rose
Of perished summers, like a rose in a book,
Kept more for ruth than pleasure—if past bloom,
Past fading also.

.   .   .   .

                She had lived
A sort of cage-bird life, born in a cage,
Accounting that to leap from perch to perch
Was act and joy enough for any bird.
Dear heaven, how silly are the things that live
In thickets, and eat berries!
                I, alas,
A wild bird scarcely fledged, was brought to her cage,   310
And she was there to meet me. Very kind.
Bring the clean water, give out the fresh seed.

She stood upon the steps to welcome me,
Calm, in black garb. I clung about her neck—
Young babes, who catch at every shred of wool
To draw the new light closer, catch and cling
Less blindly. In my ears my father's word
Hummed ignorantly, as the sea in shells,
"Love, love, my child." She, black there with my grief,
Might feel my love—she was his sister once—   320
I clung to her. A moment she seemed moved,
Kissed me with cold lips, suffered me to cling,
And drew me feebly through the hall into
The room she sat in.
                There, with some strange spasm
Of pain and passion, she wrung loose my hands
Imperiously, and held me at arm's length,
And with two grey-steel naked-bladed eyes
Searched through my face—aye, stabbed it through and through,

Through brows and cheeks and chin, as if to find
A wicked murderer in my innocent face,   330
If not here, there perhaps. Then, drawing breath,
She struggled for her ordinary calm—
And missed it rather—told me not to shrink,
As if she had told me not to lie or swear—
She "loved my father and would love me too
As long as I deserved it." Very kind.

I understood her meaning afterward:
She thought to find my mother in my face
And questioned it for that. For she, my aunt,
Had loved my father truly, as she could,   340
And hated, with the gall of gentle souls,
My Tuscan mother who had fooled away
A wise man from wise courses, a good man
From obvious duties, and depriving her,
His sister, of the household precedence,
Had wronged his tenants, robbed his native land,
And made him mad, alike by life and death,
In love and sorrow. She had pored for years
What sort of woman could be suitable
To her sort of hate, to entertain it with,   350
And so, her very curiosity
Became hate, too, and all the idealism
She ever used in life was used for hate,
Till hate, so nourished, did exceed at last
The love from which it grew, in strength and heat,
And wrinkled her smooth conscience with a sense
Of disputable virtue (say not, sin)
When Christian doctrine was enforced at church.

And thus my father's sister was to me
My mother's hater. From that day she did   360
Her duty to me (I appreciate it
In her own word as spoken to herself),
Her duty, in large measure, well pressed out
But measured always. She was generous, bland,
More courteous than was tender, gave me still
The first place—as if fearful that God's saints
Would look down suddenly and say, "Herein
You missed a point, I think, through lack of love."
Alas, a mother never is afraid
Of speaking angerly to any child,   370
Since love, she knows, is justified of love.

And I, I was a good child on the whole,
A meek and manageable child. Why not?
I did not live to have the faults of life:
There seemed more true life in my father's grave
Than in all England. Since *that* threw me off
Who fain would cleave (his latest will, they say,
Consigned me to his land), I only thought
Of lying quiet there where I was thrown
Like seaweed on the rocks, and suffering her   380
To prick me to a pattern with her pin,
Fiber from fiber, delicate leaf from leaf,
And dry out from my drowned anatomy
The last sea salt left in me.
                         So it was.
I broke the copious curls upon my head
In braids because she liked smooth-ordered hair.
I left off saying my sweet Tuscan words,
Which still at any stirring of the heart
Came up to float across the English phrase
As lilies (*Bene* or *Che che*) because   390
She liked my father's child to speak his tongue.
I learned the collects and the catechism,
The creeds, from Athanasius back to Nice,
The Articles, the Tracts *against* the times
(By no means Buonaventure's "Prick of Love"),
And various popular synopses of
Inhuman doctrines never taught by John,
Because she liked instructed piety.
I learned my complement of classic French
(Kept pure of Balzac and neologism)   400
And German also, since she liked a range
Of liberal education—tongues, not books.
I learned a little algebra, a little
Of the mathematics—brushed with extreme flounce
The circle of the sciences because
She misliked women who are frivolous.
I learned the royal genealogies
Of Oviedo, the internal laws
Of the Burmese empire, by how many feet
Mount Chimborazo outsoars Teneriffe,   410
What navigable river joins itself
To Lara, and what census of the year five
Was taken at Klagenfurt—because she liked
A general insight into useful facts.
I learned much music—such as would have been
As quite impossible in Johnson's day,

As still it might be wished—fine sleights of hand
And unimagined fingering, shuffling off
The hearer's soul through hurricanes of notes
To a noisy Tophet; and I drew . . . costumes   420
From French engravings, nereids neatly draped
(With smirks of simmering godship); I washed in
Landscapes from nature (rather say, washed out).
I danced the polka and Cellarius,
Spun glass, stuffed birds, and modeled flowers in wax
Because she liked accomplishments in girls.
I read a score of books on womanhood
To prove, if women do not think at all,
They may teach thinking (to a maiden aunt
Or else the author)—books that boldly assert   430
Their right of comprehending husband's talk
When not too deep, and even of answering
With pretty "may it please you" or "so it is"
Their rapid insight and fine aptitude,
Particular worth and general missionariness,
As long as they keep quiet by the fire
And never say "no" when the world says "aye,"
For that is fatal—their angelic reach
Of virtue, chiefly used to sit and darn,
And fatten household sinners—their, in brief,   440
Potential faculty in everything
Of abdicating power in it: she owned
She liked a woman to be womanly,
And Englishwomen, she thanked God and sighed
(Some people always sigh in thanking God),
Were models to the universe. And last,
I learned cross-stitch because she did not like
To see me wear the night with empty hands
A-doing nothing. So, my shepherdess
Was something after all (the pastoral saints   450
Be praised for it), leaning lovelorn with pink eyes
To match her shoes, when I mistook the silks;
Her head uncrushed by that round weight of hat
So strangely similar to the tortoiseshell
Which slew the tragic poet.
      By the way,
The works of women are symbolical.
We sew, sew, prick our fingers, dull our sight,
Producing what? A pair of slippers, sir,
To put on when you're weary—or a stool
To stumble over and vex you . . . "Curse that stool!"   460
Or else, at best, a cushion, where you lean

And sleep and dream of something we are not
But would be for your sake. Alas, alas!
This hurts most, this—that, after all, we are paid
The worth of our work, perhaps.
                                        In looking down
Those years of education (to return),
I wonder if Brinvilliers suffered more
In the water torture . . . flood succeeding flood
To drench the incapable throat and split the veins . . .
Than I did. Certain of your feebler souls   470
Go out in such a process; many pine
To a sick, inodorous light; my own endured:
I had relations in the Unseen and drew
The elemental nutriment and heat
From nature, as earth feels the sun at nights
Or as a babe sucks surely in the dark.
I kept the life thrust on me on the outside
Of the inner life with all its ample room
For heart and lungs, for will and intellect,
Inviolable by conventions. God,   480
I thank thee for that grace of thine!

Book II

[Slipping out of doors at dawn on her twentieth birthday, Aurora twines ivy in
her hair to celebrate her growing vocation as a poet. Her cousin Romney, inheri-
tor of the family wealth, finds her and proposes marriage in the expectation that
she will join him in his efforts to reform society and save the poor. Her refusal,
followed by the death of her aunt, leaves her to struggle alone for her living as a
writer.]

                                        I stood there fixed—   60
My arms up, like the caryatid, sole
Of some abolished temple, helplessly
Persistent in a gesture which derides
A former purpose. Yet my blush was flame,
As if from flax, not stone.
                              "Aurora Leigh,
The earliest of Auroras!"
                              Hand stretched out
I clasped, as shipwrecked men will clasp a hand,
Indifferent to the sort of palm. The tide
Had caught me at my pastime, writing down
My foolish name too near upon the sea,   70
Which drowned me with a blush as foolish. "You,
My cousin!"

The smile died out in his eyes
And dropped upon his lips, a cold dead weight,
For just a moment, "Here's a book I found!
No name writ on it—poems, by the form;
Some Greek upon the margin—lady's Greek,
Without the accents. Read it? Not a word.
I saw at once the thing had witchcraft in it,
Whereof the reading calls up dangerous spirits:
I rather bring it to the witch."

                    "My book.   80
You found it . . ."

                      "In the hollow by the stream
That beech leans down into—of which you said
The Oread in it has a Naiad's heart
And pines for waters."

                  "Thank you."

                      "Thanks to *you*
My cousin! that I have seen you not too much
Witch, scholar, poet, dreamer, and the rest,
To be a woman also."

                With a glance
The smile rose in his eyes again and touched
The ivy on my forehead, light as air.
I answered gravely, "Poets needs must be   90
Or men or women—more's the pity."

                      "Ah,
But men, and still less women, happily,
Scarce need be poets. Keep to the green wreath,
Since even dreaming of the stone and bronze
Brings headaches, pretty cousin, and defiles
The clean white morning dresses."

                      "So you judge!
Because I love the beautiful I must
Love pleasure chiefly and be overcharged
For ease and whiteness! Well, you know the world
And only miss your cousin, 'tis not much.   100
But learn this. I would rather take my part
With God's dead, who afford to walk in white
Yet spread His glory, than keep quiet here
And gather up my feet from even a step
For fear to soil my gown in so much dust.
I choose to walk at all risks— Here, if heads
That hold a rhythmic thought much ache perforce,
For my part I choose headaches,—and today's
My birthday."

     "Dear Aurora, choose instead
To cure them. You have balsams."

            "I perceive.   110
The headache is too noble for my sex.
You think the heartache would sound decenter,
Since that's the woman's special, proper ache
And altogether tolerable, except
To a woman."

  . . . .

          "There it is!—
You play beside a deathbed like a child,   180
Yet measure to yourself a prophet's place
To teach the living. None of all these things
Can women understand. You generalize—
Oh, nothing—not even grief! Your quick-breathed hearts,
So sympathetic to the personal pang,
Close on each separate knife stroke, yielding up
A whole life at each wound, incapable
Of deepening, widening a large lap of life
To hold the world-full woe. The human race
To you means such a child or such a man   190
You saw one morning waiting in the cold,
Beside that gate, perhaps. You gather up
A few such cases and, when strong, sometimes
Will write of factories and of slaves as if
Your father were a negro and your son
A spinner in the mills. All's yours and you,
All colored with your blood, or otherwise,
Just nothing to you. Why, I call you hard
To general suffering. Here's the world half-blind
With intellectual light, half-brutalized   200
With civilization, having caught the plague
In silks from Tarsus, shrieking east and west
Along a thousand railroads, mad with pain
And sin too! . . . does one woman of you all
(You who weep easily) grow pale to see
This tiger shake his cage?—does one of you
Stand still from dancing, stop from stringing pearls,
And pine and die because of the great sum
Of universal anguish? Show me a tear
Wet as Cordelia's in eyes bright as yours   210
Because the world is mad. You cannot count
That you should weep for this account, not you!
You weep for what you know. A red-haired child
Sick in a fever, if you touch him once,

Though but so little as with a fingertip,
Will set you weeping; but a million sick . . .
You could as soon weep for the rule of three
Or compound fractions. Therefore, this same world,
Uncomprehended by you, must remain
Uninfluenced by you. Women as you are,   220
Mere women, personal and passionate,
You give us doting mothers and perfect wives,
Sublime Madonnas and enduring saints!
We get no Christ from you—and verily
We shall not get a poet, in my mind."

"With which conclusion you conclude!—"
                                    "But this—
That you, Aurora, with the large live brow
And steady eyelids, cannot condescend
To play at art as children play at swords,
To show a pretty spirit chiefly admired   230
Because true action is impossible.
You never can be satisfied with praise,
Which men give women when they judge a book
Not as mere work but as mere woman's work,
Expressing the comparative respect
Which means the absolute scorn. 'Oh, excellent,
What grace, what facile turns, what fluent sweeps,
What delicate discernment . . . almost thought!
The book does honor to the sex, we hold.
Among our female authors we make room   240
For this fair writer and congratulate
The country that produces in these times
Such women, competent to' . . . spell."
                                "Stop there,"
I answered, burning through his thread of talk
With a quick flame of emotion, "You have read
My soul, if not my book, and argue well
I would not condescend . . . we will not say
To such a kind of praise (a worthless end
Is praise of all kinds), but to such a use
Of holy art and golden life. I am young,   250
And peradventure weak—you tell me so—
Through being a woman. And, for all the rest,
Take thanks for justice. I would rather dance
At fairs on tightrope till the babies dropped
Their gingerbread for joy, than shift the types
For tolerable verse, intolerable
To men who act and suffer. Better far

    Pursue a frivolous trade by serious means
    Than a sublime art frivolously."
           "You,
    Choose nobler work than either, O moist eyes   260
    And hurrying lips and heaving heart! We are young,
    Aurora, you and I. The world—look round—
    The world we're come to late is swollen hard
    With perished generations and their sins:
    The civilizer's spade grinds horribly
    On dead men's bones and cannot turn up soil
    That's otherwise than fetid. All success
    Proves partial failure; all advance implies
    What's left behind; all triumph, something crushed
    At the chariot wheels; all government, some wrong.   270
    And rich men make the poor, who curse the rich,
    Who agonize together, rich and poor,
    Under and over, in the social spasm
    And crisis of the ages. Here's an age
    That makes its own vocation! here we have stepped
    Across the bounds of time! here's nought to see
    But just the rich man and just Lazarus,
    And both in torments, with a mediate gulf,
    Though not a hint of Abraham's bosom. Who
    Being man, Aurora, can stand calmly by   280
    And view these things and never tease his soul
    For some great cure? No physic for this grief,
    In all the earth and heavens, too?"
            "You believe
    In God, for your part?—aye? that He who makes
    Can make good things from ill things, best from worst,
    As men plant tulips upon dunghills when
    They wish them finest?"
         "True. A death-heat is
    The same as life-heat, to be accurate,
    And in all nature is no death at all,
    As men account of death, so long as God   290
    Stands witnessing for life perpetually
    By being just God. That's abstract truth, I know,
    Philosophy, or sympathy with God:
    But I, I sympathize with man, not God
    (I think I was a man for chiefly this),
    And when I stand beside a dying bed
    'Tis death to me. Observe—it had not much
    Consoled the race of mastodons to know,
    Before they went to fossil, that anon
    Their place would quicken with the elephant.   300

They were not elephants but mastodons;
And I, a man, as men are now and not
As men may be hereafter, feel with men
In the agonizing present."
                              "Is it so,"
I said, "my cousin? is the world so bad,
While I hear nothing of it through the trees?
The world was always evil—but so bad?"

"So bad, Aurora. Dear, my soul is gray
With poring over the long sum of ill;
So much for vice, so much for discontent,   310
So much for the necessities of power,
So much for the connivances of fear,
Coherent in statistical despairs
With such a total of distracted life. . . .
To see it down in figures on a page,
Plain, silent, clear, as God sees through the earth
The sense of all the graves—that's terrible
For one who is not God and cannot right
The wrong he looks on. May I choose, indeed,
But vow away my years, my means, my aims,   320
Among the helpers if there's any help
In such a social strait? The common blood
That swings along my veins is strong enough
To draw me to this duty."
                              Then I spoke.
"I have not stood long on the strand of life,
And these salt waters have had scarcely time
To creep so high up as to wet my feet:
I cannot judge these tides—I shall, perhaps.
A woman's always younger than a man
At equal years because she is disallowed   330
Maturing by the outdoor sun and air
And kept in long-clothes past the age to walk.
Ah well, I know you men judge otherwise!
You think a woman ripens, as a peach,
In the cheeks chiefly. Pass it to me now;
I'm young in age, and younger still, I think,
As a woman. But a child may say amen
To a bishop's prayer and feel the way it goes,
And I, incapable to loose the knot
Of social questions, can approve, applaud   340
August compassion, Christian thoughts that shoot
Beyond the vulgar white of personal aims.
Accept my reverence."

               There he glowed on me
With all his face and eyes. "No other help?—"
Said he, "no more than so?"
               "What help?" I asked.
"You'd scorn my help—as Nature's self, you say,
Has scorned to put her music in my mouth
Because a woman's. Do you now turn round
And ask for what a woman cannot give?"

"For what she only can, I turn and ask,"   350
He answered, catching up my hands in his,
And dropping on me from his high-eaved brow
The full weight of his soul. "I ask for love,
And that, she can; for life in fellowship
Through bitter duties—that, I know she can;
For wifehood—will she?"
               "Now," I said, "may God
Be witness 'twixt us two!"—and with the word,
Meseemed I floated into a sudden light
Above his stature—"Am I proved too weak
To stand alone yet strong enough to bear   360
Such leaners on my shoulder? poor to think,
Yet rich enough to sympathize with thought?
Incompetent to sing as blackbirds can
Yet competent to love like *Him*?"
               I paused;
Perhaps I darkened, as the lighthouse will
That turns upon the sea. "It's always so.
Anything does for a wife."
               "Aurora, dear,
And dearly honored"—he pressed in at once
With eager utterance—"you translate me ill.
I do not contradict my thought of you,   370
Which is most reverent, with another thought
Found less so. If your sex is weak for art
(And I, who said so, did but honor you
By using truth in courtship), it is strong
For life and duty. Place your fecund heart
In mine, and let us blossom for the world
That wants love's color in the gray of time.
My talk, meanwhile, is arid to you, aye,
Since all my talk can only set you where
You look down coldly on the arena-heaps   380
Of headless bodies, shapeless, indistinct!
The Judgment Angel scarce would find his way
Through such a heap of generalized distress

To the individual man with lips and eyes,
Much less Aurora. Ah, my sweet, come down,
And hand in hand we'll go where yours shall touch
These victims, one by one! till, one by one,
The formless, nameless trunk of every man
Shall seem to wear a head with hair you know
And every woman catch your mother's face   390
To melt you into passion."
                         "I am a girl,"
I answered slowly. "You do well to name
My mother's face. Though far too early, alas,
God's hand did interpose 'twixt it and me,
I know so much of love as used to shine
In that face and another. Just so much;
No more indeed at all. I have not seen
So much love since, I pray you pardon me,
As answers even to make a marriage with
In this cold land of England. What you love   400
Is not a woman, Romney, but a cause:
You want a helpmate, not a mistress, sir,
A wife to help your ends—in her no end.
Your cause is noble, your ends excellent,
But I, being most unworthy of these and that,
Do otherwise conceive of love. Farewell."

"Farewell, Aurora? you reject me thus?"
He said.
        "Sir, you were married long ago.
You have a wife already whom you love;
Your social theory. Bless you both, I say.   410
For my part, I am scarcely meek enough
To be the handmaid of a lawful spouse.
Do I look a Hagar, think you?"
                              "So you jest."
"Nay, so I speak in earnest," I replied.
"You treat of marriage too much like, at least,
A chief apostle: you would bear with you
A wife . . . a sister . . . shall we speak it out?
A sister of charity."
                     "Then, must it be
Indeed farewell? And was I so far wrong
In hope and in illusion when I took   420
The woman to be nobler than the man,
Yourself the noblest woman, in the use
And comprehension of what love is—love,
That generates the likeness of itself

Through all heroic duties? so far wrong,
In saying bluntly, venturing truth on love,
'Come, human creature, love and work with me'
Instead of 'Lady, thou art wondrous fair,
And where the Graces walk before, the Muse
Will follow at the lightning of their eyes,   430
And where the Muse walks, lovers need to creep:
Turn round and love me, or I die of love.' "

With quiet indignation I broke in.
"You misconceive the question like a man
Who sees a woman as the complement
Of his sex merely. You forget too much
That every creature, female as the male,
Stands single in responsible act and thought
As also in birth and death. Whoever says
To a loyal woman 'Love and work with me'   440
Will get fair answers if the work and love,
Being good themselves, are good for her—the best
She was born for. Women of a softer mood,
Surprised by men when scarcely awake to life,
Will sometimes only hear the first word, *love*,
And catch up with it any kind of work,
Indifferent, so that dear love go with it.
I do not blame such women, though, for love
They pick much oakum; earth's fanatics make   450
Too frequently heaven's saints. But *me* your work
Is not the best for—nor your love the best,
Nor able to commend the kind of work
For love's sake merely. Ah, you force me, sir,
To be overbold in speaking of myself:
I too have my vocation—work to do,
The heavens and earth have set me since I changed
My father's face for theirs and, though your world
Were twice as wretched as you represent,
Most serious work, most necessary work
As any of the economists'. Reform,   460
Make trade a Christian possibility
And individual right no general wrong;
Wipe out earth's furrows of the Thine and Mine,
And leave one green for men to play at bowls,
With innings for them all! . . . What then, indeed,
If mortals are not greater by the head
Than any of their prosperities? what then,
Unless the artist keep up open roads
Betwixt the seen and unseen—bursting through

The best of your conventions with his best,   470
The speakable, imaginable best
God bids him speak, to prove what lies beyond
Both speech and imagination? A starved man
Exceeds a fat beast: we'll not barter, sir,
The beautiful for barley. And even so,
I hold you will not compass your poor ends
Of barley-feeding and material ease
Without a poet's individualism
To work your universal. It takes a soul
To move a body; it takes a high-souled man   480
To move the masses, even to a cleaner sty;
It takes the ideal, to blow a hair's-breadth off
The dust of the actual. Ah, your Fouriers failed
Because not poets enough to understand
That life develops from within. For me,
Perhaps I am not worthy, as you say,
Of work like this; perhaps a woman's soul
Aspires and not creates. Yet we aspire,
And yet I'll try out your perhapses, sir,
And if I fail . . . why, burn me up my straw   490
Like other false works—I'll not ask for grace;
Your scorn is better, cousin Romney. I
Who love my art would never wish it lower
To suit my stature. I may love my art.
You'll grant that even a woman may love art,
Seeing that to waste true love on anything
Is womanly, past question."
                                    I retain
The very last word which I said that day,
As you the creaking of the door, years past,
Which let upon you such disabling news   500
You ever after have been graver. He,
His eyes, the motions in his silent mouth
Were fiery points on which my words were caught,
Transfixed forever in my memory
For his sake, not their own. And yet I know
I did not love him . . . nor he me . . . that's sure . . .
And what I said is unrepented of,
As truth is always. Yet . . . a princely man!—
If hard to me, heroic for himself!
He bears down on me through the slanting years,   510
The stronger for the distance. If he had loved,
Aye, loved me, with that retributive face, . . .
I might have been a common woman now
And happier, less known and less left alone,

Perhaps a better woman after all,
With chubby children hanging on my neck
To keep me low and wise. Ah me, the vines
That bear such fruit are proud to stoop with it.
The palm stands upright in a realm of sand.
And I, who spoke the truth then, stand upright,   520
Still worthy of having spoken out the truth
By being content I spoke it though it set
Him there, me here. O woman's vile remorse,
To hanker after a mere name, a show,
A supposition, a potential love!
Does every man who names love in our lives
Become a power for that? is love's true thing
So much best to us that what personates love
Is next best? A potential love, forsooth!
I'm not so vile. No, no—he cleaves, I think,   530
This man, this image—chiefly for the wrong
And shock he gave my life in finding me
Precisely where the devil of my youth
Had set me, on those mountain peaks of hope
All glittering with the dawn-dew, all erect
And famished for the noon—exclaiming, while
I looked for empire and much tribute, "Come,
I have some worthy work for thee below.
Come, sweep my barns and keep my hospitals,
And I will pay thee with a current coin   540
Which men give women."

Book V

[Dividing her work in London between poetry and hackwork, Aurora experiences success as a writer. At twenty-nine, she meditates critically upon the limits of her accomplishment and the importance of recording "true life" in the forms that spring from the spirit. She has invested passion in her most recent book yet still is not satisfied.]

Aurora Leigh, be humble. Shall I hope
To speak my poems in mysterious tune
With man and nature?—with the lava-lymph
That trickles from successive galaxies
Still drop by drop adown the finger of God
In still new worlds?—with summer days in this
That scarce dare breathe they are so beautiful?
With spring's delicious trouble in the ground,
Tormented by the quickened blood of roots
And softly pricked by golden crocus sheaves   10

In token of the harvesttime of flowers?
With winters and with autumns—and beyond,
With the human heart's large seasons, when it hopes
And fears, joys, grieves, and loves?—with all that strain
Of sexual passion, which devours the flesh
In a sacrament of souls? with mother's breasts
Which, round the newmade creatures hanging there,
Throb luminous and harmonious like pure spheres?—
With multitudinous life, and finally,
With the great escapings of ecstatic souls, 20
Who, in a rush of too long prisoned flame,
Their radiant faces upward, burn away
This dark of the body, issuing on a world
Beyond our mortal?

. . . .

The critics say that epics have died out
With Agamemnon and the goat-nursed gods; 140
I'll not believe it. I could never deem,
As Payne Knight did (the mythic mountaineer
Who travelled higher than he was born to live,
And showed sometimes the goiter in his throat
Discoursing of an image seen through fog),
That Homer's heroes measured twelve feet high.
They were but men: his Helen's hair turned gray
Like any plain Miss Smith's who wears a front;
And Hector's infant whimpered at a plume
As yours last Friday at a turkey-cock. 150
All actual heroes are essential men,
And all men possible heroes: every age,
Heroic in proportions, double-faced,
Looks backward and before, expects a morn
And claims an epos.
                    Aye, but every age
Appears to souls who live in it (ask Carlyle)
Most unheroic. Ours, for instance, ours:
The thinkers scout it, and the poets abound
Who scorn to touch it with a fingertip:
A pewter age—mixed metal, silver-washed; 160
An age of scum, spooned off the richer past,
An age of patches for old gaberdines,
An age of mere transition, meaning nought
Except that what succeeds must shame it quite,
If God please. That's wrong thinking, to my mind,
And wrong thoughts make poor poems.

Every age,
Through being beheld too close, is ill-discerned
By those who have not lived past it. We'll suppose
Mount Athos carved, as Alexander schemed,
To some colossal statue of a man.   170
The peasants, gathering brushwood in his ear,
Had guessed as little as the browsing goats
Of form or feature of humanity
Up there—in fact, had traveled five miles off
Or ere the giant image broke on them,
Full human profile, nose and chin distinct,
Mouth, muttering rhythms of silence up the sky
And fed at evening with the blood of suns;
Grand torso—hand that flung perpetually
The largesse of a silver river down   180
To all the country pastures. 'Tis even thus
With times we live in—evermore too great
To be apprehended near.
                              But poets should
Exert a double vision; should have eyes
To see near things as comprehensively
As if afar they took their point of sight,
And distant things as intimately deep
As if they touched them. Let us strive for this.
I do distrust the poet who discerns
No character or glory in his times,   190
And trundles back his soul five hundred years,
Past moat and drawbridge, into a castle court,
To sing—oh, not of lizard or of toad
Alive in the ditch there ('twere excusable)—
But of some black chief, half knight, half sheep-lifter,
Some beauteous dame, half chattel and half queen,
As dead as must be, for the greater part,
The poems made on their chivalric bones;
And that's no wonder: death inherits death.

Nay, if there's room for poets in this world   200
A little overgrown (I think there is),
Their sole work is to represent the age—
Their age, not Charlemagne's—this live, throbbing age,
That brawls, cheats, maddens, calculates, aspires,
And spends more passion, more heroic heat
Betwixt the mirrors of its drawing rooms
Than Roland with his knights at Roncesvalles.
To flinch from modern varnish, coat or flounce,
Cry out for togas and the picturesque,

Is fatal—foolish, too. King Arthur's self   210
Was commonplace to Lady Guenever;
And Camelot to minstrels seemed as flat
As Fleet Street to our poets.
                              Never flinch,
But still, unscrupulously epic, catch
Upon the burning lava of a song
The full-veined, heaving, double-breasted Age:
That, when the next shall come, the men of that
May touch the impress with reverent hand and say,
"Behold—behold the paps we all have sucked!
This bosom seems to beat still, or at least   220
It sets ours beating: this is living art,
Which thus presents and thus records true life."

Book VI

[Two years before, Romney in his social work had met and planned to marry a working-class girl, Marian Erle, whose pure and selfless love for him won Aurora's praise. The wedding was secretly thwarted by Lady Waldemar, a selfish aristocrat who wished to marry him herself. Marian disappeared. On hearing a rumor of Lady Waldemar's impending marriage to Romney, Aurora flees to Paris. There she catches sight of Marian, pursues her, and is shocked to discover she has had a child out of wedlock. Marian explains that Lady Waldemar's henchwoman had transported her to a brothel in Paris, where she was drugged, raped, and made pregnant. Her story convinces Aurora, who invites Marian and her son to come live with her in Italy.]

                                    'Twas a room
Scarce larger than a grave, and near as bare;
Two stools, a pallet-bed; I saw the room:
A mouse could find no sort of shelter in't,
Much less a greater secret; curtainless—
The window fixed you with its torturing eye,
Defying you to take a step apart,
If peradventure you would hide a thing.
I saw the whole room, I and Marian there
Alone.
        Alone? She threw her bonnet off,   560
Then, sighing as 'twere sighing the last time,
Approached the bed and drew a shawl away:
You could not peel a fruit you fear to bruise
More calmly and more carefully than so—
Nor would you find within, a rosier flushed
Pomegranate—

                    There he lay upon his back,
The yearling creature, warm and moist with life
To the bottom of his dimples, to the ends
Of the lovely tumbled curls about his face;
For since he had been covered overmuch   570
To keep him from the light-glare, both his cheeks
Were hot and scarlet as the first live rose
The shepherd's heart blood ebbed away into,
The faster for his love. And love was here
As instant; in the pretty baby mouth,
Shut closed as if for dreaming that it sucked,
The little naked feet, drawn up the way
Of nestled birdlings; everything so soft
And tender, to the tiny holdfast hands,
Which, closing on a finger into sleep,   580
Had kept the mold of 't.
                             While we stood there dumb—
For oh, that it should take such innocence
To prove just guilt, I thought, and stood there dumb—
The light upon his eyelids pricked them wide
And, staring out at us with all their blue,
As half perplexed between the angelhood
He had been away to visit in his sleep
And our most mortal presence, gradually
He saw his mother's face, accepting it
In change for heaven itself with such a smile   590
As might have well been learned there—never moved,
But smiled on in a drowse of ecstasy,
So happy (half with her and half with heaven)
He could not have the trouble to be stirred,
But smiled and lay there. Like a rose, I said?
As red and still indeed as any rose
That blows in all the silence of its leaves,
Content in blowing to fulfil its life.

She leaned above him (drinking him as wine)
In that extremity of love 'twill pass   600
For agony or rapture, seeing that love
Includes the whole of nature, rounding it
To love—no more, since more can never be
Than just love. Self-forgot, cast out of self,
And drowning in the transport of the sight,
Her whole pale passionate face, mouth, forehead, eyes
One gaze, she stood; then, slowly as he smiled
She smiled, too, slowly, smiling unaware,
And drawing from his countenance to hers

A fainter red, as if she watched a flame 610
And stood in it aglow. "How beautiful,"
Said she.
        I answered, trying to be cold.
(Must sin have compensations, was my thought,
As if it were a holy thing like grief?
And is a woman to be fooled aside
From putting vice down with that woman's toy,
A baby?)—"Aye! the child is well enough,"
I answered. "If his mother's palms are clean
They need be glad of course in clasping such;
But if not, I would rather lay my hand, 620
Were I she, on God's brazen altar-bars,
Red-hot with burning sacrificial lambs,
Than touch the sacred curls of such a child."

She plunged her fingers in his clustering locks
As one who would not be afraid of fire;
And then with indrawn steady utterance said,
"My lamb, my lamb! although, through such as thou,
The most unclean got courage and approach
To God, once, now they cannot, even with men,
Find grace enough for pity and gentle words." 630

"My Marian," I made answer, grave and sad,
"The priest who stole a lamb to offer him
Was still a thief. And if a woman steals
(Through God's own barrier-hedges of true love,
Which fence out license in securing love)
A child like this, that smiles so in her face,
She is no mother, but a kidnapper,
And he's a dismal orphan, not a son,
Whom all her kisses cannot feed so full
He will not miss hereafter a pure home 640
To live in, a pure heart to lean against,
A pure good mother's name and memory
To hope by, when the world grows thick and bad
And he feels out for virtue."
                "Oh," she smiled
With bitter patience, "the child takes his chance;
Not much worse off in being fatherless
Than I was, fathered. He will say, belike,
His mother was the saddest creature born;
He'll say his mother lived so contrary
To joy that even the kindest, seeing her, 650
Grew sometimes almost cruel: he'll not say
She flew contrarious in the face of God

With bat wings of her vices. Stole my child—
My flower of earth, my only flower on earth,
My sweet, my beauty!" . . . Up she snatched the child
And, breaking on him in a storm of tears,
Drew out her long sobs from their shivering roots,
Until he took it for a game and stretched
His feet and flapped his eager arms like wings   660
And crowed and gurgled through his infant laugh:
"Mine, mine," she said. "I have as sure a right
As any glad proud mother in the world,
Who sets her darling down to cut his teeth
Upon her church-ring. If she talks of law,
I talk of law! I claim my mother-dues
By law—the law which now is paramount—
The common law, by which the poor and weak
Are trodden underfoot by vicious men
And loathed forever after by the good.
Let pass! I did not filch—I found the child."   670
"You found him, Marian?"
                           "Ay, I found him where
I found my curse—in the gutter, with my shame!
What have you, any of you, to say to that,
Who all are happy and sit safe and high
And never spoke before to arraign my right
To grief itself? What, what, . . . being beaten down
By hoofs of maddened oxen into a ditch,
Half-dead, whole mangled, when a girl at last
Breathes, sees . . . and finds there, bedded in her flesh
Because of the extremity of the shock,   680
Some coin of price! . . . and when a good man comes
(That's God! the best men are not quite as good)
And says, 'I dropped the coin there: take it you
And keep it—it shall pay you for the loss'—
You all put up your finger—'See the thief!
Observe what precious thing she has come to filch.
How bad those girls are!' Oh, my flower, my pet,
I dare forget I have you in my arms
And fly off to be angry with the world,
And fright you, hurt you with my tempers, till   690
You double up your lip? Why, that indeed
Is bad: a naughty mother!"
                        "You mistake,"
I interrupted; "if I loved you not,
I should not, Marian, certainly be here."

"Alas," she said, "you are so very good;
And yet I wish indeed you had never come

To make me sob until I vex the child.
It is not wholesome for these pleasure-plats
To be so early watered by our brine.
And then, who knows? he may not like me now   700
As well, perhaps, as ere he saw me fret—
One's ugly fretting! he has eyes the same
As angels, but he cannot see as deep,
And so I've kept forever in his sight
A sort of smile to please him—as you place
A green thing from the garden in a cup,
To make believe it grows there. Look, my sweet,
My cowslip-ball! we've done with that cross face,
And here's the face come back you used to like.   710
Ah, ah! he laughs! he likes me. Ah, Miss Leigh,
You're great and pure; but were you purer still—
As if you had walked, we'll say, no otherwhere
Than up and down the New Jerusalem,
And held your trailing lustring up yourself
From brushing the twelve stones, for fear of some
Small speck as little as a needle-prick,
White stitched on white—the child would keep to *me*;
Would choose his poor lost Marian, like me best;
And though you stretched your arms, cry back and cling,
As we do when God says it's time to die   720
And bids us go up higher. Leave us, then;
We two are happy. Does *he* push me off?
He's satisfied with me, as I with him."

"So soft to one, so hard to others! Nay,"
I cried, more angry that she melted me,
"We make henceforth a cushion of our faults
To sit and practice easy virtues on?
I thought a child was given to sanctify
A woman—set her in the sight of all
The clear-eyed heavens, a chosen minister   730
To do their business and lead spirits up
The difficult blue heights. A woman lives,
Not bettered, quickened toward the truth and good
Through being a mother? . . . then she's none! although
She damps her baby's cheeks by kissing them,
As we kill roses."
                    "Kill! O Christ," she said
And turned her wild sad face from side to side
With most despairing wonder in it, "What,
What have you in your souls against me then,
All of you? am I wicked, do you think?   740

God knows me, trusts me with the child; but you,
You think me really wicked?"
                              "Complaisant,"
I answered softly, "to a wrong you've done,
Because of certain profits—which is wrong
Beyond the first wrong, Marian. When you left
The pure place and the noble heart, to take
The hand of a seducer—"
                              "Whom? whose hand?
I took the hand of—"
                              Springing up erect,
And lifting up the child at full-arm's length,
As if to bear him like an oriflamme   750
Unconquerable to armies of reproach—
"By *him*," she said, "my child's head and its curls,
By these blue eyes no woman born could dare
A perjury on, I make my mother's oath,
That if I left that heart, to lighten it,
The blood of mine was still except for grief!
No cleaner maid than I was took a step
To a sadder end, no matron mother now
Looks backward to her early maidenhood
Through chaster pulses. I speak steadily;   760
And if I lie so, . . . if, being fouled in will
And paltered with in soul by devil's lust,
I dared to bid this angel take my part, . . .
Would God sit quiet, let us think, in heaven,
Nor strike me dumb with thunder? Yet I speak:
He clears me therefore. What, *seduced*'s your word!
Do wolves seduce a wandering fawn in France?
Do eagles who have pinched a lamb with claws
Seduce it into carrion? So with me.
I was not ever, as you say, seduced,   770
But simply murdered."
                              There she paused and sighed
With such a sigh as drops from agony
To exhaustion—sighing while she let the babe
Slide down upon her bosom from her arms,
And all her face's light fell after him,
Like a torch quenched in falling. Down she sank,
And sat upon the bedside with the child.

Book IX

[In Italy word reaches Aurora that Romney has been nursed by Lady Waldemar while ill, and she assumes they have married. Unannounced, he arrives at her villa. In a series of misunderstandings caused by her assumption, he attempts to explain gently to her that his home has been burned by the poor and he has renounced his idealist projects of reform. He has come to marry Marian even though he loves Aurora. Marian accepts the honor but rejects the hand, which she suggests belongs to Aurora. Finally, after Romney has revealed that the trauma has blinded him, he and Aurora acknowledge their former mistakes. In this passage she describes their first moment of union.]

But oh, the night! oh, bittersweet! oh, sweet!
O dark, O moon and stars, O ecstasy
Of darkness! O great mystery of love,
In which absorbed, loss, anguish, treason's self
Enlarges rapture—as a pebble dropped
In some full winecup overbrims the wine!
While we two sat together, leaned that night   820
So close my very garments crept and thrilled
With strange electric life, and both my cheeks
Grew red, then pale, with touches from my hair
In which his breath was—while the golden moon
Was hung before our faces as the badge
Of some sublime inherited despair,
Since ever to be seen by only one—
A voice said, low and rapid as a sigh,
Yet breaking, I felt conscious, from a smile,   830
"Thank God, who made me blind, to make me see!
Shine on, Aurora, dearest light of souls,
Which rulest forevermore both day and night!
I am happy."
           I flung closer to his breast,
As sword that after battle flings to sheath;
And in that hurtle of united souls,
The mystic motions which in common moods
Are shut beyond our sense broke in on us,
And as we sat, we felt the old earth spin
And all the starry turbulence of worlds
Swing round us in their audient circles, till,   840
If that same golden moon were overhead
Or if beneath our feet, we did not know.

A Curse for a Nation

Prologue

I heard an angel speak last night,
  And he said, "Write!
Write a Nation's curse for me,
And send it over the Western Sea."

I faltered, taking up the word:
  "Not so, my lord!
If curses must be, choose another
To send thy curse against my brother.

"For I am bound by gratitude,
  By love and blood,   10
To brothers of mine across the sea,
Who stretch out kindly hands to me."

"Therefore," the voice said, "shalt thou write
  My curse tonight.
From the summits of love a curse is driven,
As lightning is from the tops of heaven."

"Not so," I answered. "Evermore
  My heart is sore
For my own land's sins: for little feet
Of children bleeding along the street;   20

"For parked-up honors that gainsay
  The right of way;
For almsgiving through a door that is
Not open enough for two friends to kiss;

"For love of freedom which abates
  Beyond the Straits;
For patriot virtue starved to vice on
Self-praise, self-interest, and suspicion;

"For an oligarchic parliament,
  And bribes well-meant.   30
What curse to another land assign
When heavy-souled for the sins of mine?"

"Therefore," the voice said, "shalt thou write
  My curse tonight.
Because thou hast strength to see and hate
A foul thing done *within* thy gate."

"Not so," I answered once again.
  "To curse, choose men.

For I, a woman, have only known   39
How the heart melts and the tears run down."

"Therefore," the voice said, "shalt thou write
    My curse tonight.
Some women weep and curse, I say
(And no one marvels), night and day.

"And thou shalt take their part tonight,
    Weep and write.
A curse from the depths of womanhood
Is very salt, and bitter, and good."

So thus I wrote, and mourned indeed,
    What all may read.   50
And thus, as was enjoined on me,
I send it over the Western Sea.

The Curse

I.

Because ye have broken your own chain
    With the strain
Of brave men climbing a Nation's height,
Yet thence bear down with brand and thong
On souls of others—for this wrong,
    This is the curse: Write.

Because yourselves are standing straight
    In the state   60
Of Freedom's foremost acolyte,
Yet keep calm footing all the time
On writhing bondslaves—for this crime,
    This is the curse: Write.

Because ye prosper in God's name,
    With a claim
To honor in the old world's sight,
Yet do the fiend's work perfectly
In strangling martyrs—for this lie,
    This is the curse: Write.   70

II.

Ye shall watch while kings conspire
Round the people's smoldering fire,
  And, warm for your part,

Shall never dare—O shame!
To utter the thought into flame
    Which burns at your heart.
        This is the curse: Write.

Ye shall watch while nations strive
With the bloodhounds, die or survive,
    Drop faint from their jaws   80
Or throttle them backward to death;
And only under your breath
    Shall favor the cause.
        This is the curse: Write.

Ye shall watch while strong men draw
The nets of feudal law
    To strangle the weak;
And counting the sin for a sin,
Your soul shall be sadder within
    Than the word ye shall speak.   90
        This is the curse: Write.

When good men are praying erect
That Christ may avenge His elect
    And deliver the earth,
The prayer in your ears, said low,
Shall sound like the tramp of a foe
    That's driving you forth.
        This is the curse: Write.

When wise men give you their praise,
They shall praise, in the heat of the phrase,   100
    As if carried too far.
When ye boast your own charters kept true,
Ye shall blush; for the thing which ye do
    Derides what ye are.
        This is the curse: Write.

When fools cast taunts at your gate,
Your scorn ye shall somewhat abate
    As ye look o'er the wall;
For your conscience, tradition, and name
Explode with a deadlier blame   110
    Than the worst of them all.
        This is the curse: Write.

Go, wherever ill deeds shall be done,
Go, plant your flag in the sun
    Beside the ill-doers!
And recoil from clenching the curse

Of God's witnessing Universe
  With a curse of yours.
    This is the curse: Write.

1860

A Musical Instrument

I.

What was he doing, the great god Pan,
  Down in the reeds by the river?
Spreading ruin and scattering ban,
Splashing and paddling with hoofs of a goat,
And breaking the golden lilies afloat
  With the dragonfly on the river.

II.

He tore out a reed, the great god Pan,
  From the deep cool bed of the river:
The limpid water turbidly ran,
And the broken lilies a-dying lay,   10
And the dragonfly had fled away
  Ere he brought it out of the river.

III.

High on the shore sat the great god Pan,
  While turbidly flowed the river,
And hacked and hewed as a great god can,
With his hard bleak steel at the patient reed,
Till there was not a sign of the leaf indeed
  To prove it fresh from the river.

IV.

He cut it short, did the great god Pan
  (How tall it stood in the river!),   20
Then drew the pith, like the heart of a man,
Steadily from the outside ring,
And notched the poor dry empty thing
  In holes, as he sat by the river.

V.

"This is the way," laughed the great god Pan
  (Laughed while he sat by the river),

"The only way, since gods began
To make sweet music, they could succeed."
Then, dropping his mouth to a hole in the reed,
   He blew in power by the river.   30

VI.

Sweet, sweet, sweet, O Pan!
   Piercing sweet by the river!
Blinding sweet, O great god Pan!
The sun on the hill forgot to die,
And the lilies revived, and the dragonfly
   Came back to dream on the river.

VII.

Yet half a beast is the great god Pan,
   To laugh as he sits by the river,
Making a poet out of a man:
The true gods sigh for the cost and pain—   40
For the reed which grows nevermore again
   As a reed with the reeds in the river.

1862

FRANCES ANNE ("FANNY") KEMBLE

(1809–1893)

❧

Kemble was born into a family of actors: her father was Charles Kemble, her aunt,
Mrs. Siddons. She was educated in France. When bankruptcy threatened her father's the-
ater, she became an acclaimed actress, playing Juliet at Covent Garden when she was
twenty. Her early publications include two plays, Francis the First *(1832) and* The
Star of Seville *(1837). An American tour with her father in 1833 introduced her to*
Pierce Butler, a Southern slaveholder; their unhappy marriage ended in divorce in 1848,
but she continued to live primarily in the United States for twenty years and returned
definitively to England only in 1877. Her collection of Poems *(1844), was dedicated to*
her American friend Katharine Sedgwick. A second volume of Poems *appeared in 1866,*
revised in 1883; George Bethune praised her "bold" versification, of which her fifteen-line
sonnet is a conspicuous example. Although she won her fame as an actress and public
reader of Shakespeare, her voice also won respect in the abolitionist movement. Her Jour-
nal of a Residence in America (1835) and its sequel, Journal of a Residence on a
Georgian Plantation in 1838–9 *(1863), criticized slavery; Henry James called it*
"one of the most animated autobiographies in the language." Her frank memoirs of her
life in the theatrical world, Records of a Girlhood *(1878),* Records of Later Life
(1882), and Further Records, 1848–83 *(1890) scandalized readers.*

Sonnet

There's not a fiber in my trembling frame
That does not vibrate when thy step draws near,
There's not a pulse that throbs not when I hear
Thy voice, thy breathing, nay, thy very name.
When thou art with me, every sense seems dull,
And all I am, or know, or feel, is thee;
My soul grows faint, my veins run liquid flame,
And my bewildered spirit seems to swim

In eddying whirls of passion, dizzily.
When thou art gone, there creeps into my heart   10
A cold and bitter consciousness of pain:
The light, the warmth of life, with thee depart,
And I sit dreaming o'er and o'er again
Thy greeting clasp, thy parting look, and tone;
And suddenly I wake—and am alone.

1844

Fragment

*From an Epistle Written When the Thermometer
Stood at 98° in the Shade*

Oh! for the temperate airs that blow
    Upon that darling of the sea,
Where neither sunshine, rain, nor snow
    For three days hold supremacy,
But ever-varying skies contend
The blessings of all climes to lend,
To make that tiny, wave-rocked isle,
In never-fading beauty smile.
England, oh England! for the breeze
That slowly stirs thy forest trees!   10
Thy ferny brooks, thy mossy fountains,
Thy beechen woods, thy heathery mountains,
Thy lawny uplands, where the shadow
    Of many a giant oak is sleeping;
The tangled copse, the sunny meadow,
    Through which the summer rills run weeping.
Oh, land of flowers! while sinking here
    Beneath the Dog Star of the West,
The music of the waves I hear
    That cradle thee upon their breast.   20
Fresh o'er thy rippling cornfields fly
    The wild winged breezes of the sea,
While from thy smiling summer sky
    The ripening sun looks tenderly.
And thou—to whom through all this heat
    My parboiled thoughts still fondly turn,
Oh! in what "shady blest retreat"
    Art thou ensconced, while here I burn?
Across the lawn, in the deep glade,
Where hand in hand we oft have strayed,   30
Or communed sweetly, side by side,

Hear'st thou the chiming ocean tide,
As gently on the pebbly beach
   It lays its head, then ebbs away,
Or round the rocks, with nearer reach,
   Throws up a cloud of silvery spray?
Or to the firry woods, that shed
   Their spicy odors to the sun,
Goest thou with meditative tread,
   Thinking of all things that are done   40
Beneath the sky?—a great big thought,
   Of which I know you're very fond.
For me, my mind is solely wrought
   To this one wish: O! in a pond
Would I were over head and ears!
   (Of a *cold* ducking I've no fears)
Or anywhere where I am not;
   For, bless the heat! it is too hot!

1844

The Black Wallflower

I found a flower in a desolate plot,
Where no man wrought—by a deserted cot,
Where no man dwelt; a strange, dark-colored gem,
Black heavy buds on a pale leafless stem;
I plucked it, wondering, and with it hied
To my brave May; and showing it, I cried:
"Look, what a dismal flower! did ever bloom
Born of our earth and air wear such a gloom?
It looks as it should grow out of a tomb:
Is it not mournful?" "No," replied the child;   10
And gazing on it thoughtfully, she smiled.
She knows each word of that great book of God,
Spread out between the blue sky and the sod:
"There are no mournful flowers—they are all glad;
This is a solemn one, but not a sad."

Lo! with the dawn the black buds opened slowly;
Within each cup a color deep and holy
As sacrificial blood glowed rich and red,
And through the velvet tissue mantling spread,
While in the midst of this dark crimson heat   20
A precious golden heart did throb and beat;
Through ruby leaves the morning light did shine,
Each mournful bud had grown a flower divine;

And bittersweet to senses and to soul,
A breathing came from them that filled the whole
Of the surrounding tranced and sunny air
With its strange fragrance, like a silent prayer.
Then cried I, "From the earth's whole wreath I'll borrow
No flower but thee! thou exquisite type of sorrow!"

1883

CHARLOTTE BRONTË

pseud., Currer Bell (1816–1855)

The third of Patrick Brontë's six children, Charlotte suffered the loss of her mother in
1821, followed three years later by the deaths of her two older sisters, Maria and
Elizabeth, who caught typhoid fever and tuberculosis at the harsh boarding school to
which the four oldest girls had been sent. She and Emily returned to Haworth to be edu-
cated with Anne and their brother Branwell; in 1831–32 she studied at Roe Head
School, then taught there, going on to work as a governess. Although her poverty forced
her to pursue one of the few professions available to middle-class women, Charlotte felt
bitterly the intellectual aridity of her work and the social degradation of her role. Her
grim experiences as student and teacher later provided creative material for Jane Eyre
(1847). In 1842, she quit work as a governess to study with Emily in Brussels, in the
hope that a gift from their aunt would enable them to establish a school of their own.
When Aunt Branwell died a few months later, Emily returned home. But Charlotte
taught a second year in Brussels, having fallen in love with the headmaster, Constantin
Héger, who was married, Catholic, and unreceptive to her passion. Her "soul's anguish"
sent her back to England, and ultimately back to the writing that has made her famous.

With her two younger sisters and Branwell, Charlotte had begun in 1826 to com-
pose plays, stories, and poems about an imaginary African kingdom, inspired by a set of
wooden soldiers. Her year and a half away at Roe Head led to a split in the Glass
Town saga: Gondal became the separate (and secret) domain of Emily and Anne, and
Angria became the domain of Charlotte and Branwell. The narratives interspersed with
poems were transcribed in fine print to look like bound books. Charlotte continued to
write Angrian poems and narrative into her years at Roe Head, as she recounts in "We
wove a web in childhood," a poem which represents a vision cut off by the pedestrian
question of another teacher.

At twenty-one, while working as a governess, she looked to Robert Southey for advice
on assuming a literary occupation. In his 1837 response, Southey praised the young poet,
saying "You evidently possess, and in no inconsiderable degree, what Wordsworth calls
the 'faculty of verse.'" Despite this encouragement, he cautioned Charlotte against her
new vocation: "Literature cannot be the business of a woman's life, and it ought not be.

The more she is engaged in her proper duties, the less leisure she will have for it."
Though Southey's advice temporarily arrested Charlotte's public literary endeavors, she
eventually arranged the pseudonymous publication of Poems by Currer, Ellis, and
Acton Bell *(1846). To her publisher she wrote: "No matter—whether known or un-*
known—misjudged or the contrary—I am resolved not to write otherwise. I shall bend
as my powers tend" (September 21, 1849).

As "Currer," Charlotte shifted genres to publish her best-loved novel, Jane Eyre
(1848); a realist narrative about paired heroines set in the period of frame-breaking,
Shirley *(1850); and the school novel* Villette *(1853), which returns to themes an-*
nounced in her first novel, The Professor, *which did not see print until 1857, after her*
death. Unlike Anne, Charlotte drew much attention for the display of talents in her fic-
tion. The novelist Margaret Oliphant described Jane Eyre *as "the most alarming revo-*
lution of modern times." George Eliot exclaimed: "What passion, what fire in her!"
Elizabeth Gaskell's exceptional 1857 biography secured Charlotte's fame.

[He is gone and all grandeur has fled from the mountain]

He is gone and all grandeur has fled from the mountain,
All beauty departed from stream and from fountain.
  A dark veil is hung
O'er the bright sky of gladness,
  And where birds sweetly sung,
There's a murmur of sadness.
The wind sings with a warning tone
 Through many a shadowy tree:
I hear in every passing moan
 The voice of destiny.

Then, oh lord of the waters! the great and all-seeing,
Preserve in thy mercy his safety and being.
  May he trust in thy might
When the dark storm is howling
  And the blackness of night
Over Heaven is scowling.
But may the sea flow glidingly
 With gentle summer waves,
And silent may all tempests lie,
 Chained in vast Aeolian caves!

Yet though ere he returns long years will have vanished,
Sweet hope from my bosom shall never be banished.
  I'll think of the time
When his step lightly bounding
  Shall be heard on the rock
Where the cataract is sounding,
When the banner of his Father's host

Shall be unfurled on high
To welcome back the pride and boast
   Of England's chivalry.

Yet tears will flow forth while of hope I am singing;
Still despair her dark shadow is over me flinging.
     But when he's far away
   I will pluck the wildflower
     On bank and on brae
   At the still moonlight hour,
And I will twine for him a wreath
   Low in the fairy's dell.
Methought I heard the night wind breathe
   That solemn word, *Farewell*!

1832 / 1917

[We wove a web in childhood]

We wove a web in childhood,
   A web of sunny air;
We dug a spring in infancy
   Of water pure and fair;

We sowed in youth a mustard seed,
   We cut an almond rod;
We are now grown up to riper age—
   Are they withered in the sod?

Are they blighted, failed, and faded,
   Are they moldered back to clay?   10
For life is darkly shaded,
   And its joys fleet fast away.

Faded! the web is still of air,
   But how its folds are spread,
And from its tints of crimson clear
   How deep a glow is shed.
The light of an Italian sky
Where clouds of sunset lingering lie
   Is not more ruby-red.

But the spring was under a mossy stone,   20
   Its jet may gush no more.
Hark! skeptic, bid thy doubts be gone.
   Is that a feeble roar
Rushing around thee? Lo! the tide
Of waves where armed fleets may ride,

Sinking and swelling, frowns and smiles—
An ocean with a thousand isles
    And scarce a glimpse of shore.

The mustard seed in distant land
    Bends down a mighty tree,   30
The dry unbudding almond wand
    Has touched eternity.
There came a second miracle
Such as on Aaron's scepter fell,
And sapless grew like life from heath
Bud, bloom, and fruit in mingling wreath
All twined the shrivelled offshoot round,
As flowers lie on the long grave mound.

Dream that stole o'er us in the time
When life was in its vernal clime,
Dream that still faster o'er us steals   40
    As the mild star of spring declining
The advent of that day reveals
    That glows in Sirius' fiery shining:
Oh! as thou swellest, and as the scenes
    Cover this cold world's darkest features,
Stronger each change my spirit weans
    To bow before thy godlike creatures.

When I sat neath a strange roof-tree
With nought I knew or loved round me,   50
Oh, how my heart shrank back to thee;
Then I felt how fast thy ties had bound me.

That hour, that bleak hour when the day
    Closed in the cold autumn's gloaming,
When the clouds hung so bleak and drear and gray
    And a bitter wind through their folds was roaming,

There shone no fire on the cheerless hearth,
    In the chamber there gleamed no taper's twinkle.
Within, neither sight nor sound of mirth,
    Without, but the blast and the sleet's chill sprinkle.   60

Then sadly I longed for my own dear home,
    For a sight of the old familiar faces;
I drew near the casement and sat in its gloom
    And looked forth on the tempest's desolate traces.

Ever anon that wolfish breeze
    The dead leaves and sere from their boughs was shaking,

And I gazed on the hills through the leafless trees
   And felt as if my heart was breaking.

Where was I ere an hour had passed?
Still listening to that dreary blast,   70
Still in that mirthless lifeless room,
Cramped, chilled, and deadened by its gloom?

No! thanks to that bright darling dream.
Its power had shot one kindling gleam,
Its voice had sent one wakening cry,
And bade me lay my sorrows by,
And called me earnestly to come,
And borne me to my moorland home.
I heard no more the senseless sound
Of task and chat that hummed around;   80
I saw no more that grisly night,
Closing the day's sepulchral light.

The vision's spell had deepened o'er me:
Its lands, its scenes were spread before me;
In one short hour a hundred homes
Had roofed me with their lordly domes,
And I had sat by fires whose light
Flashed wide o'er halls of regal height,
And I had seen them come and go
Whose forms gave radiance to the glow,   90
And I had heard the matted floor
Of anteroom and corridor
Shake to some half-remembered tread
Whose haughty firmness woke even dread,
As through the curtained portal strode
Some spurred and fur-wrapped demigod
Whose ride through that tempestuous night
   Had added somewhat of a frown
To brows that shadowed eyes of light
   Fit to flash fire from Scythian crown,   100
Till sweet salute from lady gay
Chased that unconscious scowl away.
And then the savage fur cap doffed,
   The Georgian mantel laid aside,
The satrap stretched on cushion soft,
   His loved and chosen by his side;
That hand, that in its horseman's glove
   Looked fit for nought but bridle rein,
Caresses now its ladylove
   With fingers white that show no stain   110

They got in hot and jarring strife,
When hate or honor warred with life—
Nought redder than the roseate ring
That glitters fit for eastern king.

In one proud household where the sound
Of life and stir rang highest round,
Hall within hall burned starry bright,
And light gave birth to richer light,
Grandly its social tone seemed strung,
Wildly its keen excitement rung,   120
And hundreds, mid its splendors free,
Moved with unfettered liberty,
Not gathered to a lordly feast,
But each a self-invited guest.
It was the kingly custom there
That each at will the house should share.

I saw the master not alone,
He crossed me in a vast saloon,
Just seen then sudden vanishing
As laughingly he joined the ring   130
That closed around a dazzling fire
And listened to a trembling lyre.
He was in light and licensed mood,
Fierce gaiety had warmed his blood,
Kindled his dark and brilliant eye
And toned his lips' full melody.

I saw him take a little child
    That stretched its arms and called his name.
It was his own, and half he smiled
    As the small eager creature came   140
Nestling upon his stately breast,
    And its fair curls and forehead laying
To what but formed a fevered nest—
    Its father's cheek where curls were straying
Thicker and darker on a bloom
Whose hectic brightness boded doom.

He kissed it and a deeper blush
Rose to the already crimson flush,
And a wild sadness flung its grace
Over his grand and Roman face.   150
The little, heedless, lovely thing
Lulled on the bosom of a king,
Its fingers mid his thick locks twining,
Pleased with their rich and wreathed shining,

Dreamed not what thoughts his soul were haunting
Nor why his heart so high was panting.

I went out in a summer night,
    My path lay o'er a lonesome waste,
Slumbering and still in clear moonlight,
    A noble road was o'er it traced.   160
Far as the eye of man could see
    No shade upon its surface stirred;
All slept in mute tranquillity
    Unbroke by step or wind or word.

That waste had been a battle-plain;
    Headstones were reared in the waving fern.
There they had buried the gallant slain
    That dust to its own dust might return.
And one black marble monument
    Rose where the heather was rank and deep;   170
Its base was hid with the bracken and bent,
    Its sides were bare to the night wind's sweep.

A Victory carved in polished stone
    Her trumpet to her cold lips held,
And strange it seemed as she stood alone
That not a single note was blown,
    That not a whisper swelled.

It was Camalia's ancient field,
    I knew the desert well,
For traced around a sculptured shield   180
These words the summer moon revealed:
    "Here brave Macarthy fell!
The men of Keswick leading on.
Their first, their best, their noblest one,
    He did his duty well."

I now heard the far clatter of hoofs on the hard and milk-white road, the great
highway that turns in a bend from Free-Town, and stretches on to the West.
Two horsemen rode slowly up in the moonlight and leaving the path struck
deep into the moor, galloping through heather to their chargers' breasts.

"Hah!" said one of them as he flung himself from his steed and walked for-
ward to the monument; "Hah! Edward, here's my kinsman's tomb. Now for the
bugle sound! He must have his requiem or he will trouble me. The bell tolled
for him in Alderwood on the eve of the conflict. I heard it myself, and though
then but a very little child, I remember well how my mother trembled as she sat
in the drawing room of the manor house and listened while that unaccountable
and supernatural sound was booming so horribly through the woods. Edward,
begin."

Never shall I, Charlotte Brontë, forget what a voice of wild and wailing music now came thrillingly to my mind's—almost to my body's—ear; nor how distinctly I, sitting in the schoolroom at Roe Head, saw the Duke of Zamorna leaning against that obelisk, with the mute marble Victory above him, the fern waving at his feet, his black horse turned loose grazing among the heather, the moonlight so mild and so exquisitely tranquil, sleeping upon that vast and vacant road, and the African sky quivering and shaking with stars expanded above all. I was quite gone. I had really utterly forgot where I was and all the gloom and cheerlessness of my situation. I felt myself breathing quick and short as I beheld the Duke lifting up his sable crest, which undulated as the plume of a hearse waves to the wind, and knew that that music which seems as mournfully triumphant as the scriptural verse

> Oh grave, where is thy sting?
> Oh death, where is thy victory?

was exciting him and quickening his ever rapid pulse.

"Miss Brontë, what are you thinking about?" said a voice that dissipated all the charm, and Miss Lister thrust her little rough black head into my face! *Sic transit* &c.

1835 / 1913

The Teacher's Monologue

The room is quiet, thoughts alone
    People its mute tranquillity;
The yoke put off, the long task done—
    I am, as it is bliss to be,
Still and untroubled. Now, I see,
    For the first time, how soft the day
O'er waveless water, stirless tree,
    Silent and sunny, wings its way
Now, as I watch that distant hill,
    So faint, so blue, so far removed,   10
Sweet dreams of home my heart may fill,
    That home where I am known and loved:
It lies beyond; yon azure brow
    Parts me from all earth holds for me;
And morn and eve, my yearnings flow,
    Thitherward tending, changelessly.
My happiest hours, aye! all the time,
    I love to keep in memory,
Lapsed among moors, ere life's first prime
    Decayed to dark anxiety.   20

Sometimes, I think a narrow heart
    Makes me thus mourn those far away,

And keeps my love so far apart
   From friends and friendships of today;
Sometimes, I think 'tis but a dream
   I treasure up so jealously,
All the sweet thoughts I live on seem
   To vanish into vacancy.
And then this strange, coarse world around
   Seems all that's palpable and true,   30
And every sight and every sound
   Combines my spirit to subdue
To aching grief; so void and lone
   Is life and earth—so worse than vain
The hopes that in my own heart sown,
   And cherished by such sun and rain
As joy and transient sorrow shed,
   Have ripened to a harvest there:
Alas! methinks I hear it said,
   "Thy golden sheaves are empty air."   40
All fades away; my very home
   I think will soon be desolate;
I hear, at times, a warning come
   Of bitter partings at its gate;
And, if I should return and see
   The hearth fire quenched, the vacant chair,
And hear it whispered mournfully
   That farewells have been spoken there,
What shall I do and whither turn?
Where look for peace? When cease to mourn?   50

*   *   **

'Tis not the air I wished to play,
   The strain I wished to sing;
My wilful spirit slipped away
   And struck another string.
I neither wanted smile nor tear,
   Bright joy nor bitter woe,
But just a song that sweet and clear,
   Though haply sad, might flow.

A quiet song, to solace me
   When sleep refused to come;   60
A strain to chase despondency
   When sorrowful for home.
In vain I try; I cannot sing;
   All feels so cold and dead;
No wild distress, no gushing spring
   Of tears in anguish shed;

But all the impatient gloom of one
   Who waits a distant day,
When, some great task of suffering done,
   Repose shall toil repay.   70
For youth departs, and pleasure flies,
   And life consumes away,
And youth's rejoicing ardor dies
   Beneath this drear delay;

And patience, weary with her yoke,
   Is yielding to despair,
And health's elastic spring is broke
   Beneath the strain of care.
Life will be gone ere I have lived;
   Where now is life's first prime?   80
I've worked and studied, longed and grieved,
   Through all that rosy time.

To toil, to think, to long, to grieve—
   Is such my future fate?
The morn was dreary, must the eve
   Be also desolate?
Well, such a life at least makes death
   A welcome, wished-for friend;
Then, aid me, reason, patience, faith,
   To suffer to the end!   90

1837 / 1846

Apostasy

This last denial of my faith,
   Thou, solemn priest, hast heard;
And though upon my bed of death,
   I call not back a word.
Point not to thy Madonna, priest,
   Thy sightless saint of stone:
She cannot from this burning breast
   Wring one repentant moan.

Thou sayest that, when a sinless child,
   I duly bent the knee   10
And prayed to what in marble smiled
   Cold, lifeless, mute on me.
I did. But listen! Children spring
   Full soon to riper youth;
And for love's vow and wedlock's ring,
   I sold my early truth.

'Twas not a gray, bare head, like thine,
   Bent o'er me, when I said,
"That land and God and Faith are mine,
   For which thy fathers bled."   20
I see thee not—my eyes are dim—
   But well I hear thee say,
"O daughter, cease to think of him
   Who led thy soul astray.

"Between you lies both space and time;
   Let leagues and years prevail
To turn thee from the path of crime,
   Back to the Church's pale."
And did I need that thou shouldst tell
   What mighty barriers rise   30
To part me from that dungeon cell
   Where my loved Walter lies?

And did I need that thou shouldst taunt
   My dying hour at last,
By bidding his worn spirit pant
   No more for what is past?
Priest—*must* I cease to think of him?
   How hollow rings that word!
Can time, can tears, can distance dim
   The memory of my lord?   40

I said before, I saw not thee,
   Because, an hour agone,
Over my eyeballs, heavily,
   The lids fell down like stone.
But still my spirit's inward sight
   Beholds his image beam
As fixed, as clear, as burning bright,
   As some red planet's gleam.

Talk not of thy Last Sacrament,
   Tell not thy beads for me;   50
Both rite and prayer are vainly spent
   As dews upon the sea.
Speak not one word of Heaven above,
   Rave not of Hell's alarms;
Give me but back my Walter's love,
   Restore me to his arms!

Then will the bliss of Heaven be won;
   Then will Hell shrink away,
As I have seen night's terrors shun

The conquering steps of day.   60
  'Tis my religion thus to love,
    My creed thus fixed to be;
Not death shall shake, nor priestcraft break
    My rock-like constancy!

Now go, for at the door there waits
    Another stranger guest;
He calls—I come—my pulse scarce beats,
    My heart fails in my breast.
Again that voice—how far away,
    How dreary sounds that tone!   70
And I, methinks, am gone astray
    In trackless wastes and lone.

I fain would rest a little while:
    Where can I find a stay,
Till dawn upon the hills shall smile
    And show some trodden way?
"I come! I come!" in haste she said,
  " 'Twas Walter's voice I heard!"
Then up she sprang—but fell back dead,
    His name her latest word.   80

1837 / 1846

[He saw my heart's woe—discovered my soul's anguish]

He saw my heart's woe—discovered my soul's anguish,
  How in fever, in thirst, in atrophy it pined;
Knew he could heal, yet looked and let it languish,
  To its moans spirit-deaf, to its pangs spirit-blind.

But once a year he heard a whisper low and dreary
  Appealing for aid, entreating some reply.
Only when sick, soul-worn, and torture-weary,
  Breathed I that prayer—heaved I that sigh.

He was mute as is the grave—he stood stirless as a tower.
  At last I looked up and saw I prayed to stone: 10
I asked help of that which to help had no power;
  I sought love where love was utterly unknown.

Idolater I kneeled to an idol cut in rock.
  I might have slashed my flesh and drawn my heart's best blood:
The granite god had felt no tenderness, no shock;
  My Baal had not seen nor heard nor understood.

In dark remorse I rose; I rose in darker shame;
  Self-condemned I withdrew to an exile from my kind;

A solitude I sought where mortal never came,
   Hoping, in its wilds, forgetfulness to find.   20

Now, Heaven, heal the wound which I still deeply feel;
   Thy glorious hosts look not in scorn on our poor race;
Thy King eternal doth no iron judgment deal
   On suffering worms who seek forgiveness, comfort, grace.

He gave our hearts to love, He will not love despise,
   E'en if the gift be lost, as mine was long ago.
He will forgive the fault—will bid the offender rise,
   Wash out with dews of bliss the fiery brand of woe;

And give a sheltered place beneath the unsullied throne,
   Whence the soul redeemed may mark time's fleeting course
      round earth   30
And know its trials overpast, its sufferings gone,
   And feel the peril past of death's immortal birth.

1847 / 1915

EMILY JANE BRONTË

pseud., Ellis Bell (1818–1848)

Author of Wuthering Heights *(1847), the reclusive Emily was also the most prolific and accomplished poet of the Brontë sisters. Shortly after her father, Patrick Brontë, became minister at Haworth, her mother died in 1821. In 1824–25 she and her three older sisters attended the Cowan Bridge School; there Maria and Elizabeth caught typhoid fever and tuberculosis and died. The surviving girls were taught at home with their brother Branwell by their aunt Elizabeth Branwell. Emily went briefly to boarding school in 1835, taught half a year at Law Hill school in 1837, and spent another year in Belgium with Charlotte, studying French at the school of Constantin Héger in 1842. In Héger's view, "she should have been a man—a great navigator. . . . Her strong, imperious will would never have been daunted by opposition or difficulty." Not surprisingly, Emily was unhappy at school. Her "chainless soul" needed the freedom of the moors that surround Haworth parsonage: "To transplant her was to kill her." Her brother's return in disgrace from his position as tutor, addicted to alcohol and opium, shattered the peace of their home. Emily nursed him on his deathbed, then succumbed to tuberculosis and died two months later.*

As children, the four surviving Brontës invested their lively imaginations in developing a fantasy world around a set of wooden soldiers. Emily and Anne created their own fantastical world of Gondal, depicting in verse and prose the legends, myths, and sagas of an imaginary North Pacific kingdom. While Anne eventually lost interest in the poetic chronicle, Emily continued to compose Gondal poems throughout her brief adult life.

When Charlotte discovered Emily's verse and promoted the publication of Poems by Currer, Ellis, and Acton Bell *(1846), Emily expunged all reference to Gondal from the twenty-one poems she hesitantly offered for the collection. Only after her death were full selections of the Gondal poetry published, but even the editions of 1846 and 1850 revealed what Charlotte called their "peculiar music—wild, melancholy, and elevating." Emily's intensely dramatized expressions of emotion and fluid movement among personae have surprised and impressed readers, but only two copies of the volume sold at first. In midcentury, she was known instead for* Wuthering Heights, *published in*

December 1847, whose "brutal" Byronic hero and primal passions shocked reviewers and alarmed even Charlotte. Echoing the critics who thought "no woman could write Wuthering Heights," Anne Mellor has argued that Brontë in her life, poetry, and novel conformed to a "masculine" model of Romanticism.

For Algernon Charles Swinburne, Brontë hit "the pure note of absolutely right expression for things inexpressible in full by prose." Charlotte Mew, who at one time hoped to edit the poems, found in them a tension between Brontë's stance of self-sufficient aloofness and her vision of violent sparks in a spectacle of "trackless starless darkness." Virginia Woolf predicted in The Common Reader that "her poems will perhaps outlast her novel."

[High waving heather neath stormy blasts bending]

High waving heather neath stormy blasts bending,
   Midnight and moonlight and bright shining stars;
Darkness and glory rejoicingly blending,
Earth rising to heaven and heaven descending,
Man's spirit away from its drear dungeon sending,
   Bursting the fetters and breaking the bars.

All down the mountainsides, wild forests lending
   One mighty voice to the life-giving wind;
Rivers their banks in the jubilee rending,
Fast through the valleys a reckless course wending,   10
Wilder and deeper their waters extending,
   Leaving a desolate desert behind.

Shining and lowering and swelling and dying,
   Changing forever from midnight to noon;
Roaring like thunder, like soft music sighing,
Shadows on shadows advancing and flying,
Lightning-bright flashes the deep gloom defying,
   Coming as swiftly, and fading as soon.

1836 / 1902

[Fall, leaves, fall; die, flowers, away]

Fall, leaves, fall; die, flowers, away;
Lengthen, night, and shorten, day!
Every leaf speaks bliss to me,
Fluttering from the autumn tree.
I shall smile when wreaths of snow
Blossom where the rose should grow;
I shall sing when night's decay
Ushers in a drearier day.

c.1838 / 1910

[And now the house-dog stretched once more]

And now the house-dog stretched once more
His limbs upon the glowing floor;
The children half resumed their play,
Though from the warm hearth scared away.
The goodwife left her spinning wheel
And spread with smiles the evening meal;
The shepherd placed a seat and pressed
To their poor fare his unknown guest.
And he unclasped his mantle now,
And raised the covering from his brow;   10
Said, "Voyagers by land and sea
Were seldom feasted daintily";
And checked his host by adding stern
He'd no refinement to unlearn.
A silence settled on the room;
The cheerful welcome sank to gloom;
But not those words, though cold and high,
So froze their hospitable joy.
No—there was something in his face,
Some nameless thing they could not trace,   20
And something in his voice's tone
Which turned their blood as chill as stone.
The ringlets of his long black hair
Fell o'er a cheek most ghastly fair.
Youthful he seemed—but worn as they
Who spend too soon their youthful day.
When his glance drooped, 'twas hard to quell
Unbidden feelings' sudden swell;
And pity scarce her tears could hide,
So sweet that brow with all its pride;
But when upraised his eye would dart
An icy shudder through the heart,
Compassion changed to horror then
And fear to meet that gaze again.
It was not hatred's tiger-glare,
Nor the wild anguish of despair;
It was not useless misery,
Which mocks at friendship's sympathy.
No—lightning all unearthly shone
Deep in that dark eye's circling zone,   40
Such withering lightning as we deem
None but a specter's look may beam;
And glad they were when he turned away
And wrapped him in his mantle gray,

Leaned down his head upon his arm
And veiled from view their basilisk charm.

1839 / 1902

[There was a time when my cheek burned]

There was a time when my cheek burned
To give such scornful fiends the lie;
Ungoverned nature madly spurned
The law that bade it not defy.
O, in the days of ardent youth
I would have given my life for truth.

For truth, for right, for liberty
I would have gladly, freely died;
And now I calmly hear and see
The vain man smile, the fool deride—   10
Though not because my heart is tame,
Though not for fear, though not for shame.

My soul still chafes at every tone
Of selfish and self-blinded error;
My breast still braves the world alone,
Steeled as it ever was to terror;
Only I know, howe'er I frown,
The same world will go rolling on.

1839 / 1910

The Night Wind

In summer's mellow midnight,
A cloudless moon shone through
Our open parlor window
And rose trees wet with dew.

I sat in silent musing,
The soft wind waved my hair;
It told me Heaven was glorious
And sleeping Earth was fair.

I needed not its breathing
To bring such thoughts to me;   10
But still it whispered lowly,
"How dark the woods will be!

"The thick leaves in my murmur
Are rustling like a dream,

And all their myriad voices
Instinct with spirit seem."

I said, "Go, gentle singer,
Thy wooing voice is kind,
But do not think its music
Has power to reach my mind.   20

"Play with the scented flower,
The young tree's supple bough,
And leave my human feelings
In their own course to flow."

The wanderer would not leave me;
Its kiss grew warmer still—
"O come," it sighed so sweetly,
"I'll win thee 'gainst thy will.

"Have we not been from childhood friends?
Have I not loved thee long?   30
As long as thou hast loved the night
Whose silence wakes my song.

"And when thy heart is laid at rest
Beneath the churchyard stone,
I shall have time enough to mourn,
And thou to be alone"—

                                          1840 / 1850

Song

The linnet in the rocky dells,
    The moor-lark in the air,
The bee among the heather bells
    That hide my lady fair:

The wild deer browse above her breast;
    The wild birds raise their brood;
And they, her smiles of love caressed,
    Have left her solitude!

I ween, that when the grave's dark wall
    Did first her form retain,   10
They thought their hearts could ne'er recall
    The light of joy again.

They thought the tide of grief would flow
    Unchecked through future years;

But where is all their anguish now,
    And where are all their tears?

Well, let them fight for honor's breath,
    Or pleasure's shade pursue—
The dweller in the land of death
    Is changed and careless, too.   20

And if their eyes should watch and weep
    Till sorrow's source were dry,
She would not, in her tranquil sleep,
    Return a single sigh!

Blow, west wind, by the lonely mound,
    And murmur, summer streams—
There is no need of other sound
    To soothe my lady's dreams.

1844 / 1846

The Philosopher

"Enough of thought, philosopher!
    Too long hast thou been dreaming
Unlightened in this chamber drear
    While summer's sun is beaming!
Space-sweeping soul, what sad refrain
Concludes thy musings once again?

" 'Oh, for the time when I shall sleep
    Without identity
And never care how rain may steep
    Or snow may cover me!   10
No promised heaven, these wild desires
    Could all or half fulfill;
No threatened hell, with quenchless fires,
    Subdue this quenchless will!' "

"So said I and still say the same;
    Still, to my death, will say—
Three gods within this little frame
    Are warring, night and day;
Heaven could not hold them all, and yet
    They all are held in me;   20
And must be mine till I forget
    My present entity!
Oh, for the time, when in my breast
    Their struggles will be o'er!

Oh, for the day, when I shall rest,
   And never suffer more!"

"I saw a spirit, standing, man,
   Where thou dost stand—an hour ago,
And round his feet three rivers ran,
   Of equal depth and equal flow—   30
A golden stream—and one like blood;
   And one like sapphire seemed to be;
But where they joined their triple flood
   It tumbled in an inky sea.
The spirit sent his dazzling gaze
   Down through that ocean's gloomy night;
Then kindling all with sudden blaze,
   The glad deep sparkled wide and bright—
White as the sun, far, far more fair
   Than its divided sources were!"   40

"And even for that spirit, seer,
   I've watched and sought my lifetime long;
Sought him in heaven, hell, earth, and air,
   And endless search, and always wrong.
Had I but seen his glorious eye
   Once light the clouds that 'wilder me,
I ne'er had raised this coward cry
   To cease to think and cease to be;
I ne'er had called oblivion blest
   Nor, stretching eager hands to death,   50
Implored to change for senseless rest
   This sentient soul, this living breath.
Oh, let me die—that power and will
   Their cruel strife may close,
And conquered good and conquering ill
   Be lost in one repose!"

                                        1845

Remembrance

Cold in the earth—and the deep snow piled above thee,
   Far, far removed, cold in the dreary grave!
Have I forgot, my only love, to love thee,
   Severed at last by time's all-severing wave?

Now, when alone, do my thoughts no longer hover
   Over the mountains, on that northern shore,
Resting their wings where heath and fern leaves cover
   Thy noble heart forever, evermore?

Cold in the earth—and fifteen wild Decembers
    From those brown hills have melted into spring: 10
Faithful, indeed, is the spirit that remembers
    After such years of change and suffering!

Sweet love of youth, forgive if I forget thee
    While the world's tide is bearing me along;
Other desires and other hopes beset me,
    Hopes which obscure, but cannot do thee wrong!

No later light has lightened up my heaven,
    No second morn has ever shone for me;
All my life's bliss from thy dear life was given,
    All my life's bliss is in the grave with thee.   20

But when the days of golden dreams had perished,
    And even despair was powerless to destroy,
Then did I learn how existence could be cherished,
    Strengthened, and fed, without the aid of joy.

Then did I check the tears of useless passion—
    Weaned my young soul from yearning after thine;
Sternly denied its burning wish to hasten
    Down to that tomb already more than mine.

And, even yet, I dare not let it languish,
    Dare not indulge in memory's rapturous pain;   30
Once drinking deep of that divinest anguish,
    How could I seek the empty world again?

                     1845 / 1846

Stars

Ah! why, because the dazzling sun
    Restored our earth to joy,
Have you departed, every one,
    And left a desert sky?

All through the night your glorious eyes
    Were gazing down in mine,
And with a full heart's thankful sighs
    I blessed that watch divine.

I was at peace and drank your beams
    As they were life to me;   10
And reveled in my changeful dreams,
    Like petrel on the sea.

Thought followed thought, star followed star
  Through boundless regions on;
While one sweet influence, near and far,
  Thrilled through and proved us one!

Why did the morning dawn to break
  So great, so pure a spell,
And scorch with fire the tranquil cheek
  Where your cool radiance fell?   20

Blood-red he rose, and arrow-straight
  His fierce beams struck my brow;
The soul of nature sprang, elate,
  But *mine* sank sad and low!

My lids closed down, yet through their veil
  I saw him blazing still,
And steep in gold the misty dale
  And flash upon the hill.

I turned me to the pillow then,
  To call back night and see   30
Your worlds of solemn light again
  Throb with my heart and me!

It would not do—the pillow glowed,
  And glowed both roof and floor;
And birds sang loudly in the wood,
  And fresh winds shook the door;

The curtains waved, the wakened flies
  Were murmuring round my room,
Imprisoned there, till I should rise
  And give them leave to roam.   40

O stars, and dreams, and gentle night;
  O night and stars, return!
And hide me from the hostile light
  That does not warm, but burn;

That drains the blood of suffering men;
  Drinks tears, instead of dew;
Let me sleep through his blinding reign
  And only wake with you!

1845 / 1846

The Prisoner

A Fragment

In the dungeon crypts, idly did I stray,
Reckless of the lives wasting there away;
"Draw the ponderous bars; open, warder stern!"
He dared not say me nay—the hinges harshly turn.

"Our guests are darkly lodged," I whispered, gazing through
The vault whose grated eye showed heaven more gray than blue.
(This was when glad spring laughed in awaking pride.)
"Aye, darkly lodged enough!" returned my sullen guide.

Then, God forgive my youth, forgive my careless tongue!
I scoffed, as the chill chains on the damp flagstones rung;   10
"Confined in triple walls, art thou so much to fear,
That we must bind thee down and clench thy fetters here?"

The captive raised her face; it was as soft and mild
As sculptured marble saint or slumbering, unweaned child;
It was so soft and mild, it was so sweet and fair,
Pain could not trace a line nor grief a shadow there!

The captive raised her hand and pressed it to her brow:
"I have been struck," she said, "and I am suffering now;
Yet these are little worth, your bolts and irons strong;
And were they forged in steel they could not hold me long."   20

Hoarse laughed the jailor grim: "Shall I be won to hear;
Dost think, fond dreaming wretch, that *I* shall grant thy prayer?
Or, better still, wilt melt my master's heart with groans?
Ah, sooner might the sun thaw down these granite stones!

"My master's voice is low, his aspect bland and kind,
But hard as hardest flint the soul that lurks behind;
And I am rough and rude, yet not more rough to see
Than is the hidden ghost that has its home in me!"

About her lips there played a smile of almost scorn:
"My friend," she gently said, "you have not heard me mourn;   30
When you my kindred's lives, *my* lost life, can restore,
Then may I weep and sue—but never, friend, before!

"Still, let my tyrants know, I am not doomed to wear
Year after year in gloom and desolate despair;
A messenger of hope comes every night to me,
And offers, for short life, eternal liberty.

"He comes with western winds, with evening's wandering airs,
With that clear dusk of heaven that brings the thickest stars;
Winds take a pensive tone, and stars a tender fire,
And visions rise and change, that kill me with desire.   40

"Desire for nothing known in my maturer years,
When joy grew mad with awe at counting future tears;
When, if my spirit's sky was full of flashes warm,
I knew not whence they came, from sun or thunderstorm.

"But first a hush of peace, a soundless calm descends;
The struggle of distress and fierce impatience ends;
Mute music soothes my breast—unuttered harmony
That I could never dream till earth was lost to me.

"Then dawns the invisible, the unseen its truth reveals;
My outward sense is gone, my inward essence feels—   50
Its wings are almost free, its home, its harbor found;
Measuring the gulf it stoops—and dares the final bound!

"Oh, dreadful is the check—intense the agony—
When the ear begins to hear and the eye begins to see;
When the pulse begins to throb, the brain to think again,
The soul to feel the flesh and the flesh to feel the chain!

"Yet I would lose no sting, would wish no torture less;
The more that anguish racks, the earlier it will bless;
And robed in fires of hell, or bright with heavenly shine,
If it but herald death, the vision is divine."   60

She ceased to speak, and we, unanswering, turned to go—
We had no further power to work the captive woe;
Her cheek, her gleaming eye, declared that man had given
A sentence unapproved and overruled by heaven.

                                                1845 / 1846

[No coward soul is mine]

No coward soul is mine,
No trembler in the world's storm-troubled sphere:
I see Heaven's glories shine,
And faith shines equal, arming me from fear.

O God within my breast,
Almighty, ever-present Deity!
Life, that in me hast rest,
As I, Undying Life, have power in thee!

Vain are the thousand creeds
That move men's hearts, unutterably vain;   10
Worthless as withered weeds
Or idlest froth amid the boundless main

To waken doubt in one
Holding so fast by thy infinity,
So surely anchored on
The steadfast rock of immortality.

With wide-embracing love
Thy spirit animates eternal years,
Pervades and broods above,
Changes, sustains, dissolves, creates, and rears.   20

Though earth and moon were gone,
And suns and universes ceased to be,
And thou wert left alone,
Every existence would exist in thee.

There is not room for death,
Nor atom that his might could render void:
Since thou art Being and Breath,
And what thou art may never be destroyed.

1846 / 1850

George Eliot

pseud. of Mary Ann Evans (1819–1880)

Evans grew up in the rural world described later in her novels: her father was an estate agent, a post assumed in time by her brother Isaac, whose close relationship with her provided the model for Mill on the Floss *and the poem "Brother and Sister." When her mother died, she returned home from boarding school to become her father's housekeeper in her teens. At home she continued her studies, taking tutorials in German and Italian, Greek and Latin, and reading widely in poetry and philosophy. Although educated in an Evangelical milieu, she rejected religion in her twenties, and at the behest of a free-thinking friend translated in 1844 David Friedrich Strauss's* Das Leben Jesu *(an attempt to show the Bible to be mythical, not historical). For Virginia Woolf, Eliot was "one of the most learned women—or men—of her time."*

When her father's death released her from domestic service at thirty, she moved to London, where her career as a writer took shape. She was the assistant editor of the radical Westminster Review; *for this quarterly she wrote her programmatic review, "Silly Novels by Lady Novelists," before she launched on her own career as a novelist. For twenty-five years, from 1853 until his death, she lived with George Henry Lewes, a married journalist unable to obtain a divorce from his unfaithful wife. The scandal of this relationship created a rupture with her family and isolated her from London society; "proper" women shunned her weekly receptions. Emily Dickinson therefore thought Evans's life was "a Doom of Fruit without the Bloom," but she ranked her work second only to that of Barrett Browning. With her writing Evans helped support the three children of Lewes: she received £12,000 for* Adam Bede *(1859) and £7,000 for* Romola *(1863). After his death in 1878, she completed the publication of his last work; she married a younger admirer, John Cross, in 1880 (regaining respectability in her family's eyes), but died seven months later.*

Lewes encouraged her to write under the cover of a pseudonym that reflected her debt to him as well as her admiration of George Sand: Scenes of Clerical Life *(1857–58) was followed by the two novels already mentioned and five others,* The Mill on the Floss *(1860),* Silas Marner *(1861),* Felix Holt, the Radical *(1866),* Middlemarch *(1871–72), and* Daniel Deronda *(1876). Her fiction explores the sexual double standard and the disparate social treatment of men's and women's aspirations. Henry James admired her as a humorist and philosopher whose "touches" gained strength from the play of thought.*

Although her reputation rests upon her novels, Evans, who admired Aurora Leigh, also wrote several verse narratives, as well as shorter lyrics. Most of her narrative personae in the fiction are masculine, but she teasingly endorsed a contradictory "feminine style" as "the truest representation of life." Her poetic dramas permitted her to experiment with female voices. The heroine of The Spanish Gypsy *(1868), Fedalma, finds herself caught between private and public roles, in both of which she is the object of male struggles for power.* The Legend of Jubal *(1869) rewrites the story of the Fall. Like Mme. de Staël and Barrett Browning, she examined, in* Armgart *(1870), the conflict of goals for the woman artist. The heroine, a singer, rejects her suitor's claim that "home delights" comprehend the fullness of womanhood and responds, "I am an artist by my birth—/ By the same warrant that I am a woman." Some of her most modern poetry remained in manuscript, perhaps because of its pessimistic tone.*

A Minor Prophet

I have a friend, a vegetarian seer,
By name Elias Baptist Butterworth,
A harmless, bland, disinterested man,
Whose ancestors in Cromwell's day believed
The Second Advent certain in five years,
But when King Charles the Second came instead,
Revised their date and sought another world:
I mean not heaven, but—America.
A fervid stock, whose generous hope embraced
The fortunes of mankind, not stopping short   10
At rise of leather, or the fall of gold,
Nor listening to the voices of the time
As housewives listen to a cackling hen,
With wonder whether she has laid her egg
On their own nest egg. Still they did insist
Somewhat too wearisomely on the joys
Of their Millennium, when coats and hats
Would all be of one pattern, books and songs
All fit for Sundays, and the casual talk
As good as sermons preached extempore.   20

And in Elias the ancestral zeal
Breathes strong as ever, only modified
By transatlantic air and modern thought.
You could not pass him in the street and fail
To note his shoulders' long declivity,

Beard to the waist, swan neck, and large pale eyes;
Or, when he lifts his hat, to mark his hair
Brushed back to show his great capacity—
A full grain's length at the angle of the brow
Proving him witty, while the shallower men   30
Only seem witty in their repartees.
Not that he's vain, but that his doctrine needs
The testimony of his frontal lobe.
On all points he adopts the latest views;
Takes for the key of universal Mind
The "levitation" of stout gentlemen;
Believes the rappings are not spirits' work
But the Thought-atmosphere's, a steam of brains
In correlated force of raps, as proved
By motion, heat, and science generally;   40
The spectrum, for example, which has shown
The selfsame metals in the sun as here;
So the Thought-atmosphere is everywhere:
High truths that glimmered under other names
To ancient sages, whence good scholarship
Applied to Eleusinian mysteries—
The Vedas—Tripitaka—Vendidad—
Might furnish weaker proof for weaker minds
That Thought was rapping in the hoary past,
And might have edified the Greeks by raps   50
At the greater Dionysia, if their ears
Had not been filled with Sophoclean verse.
And when all Earth is vegetarian—
When, lacking butchers, quadrupeds die out,
And less Thought-atmosphere is reabsorbed
By nerves of insects parasitical,
Those higher truths, seized now by higher minds
But not expressed (the insects hindering)
Will either flash out into eloquence
Or, better still, be comprehensible   60
By rappings simply, without need of roots.

'Tis on this theme—the vegetarian world—
That good Elias willingly expands:
He loves to tell in mildly nasal tones
And vowels stretched to suit the widest views
The future fortunes of our infant Earth—
When it will be too full of humankind
To have the room for wilder animals.
Saith he, Sahara will be populous

With families of gentlemen retired   70
From commerce in more Central Africa,
Who order coolness as we order coal,
And have a lobe anterior strong enough
To think away the sandstorms. Science thus
Will leave no spot on this terraqueous globe
Unfit to be inhabited by man,
The chief of animals: all meaner brutes
Will have been smoked and elbowed out of life.
No lions then shall lap Caffrarian pools,
Or shake the Atlas with their midnight roar: 80
Even the slow, slime-loving crocodile,
The last of animals to take a hint,
Will then retire forever from a scene
Where public feeling strongly sets against him.
Fishes may lead carnivorous lives obscure
But must not dream of culinary rank
Or being dished in good society.
Imagination in that distant age,
Aiming at fiction called historical,
Will vainly try to reconstruct the times   90
When it was men's preposterous delight
To sit astride live horses, which consumed
Materials for incalculable cakes;
When there were milkmaids who drew milk from cows
With udders kept abnormal for that end
Since the rude mythopœic period
Of Aryan dairymen, who did not blush
To call their milkmaid and their daughter one—
Helplessly gazing at the Milky Way,
Nor dreaming of the astral coconuts   100
Quite at the service of posterity.
'Tis to be feared, though, that the duller boys,
Much given to anachronisms and nuts
(Elias has confessed boys will be boys),
May write a jockey for a centaur, think
Europa's suitor was an Irish bull,
Æsop a journalist who wrote up Fox,
And Bruin a chief swindler upon 'Change.
Boys will be boys, but dogs will all be moral,
With longer alimentary canals   110
Suited to diet vegetarian.
The uglier breeds will fade from memory
Or, being palæontological,
Live but as portraits in large learned books,

Distasteful to the feelings of an age
Nourished on purest beauty. Earth will hold
No stupid brutes, no cheerful queernesses,
No naïve cunning, grave absurdity.
Wart-pigs with tender and parental grunts,
Wombats much flattened as to their contour,   120
Perhaps from too much crushing in the ark,
But taking meekly that fatality;
The serious cranes, unstung by ridicule;
Long-headed, short-legged, solemn-looking curs,
(Wise, silent critics of a flippant age);
The silly straddling foals, the weak-brained geese
Hissing fallaciously at sound of wheels—
All these rude products will have disappeared
Along with every faulty human type.
By dint of diet vegetarian   130
All will be harmony of hue and line,
Bodies and minds all perfect, limbs well turned,
And talk quite free from aught erroneous.

Thus far Elias in his seer's mantle:
But at this climax in his prophecy
My sinking spirits, fearing to be swamped,
Urge me to speak. "High prospects these, my friend,
Setting the weak carnivorous brain astretch;
We will resume the thread another day."
"Tomorrow," cries Elias, "at this hour?"   140
"No, not tomorrow—I shall have a cold—
At least I feel some soreness—this endemic—
Good-bye."

       No tears are sadder than the smile
With which I quit Elias. Bitterly
I feel that every change upon this earth
Is bought with sacrifice. My yearnings fail
To reach that high apocalyptic mount
Which shows in bird's-eye view a perfect world
Or enter warmly into other joys
Than those of faulty, struggling human kind.   150
That strain upon my soul's too feeble wing
Ends in ignoble floundering: I fall
Into shortsighted pity for the men
Who living in those perfect future times
Will not know half the dear imperfect things
That move my smiles and tears—will never know
The fine old incongruities that raise

My friendly laugh; the innocent conceits
That like a needless eyeglass or black patch
Give those who wear them harmless happiness;   160
The twists and cracks in our poor earthenware,
That touch me to more conscious fellowship
(I am not myself the finest Parian)
With my coevals. So poor Colin Clout,
To whom raw onion gives prospective zest,
Consoling hours of dampest wintry work,
Could hardly fancy any regal joys
Quite unimpregnate with the onion's scent:
Perhaps his highest hopes are not all clear
Of waftings from that energetic bulb—   170
'Tis well that onion is not heresy.
Speaking in parable, I am Colin Clout.
A clinging flavor penetrates my life—
My onion is imperfectness: I cleave
To nature's blunders, evanescent types
Which sages banish from Utopia.
"Not worship beauty?" say you. Patience, friend.
I worship in the temple with the rest;
But by my hearth I keep a sacred nook
For gnomes and dwarfs, duck-footed waddling elves   180
Who stitched and hammered for the weary man
In days of old. And in that piety
I clothe ungainly forms inherited
From toiling generations, daily bent
At desk, or plow, or loom, or in the mine,
In pioneering labors for the world.
Nay, I am apt when floundering, confused
From too rash flight, to grasp at paradox,
And pity future men who will not know
A keen experience with pity blent,   190
The pathos exquisite of lovely minds
Hid in harsh forms—not penetrating them
Like fire divine within a common bush
Which glows transfigured by the heavenly guest,
So that men put their shoes off; but encaged
Like a sweet child within some thick-walled cell,
Who leaps and fails to hold the window bars,
But having shown a little dimpled hand,
Is visited thenceforth by tender hearts,
Whose eyes keep watch about the prison walls.   200
A foolish, nay, a wicked paradox!
For purest pity is the eye of love

Melting at sight of sorrow; and to grieve
Because it sees no sorrow shows a love
Warped from its truer nature, turned to love
Of merest habit, like the miser's greed.
But I am Colin still: my prejudice
Is for the flavor of my daily food.
Not that I doubt the world is growing still,
As once it grew from chaos and from night;   210
Or have a soul too shrunken for the hope
Which dawned in human breasts, a double morn,
With earliest watchings of the rising light
Chasing the darkness; and through many an age
Has raised the vision of a future time
That stands an angel with a face all mild
Spearing the demon. I too rest in faith
That man's perfection is the crowning flower
Toward which the urgent sap in life's great tree
Is pressing—seen in puny blossoms now,   220
But in the world's great morrows to expand
With broadest petal and with deepest glow.

Yet, see the patched and plodding citizen
Waiting upon the pavement with the throng
While some victorious world-hero makes
Triumphal entry, and the peal of shouts
And flash of faces neath uplifted hats
Run like a storm of joy along the streets!
He says, "God bless him!" almost with a sob,
As the great hero passes: he is glad   230
The world holds mighty men and mighty deeds;
The music stirs his pulses like strong wine,
The moving splendor touches him with awe—
'Tis glory shed around the common weal,
And he will pay his tribute willingly,
Though with the pennies earned by sordid toil.
Perhaps the hero's deeds have helped to bring
A time when every honest citizen
Shall wear a coat unpatched. And yet he feels
More easy fellowship with neighbors there   240
Who look on, too; and he will soon relapse
From noticing the banners and the steeds
To think with pleasure there is just one bun
Left in his pocket, that may serve to tempt
The wide-eyed lad, whose weight is all too much
For that young mother's arms: and then he falls
To dreamy picturing of sunny days

When he himself was a small big-cheeked lad
In some far village where no heroes came,
And stood a listener 'twixt his father's legs   250
In the warm firelight, while the old folk talked
And shook their heads and looked upon the floor;
And he was puzzled, thinking life was fine—
The bread and cheese so nice all through the year,
And Christmas sure to come. Oh that good time!
He, could he choose, would have those days again
And see the dear old-fashioned things once more.
But soon the wheels and drums have all passed by
And tramping feet are heard like sudden rain:
The quiet startles our good citizen;   260
He feels the child upon his arms and knows
He is with the people making holiday
Because of hopes for better days to come.
But hope to him was like the brilliant west,
Telling of sunrise in a world unknown,
And from that dazzling curtain of bright hues
He turned to the familiar face of fields
Lying all clear in the calm morning land.

Maybe 'tis wiser not to fix a lens
Too scrutinizing on the glorious times   270
When Barbarossa shall arise and shake
His mountain, good King Arthur come again,
And all the heroes of such giant soul
That, living once to cheer mankind with hope,
They had to sleep until the time was ripe
For greater deeds to match their greater thought.
Yet no! the earth yields nothing more divine
Than high prophetic vision—than the seer
Who, fasting from man's meaner joy, beholds
The paths of beauteous order and constructs   280
A fairer type to shame our low content.
But prophecy is like potential sound
Which turned to music seems a voice sublime
From out the soul of light; but turns to noise
In scrannel pipes, and makes all ears averse.

The faith that life on earth is being shaped
To glorious ends, that order, justice, love
Mean man's completeness, mean effect as sure
As roundness in the dewdrop—that great faith
Is but the rushing and expanding stream   290

Of thought, of feeling, fed by all the past.
Our finest hope is finest memory,
As they who love in age think youth is blest
Because it has a life to fill with love.
Full souls are double mirrors, making still
An endless vista of fair things before
Repeating things behind; so faith is strong
Only when we are strong, shrinks when we shrink.
It comes when music stirs us, and the chords
Moving on some grand climax shake our souls   300
With influx new that makes new energies.
It comes in swellings of the heart and tears
That rise at noble and at gentle deeds—
At labors of the master artist's hand
Which, trembling, touches to a finer end,
Trembling before an image seen within.
It comes in moments of heroic love,
Unjealous joy in joy not made for us—
In conscious triumph of the good within
Making us worship goodness that rebukes.   310
Even our failures are a prophecy,
Even our yearnings and our bitter tears
After that fair and true we cannot grasp,
As patriots who seem to die in vain
Make liberty more sacred by their pangs.

Presentiment of better things on earth
Sweeps in with every force that stirs our souls
To admiration, self-renouncing love,
Or thoughts, like light, that bind the world in one:
Sweeps like the sense of vastness, when at night   320
We hear the roll and dash of waves that break
Nearer and nearer with the rushing tide,
Which rises to the level of the cliff
Because the wide Atlantic rolls behind,
Throbbing respondent to the far-off orbs.

1865

In a London Drawingroom

The sky is cloudy, yellowed by the smoke.
For view there are the houses opposite,
Cutting the sky with one long line of wall
Like solid fog: far as the eye can stretch

Monotony of surface and of form
Without a break to hang a guess upon.
No bird can make a shadow as it flies,
For all its shadow, as in ways o'erhung
By thickest canvas, where the golden rays
Are clothed in hemp. No figure lingering   10
Pauses to feed the hunger of the eye
Or rest a little on the lap of life.
All hurry on and look upon the ground
Or glance unmarking at the passersby.
The wheels are hurrying, too, cabs, carriages
All closed, in multiplied identity.
The world seems one huge prison-house and court
Where men are punished at the slightest cost,
With lowest rate of color, warmth, and joy.

                         1865 / 1989

O May I Join the Choir Invisible

Longum illud tempus, quum non ero, magis me movet, quam hoc exiguum.
                              —CICERO, *ad.Att., xii. 18.*

O may I join the choir invisible
Of those immortal dead who live again
In minds made better by their presence: live
In pulses stirred to generosity,
In deeds of daring rectitude, in scorn
For miserable aims that end with self,
In thoughts sublime that pierce the night like stars,
And with their mild persistence urge man's search
To vaster issues.
                         So to live is heaven:
To make undying music in the world,   10
Breathing as beauteous order that controls
With growing sway the growing life of man.
So we inherit that sweet purity
For which we struggled, failed, and agonized
With widening retrospect that bred despair.
Rebellious flesh that would not be subdued,
A vicious parent shaming still its child,
Poor anxious penitence, is quick dissolved;
Its discords, quenched by meeting harmonies,
Die in the large and charitable air.   20

And all our rarer, truer self,
That sobbed religiously in yearning song,
That watched to ease the burden of the world,
Laboriously tracing what must be
And what may yet be better—saw within
A worthier image for the sanctuary
And shaped it forth before the multitude
Divinely human, raising worship so
To higher reverence more mixed with love—
That better self shall live till human time   30
Shall fold its eyelids and the human sky
Be gathered like a scroll within the tomb
Unread for ever.
                    This is life to come,
Which martyred men have made more glorious
For us who strive to follow. May I reach
That purest heaven, be to other souls
The cup of strength in some great agony,
Enkindle generous ardor, feed pure love,
Beget the smiles that have no cruelty—
Be the sweet presence of a good diffused   40
And, in diffusion, ever more intense.
So shall I join the choir invisible,
Whose music is the gladness of the world.

                                        1867 / 1874

From *The Spanish Gypsy*
[*Should I long that dark were fair?*]

Should I long that dark were fair?
Say, O song!
Lacks my love aught, that I should long?

Dark the night, with breath all flowers
And tender broken voice that fills
With ravishment the listening hours:
Whisperings, wooings,
Liquid ripples and soft ring-dove cooings
In low-toned rhythm that love's aching stills.
Dark the night,
Yet is she bright,   10
For in her dark she brings the mystic star,
Trembling yet strong, as is the voice of love,
From some unknown afar.

O radiant dark! O darkly fostered ray!
Thou hast a joy too deep for shallow day.

[*The world is great: the birds all fly from me*]

The world is great: the birds all fly from me;
The stars are golden fruit upon a tree,
All out of reach: my little sister went,
      And I am lonely.

The world is great: I tried to mount the hill
Above the pines, where the light lies so still.
But it rose higher; little Lisa went,
      And I am lonely.

The world is great: the wind comes rushing by—
I wonder where it comes from; seabirds cry   10
And hurt my heart: my little sister went,
      And I am lonely.

The world is great: the people laugh and talk
And make loud holiday—how fast they walk!
I'm lame; they push me: little Lisa went,
      And I am lonely.

Song of the Zíncali

All things journey: sun and moon,
Morning, noon, and afternoon,
    Night and all her stars.
'Twixt the east and western bars
    Round they journey,
      Come and go!
    We go with them!
For to roam and ever roam
Is the Zíncali's loved home.

Earth is good: the hillside breaks   10
By the ashen roots and makes
    Hungry nostrils glad;
Then we run till we are mad
    Like the horses,
      And we cry,
    None shall catch us!
Swift winds wing us—we are free—
Drink the air—Zíncali!

Falls the snow: the pine-branch split,
Call the fire out, see it flit,   20
    Through the dry leaves run,
Spread and glow, and make a sun
    In the dark tent—
        O warm dark!
    Warm as conies!
Strong fire loves us, we are warm!
Who the Zíncali shall harm?

Onward journey: fires are spent;
Sunward, sunward! lift the tent,   30
    Run before the rain,
Through the pass, along the plain.
    Hurry, hurry,
        Lift us, wind!
    Like the horses.
For to roam and ever roam
Is the Zíncali's loved home.

1868

Brother and Sister

I.

I cannot choose but think upon the time
When our two lives grew like two buds that kiss
At lightest thrill from the bee's swinging chime
Because the one so near the other is.

He was the elder and a little man
Of forty inches, bound to show no dread,
And I the girl that puppy-like now ran,
Now lagged behind my brother's larger tread.

I held him wise, and when he talked to me
Of snakes and birds, and which God loved the best,   10
I thought his knowledge marked the boundary
Where men grew blind, though angels knew the rest.

    If he said, "Hush!" I tried to hold my breath
    Wherever he said, "Come!" I stepped in faith.

II.

Long years have left their writing on my brow,
But yet the freshness and the dew-fed beam

Of those young mornings are about me now,
When we two wandered toward the far-off stream

With rod and line. Our basket held a store
Baked for us only, and I thought with joy   20
That I should have my share, though he had more,
Because he was the elder and a boy.

The firmaments of daisies since to me
Have had those mornings in their opening eyes,
The bunchèd cowslip's pale transparency
Carries that sunshine of sweet memories,

    And wild-rose branches take their finest scent
    From those blest hours of infantine content.

III.

Our mother bade us keep the trodden ways,
Stroked down my tippet, set my brother's frill,   30
Then with the benediction of her gaze
Clung to us lessening, and pursued us still

Across the homestead to the rookery elms,
Whose tall old trunks had each a grassy mound,
So rich for us, we counted them as realms
With varied products: here were earth-nuts found,

And here the lady-fingers in deep shade;
Here sloping toward the moat the rushes grew,
The large to split for pith, the small to braid;
While over all the dark rooks cawing flew,   40

    And made a happy strange solemnity,
    A deep-toned chant from life unknown to me.

IV.

Our meadow path had memorable spots:
One where it bridged a tiny rivulet,
Deep hid by tangled blue forget-me-nots;
And all along the waving grasses met

My little palm or nodded to my cheek,
When flowers with upturned faces gazing drew
My wonder downward, seeming all to speak
With eyes of souls that dumbly heard and knew.   50

Then came the copse, where wild things rushed
    unseen,
And black-scathed grass betrayed the past abode

Of mystic gypsies, who still lurked between
Me and each hidden distance of the road.

A gypsy once had startled me at play,
Blotting with her dark smile my sunny day.

V.

Thus rambling we were schooled in deepest lore,
And learned the meanings that give words a soul,
The fear, the love, the primal passionate store,
Whose shaping impulses make manhood whole.   60

Those hours were seed to all my after good;
My infant gladness, through eye, ear, and touch,
Took easily as warmth a various food
To nourish the sweet skill of loving much.

For who in age shall roam the earth and find
Reasons for loving that will strike out love
With sudden rod from the hard year-pressed mind?
Were reasons sown as thick as stars above,

'Tis love must see them, as the eye sees light:
Day is but number to the darkened sight.   70

VI.

Our brown canal was endless to my thought;
And on its banks I sat in dreamy peace,
Unknowing how the good I loved was wrought,
Untroubled by the fear that it would cease.

Slowly the barges floated into view,
Rounding a grassy hill to me sublime
With some unknown beyond it, whither flew
The parting cuckoo toward a fresh springtime.

The wide-arched bridge, the scented elder flowers,
The wondrous watery rings that died too soon;   80
The echoes of the quarry, the still hours
With white robe sweeping-on the shadeless noon,

Were but my growing self, are part of me,
My present past, my root of piety.

VII.

Those long days measured by my little feet
Had chronicles which yield me many a text;

Where irony still finds an image meet
Of full-grown judgments in this world perplexed.

One day my brother left me in high charge,
To mind the rod while he went seeking bait,   90
And bade me, when I saw a nearing barge,
Snatch out the line, lest he should come too late.

Proud of the task, I watched with all my might
For one whole minute, till my eyes grew wide,
Till sky and earth took on a strange new light
And seemed a dreamworld floating on some tide—

  A fair pavilioned boat for me alone,
  Bearing me onward through the vast unknown.

VIII.

But sudden came the barge's pitch-black prow,
Nearer and angrier came my brother's cry,   100
And all my soul was quivering fear, when lo!
Upon the imperiled line, suspended high,

A silver perch! My guilt that won the prey
Now turned to merit, had a guerdon rich
Of hugs and praises, and made merry play,
Until my triumph reached its highest pitch

When all at home were told the wondrous feat,
And how the little sister had fished well.
In secret, though my fortune tasted sweet,
I wondered why this happiness befell.   110

  "The little lass had luck," the gardener said:
  And so I learned, luck was with glory wed.

IX.

We had the selfsame world enlarged for each
By loving difference of girl and boy:
The fruit that hung on high beyond my reach
He plucked for me, and oft he must employ

A measuring glance to guide my tiny shoe
Where lay firm stepping-stones, or call to mind
"This thing I like my sister may not do,
For she is little, and I must be kind."   120

Thus boyish will the nobler mastery learned
Where inward vision over impulse reigns,

Widening its life with separate life discerned,
A like unlike, a self that self restrains.

His years with others must the sweeter be
For those brief days he spent in loving me.

X.

His sorrow was my sorrow, and his joy
Sent little leaps and laughs through all my frame;
My doll seemed lifeless, and no girlish toy
Had any reason when my brother came.   130

I knelt with him at marbles, marked his fling
Cut the ringed stem and make the apple drop,
Or watched him winding close the spiral string
That looped the orbits of the humming top.

Grasped by such fellowship my vagrant thought
Ceased with dream-fruit dream-wishes to fulfil;
My aerie-picturing fantasy was taught
Subjection to the harder, truer skill

That seeks with deeds to grave a thought-tracked line,
And by "what is," "what will be" to define.   140

XI.

School parted us; we never found again
That childish world where our two spirits mingled
Like scents from varying roses that remain
One sweetness nor can evermore be singled.

Yet the twin habit of that early time
Lingered for long about the heart and tongue:
We had been natives of one happy clime,
And its dear accent to our utterance clung.

Till the dire years whose awful name is Change
Had grasped our souls still yearning in divorce,   150
And pitiless shaped them in two forms that range
Two elements which sever their life's course.

But were another childhood world my share,
I would be born a little sister there.

1869 / 1874

Erinna

"Erinna died in early youth when chained by her mother to the spinning-wheel. She had as yet known the charm of existence in imagination alone. Her poem called 'The Spindle'—Ἠλακάτη—containing only 300 hexameter verses, in which she probably expressed the restless and aspiring thoughts which crowded on her youthful mind as she pursued her monotonous work, has been deemed by many of the ancients of such high poetic merit as to entitle it to a place beside the epics of Homer." (Müller, History of Greek Literature) Four lines of the Ἠλακάτη are extant. The dialect is a mixture of Doric and Æolic spoken at Rhodes, where Erinna was born; the date about B.C. 612:

Τούτω κὴς Ἀΐδαν κενεα διανήχεται ἀχω.
σιγᾶ δ' ἐν νεκύεσσι τὸ δὲ σκότος ὕσσε κατέρρει.
—*Stob. Flor. cxviii,4*

πομπίλε, ναύταισιν πέμπων πλόον εὔπλοον ἰχθύ
πομπεύσαις πρύμναθεν ἐμάν ἀδεῖαν ἕταιραν.
—*Athanaeus, vii. 283*

1.

'Twas in the isle that Helios saw
Uprising from the sea a flower-tressed bride
To meet his kisses—Rhodes, the filial pride
    Of god-taught craftsmen who gave art its law:
    She held the spindle as she sat,
    Erinna with the thick-coiled mat
    Of raven hair and deepest agate eyes,
    Gazing with a sad surprise
    At surging visions of her destiny
    To spin the byssus drearily   10
    In insect labor, while the throng
Of gods and men wrought deeds that poets wrought in song

2.

    Visions of ocean-wreathed Earth
Shone through with light of epic rhapsody
Where Zeus looked with Olympus and the sea
    Smiled back with Aphrodite's birth;
    Where heroes sailed on daring quests
    In ships that knew and loved their guests;
    Where the deep-bosomed matron and sweet maid
    Died for others unafraid;   20
    Where Pindus echoed to the Ionian shore
    Songs fed with action and the lore

Of primal work, where Themis saw
Brute fear beneath her rod ennobled into awe.

3.

Hark, the passion in her eyes
Changes to melodic cries
Lone she pours her lonely pain.
Song unheard is not in vain:
The god within us plies
His shaping power and molds in speech   30
Harmonious a statue of our sorrow,
Till suffering turn beholding and we borrow,
Gazing on self apart, the wider reach
Of solemn souls that contemplate
And slay with full-beamed thought the darling dragon Hate.

4.

"Great Cybele, whose ear doth love
The piercing flute, why is my maiden wail
Like hers, the loved twice lost, whose dear hands pale
Yearning, severed seemed to move
Thin phantoms on the night-black air?   40
But thou art deaf to human care:
Thy breasts impartial cherish with their food
Strength alike of ill and good.
The dragon and the hero, friend and foe,
Who makes the city's weal, and who its woe,
All draw their strength from thee; and what I draw
Is rage divine in limbs fast bound by narrow law.

5.

But Pallas, thou dost choose and bless
The nobler cause, thy maiden height
And terrible beauty marshaling the fight   50
Inspire weak limbs with steadfastness.
Thy virgin breast uplifts
The direful aegis, but thy hand
Wielded its weapon with benign command
In rivalry of highest gifts
With strong Poseidon whose earth-shaking roll
Matched not the delicate tremors of thy spear,
Piercing Athenian land and drawing thence
With conquering beneficence
Thy subtly chosen dole,   60

The sacred olive fraught with light and plenteous cheer.
What, though thou pliest the distaff and the loom?
    Counsel is thine, to sway the doubtful doom
    Of cities with a leaguer at their gate;
    Thine the device that snares the hulk elate
Of purblind force and saves the hero or the state."

*c.*1875 / 1989

JEAN INGELOW

pseud., Orris (1820–1897)

༚᨞༚

Ingelow was educated by governesses in the comfortable if strictly Evangelical environ-ment of a banker's family, where the children produced their own periodical. At fourteen she was given a room to herself and began to write poetry on the inside of its shutters. A friend of the Taylors, she sent poems to Youth's Magazine *under a pseudonym, and her stories for children,* Tales of Orris *(1860),* Studies for Stories *(1864),* Stories Told to a Child *(1865), and above all* Mopsa the Fairy *(1869), continue to be ad-mired. Of her novels Walter de la Mare observed that they were "oddly unreal, mean-dering, but with occasional glints of penetrating imagination"; these included* Off the Skelligs *(1872) and its sequel,* Fated to be Free *(1875).*

Her poetry for adults bears the imprint of friendships with Tennyson, Browning, Christina Rossetti, and Dora Greenwell, who considered her poetry "exquisite." She strove for refinement and pathos; poetry, she thought, "is sweetest when it keeps clear of ladies and gentlemen." Rossetti believed Ingelow "would be a formidable rival to most men, and to any woman." A Rhyming Chronicle of Incidents and Feelings *(1850) was followed by three volumes of* Poems *(1863, 1880, 1885), which went through many editions in both England and America, where over two hundred thousand copies were sold; by 1875 she had earned £1,308. With her earnings she undertook charities, including weekly "copyright dinners" served to the convalescent poor. Her best-known ballad was "The High Tide on the Coast of Lincolnshire, 1571"; Vita Sackville-West, however, thought "Divided" her "one really excellent poem."*

Divided

I.

An empty sky, a world of heather,
  Purple of foxglove, yellow of broom;
We two among them wading together,
  Shaking out honey, treading perfume.

Crowds of bees are giddy with clover,
 Crowds of grasshoppers skip at our feet,
Crowds of larks at their matins hang over,
 Thanking the Lord for a life so sweet.

Flusheth the rise with her purple favor,
 Gloweth the cleft with her golden ring,
'Twixt the two, brown butterflies waver,
 Lightly settle, and sleepily swing.

We two walk till the purple dieth
 And short dry grass under foot is brown,
But one little streak at a distance lieth,
 Green like a ribbon to prank the down.

II.

Over the grass we stepped unto it,
 And God, He knoweth how blithe we were!
Never a voice to bid us eschew it—
 Hey the green ribbon that showed so fair!

Hey the green ribbon! we kneeled beside it,
 We parted the grasses dewy and sheen;
Drop over drop, there filtered and slided
 A tiny bright beck that trickled between.

Tinkle, tinkle, sweetly it sung to us,
 Light was our talk as of fairy bells—
Fairy wedding bells faintly rung to us
 Down in their fortunate parallels.

Hand in hand, while the sun peered over,
 We lapped the grass on that youngling spring:
Swept back its rushes, smoothed its clover,
 And said, "Let us follow it westering."

III.

A dapple sky, a world of meadows,
 Circling above us the black rooks fly
Forward, backward; lo, their dark shadows
 Flit on the blossoming tapestry—

Flit on the beck, for her long grass parteth
 As hair from a maid's bright eyes blown back;
And lo, the sun like a lover darteth
 His flattering smile on her wayward track.

10

20

30

40

Sing on! we sing in the glorious weather,
   Till one steps over the tiny strand,
So narrow, in sooth, that still together
   On either brink we go hand in hand.

The beck grows wider; the hands must sever.
   On either margin, our songs all done,
We move apart while she singeth ever,
   Taking the course of the stooping sun.

He prays, "Come over"—I may not follow;
   I cry, "Return"—but he cannot come: 50
We speak, we laugh, but with voices hollow;
   Our hands are hanging, our hearts are numb.

IV.

A breathing sigh, a sigh for answer,
   A little talking of outward things:
The careless beck is a merry dancer,
   Keeping sweet time to the air she sings.

A little pain when the beck grows wider;
   "Cross to me now—for her wavelets swell."
"I may not cross"—and the voice beside her
   Faintly reacheth, though heeded well.   60

No backward path; ah! no returning;
   No second crossing that ripple's flow:
"Come to me now, for the west is burning;
   Come ere it darkens"—"Ah, no! ah, no!"

Then cries of pain, and arms outreaching—
   The beck grows wider and swift and deep:
Passionate words as of one beseeching—
   The loud beck drowns them; we walk and weep.

V.

A yellow moon in splendor drooping,
   A tired queen with her state oppressed,   70
Low by rushes and swordgrass stooping,
   Lies she soft on the waves at rest.

The desert heavens have felt her sadness;
   Her earth will weep her some dewy tears;
The wild beck ends her tune of gladness
   And goeth stilly, as soul that fears.

We two walk on in our grassy places
    On either marge of the moonlit flood,
With the moon's own sadness in our faces,
    Where joy is withered, blossom and bud.   80

VI.

A shady freshness, chafers whirring,
    A little piping of leaf-hid birds;
A flutter of wings, a fitful stirring,
    A cloud to the eastward snowy as curds.

Bare glassy slopes, where kids are tethered;
    Round valleys like nests all ferny-lined;
Round hills, with fluttering treetops feathered,
    Swell high in their freckled robes behind.

A rose-flush tender, a thrill, a quiver,
    When golden gleams to the treetops glide;   90
A flashing edge for the milk-white river,
    The beck, a river—with still sleek tide.

Broad and white, and polished as silver,
    On she goes under fruit-laden trees;
Sunk in leafage cooeth the culver,
    And 'plaineth of love's disloyalties.

Glitters the dew and shines the river,
    Up comes the lily and dries her bell;
But two are walking apart forever
    And wave their hands for a mute farewell.   100

VII.

A braver swell, a swifter sliding;
    The river hasteth, her banks recede:
Wing-like sails on her bosom gliding
    Bear down the lily and drown the reed.

Stately prows are rising and bowing
    (Shouts of mariners winnow the air),
And level sands for banks endowing
    The tiny green ribbon that showed so fair.

While, O my heart! as white sails shiver,
    And crowds are passing, and banks stretch wide,   110
How hard to follow, with lips that quiver,
    That moving speck on the far-off side!

.Farther, farther—I see it—know it—
My eyes brim over, it melts away:
Only my heart to my heart shall show it
    As I walk desolate day by day.

VIII.

And yet I know past all doubting, truly—
    And knowledge greater than grief can dim—
I know, as he loved, he will love me duly—
    Yea, better—e'en better than I love him.   120

And as I walk by the vast calm river,
    The awful river so dread to see,
I say, "Thy breadth and thy depth forever
    Are bridged by his thoughts that cross to me."

1863

The High Tide on the Coast of Lincolnshire, 1571

The old mayor climbed the belfry tower,
    The ringers ran by two, by three;
"Pull, if ye never pulled before;
    Good ringers, pull your best," quoth he.
"Play uppe, play uppe, O Boston bells!
Ply all your changes, all your swells,
    Play uppe 'The Brides of Enderby.'."

Men say it was a stolen tyde—
    The Lord that sent it, He knows all;
But in myne ears doth still abide   10
    The message that the bells let fall:
And there was naught of strange, beside
The flight of mews and peewits pied
    By millions crouched on the old sea wall.

I sat and spun within the doore,
    My thread break off, I raised myne eyes;
The level sun, like ruddy ore,
    Lay sinking in the barren skies;
And dark against day's golden death
She moved where Lindis wandereth,   20
    My sonne's faire wife, Elizabeth.

"Cusha! Cusha! Cusha!" calling,
Ere the early dews were falling,
Farre away I heard her song,

"Cusha! Cusha!" all along;
Where the reedy Lindis floweth,
    Floweth, floweth,
From the meads where melick groweth
Faintly came her milking song—

"Cusha! Cusha! Cusha!" calling,   30
"For the dews will soone be falling;
Leave your meadow grasses mellow,
    Mellow, mellow;
Quit your cowslips, cowslips yellow;
Come uppe, Whitefoot, come uppe, Lightfoot;
Quit the stalks of parsley hollow,
    Hollow, hollow;
Come uppe, Jetty, rise and follow,
From the clovers lift your head;
Come uppe, Whitefoot, come uppe, Lightfoot,   40
Come uppe, Jetty, rise and follow,
Jetty to the milking shed."

If it be long, aye, long ago,
    When I beginne to think howe long,
Againe I hear the Lindis flow,
    Swift as an arrowe, sharpe and strong;
And all the aire, it seemeth mee,
Bin full of floating bells (sayth shee),
That ring the tune of Enderby.

Alle fresh the level pasture lay,   50
    And not a shadowe mote be seene
Save where, full fyve good miles away,
    The steeple towered from out the greene;
And lo! the great bell farre and wide
Was heard in all the countryside
That Saturday at eventide.

The swanherds, where their sedges are,
    Moved on in sunset's golden breath,
The shepherde lads I heard afarre,
    And my sonne's wife, Elizabeth;   60
Till floating o'er the grassy sea
Came downe that kyndly message free,
"The Brides of Mavis Enderby."

Then some looked uppe into the sky,
    And all along where Lindis flows,
To where the goodly vessels lie
    And where the lordly steeple shows.

They sayde, "And why should this thing be?
What danger lowers by land or sea?
They ring the tune of Enderby!   70

"For evil news from Mablethorpe,
  Of pyrate galleys warping down;
For shippes ashore beyond the scorpe,
  They have not spared to wake the towne;
But while the west bin red to see,
And storms be none, and pyrates flee,
Why ring 'The Brides of Enderby'?"

I looked without, and lo! my sonne
  Came riding downe with might and main:
He raised a shout as he drew on,   80
  Till all the welkin rang again,
"Elizabeth! Elizabeth!
(A sweeter woman ne'er drew breath
Than my sonne's wife, Elizabeth.)

"The olde sea wall," he cried, "is downe,
  The rising tide comes on apace,
And boats adrift in yonder towne
  Go sailing uppe the marketplace."
He shook as one that looks on death:
"God save you, mother!" straight he saith;   90
"Where is my wife, Elizabeth?"

"Good sonne, where Lindis winds her way,
  With her two bairns I marked her long;
And ere young bells beganne to play,
  Afar I heard her milking song."
He looked across the grassy lea,
To right, to left, "Ho, Enderby!"
They rang "The Brides of Enderby"!

With that he cried and beat his breast;
For lo! along the river's bed   100
A mighty eygre reared his crest
  And uppe the Lindis raging sped.
It swept with thunderous noises loud;
Shaped like a curling snow-white cloud,
Or like a demon in a shroud.

And rearing Lindis, backward pressed,
  Shook all her trembling bankes amaine;
Then madly at the eygre's breast
  Flung uppe her weltering walls again.
Then bankes came downe with ruin and rout—   110

Then beaten foam flew round about—
Then all the mighty floods were out.

So farre, so fast the eygre drave,
 The heart had hardly time to beat
Before a shallow seething wave
 Sobbed in the grasses at oure feet:
The feet had hardly time to flee
Before it brake against the knee
And all the world was in the sea.

Upon the roofe we sate that night,   120
 The noise of bells went sweeping by;
I marked the lofty beacon light
 Stream from the church tower, red and high—
A lurid mark and dread to see;
And awesome bells they were to mee,
That in the dark rang "Enderby."

They rang the sailor lads to guide
 From roofe to roofe who fearless rowed;
And I—my sonne was at my side,
 And yet the ruddy beacon glowed;   130
And yet he moaned beneath his breath,
"O come in life, or come in death!
O lost! my love, Elizabeth."

And didst thou visit him no more?
 Thou didst, thou didst, my daughter deare;
The waters laid thee at his doore
 Ere yet the early dawn was clear.
The pretty bairns in fast embrace,
The lifted sun shone on thy face,
Downe drifted to thy dwelling place.   140

That flow strewed wrecks about the grass,
 That ebbe swept out the flocks to sea;
A fatal ebbe and flow, alas!
 To manye more than myne and mee:
But each will mourn his own (she saith);
And sweeter woman ne'er drew breath
Than my sonne's wife, Elizabeth.

I shall never hear her more
By the reedy Lindis shore,
"Cusha! Cusha! Cusha!" calling,   150
Ere the early dews be falling;
I shall never hear her song,
"Cusha! Cusha!" all along

Where the sunny Lindis floweth,
 Goeth, floweth;
From the meads where melick groweth,
When the water, winding down,
Onward floweth to the town.

I shall never see her more
Where the reeds and rushes quiver,
 Shiver, quiver;   160
Stand beside the sobbing river,
Sobbing, throbbing, in its falling
To the sandy lonesome shore;
I shall never hear her calling,
"Leave your meadow grasses mellow,
 Mellow, mellow;
Quit your cowslips, cowslips yellow;
Come uppe, Whitefoot, come uppe, Lightfoot;
Quit your pipes of parsley hollow,   170
 Hollow, hollow;
Come uppe, Lightfoot, rise and follow;
 Lightfoot, Whitefoot,
From your clovers lift the head:
Come uppe, Jetty, follow, follow,
Jetty, to the milking shed."

          1863

Work

Like coral insects multitudinous,
 The minutes are whereof our life is made.
 They build it up, as in the deep's blue shade
It grows, it comes to light, and then and thus
For both there is an end. The populous
 Sea-blossoms close, our minutes that have paid
 Life's debt of work are spent; the work is laid
Before our feet that shall come after us.
We may not stay to watch if it will speed:
 The bard if on some luter's string his song   10
Live sweetly yet; the hero if his star
Doth shine. Work is its own best earthly meed,
 Else have we none more than the sea-born throng
Who wrought those marvelous isles that bloom afar.

          1871

ANNE BRONTË

pseud., Acton Bell (1820–1849)

The Brontë family was literary: Anne's clergyman father dabbled in poetry and collected sermons, her mother wrote essays, and the six children read avidly, ranging from Aesop and the Arabian Nights *to Scott and Byron. After the early death of their mother from cancer, they were raised by a strict Methodist aunt. Unlike her older sisters, Anne was educated primarily at home in Haworth, Yorkshire. Her unwavering religious and moral didacticism has been attributed to her mentors' potent and nearly exclusive influence.*

Anne began writing poetry as a child in a group project with her sisters and brother. In collaboration with Emily, she created a sequence of poems depicting the fantasy kingdom of Gondal. Both contributed to the only volume of poetry published by the Brontë sisters in their lifetimes, Poems of Currer, Ellis, and Acton Bell *(1846). The text as a whole was heralded in the 1846* Critic *as "a ray of sunshine . . . good, wholesome, refreshing, vigorous poetry." Critical response to the portion by "Acton Bell" was generally negative, however. A review in* The Athenaeum *proclaimed that "indulgences of affection" alone would render Anne's poetry "music"—ironically, since a number of her poems were transcribed in songbooks, to hymn meters. Though Anne is usually disparaged as the least gifted of the sisters, her poetic contributions and the novels,* Agnes Grey *(1847), which describes the life of a governess, and* The Tenant of Wildfell Hall *(1848), which draws on Branwell's dissolute collapse, are currently being reassessed. Her reputation in the past was largely shaped by Charlotte's condescending portrait of her as a "nun-like" governess who "wanted the power, the fire, the originality" of Emily, but recent critics have admired her realistic prose and have found, as Augustine Birrell did in 1887, that "her verses have a tender pathos of their own."*

Lines Composed in a Wood on a Windy Day

My soul is awakened, my spirit is soaring
    And carried aloft on the wings of the breeze;

For above and around me the wild wind is roaring,
   Arousing to rapture the earth and the seas.

The long withered grass in the sunshine is glancing,
   The bare trees are tossing their branches on high,
The dead leaves beneath them are merrily dancing,
   The white clouds are scudding across the blue sky.

I wish I could see how the ocean is lashing
   The foam of its billows to whirlwinds of spray;   10
I wish I could see how its proud waves are dashing,
   And hear the wild roar of their thunder today!

1842 / 1846

A Prayer

My God, Oh let me call Thee mine!
   Weak, wretched sinner though I be,
My trembling soul would fain be Thine;
   My feeble faith still clings to Thee.

Not only for the past I grieve,
   The future fills me with dismay;
Unless Thou hasten to relieve,
   I know my heart will fall away.

I cannot say my faith is strong,
   I dare not hope my love is great;   10
But strength and love to Thee belong:
   Oh, do not leave me desolate!

I know I owe my all to Thee.
   Oh, take this heart I cannot give;
Do Thou my Strength, my Savior be,
   And make me to Thy glory live!

1844 / 1850

Last Lines

A dreadful darkness closes in
   On my bewildered mind;
O let me suffer and not sin,
   Be tortured yet resigned.

Through all this world of blinding mist
   Still let me look to thee,

And give me courage to resist
    The Tempter till he flee.

Weary I am—O give me strength,
    And leave me not to faint.   10
Say thou wilt comfort me at length
    And pity my complaint.

I've begged to serve thee heart and soul,
    To sacrifice to thee
No niggard portion, but the whole
    Of my identity.

I hoped amid the brave and strong
    My portioned task might lie,
To toil amid the laboring throng
    With purpose keen and high;   20

But thou hast fixed another part,
    And thou hast fixed it well;
I said so with my breaking heart
    When first the anguish fell.

For thou hast taken my delight
    And hope of life away
And bid me watch the painful night
    And wait the weary day.

The hope and the delight were thine:
    I bless thee for their loan;   30
I gave thee, while I deemed them mine,
    Too little thanks, I own.

Shall I with joy thy blessings share
    And not endure their loss?
Or hope the martyr's crown to wear
    And cast away the cross?

These weary hours will not be lost,
    These days of passive misery,
These nights of darkness, anguish-tossed,
    If I can fix my heart on thee.   40

Weak and weary though I lie,
    Crushed with sorrow, worn with pain,
I may lift to heaven mine eye
    And strive and labor not in vain:

That inward strife against the sins
    That ever wait on suffering

To watch and strike where first begins
  Each ill that would corruption bring;

That secret labor to sustain
  With humble patience every blow;   50
To gather fortitude from pain
  And hope and holiness from woe.

Thus let me serve thee from my heart,
  Whatever be my written fate,
Whether thus early to depart
  Or yet a while to wait.

If Thou shouldst bring me back to life,
  More humbled I should be,
More wise, more strengthened for the strife,
  More apt to lean on thee.   60

Should Death be standing at the gate,
  Thus should I keep my vow;
But Lord, whate'er my future fate,
  So let me serve thee now.

1849 / 1850

DORA GREENWELL

(1821–1882)

Daughter of a magistrate, Greenwell was first educated by governesses, then taught herself Latin and modern languages. She taught and did parish work with her brother, a minister in Lancashire, then moved in 1854 with her mother to Durham, where she worked among paupers. In 1871, after her mother's death, she moved to London. An invalid for many years, she nonetheless made philanthropic visits to prisons and asylums.

A friend of the feminist Josephine Butler, Greenwell supported women's suffrage and education; her essay on "Our Single Women" portrayed women who long to profit from their gifts, "better content to plant potatoes in any yet discovered bush" than to pass a comfortable life "fenced in with a thousand unmeaning restrictions." Her interest in philosophy and economics led her to write on juvenile delinquency and the mentally disabled; she also devoted poems to Italian nationalism, the Lancashire cotton famine, the East African slave trade, and the American Civil War.

Even more important for the body of her work was her quietist and mystical form of Anglicanism, which tightened her links to the poets Christina Rossetti and Jean Ingelow. During the eighteen years she spent in Durham, she produced a volume of spiritual reflections, The Patience of Hope *(1860), dedicated to Butler, which was introduced in the United States by Whittier; she also wrote biographies of the Dominican monk Lacordaire (1867) and the Quaker John Woolman (1871). Her* Poems *(1848) and* Stories That Might be True, with Other Poems *(1850) convey her love of Tennyson and Browning. Her later volumes of poetry were* Carmina Crucis *(1869),* Songs of Salvation *(1873),* The Soul's Legend *(1873), and* Camera Obscura *(1876).*

To Elizabeth Barrett Browning in 1851

I lose myself within thy mind—from room
   To goodly room thou leadest me, and still
   Dost show me of thy glory more, until

My soul, like Sheba's Queen, faints, overcome,
And all my spirit dies within me, numb,
   Sucked in by thine, a larger star, at will;
   And hasting like thy bee, my hive to fill,
I "swoon for very joy" amid thy bloom;
Till—not like that poor bird (as poets feign)
   That tried against the lutenist's her skill,   10
   Crowding her thick precipitate notes, until
Her weak heart break above the contest vain—
   Did not thy strength a nobler thought instill,
I feel as if I ne'er could sing again!

1851 / 1861

To Elizabeth Barrett Browning in 1861

I praised thee not while living; what to thee
   Was praise of mine? I mourned thee not when dead;
   I only loved thee—love thee! oh thou fled
Fair spirit, free at last where all are free,
I only love thee, bless thee, that to me
   Forever thou hast made the rose more red,
   More sweet each word by olden singers said
In sadness or by children in their glee;
   Once, only once in life I heard thee speak,
   Once, only once I kissed thee on the cheek,   10
And met thy kiss and blessing; scarce I knew
Thy smile, I only loved thee, only grew,
   Through wealth, through strength of thine, less poor, less weak;
   Oh, what hath death with souls like thine to do?

1861

Old Letters: II

Oft have I bent my gaze
Adown our life's steep edge with eyeballs dim
   And thirsting soul, aweary of the day's
Hot parching dust and glare; this well is deep,
   Too seldom rise the waters to its brim,
And I had nought to draw with! oft in sleep
I felt them touch my very lips, and flow
All o'er my forehead and my hands, but lo,
I waked and thirsted; looking down, I knew
Each pebble lying at the base, that drew   10
   A glimmer from the sunbeam; round the rim

I knew each flower, each forkèd fern that through
The stone did thrust its tongue, each moss that grew
Far down its cool and slippery sides—I knew
All but the water's freshness.

                              Now I yearn
No more in vain, no longer need I stoop
    So wistful o'er the well, for like an urn
Is thy pure soul to me, wherein I scoop
    The waters as I list, and still return.

                                        1861

A Scherzo
(A Shy Person's Wishes)

With the wasp at the innermost heart of a peach,
On a sunny wall out of tiptoe reach,
With the trout in the darkest summer pool,
With the fern seed clinging behind its cool
Smooth frond, in the chink of an aged tree,
In the woodbine's horn with the drunken bee,
With the mouse in its nest in a furrow old,
With the chrysalis wrapped in its gauzy fold;
With things that are hidden, and safe, and bold,
With things that are timid, and shy, and free,   10
Wishing to be;
With the nut in its shell, with the seed in its pod,
With the corn as it sprouts in the kindly clod,
Far down where the secret of beauty shows
In the bulb of the tulip, before it blows;
With things that are rooted, and firm, and deep,
Quiet to lie, and dreamless to sleep;
With things that are chainless, and tameless, and proud,
With the fire in the jagged thundercloud,
With the wind in its sleep, with the wind in its waking,
With the drops that go to the rainbow's making,   20
Wishing to be with the light leaves shaking,
Or stones on some desolate highway breaking;
Far up on the hills, where no foot surprises
The dew as it falls or the dust as it rises;
To be couched with the beast in its torrid lair
Or drifting on ice with the polar bear,
With the weaver at work at his quiet loom;
Anywhere, anywhere, out of this room!

                                        1867

The Sunflower

Till the slow daylight pale,
  A willing slave, fast bound to one above,
I wait; he seems to speed, and change, and fail;
  I know he will not move.

I lift my golden orb
  To his, unsmitten when the roses die,
And in my broad and burning disk absorb
  The splendors of his eye.

His eye is like a clear
  Keen flame that searches through me: I must droop   10
Upon my stalk, I cannot reach his sphere;
  To mine he cannot stoop.

I win not my desire,
  And yet I fail not of my guerdon; lo!
A thousand flickering darts and tongues of fire
  Around me spread and glow.

All rayed and crowned, I miss
  No queenly state until the summer wane,
The hours flit by; none knoweth of my bliss,
  And none has guessed my pain.   20

I follow one above,
  I track the shadow of his steps, I grow
Most like to him I love
  Of all that shines below.

1875

To Christina Rossetti

Thou hast filled me a golden cup
With a drink divine that glows,
With the bloom that is shining up
From the heart of the folded rose.
The grapes in their amber glow
And the strength of the blood-red wine
All mingle and change and flow
In this golden cup of thine,
With the scent of the curling vine,
With the balm of the rose's breath—   10
For the voice of love is thine,
And thine is the song of death!

1875 / 1885

Demeter and Cora

"Speak, daughter, speak; art speaking now?"
"Seek, mother, seek; art seeking thou
Thy dear-loved Cora?" "Daughter sweet,
I bend unto the earth my ear
To catch the sound of coming feet;
I listen long, but only hear
The deep dark waters running clear."
"Oh! my great mother, now the heat
Of thy strong heart in thickened beat
Hath reached thy Cora in her gloom,   10
Is it well with thee, my mother—tell?"
"Is it well with thee, my daughter?" "Well
Or ill I know not; I, through fate,
Queen of a wide unmeasured tomb,
Know not if it be love or hate
That holds me fast, but I am bound
Forever! What if I am found
Of thee, my mother; still the bars
Are round me, and the girdling night
Hath passed within my soul! the stars   20
Have risen[1] on me, but the light
Hath gone forever." "Daughter, tell,
Doth thy dark lord, the King of Hell,
Still love thee?" "Oh, too well, too well
He loves! he binds with unwrought chain.
I was not born to be thy mate,
Aïdes! nor the Queen of pain:
I was thy daughter Cora, vowed
To gladness in thy world above;
I loved the daffodil, I love   30
All lovely, free, and gentle things
Beloved of thee! a sound of wings
Is with me in captivity
Of birds, and bees, with her that sings,
The shrill Cicula, ever gay
In noon's white heat." "But, daughter, say
Dost love Aïdes?" "Now too bold
Thy question, mother; this be told,
I leave him not for love, for gold;
One lot we share, one life we know.   40
The lord is he of wealth and rest,

1. "When night has once passed into a human soul it never leaves it, though the stars may rise."—Victor Hugo

As well as king of death and pain;
He folds me to a kingly breast,
He yields to me a rich domain.
I leave him not for aught above,
For any God's unsteadfast love
Or fairest mortal form below;
Thou hast left heaven for earth; and thou
For thy poor Cora's sake, self-driven,
Hast fled its sunny heights in scorn   50
And hate, of Zeus unforgiven!
Do mortals love thee?" "Daughter, yea.
They call me their great mother. Corn
And wine I give them when they pray;
Their love for me their little day
Of life lasts out; perchance they knew
It was not love for them that drew
Me down to wander where the vine
Is sweet to me, and breath of kine.
Art listening now, my Cora dear?   60
Art listening now, my child—art near?
Oh, that thy kiss upon my cheek
Were warm! thy little hand in mine
Once more! Yet, let me hear thee speak,
And tell me of that garden rare,
And of thy flowers, dark, fiery, sweet,
That never breathe the upper air."
"Oh, mother, they are fair, are fair;
Large-leaved are they, large-blossomed, frail,
And beautiful. No vexing gale   70
Comes ever nigh them; fed with fire
They kindle in a torchlike flame
Half ecstasy, half tender shame
Of bloom that must so soon expire.
But, mother, tell me of the wet
Cool primrose! of the lilac bough
And its warm gust of rapture, met
In summer days!—art listening yet?"
"Art near me, O my Cora, now?"

1876

The Homeward Lane

Sehst du sehr geblässlich aus?
Seyst getrost! du bist zu Haus.
—HEINE

My soul within me yearned
For home; not yet appeared
The father's house in sight:
I saw no kindled light
In gleaming windowpane,
No forms arrayed in white
Came forth, yet was I cheered
At heart: I knew I neared
My home, and kept aright
The way.

    My footsteps turned   10
Adown a well-known lane,
Lone, quiet; on each side
A grassy margin wide,
And hedgerows freshened to the deepened stain
Left by warm summer rain.
O'er all a sparkle wet;
An odor dank and cool
From balsam poplars set
Within the hedge, and yet
A sunset flash from many a tiny pool.   20

Then saw I on a gate
Two men in garments plain,
That leaned, as in the summer evenings late
Men lean; of common things
And themes, to dwellers in the country dear,
If husbandman or kings,
They spake, nor ceased their talk as I drew near;
But with a quiet smile
One open held the gate;
The other spake, "For thee, I said, long while   30
Here would I stand and wait."[1]

But when I would have turned within, I saw
A sandy heath forlorn
That stretched, whereon an aged woman, bent
With care and toil outworn,

---

1. In allusion to Psalms 84:10—a favorite one with an aged relation, expressive of contentment in the prospect of being a mere "doorkeeper in the house of God."

Stooped down to pluck a small white rose[2] that grew
As if it lived but with its leaves to strew
The thin light soil, nor seemed, sun-fed, the dew
To need, beset with many a grieving thorn;
But when she, turning, lifted up her head,   40
I looked upon the face
Of one long loved by me and with the dead
Long numbered; there no trace
Of age or pain I read,
But in her deep-set eye
Dwelt untold ecstasy,
And in her smile was bliss,
And rapture in her kiss,
And heaven in her embrace.

1876

Home

Two birds within one nest;
Two hearts within one breast;
    Two spirits in one fair,
    Firm league of love and prayer,
Together bound for aye, together blest.

An ear that waits to catch
A hand upon the latch;
A step that hastens its sweet rest to win;
    A world of care without,
    A world of strife shut out,
A world of love shut in.

1876

2. *Rosa spinossima*, the small white Burnet rose.

CHRISTINA GEORGINA ROSSETTI

pseud., Ellen Alleyne (1830–1894)

The youngest child of an Italian political refugee, a professor of Italian at Kings' College, and niece of the novelist Dr. John William Polidori, Rossetti grew up in a circle of poets and artists interested in politics and passionate about poetry, especially Dante. At about fifteen she suffered a nervous breakdown, but published a volume called Verses *two years later in 1847. In 1848 her brothers formed the Pre-Raphaelite Brotherhood, from which as a woman she was barred, but to whose journal* The Germ *she was allowed to contribute. Her brother William Michael Rossetti called her the "Queen of the Pre-Raphaelites." For a few years she and her mother taught literature and for thirty years she earned between £10 and £40 a year from her writing. Her older sister, Maria, became an Anglican nun.*

Rossetti was increasingly reclusive: Graves' disease disfigured her face from 1871, and in the nineties she contracted cancer. Yet her morbidity was balanced by exquisite playfulness. To her older brother she mockingly complained, "If only my figure would shrink somewhat! For a fat poetess is incongruous, especially when seated by the grave of buried hope."

Rossetti's autobiographical Künstlerroman, Maude *(composed when she was nineteen but not published until 1897), announces motifs of renunciation, religious devotion, and the costs of art to women. (Twice her religious beliefs led her to break off engagements with men she loved.) The same themes return in her poetry and in her correspondence with the poets Dora Greenwell and Jean Ingelow. Rossetti was an associate of the Anglican Sisters of Mercy, but poetry, not "rescue" work with young prostitutes, was her real calling, as* Goblin Market and Other Poems *(1862) made manifest. She admired Dante, Plato, Tennyson, and among the women of the period, Jean Ingelow, Augusta Webster, and especially Barrett Browning, whose sonnets she echoed in the sequence "Monna Innominata" in* A Pageant and Other Poems *(1881).*

Alice Meynell found the "thinnest beaten gold" in Rossetti's slender poems for children, gathered in Sing-Song: A Nursery Rhyme Book *(1872; expanded 1893). A major part of her corpus was devotional: meditations on Biblical lines or explorations of spiritual conflict. The critic George Saintsbury acclaimed her "astonishingly true and*

*new note of poetry," which deepened and varied in her later volumes. Some of her finest
work was edited posthumously by her brother William.*

Song

When I am dead, my dearest,
   Sing no sad songs for me;
Plant thou no roses at my head,
   Nor shady cypress tree:
Be the green grass above me
   With showers and dewdrops wet;
And if thou wilt, remember,
   And if thou wilt, forget.

I shall not see the shadows,
   I shall not feel the rain;
I shall not hear the nightingale
   Sing on, as if in pain:
And dreaming through the twilight
   That doth not rise nor set,
Haply I may remember,
   And haply may forget.

            1848 / 1862

Song

She sat and sang alway
   By the green margin of a stream,
Watching the fishes leap and play
   Beneath the glad sunbeam.

I sat and wept alway
   Beneath the moon's most shadowy beam,
Watching the blossoms of the May
   Weep leaves into the stream.

I wept for memory;
   She sang for hope that is so fair:
My tears were swallowed by the sea;
   Her songs died on the air.

            1848 / 1862

[Some ladies dress in muslin full and white]

Some ladies dress in muslin full and white,
Some gentlemen in cloth succinct and black;
Some patronise a dog-cart, some a hack,
    Some think a painted clarence only right.
    Youth is not always such a pleasing sight:
Witness a man with tassels on his back;
Or woman in a great-coat like a sack,
    Towering above her sex with horrid height.
If all the world were water fit to drown,
    There are some whom you would not teach to swim,   10
Rather enjoying if you saw them sink:
Certain old ladies dressed in girlish pink,
With roses and geraniums on their gown.
    Go to the basin, poke them o'er the rim—

c. 1848 / 1896

After Death

The curtains were half drawn, the floor was swept
    And strewn with rushes, rosemary and may
    Lay thick upon the bed on which I lay,
Where through the lattice ivy shadows crept.
He leaned above me, thinking that I slept
    And could not hear him; but I heard him say,
    "Poor child, poor child," and as he turned away
Came a deep silence, and I knew he wept.
He did not touch the shroud, or raise the fold
    That hid my face, or take my hand in his,   10
    Or ruffle the smooth pillows for my head:
    He did not love me living; but once dead
He pitied me; and very sweet it is
To know he still is warm though I am cold.

1849 / 1862

On Keats

A garden in a garden, a green spot
    Where all is green: most fitting slumber place
    For the strong man grown weary of a race
Soon over. Unto him a goodly lot
Hath fallen in fertile ground; there thorns are not,
    But his own daisies; silence, full of grace,
    Surely hath shed a quiet on his face:

His earth is but sweet leaves that fell and rot.
What was his record of himself, ere he
    Went from us? *Here lies one whose name was writ*   10
  In water. While the chilly shadows flit
      Of sweet Saint Agnes' Eve, while basil springs,
      His name in every humble heart that sings
Shall be a fountain of love, verily.

1849 / 1896

A Pause

They made the chamber sweet with flowers and leaves
  And the bed sweet with flowers on which I lay,
  While my soul, love-bound, loitered on its way.
I did not hear the birds about the eaves,
Nor hear the reapers talk among the sheaves:
  Only my soul kept watch from day to day,
  My thirsty soul kept watch for one away—
Perhaps he loves, I thought, remembers, grieves.
At length there came the step upon the stair,
  Upon the lock the old familiar hand: 10
Then first my spirit seemed to scent the air
  Of Paradise; then first the tardy sand
Of time ran golden; and I felt my hair
  Put on a glory, and my soul expand.

1853 / 1896

The World

By day she woos me, soft, exceeding fair:
  But all night, as the moon, so changeth she;
  Loathsome and foul with hideous leprosy
And subtle serpents gliding in her hair.
By day she woos me to the outer air,
  Ripe fruits, sweet flowers, and full satiety:
  But through the night, a beast, she grins at me,
A very monster void of love and prayer.
By day she stands a lie; by night she stands
  In all the naked horror of the truth   10
With pushing horns and clawed and clutching hands.
Is this a friend, indeed, that I should sell
  My soul to her, give her my life and youth,
Till my feet, cloven too, take hold on hell?

1854 / 1862

A Soul

She stands as pale as Parian statues stand;
   Like Cleopatra when she turned at bay
   And felt her strength above the Roman sway,
And felt the aspic writhing in her hand.
Her face is steadfast toward the shadowy land,
   For dim beyond it looms the land of day:
   Her feet are steadfast all the arduous way
That foot-track doth not waver on the sand.
She stands there like a beacon through the night,
   A pale clear beacon where the storm-drift is—   10
She stands alone, a wonder deathly white:
She stands there patient nerved with inner might,
   Indomitable in her feebleness,
Her face and will athirst against the light.

                    1854 / 1896

Cobwebs

It is a land with neither night nor day,
   Nor heat nor cold, nor any wind nor rain,
   Nor hills nor valleys; but one even plain
Stretches through long unbroken miles away,
While through the sluggish air a twilight gray
   Broodeth: no moons or seasons wax and wane,
   No ebb and flow are there along the main,
No bud-time, no leaf-falling there for aye,
No ripple on the sea, no shifting sand,
   No beat of wings to stir the stagnant space,   10
No pulse of life through all the loveless land
And loveless sea; no trace of days before,
   No guarded home, no toil-won resting place
No future hope, no fear forevermore.

                    1855 / 1896

Shut Out

The door was shut. I looked between
   Its iron bars and saw it lie,
   My garden, mine, beneath the sky,
Pied with all flowers bedewed and green:

From bough to bough the songbirds crossed,
   From flower to flower the moths and bees;

With all its nests and stately trees
It had been mine, and it was lost.

A shadowless spirit kept the gate,
Blank and unchanging like the grave.   10
I, peering through, said, "Let me have
Some buds to cheer my outcast state."

He answered not. "Or give me, then,
But one small twig from shrub or tree;
And bid my home remember me
Until I come to it again."

The spirit was silent, but he took
Mortar and stone to build a wall;
He left no loophole great or small
Through which my straining eyes might look.   20

So now I sit here quite alone,
Blinded with tears; nor grieve for that,
For nought is left worth looking at
Since my delightful land is gone.

A violet bed is budding near,
Wherein a lark has made her nest:
And good they are, but not the best;
And dear they are, but not so dear.

1856 / 1862

In an Artist's Studio

One face looks out from all his canvases,
One selfsame figure sits or walks or leans:
We found her hidden just behind those screens,
That mirror gave back all her loveliness.
A queen in opal or in ruby dress,
A nameless girl in freshest summer greens,
A saint, an angel—every canvas means
The same one meaning, neither more nor less.
He feeds upon her face by day and night,
And she with true kind eyes looks back on him,   10
Fair as the moon and joyful as the light:
Not wan with waiting, not with sorrow dim;
Not as she is, but was when hope shone bright;
Not as she is, but as she fills his dream.

1856 / 1896

Winter: My Secret

I, tell my secret? No indeed, not I:
Perhaps someday, who knows?
But not today; it froze, and blows, and snows,
And you're too curious: fie!
You want to hear it? well—
Only, my secret's mine, and I won't tell.

Or, after all, perhaps there's none:
Suppose there is no secret after all,
But only just my fun.
Today's a nipping day, a biting day;   10
In which one wants a shawl,
A veil, a cloak, and other wraps:
I cannot ope to everyone who taps,
And let the drafts come whistling through my hall;
Come bounding and surrounding me,
Come buffeting, astounding me,
Nipping and clipping through my wraps and all.
I wear my mask for warmth: whoever shows
His nose to Russian snows
To be pecked at by every wind that blows?   20
You would not peck? I thank you for goodwill,
Believe, but leave that truth untested still.

Spring's an expansive time: yet I don't trust
March with its peck of dust,
Nor April with its rainbow-crowned brief showers,
Nor even May, whose flowers
One frost may wither through the sunless hours.

Perhaps some languid summer day,
When drowsy birds sing less and less,
And golden fruit is ripening to excess,   30
If there's not too much sun nor too much cloud,
And the warm wind is neither still nor loud,
Perhaps my secret I may say,
Or you may guess.

1857 / 1862

Uphill

Does the road wind uphill all the way?
    Yes, to the very end.
Will the day's journey take the whole long day?
    From morn to night, my friend.

But is there for the night a resting place?
  A roof for when the slow dark hours begin.
May not the darkness hide it from my face?
  You cannot miss that inn.

Shall I meet other wayfarers at night?
  Those who have gone before.
Then must I knock or call when just in sight?
  They will not keep you standing at that door.

Shall I find comfort, travel-sore and weak?
  Of labor you shall find the sum.
Will there be beds for me and all who seek?
  Yea, beds for all who come.

1858 / 1861

At Home

When I was dead, my spirit turned
  To seek the much frequented house:
I passed the door and saw my friends
  Feasting beneath green orange boughs;
From hand to hand they pushed the wine,
  They sucked the pulp of plum and peach;
They sang, they jested, and they laughed,
  For each was loved of each.

I listened to their honest chat:
  Said one, "Tomorrow we shall be
Plod plod along the featureless sands
  And coasting miles and miles of sea."
Said one, "Before the turn of tide
  We will achieve the eyrie-seat."
Said one, "Tomorrow shall be like
  Today, but much more sweet."

"Tomorrow," said they, strong with hope,
  And dwelt upon the pleasant way.
"Tomorrow," cried they one and all,
  While no one spoke of yesterday.
Their life stood full at blessed noon;
  I, only I, had passed away:
"Tomorrow, and today," they cried;
  I was of yesterday.

I shivered comfortless but cast
  No chill across the tablecloth;

I, all forgotten, shivered, sad
   To stay and yet to part how loath:
I passed from the familiar room,
   I who from love had passed away,   30
Like the remembrance of a guest
   That tarrieth but a day.

1858 / 1862

From House to Home

The first was like a dream through summer heat,
   The second like a tedious numbing swoon
While the half-frozen pulses lagged to beat
   Beneath a winter moon.

"But," says my friend, "what was this thing and where?"
   It was a pleasure-place within my soul,
An earthly paradise supremely fair
   That lured me from the goal.

The first part was a tissue of hugged lies;
   The second was its ruin fraught with pain: 10
Why raise the fair delusion to the skies
   But to be dashed again?

My castle stood of white transparent glass
   Glittering and frail with many a fretted spire,
But when the summer sunset came to pass
   It kindled into fire.

My pleasaunce was an undulating green,
   Stately with trees whose shadows slept below,
With glimpses of smooth garden beds between,
   Like flame or sky or snow.   20

Swift squirrels on the pastures took their ease,
   With leaping lambs safe from the unfeared knife;
All singing birds rejoicing in those trees
   Fulfilled their careless life.

Wood-pigeons cooed there, stockdoves nestled there,
   My trees were full of songs and flowers and fruit,
Their branches spread a city to the air
   And mice lodged in their root.

My heath lay farther off, where lizards lived
   In strange metallic mail, just spied and gone,   30
Like darted lightnings here and there perceived
   But nowhere dwelt upon.

Frogs and fat toads were there to hop or plod
   And propagate in peace, an uncouth crew,
Where velvet-headed rushes, rustling, nod
     And spill the morning dew.

All caterpillars throve beneath my rule,
   With snails and slugs in corners out of sight;
I never marred the curious sudden 'stool
     That perfects in a night.   40

Safe in his excavated gallery
   The burrowing mole groped on from year to year;
No harmless hedgehog curled, because of me,
     His prickly back for fear.

Ofttimes one like an angel walked with me,
   With spirit-discerning eyes like flames of fire
But deep as the unfathomed endless sea,
     Fulfilling my desire.

And sometimes like a snowdrift he was fair,
   And sometimes like a sunset glorious red,
And sometimes he had wings to scale the air,   50
     With aureole round his head.

We sang our songs together by the way,
Calls and recalls and echoes of delight;
So communed we together all the day,
     And so in dreams by night.

I have no words to tell what way we walked,
   What unforgotten path now closed and sealed;
I have no words to tell all things we talked,
     All things that he revealed.   60

This only can I tell: that hour by hour
   I waxed more feastful, lifted up and glad;
I felt no thorn-prick when I plucked a flower,
     Felt not my friend was sad.

"Tomorrow," once I said to him with smiles;
   "Tonight," he answered gravely and was dumb,
But pointed out the stones that numbered miles
     And miles and miles to come.

"Not so," I said. "Tomorrow shall be sweet;
   Tonight is not so sweet as coming days."   70
Then first I saw that he had turned his feet,
     Had turned from me his face:

Running and flying miles and miles he went,
  But once looked back to beckon with his hand
And cry: "Come home, O love, from banishment:
    Come to the distant land—"

That night destroyed me like an avalanche;
  One night turned all my summer back to snow:
Next morning not a bird upon my branch,
    Not a lamb woke below;   80

No bird, no lamb, no living breathing thing;
  No squirrel scampered on my breezy lawn,
No mouse lodged by his hoard—all joys took wing
    And fled before that dawn.

Azure and sun were starved from heaven above,
  No dew had fallen but biting frost lay hoar:
O love, I knew that I should meet my love,
    Should find my love no more.

"My love no more," I muttered, stunned with pain:
  I shed no tear, I wrung no passionate hand,   90
Till something whispered: "You shall meet again,
    Meet in a distant land."

Then with a cry like famine I arose,
  I lit my candle, searched from room to room,
Searched up and down; a war of winds that froze
    Swept through the blank of gloom.

I searched day after day, night after night;
  Scant change there came to me of night or day:
"No more," I wailed, "no more," and trimmed my light,
    And gnashed but did not pray,   100

Until my heart broke and my spirit broke:
  Upon the frost-bound floor I stumbled, fell,
And moaned, "It is enough: withhold the stroke.
    Farewell, O love, farewell."

Then life swooned from me. And I heard the song
  Of spheres and spirits rejoicing over me:
One cried, "Our sister, she hath suffered long—"
    One answered, "Make her see—"

One cried, "Oh blessèd she who no more pain,
  Who no more disappointment shall receive—"   110
One answered, "Not so: she must live again;
    Strengthen thou her to live."

So while I lay entranced a curtain seemed
   To shrivel with crackling from before my face;
Across mine eyes a waxing radiance beamed
    And showed a certain place.

I saw a vision of a woman, where
   Night and new morning strive for domination;
Incomparably pale, and almost fair,
    And sad beyond expression.   120

Her eyes were like some fire-enshrining gem,
   Were stately like the stars, and yet were tender;
Her figure charmed me like a windy stem,
    Quivering and drooped and slender.

I stood upon the outer barren ground,
   She stood on inner ground that budded flowers;
While circling in their never-slackening round
    Danced by the mystic hours.

But every flower was lifted on a thorn,
   And every thorn shot upright from its sands   130
To gall her feet; hoarse laughter pealed in scorn
    With cruel clapping hands.

She bled and wept, yet did not shrink; her strength
   Was strung up until daybreak of delight:
She measured measureless sorrow toward its length,
    And breadth, and depth, and height.

Then marked I how a chain sustained her form,
   A chain of living links not made nor riven:
It stretched sheer, up through lightning, wind, and storm,
    And anchored fast in heaven.   140

One cried, "How long? yet founded on the Rock
   She shall do battle, suffer, and attain—"
One answered, "Faith quakes in the tempest shock:
    Strengthen her soul again."

I saw a cup sent down and come to her,
   Brimful of loathing and of bitterness:
She drank with livid lips that seemed to stir
    The depth, not make it less.

But as she drank I spied a hand distill
   New wine and virgin honey; making it   150
First bittersweet, then sweet, indeed, until
    She tasted only sweet.

Her lips and cheeks waxed rosy-fresh and young;
   Drinking, she sang, "My soul shall nothing want,"
And drank anew; while soft a song was sung,
   A mystical slow chant.

One cried, "The wounds are faithful of a friend:
   The wilderness shall blossom as a rose—"
One answered, "Rend the veil, declare the end,
   Strengthen her ere she goes."   160

Then earth and heaven were rolled up like a scroll;
   Time and space, change and death, had passed away;
Weight, number, measure, each had reached its whole;
   The day had come, that day.

Multitudes—multitudes—stood up in bliss,
   Made equal to the angels, glorious, fair;
With harps, palms, wedding garments, kiss of peace,
   And crowned and haloed hair.

They sang a song, a new song in the height,
   Harping with harps to Him Who is strong and true: 170
They drank new wine, their eyes saw with new light,
   Lo, all things were made new.

Tier beyond tier they rose and rose and rose
   So high that it was dreadful, flames with flames:
No man could number them, no tongue disclose
   Their secret sacred names.

As though one pulse stirred all, one rush of blood
   Fed all, one breath swept through them myriad-voiced,
They struck their harps, cast down their crowns, they stood
   And worshipped and rejoiced.   180

Each face looked one way like a moon new-lit,
   Each face looked one way towards its Sun of Love;
Drank love and bathed in love and mirrored it
   And knew no end thereof.

Glory touched glory on each blessèd head,
   Hands locked dear hands never to sunder more:
These were the new-begotten from the dead
   Whom the great birthday bore.

Heart answered heart, soul answered soul at rest,
   Double against each other, filled, sufficed: 190
All loving, loved of all; but loving best
   And best beloved of Christ.

I saw that one who lost her love in pain,
    Who trod on thorns, who drank the loathsome cup;
The lost in night, in day was found again;
    The fallen was lifted up.

They stood together in the blessèd noon,
    They sang together through the length of days;
Each loving face bent Sunwards like a moon
    New-lit with love and praise.   200

Therefore, O friend, I would not if I might
    Rebuild my house of lies, wherein I joyed
One time to dwell: my soul shall walk in white,
    Cast down but not destroyed.

Therefore in patience I possess my soul;
    Yea, therefore as a flint I set my face,
To pluck down, to build up again the whole—
    But in a distant place.

These thorns are sharp, yet I can tread on them;
    This cup is loathsome, yet He makes it sweet: 210
My face is steadfast toward Jerusalem,
    My heart remembers it.

I lift the hanging hands, the feeble knees—
    I, precious more than seven times molten gold—
Until the day when from His storehouses
    God shall bring new and old;

Beauty for ashes, oil of joy for grief,
    Garment of praise for spirit of heaviness—
Although today I fade as doth a leaf,
    I languish and grow less.   220

Although today He prunes my twigs with pain,
    Yet doth His blood nourish and warm my root:
Tomorrow I shall put forth buds again
    And clothe myself with fruit.

Although today I walk in tedious ways,
    Today His staff is turned into a rod,
Yet will I wait for Him the appointed days
    And stay upon my God.

1858 / 1862

The Convent Threshold

There's blood between us, love, my love,
There's father's blood, there's brother's blood;
And blood's a bar I cannot pass:
I choose the stairs that mount above,
Stair after golden skyward stair,
To city and to sea of glass.
My lily feet are soiled with mud,
With scarlet mud, which tells a tale
Of hope that was, of guilt that was,
Of love that shall not yet avail;   10
Alas, my heart, if I could bare
My heart, this selfsame stain is there:
I seek the sea of glass and fire
To wash the spot, to burn the snare;
Lo, stairs are meant to lift us higher:
Mount with me, mount the kindled stair.

Your eyes look earthward, mine look up.
I see the far-off city grand,
Beyond the hills a watered land,
Beyond the gulf a gleaming strand   20
Of mansions where the righteous sup;
Who sleep at ease among their trees,
Or wake to sing a cadenced hymn
With cherubim and seraphim;
They bore the Cross, they drained the cup,
Racked, roasted, crushed, wrenched limb from limb,
They, the offscouring of the world:
The heaven of starry heavens unfurled,
The sun before their face is dim.

You, looking earthward, what see you?   30
Mild-white, wine-flushed among the vines,
Up and down leaping, to and fro,
Most glad, most full, made strong with wines,
Blooming as peaches pearled with dew,
Their golden windy hair afloat,
Love music warbling in their throat,
Young men and women come and go.

You linger, yet the time is short:
Flee for your life, gird up your strength
To flee; the shadows stretched at length   40
Show that day wanes, that night draws nigh;
Flee to the mountain, tarry not.
Is this a time for smile and sigh,

For songs among the secret trees
Where sudden bluebirds nest and sport?
The time is short and yet you stay:
Today, while it is called today,
Kneel, wrestle, knock, do violence, pray;
Today is short, tomorrow nigh:
Why will you die? why will you die? 50

You sinned with me a pleasant sin:
Repent with me, for I repent.
Woe's me the lore I must unlearn!
Woe's me that easy way we went,
So rugged when I would return!
How long until my sleep begin,
How long shall stretch these nights and days?
Surely, clean angels cry, she prays;
She laves her soul with tedious tears—
How long must stretch these years and years? 60

I turn from you my cheeks and eyes,
My hair which you shall see no more—
Alas for joy that went before,
For joy that dies, for love that dies.
Only my lips still turn to you,
My livid lips that cry, Repent.
Oh weary life, oh weary Lent,
Oh weary time whose stars are few.

How should I rest in Paradise,
Or sit on steps of heaven alone? 70
If saints and angels spoke of love
Should I not answer from my throne:
Have pity upon me, ye my friends,
For I have heard the sound thereof.
Should I not turn with yearning eyes,
Turn earthward with a pitiful pang?
Oh, save me from a pang in heaven.
By all the gifts we took and gave,
Repent, repent, and be forgiven.
This life is long, but yet it ends; 80
Repent and purge your soul and save:
No gladder song the morning stars
Upon their birthday morning sang
Then Angels sing when one repents.

I tell you what I dreamed last night:
A spirit with transfigured face,
Fire-footed clomb an infinite space.

I heard his hundred pinions clang,
Heaven-bells rejoicing rang and rang,
Heaven-air was thrilled with subtle scents,   90
Worlds spun upon their rushing cars.
He mounted, shrieking: "Give me light."
Still light was poured on him, more light;
Angels, archangels he outstripped,
Exultant in exceeding might,
And trod the skirts of cherubim.
Still "Give me light," he shrieked, and dipped
His thirsty face and drank a sea,
Athirst with thirst it could not slake.
I saw him, drunk with knowledge, take   100
From arching brows the aureole crown—
His locks writhed like a cloven snake—
He left his throne to grovel down
And lick the dust of seraphs' feet:
For what is knowledge duly weighed?
Knowledge is strong, but love is sweet;
Yea, all the progress he had made
Was but to learn that all is small
Save love, for love is all in all.

I tell you what I dreamed last night: 110
It was not dark, it was not light,
Cold dews had drenched my plenteous hair
Through clay; you came to seek me there.
And "Do you dream of me?" you said.
My heart was dust that used to leap
To you; I answered half asleep:
"My pillow is damp, my sheets are red,
There's a leaden tester to my bed—
Find you a warmer playfellow,
A warmer pillow for your head,   120
A kinder love to love than mine."
You wrung your hands, while I like lead
Crushed downwards through the sodden earth,
You smote your hands but not in mirth,
And reeled but were not drunk with wine.

For all night long I dreamed of you:
I woke and prayed against my will,
Then slept to dream of you again.
At length I rose and knelt and prayed—
I cannot write the words I said,
My words were slow, my tears were few;
But through the dark my silence spoke

Like thunder. When this morning broke,
My face was pinched, my hair was gray,
And frozen blood was on the sill
Where stifling in my struggle I lay.

If now you saw me you would say:
Where is the face I used to love?
And I would answer: Gone before;
It tarries veiled in Paradise.   140
When once the morning star shall rise,
When earth with shadow flees away
And we stand safe within the door,
Then you shall lift the veil thereof.
Look up, rise up: for far above
Our palms are grown, our place is set;
There we shall meet, as once we met,
And love with old familiar love.

1858 / 1862

L.E.L.

"Whose heart was breaking for a little love."

Downstairs I laugh, I sport and jest with all;
    But in my solitary room above
I turn my face in silence to the wall;
    My heart is breaking for a little love.
        Though winter frosts are done,
        And birds pair every one,
And leaves peep out, for springtide is begun.

I feel no spring, while spring is well-nigh blown,
    I find no nest, while nests are in the grove.
Woe's me for mine own heart that dwells alone,   10
    My heart that breaketh for a little love,
        While, golden in the sun,
        Rivulets rise and run,
While lilies bud, for springtide is begun.

All love, are loved, save only I; their hearts
    Beat warm with love and joy, beat full thereof:
They cannot guess, who play the pleasant parts,
    My heart is breaking for a little love.
        While beehives wake and whir,
        And rabbit thins his fur,   20
In living spring that sets the world astir.

I deck myself with silks and jewelry,
   I plume myself like any mated dove.
They praise my rustling show, and never see
   My heart is breaking for a little love.
      While sprouts green lavender
      With rosemary and myrrh,
For in quick spring the sap is all astir.

Perhaps some saints in glory guess the truth,
   Perhaps some angels read it as they move,   30
And cry one to another full of ruth,
   "Her heart is breaking for a little love."
      Though other things have birth,
      And leap and sing for mirth,
When springtime wakes and clothes and feeds the earth.

Yet saith a saint, "Take patience for thy scathe";
   Yet saith an angel, "Wait, and thou shalt prove
True best is last, true life is born of death,
   O thou, heartbroken for a little love.
      Then love shall fill thy girth,   40
      And love make fat thy dearth,
When new spring builds new heaven and clean new earth."

                        1859 / 1866

Goblin Market

Morning and evening,
Maids heard the goblins cry:
"Come buy our orchard fruits,
Come buy, come buy:
Apples and quinces,
Lemons and oranges,
Plump unpecked cherries,
Melons and raspberries,
Bloom-down-cheeked peaches,
Swart-headed mulberries,   10
Wild free-born cranberries,
Crab apples, dewberries,
Pineapples, blackberries,
Apricots, strawberries—
All ripe together
In summer weather—
Morns that pass by,
Fair eves that fly;
Come buy, come buy:

Our grapes fresh from the vine,   20
Pomegranates full and fine,
Dates and sharp bullaces,
Rare pears and greengages,
Damsons and bilberries;
Taste them and try:
Currants and gooseberries,
Bright-fire-like barberries,
Figs to fill your mouth,
Citrons from the South,
Sweet to tongue and sound to eye;   30
Come buy, come buy."

Evening by evening,
Among the brookside rushes,
Laura bowed her head to hear,
Lizzie veiled her blushes:
Crouching close together
In the cooling weather,
With clasping arms and cautioning lips,
With tingling cheeks and fingertips.
"Lie close," Laura said,   40
Pricking up her golden head.
"We must not look at goblin men,
We must not buy their fruits:
Who knows upon what soil they fed
Their hungry thirsty roots?"
"Come buy," call the goblins
Hobbling down the glen.
"Oh," cried Lizzie, "Laura, Laura,
You should not peep at goblin men."
Lizzie covered up her eyes,   50
Covered close lest they should look;
Laura reared her glossy head
And whispered like the restless brook,
"Look, Lizzie, look, Lizzie,
Down the glen tramp little men.
One hauls a basket,
One bears a plate,
One lugs a golden dish
Of many pounds weight.
How fair the vine must grow   60
Whose grapes are so luscious;
How warm the wind must blow
Through those fruit bushes."
"No," said Lizzie, "No, no, no.

Their offers should not charm us,
Their evil gifts would harm us."
She thrust a dimpled finger
In each ear, shut eyes, and ran;
Curious Laura chose to linger,
Wondering at each merchant man: 70
One had a cat's face,
One whisked a tail,
One tramped at a rat's pace,
One crawled like a snail,
One like a wombat prowled obtuse and furry,
One like a ratel tumbled hurry-scurry.
She heard a voice like voice of doves
Cooing all together:
They sounded kind and full of loves
In the pleasant weather.   80

Laura stretched her gleaming neck
Like a rush-imbedded swan,
Like a lily from the beck,
Like a moonlit poplar branch,
Like a vessel at the launch
When its last restraint is gone.

Backwards up the mossy glen
Turned and trooped the goblin men,
With their shrill repeated cry,
"Come buy, come buy."   90
When they reached where Laura was
They stood stock still upon the moss,
Leering at each other,
Brother with queer brother;
Signaling each other,
Brother with sly brother.
One set his basket down,
One reared his plate;
One began to weave a crown
Of tendrils, leaves and rough nuts brown   100
(Men sell not such in any town);
One heaved the golden weight
Of dish and fruit to offer her:
"Come buy, come buy," was still their cry.

Laura stared but did not stir,
Longed but had no money:
The whisk-tailed merchant bade her taste
In tones as smooth as honey,

The cat-faced purred,
The rat-paced spoke a word   110
Of welcome, and the snail-paced even was heard;
One parrot-voiced and jolly
Cried "Pretty Goblin" still for "Pretty Polly"—
One whistled like a bird.

But sweet-tooth Laura spoke in haste:
"Good folk, I have no coin;
To take were to purloin.
I have no copper in my purse,
I have no silver either,
And all my gold is on the furze   120
That shakes in windy weather
Above the rusty heather."
"You have much gold upon your head,"
They answered all together:
"Buy from us with a golden curl."
She clipped a precious golden lock,
She dropped a tear more rare than pearl,
Then sucked their fruit globes fair or red:
Sweeter than honey from the rock.
Stronger than man-rejoicing wine,   130
Clearer than water flowed that juice;
She never tasted such before,
How should it cloy with length of use?
She sucked and sucked and sucked the more
Fruits which that unknown orchard bore;
She sucked until her lips were sore;
Then flung the emptied rinds away
But gathered up one kernel-stone,
And knew not was it night or day
As she turned home alone.   140

Lizzie met her at the gate
Full of wise upbraidings:
"Dear, you should not stay so late,
Twilight is not good for maidens;
Should not loiter in the glen
In the haunts of goblin men.
Do you not remember Jeanie,
How she met them in the moonlight,
Took their gifts both choice and many,
Ate their fruits and wore their flowers   150
Plucked from bowers
Where summer ripens at all hours?
But ever in the noonlight

She pined and pined away;
Sought them by night and day,
Found them no more but dwindled and grew gray;
Then fell with the first snow,
While to this day no grass will grow
Where she lies low:
I planted daisies there a year ago   160
That never blow.
You should not loiter so."
"Nay, hush," said Laura,
"Nay, hush, my sister:
I ate and ate my fill,
Yet my mouth waters still;
Tomorrow night I will
Buy more," and kissed her.
"Have done with sorrow;
I'll bring you plums tomorrow,   170
Fresh on their mother twigs,
Cherries worth getting;
You cannot think what figs
My teeth have met in,
What melons, icy-cold,
Piled on a dish of gold
Too huge for me to hold,
What peaches with a velvet nap,
Pellucid grapes without one seed:
Odorous indeed must be the mead   180
Whereon they grow, and pure the wave they drink,
With lilies at the brink,
And sugar-sweet their sap."

Golden head by golden head,
Like two pigeons in one nest,
Folded in each other's wings,
They lay down in their curtained bed:
Like two blossoms on one stem,
Like two flakes of new-fallen snow,
Like two wands of ivory   190
Tipped with gold for awful kings.
Moon and stars gazed in at them,
Wind sang to them lullaby,
Lumbering owls forbore to fly,
Not a bat flapped to and fro
Round their rest:
Cheek to cheek and breast to breast,
Locked together in one nest.

Early in the morning
When the first cock crowed his warning,
Neat like bees, as sweet and busy,
Laura rose with Lizzie;
Fetched in honey, milked the cows,
Aired and set to rights the house,
Kneaded cakes of whitest wheat,
Cakes for dainty mouths to eat,
Next churned butter, whipped up cream,
Fed their poultry, sat and sewed;
Talked as modest maidens should:
Lizzie with an open heart,
Laura in an absent dream,
One content, one sick in part;
One warbling for the mere bright day's delight,
One longing for the night.

At length slow evening came:
They went with pitchers to the reedy brook;
Lizzie most placid in her look,
Laura most like a leaping flame.
They drew the gurgling water from its deep;
Lizzie plucked purple and rich golden flags,
Then turning homewards said: "The sunset flushes
Those furthest loftiest crags;
Come, Laura, not another maiden lags,
No willful squirrel wags;
The beasts and birds are fast asleep."
But Laura loitered still among the rushes
And said the bank was steep.

And said the hour was early still,
The dew not fallen, the wind not chill—
Listening ever, but not catching
The customary cry,
"Come buy, come buy,"
With its iterated jingle
Of sugar-baited words;
Not for all her watching
Once discerning even one goblin
Racing, whisking, tumbling, hobbling,
Let alone the herds
That used to tramp along the glen,
In groups or single,
Of brisk fruit-merchant men.
Till Lizzie urged, "O Laura, come;
I hear the fruit-call but I dare not look—

200

210

220

230

240

You should not loiter longer at this brook;
Come with me home.
The stars rise, the moon bends her arc,
Each glowworm winks her spark;
Let us get home before the night grows dark:
For clouds may gather,
Though this is summer weather,   250
Put out the lights and drench us through;
Then if we lost our way what should we do?"

Laura turned cold as stone
To find her sister heard that cry alone,
That goblin cry,
"Come buy our fruits, come buy."
Must she then buy no more such dainty fruit?
Must she no more such succous pasture find,
Gone deaf and blind?
Her tree of life drooped from the root: 260
She said not one word in her heart's sore ache;
But peering through the dimness, nought discerning,
Trudged home, her pitcher dripping all the way;
So crept to bed, and lay
Silent till Lizzie slept;
Then sat up in a passionate yearning,
And gnashed her teeth for baulked desire, and wept
As if her heart would break.

Day after day, night after night,
Laura kept watch in vain   270
In sullen silence of exceeding pain.
She never caught again the goblin cry:
"Come buy, come buy";
She never spied the goblin men
Hawking their fruits along the glen.
But when the noon waxed bright
Her hair grew thin and gray;
She dwindled, as the fair full moon doth turn
To swift decay and burn
Her fire away.   280

One day remembering her kernel-stone,
She set it by a wall that faced the south;
Dewed it with tears, hoped for a root,
Watched for a waxing shoot,
But there came none;
It never saw the sun,
It never felt the trickling moisture run;

While with sunk eyes and faded mouth
She dreamed of melons, as a traveler sees
False waves in desert drought   290
With shade of leaf-crowned trees,
And burns the thirstier in the sandful breeze.

She no more swept the house,
Tended the fowls or cows,
Fetched honey, kneaded cakes of wheat,
Brought water from the brook;
But sat down listless in the chimney-nook
And would not eat.

Tender Lizzie could not bear
To watch her sister's cankerous care   300
Yet not to share.
She night and morning
Caught the goblins' cry:
"Come buy our orchard fruits,
Come buy, come buy"—
Beside the brook, along the glen,
She heard the tramp of goblin men,
The voice and stir
Poor Laura could not hear;
Longed to buy fruit to comfort her   310
But feared to pay too dear.
She thought of Jeanie in her grave,
Who should have been a bride,
But who for joys brides hope to have
Fell sick and died
In her gay prime,
In earliest wintertime,
With the first glazing rime,
With the first snowfall of crisp wintertime.

Till Laura dwindling   320
Seemed knocking at Death's door:
Then Lizzie weighed no more
Better and worse,
But put a silver penny in her purse,
Kissed Laura, crossed the heath with clumps of furze
At twilight, halted by the brook—
And for the first time in her life
Began to listen and look.

Laughed every goblin
When they spied her peeping;   330
Came towards her hobbling,

Flying, running, leaping,
Puffing and blowing,
Chuckling, clapping, crowing,
Clucking and gobbling,
Mopping and mowing,
Full of airs and graces,
Pulling wry faces,
Demure grimaces,
Cat-like and rat-like,   340
Ratel- and wombat-like,
Snail-paced in a hurry,
Parrot-voiced and whistler,
Helter-skelter, hurry-scurry,
Chattering like magpies,
Fluttering like pigeons,
Gliding like fishes—
Hugged her and kissed her,
Squeezed and caressed her;
Stretched up their dishes,   350
Panniers, and plates:
"Look at our apples
Russet and dun,
Bob at our cherries,
Bite at our peaches,
Citrons and dates,
Grapes for the asking,
Pears red with basking
Out in the sun,
Plums on their twigs;   360
Pluck them and suck them,
Pomegranates, figs—"

"Good folk," said Lizzie,
Mindful of Jeanie:
"Give me much and many"—
Held out her apron,
Tossed them her penny.
"Nay, take a seat with us,
Honor and eat with us,"
They answered grinning.   370
"Our feast is but beginning.
Night yet is early,
Warm and dew-pearly,
Wakeful and starry:
Such fruits as these
No man can carry;

Half their bloom would fly,
Half their dew would dry,
Half their flavor would pass by.
Sit down and feast with us,   380
Be welcome guest with us,
Cheer you and rest with us—"

"Thank you," said Lizzie. "But one waits
At home alone for me:
So without further parleying,
If you will not sell me any
Of your fruits though much and many,
Give me back my silver penny
I tossed you for a fee—"
They began to scratch their pates,   390
No longer wagging, purring,
But visibly demurring,
Grunting and snarling.
One called her proud,
Cross-grained, uncivil;
Their tones waxed loud,
Their looks were evil.
Lashing their tails
They trod and hustled her,
Elbowed and jostled her,   400
Clawed with their nails,
Barking, mewing, hissing, mocking,
Tore her gown and soiled her stocking,
Twitched her hair out by the roots,
Stamped upon her tender feet,
Held her hands and squeezed their fruits
Against her mouth to make her eat.

White and golden Lizzie stood,
Like a lily in a flood—
Like a rock of blue-veined stone   410
Lashed by tides obstreperously—
Like a beacon left alone
In a hoary roaring sea,
Sending up a golden fire—
Like a fruit-crowned orange tree,
White with blossoms honey-sweet,
Sore beset by wasp and bee—
Like a royal virgin town
Topped with gilded dome and spire

Close beleaguered by a fleet   420
Mad to tug her standard down.

One may lead a horse to water,
Twenty cannot make him drink.
Though the goblins cuffed and caught her,
Coaxed and fought her,
Bullied and besought her,
Scratched her, pinched her black as ink,
Kicked and knocked her,
Mauled and mocked her,
Lizzie uttered not a word;   430
Would not open lip from lip
Lest they should cram a mouthful in;
But laughed in heart to feel the drip
Of juice that syruped all her face,
And lodged in dimples of her chin,
And streaked her neck, which quaked like curd.
At last the evil people
Worn out by her resistance
Flung back her penny, kicked their fruit
Along whichever road they took,   440
Not leaving root or stone or shoot;
Some writhed into the ground,
Some dived into the brook
With ring and ripple,
Some scudded on the gale without a sound,
Some vanished in the distance.

In a smart, ache, tingle,
Lizzie went her way;
Knew not was it night or day;
Sprang up the bank, tore through the furze,   450
Threaded copse and dingle,
And heard her penny jingle
Bouncing in her purse,
Its bounce was music to her ear.
She ran and ran
As if she feared some goblin man
Dogged her with gibe or curse
Or something worse:
But not one goblin scurried after,
Nor was she pricked by fear;   460
The kind heart made her windy-paced
That urged her home quite out of breath with haste
And inward laughter.

She cried, "Laura," up the garden,
"Did you miss me?
Come and kiss me.
Never mind my bruises,
Hug me, kiss me, suck my juices
Squeezed from goblin fruits for you,
Goblin pulp and goblin dew.   470
Eat me, drink me, love me;
Laura, make much of me:
For your sake I have braved the glen
And had to do with goblin merchant men."

Laura started from her chair,
Flung her arms up in the air,
Clutched her hair.
"Lizzie, Lizzie, have you tasted
For my sake the fruit forbidden?
Must your light like mine be hidden,   480
Your young life like mine be wasted,
Undone in mine undoing
And ruined in my ruin,
Thirsty, cankered, goblin-ridden?—"
She clung about her sister,
Kissed and kissed and kissed her:
Tears once again
Refreshed her shrunken eyes,
Dropping like rain
After long sultry drouth;   490
Shaking with anguish, fear, and pain,
She kissed and kissed her with a hungry mouth.

Her lips began to scorch,
That juice was wormwood to her tongue;
She loathed the feast:
Writhing as one possessed she leaped and sung,
Rent all her robe, and wrung
Her hands in lamentable haste
And beat her breast.
Her locks streamed like the torch   500
Borne by a racer at full speed,
Or like the mane of horses in their flight,
Or like an eagle when she stems the light
Straight toward the sun,
Or like a caged thing freed,
Or like a flying flag when armies run.

Swift fire spread through her veins, knocked at her heart,
Met the fire smoldering there,
And overbore its lesser flame;
She gorged on bitterness without a name;   510
Ah! fool, to choose such part
Of soul-consuming care!
Sense failed in the mortal strife:
Like the watchtower of a town
Which an earthquake shatters down,
Like a lightning-stricken mast,
Like a wind-uprooted tree
Spun about,
Like a foam-topped waterspout
Cast down headlong in the sea,   520
She fell at last;
Pleasure past and anguish past,
Is it death or is it life?

Life out of death.
That night long Lizzie watched by her,
Counted her pulse's flagging stir,
Felt for her breath,
Held water to her lips, and cooled her face
With tears and fanning leaves:
But when the first birds chirped about their eaves,   530
And early reapers plodded to the place
Of golden sheaves,
And dew-wet grass
Bowed in the morning winds so brisk to pass,
And new buds with new day
Opened of cuplike lilies on the stream,
Laura awoke as from a dream,
Laughed in the innocent old way,
Hugged Lizzie but not twice or thrice;
Her gleaming locks showed not one thread of gray,   540
Her breath was sweet as May,
And light danced in her eyes.

Days, weeks, months, years
Afterwards, when both were wives
With children of their own,
Their mother-hearts beset with fears,
Their lives bound up in tender lives,
Laura would call the little ones
And tell them of her early prime,
Those pleasant days long gone   550
Of not-returning time;

Would talk about the haunted glen,
The wicked, quaint fruit-merchant men,
Their fruits like honey to the throat
But poison in the blood
(Men sell not such in any town);
Would tell them how her sister stood
In deadly peril to do her good
And win the fiery antidote;
Then joining hands to little hands   560
Would bid them cling together,
"For there is no friend like a sister
In calm or stormy weather;
To cheer one on the tedious way,
To fetch one if one goes astray,
To lift one if one totters down,
To strengthen whilst one stands."

1859 / 1862

On the Wing

Once in a dream (for once I dreamed of you)
　We stood together in an open field;
　Above our heads two swift-winged pigeons wheeled,
Sporting at ease and courting full in view.
When loftier still a broadening darkness flew,
　Down-swooping, and a ravenous hawk revealed;
　Too weak to fight, too fond to fly, they yield;
So farewell, life and love and pleasures new.
Then as their plumes fell fluttering to the ground,
　Their snow-white plumage flecked with crimson drops,
　　I wept, and thought I turned towards you to weep:
　But you were gone; while rustling hedgerow tops
Bent in a wind which bore to me a sound
　Of far-off piteous bleat of lambs and sheep.

1862 / 1866

[If a Mouse Could Fly]

If a mouse could fly,
　Or if a crow could swim,
Or if a sprat could walk and talk,
　I'd like to be like him.

If a mouse could fly,
　He might fly away;

Or if a crow could swim,
　　It might turn him gray;
Or if a sprat could walk and talk,
　　What would he find to say?　　　　　10

1872

[O Lady Moon, your horns point toward the east]

O Lady Moon, your horns point toward the east:
　　Shine, be increased;
O Lady Moon, your horns point toward the west:
　　Wane, be at rest.

1872

[Brown and furry]

Brown and furry
Caterpillar in a hurry,
Take your walk
To the shady leaf, or stalk,
Or what not,
Which may be the chosen spot.
No toad spy you,
Hovering bird of prey pass by you;
Spin and die
To live again a butterfly.　　　　　10

1872

[If a pig wore a wig]

If a pig wore a wig,
　　What could we say?
Treat him as a gentleman,
　　And say "Good day."

If his tail chanced to fail,
　　What could we do?—
Send him to the tailoress
　　To get one new.

1872

A Christmas Carol

In the bleak midwinter
　　Frosty wind made moan,
Earth stood hard as iron,
　　Water like a stone;
Snow had fallen, snow on snow,
　　Snow on snow,
In the bleak midwinter
　　Long ago.

Our God, Heaven cannot hold Him
　　Nor earth sustain;   10
Heaven and earth shall flee away
　　When He comes to reign:
In the bleak midwinter
　　A stable-place sufficed
The Lord God Almighty
　　Jesus Christ.

Enough for Him whom cherubim
　　Worship night and day,
A breastful of milk
　　And a mangerful of hay;   20
Enough for Him whom angels
　　Fall down before,
The ox and ass and camel
　　Which adore.

Angels and archangels
May have gathered there,
Cherubim and seraphim
　　Thronged the air,
But only His mother
　　In her maiden bliss   30
Worshipped the beloved
　　With a kiss.

What can I give Him,
　　Poor as I am?
If I were a shepherd
　　I would bring a lamb,
If I were a wise man
　　I would do my part—
Yet what I can I give Him,
　　Give my heart.   40

1875

Passing and Glassing

All things that pass
Are woman's looking-glass;
They show her how her bloom must fade,
And she herself be laid
With withered roses in the shade;
  With withered roses and the fallen peach,
  Unlovely, out of reach
    Of summer joy that was.

All things that pass
Are woman's tiring-glass;   10
The faded lavender is sweet,
Sweet the dead violet
Culled and laid by and cared for yet;
  The dried-up violets and dried lavender,
  Still sweet, may comfort her,
    Nor need she cry Alas!

All things that pass
Are wisdom's looking-glass;
Being full of hope and fear, and still
Brimful of good or ill,   20
According to our work and will;
  For there is nothing new beneath the sun;
  Our doings have been done,
    And that which shall be was.

                                        1881

Sonnet 10
From *Monna Innominata*

Con miglior corso e con migliore stella.   —DANTE
La vita fugge e non s'arresta un' ora.   —PETRARCA

Time flies, hope flags, life plies a wearied wing;
  Death following hard on life gains ground apace;
  Faith runs with each and rears an eager face,
Outruns the rest, makes light of everything,
Spurns earth, and still finds breath to pray and sing;
  While love ahead of all uplifts his praise,
  Still asks for grace and still gives thanks for grace,
Content with all day brings and night will bring.
Life wanes; and when love folds his wings above
  Tired hope, and less we feel his conscious pulse,   10

Let us go fall asleep, dear friend, in peace:
A little while, and age and sorrow cease;
A little while, and life reborn annuls
Loss and decay and death, and all is love.

1881

Sonnet 6
From *Later Life: A Double Sonnet of Sonnets*

We lack, yet cannot fix upon the lack:
Not this, nor that; yet somewhat, certainly.
We see the things we do not yearn to see
Around us—and what see we glancing back?
Lost hopes that leave our hearts upon the rack,
Hopes that were never ours yet seemed to be,
For which we steered on life's salt stormy sea
Braving the sunstroke and the frozen pack.
If thus to look behind is all in vain.
And all in vain to look to left or right,   10
Why face we not our future once again,
Launching with hardier hearts across the main,
Straining dim eyes to catch the invisible sight,
And strong to bear ourselves in patient pain?

1881

Advent

Earth grown old yet still so green,
        Deep beneath her crust of cold,
Nurses fire unfelt, unseen—
        Earth grown old.

        We who live are quickly told:
Millions more lie hid between
        Inner swathings of her fold.

When will fire break up her screen?
        When will life burst through her mold?
Earth, earth, earth, thy cold is keen,   10
        Earth grown old.

1885

[Stroke a flint, and there is nothing to admire]

Stroke a flint, and there is nothing to admire:
Strike a flint, and forthwith flash out sparks of fire.

1893

[Sleeping at last, the trouble and tumult over]

Sleeping at last, the trouble and tumult over,
Sleeping at last, the struggle and horror past,
Cold and white, out of sight of friend and of lover,
    Sleeping at last.

No more a tired heart downcast or overcast,
No more pangs that wring or shifting fears that hover,
Sleeping at last in a dreamless sleep locked fast.

Fast asleep. Singing birds in their leafy cover
Cannot wake her, nor shake her the gusty blast.
Under the purple thyme and the purple clover   10
    Sleeping at last.

c. 1893 / 1896

EMILY JANE PFEIFFER

née Davis (1827–1890)

The bankruptcy of Emily Davis's grandfather impeded her formal education, but her artistic gifts were encouraged; while still in her teens, she gathered tales, music, and illustrations in The Holly Branch: An Album for 1843. *After her marriage in 1853 to Jurgen Edward Pfeiffer, a German banker, she composed* Valisneria; or A Midsummer Night's Dream *(1875), a fantasy in the mold of Sara Coleridge's* Phantasmion; *a verse drama entitled* The Wynnes of Wynhavod *(1881); and several long narrative poems:* Margaret, or The Motherless *(1861),* Gerard's Monument and Other Poems *(1873),* Glan-Alarch: His Silence and Song *(1877), and* The Rhyme of the Lady of the Rock and How It Grew *(1884). Pfeiffer's shorter verse was collected in* Poems *(1876),* Sonnets and Songs *(1880; rev. 1882),* Under the Aspens *(1882), and* Flowers of the Night *(1889). In response to her sonnets, Swinburne wrote that he was "struck by their singular power and freshness of thought."*

Between 1878 and 1885 she contributed articles on women's legal rights and feminist social issues to the Contemporary Review; Women and Work *(1888) compiles her arguments on behalf of women's education and female trade unions. Those callings that offer the highest rewards in money or consideration, she notes, are taboo or "unwomanly," while an outdated chivalric division of labor protects a male "army of incompetence." When she died, she left £2,000 for women's higher education.*

To a Moth That Drinketh of the Ripe October

I.

A moth belated, sun and zephyr-kissed,
Trembling about a pale arbutus bell,
Probing to wildering depths its honeyed cell—
A noonday thief, a downy sensualist!
Not vainly, sprite, thou drawest careless breath,
Strikest ambrosia from the cool-cupped flowers,

And flutterest through the soft, uncounted hours,
To drop at last in unawaited death;
'Tis something to be glad! and those fine thrills
Which move thee, to my lip have drawn the smile   10
Wherewith we look on joy. Drink! drown thine ills,
If ill have any part in thee; erewhile
May the pent force—thy bounded life, set free—
Fill larger sphere with equal ecstasy.

II.

With what fine organs art thou dowered, frail elf!
Thy harp is pitched too high for dull annoy,
Thy life a love feast, and a silent joy,
As mute and rapt as Passion's silent self.
I turn from thee and see the swallow sweep,
Like a winged will and the keen-scented hound   20
That snuffs with rapture at the tainted ground—
All things that freely course, that swim or leap—
Then hearing glad-voiced creatures men call dumb,
I feel my heart, oft sinking neath the weight
Of Nature's sorrow, lighten at the sum
Of Nature's joy; its half-unfolded fate
Breathes hope—for all but those beneath the ban
Of the inquisitor and tyrant, man.

                                        1878

The Lost Light

I.

I never touched thy royal hand, dead queen,
    But from afar have looked upon thy face,
    Which, calm with conquest, carried still the trace
Of many a hard-fought battle that had been.
Since thou hast done with life, its toil and teen,
    Its pains and gains, and that no further grace
    Can come to us of thee, a poorer place
Shows the lorn world—a dimlier lighted scene.

Lost queen and captain, Pallas of our band,
    Who late upon the height of glory stood,   10
Guarding from scorn—the ægis in thy hand—
    The banner of insurgent womanhood;
Who of our cause may take the high command?
    Who make with shining front our victory good?

II.

Great student of the schools, who grew to be
 The greater teacher, having wandered wide
 In lonely strength of purity and pride
Through pathless sands, unfruitful as the sea,
Now warning words—and one clear act of thee,
 Bold pioneer who shouldst have been our guide—   20
 Affirm the track which wisdom must abide.
For man is bond, the beast alone is free.

So hast thou sought a larger good, so won
 Thy way to higher law, that by thy grave,
We, thanking thee for lavish gifts, for none
 May owe thee more than that in quest so brave—
True to a light our onward feet may shun—
 Thou gavest nobler strength our strength to save.

1880

A Chrysalis

When gathering shells cast upwards by the waves
 Of progress, they who note its ebb and flow,
 Its flux and reflux, surely come to know
That the sea level rises; that dark caves
Of ignorance are flooded, and foul graves
 Of sin are cleansed, albeit the work is slow;
 Till, seeing great from less forever grow,
Law comes to mean for them the Love that saves.

And leaning down the ages, my dull ear,
 Catching their slow-ascending harmonies,
I am uplift of them, and borne more near,   10
 I feel within my flesh—laid pupa-wise—
A soul of worship, though of vision dim,
 Which links me with wing-folded cherubim.

1888

Klytemnestra

I.

Daughter of gods and men, great ruling will,
 Seething in oily rage within the sphere
 Which gods and men assign the woman here,
Till, stricken where the wound approved thee still

Mother and mortal, all the tide of ill
   Rushed through the gap, and nothing more seemed dear
   But power to wreak high ruin, nothing clear
But the long dream you waited to fulfill.

Mother and spouse, queen of the king of men,
   What fury brought Aegysthus to thy side—   10
That bearded semblant, man to outward ken,
   But else mere mawworm, made to fret man's pride?
Woman, thy foot was on thy tyrant then—
   Mother, thou wert avenged for love defied!

II.

Woman and Greek—so, doubly trained in art!—
   Spreading the purple for the conqueror's tread,
   Bowing with feline grace thy royal head,
How perfect, whelp-robbed lioness, thy part!
One wrong the more to wring the ancient smart,
   Then three swift strokes, and the slow hope blooms red,   20
   Who shamed the hero lays him with the dead,
Where nevermore his word may vex her heart.

Bold queen, what were to thee the gods of Greece?
   What had been any god of any name,
More than the lion-heart you made to cease,
   Or the live dog to all your humors tame?—
The very furies left your soul in peace
   Until Orestes' sword drove home their claim.

1888

AUGUSTA WEBSTER

née Julia Augusta Davies; pseud., Cecil Home (1837–1894)

Daughter of a family with literary connections, Augusta Davies had a good classical education, learning French, Italian, Spanish, and Greek. At the Kensington Art School, according to Ray Strachey, she "nearly dashed the prospects of women art students forever by being expelled for whistling." Davies published her first volume of verse at twenty-three: Blanche Lisle and Other Poems *(1860).*

In 1863 she married Thomas Webster, a fellow of Trinity College; she was devoted to their only daughter. In 1864 another volume of verse, Lilian Gray, *and her only novel,* Lesley's Guardians, *appeared. She translated Aeschylus'* Prometheus Bound *(1866) and Euripides'* Medea *(1868). An activist for women's education and suffrage, she demonstrated in* Housewife's Opinions *(1878) her "mother-wit" on social and domestic subjects. She was elected to the London School Board.*

Webster's poetic achievement lies in her dramatic monologues, influenced by the Brownings and Tennyson. Dramatic Studies *(1866) and* A Woman Sold and Other Poems *(1867) were praised by reviewers for their "masculine" vigor and "strength."* Portraits *(1870) juxtaposes acid social analyses and revealing self-portraits of figures like Circe and a courtesan, which one reviewer found "too painful."* A Book of Rhyme *(1881) inaugurated the Italian stanza form known as* risputi *or* stornelli *into English poetry.*

William Rossetti, in introducing the sonnet sequence Mother and Daughter *(1895), praised the "natural" beauty of these playful depictions of domestic affection; he singled out her drama* The Sentence *as equal to the work of Barrett Browning or of Christina Rossetti, who herself considered Webster next to Barrett Browning in poetic power. Vita Sackville-West commented that her poetry was "good, but powerful."*

Circe

The sun drops luridly into the west;
Darkness has raised her arms to draw him down
Before the time, not waiting as of wont

Till he has come to her behind the sea;
And the smooth waves grow sullen in the gloom
And wear their threatening purple; more and more
The plain of waters sways and seems to rise
Convexly from its level of the shores;
And low dull thunder rolls along the beach:
There will be storm at last, storm, glorious storm!   10

Oh, welcome, welcome, though it rend my bowers,
Scattering my blossomed roses like the dust,
Splitting the shrieking branches, tossing down
My riotous vines with their young half-tinged grapes
Like small round amethysts or beryls strung
Tumultuously in clusters; though it sate
Its ravenous spite among my goodliest pines,
Standing there round and still against the sky
That makes blue lakes between their somber tufts,
Or harry from my silvery olive slopes   20
Some hoary king whose gnarled fantastic limbs
Wear rugged armor of a thousand years;
Though it will hurl high on my flowery shores
The hostile wave that rives at the poor sward
And drags it down the slants, that swirls its foam
Over my terraces, shakes their firm blocks
Of great bright marbles into tumbled heaps,
And makes my pleached and mossy labyrinths,
Where the small odorous blossoms grow like stars
Strewn in the milky way, a briny marsh.   30
What matter? let it come and bring me change,
Breaking the sickly sweet monotony.

I am too weary of this long bright calm;
Always the same blue sky, always the sea
The same blue perfect likeness of the sky,
One rose to match the other that has waned,
Tomorrow's dawn the twin of yesterday's;
And every night the ceaseless crickets chirp
The same long joy, and the late strain of birds
Repeats their strain of all the even month;   40
And changelessly the petty plashing surfs
Bubble their chiming burden round the stones;
Dusk after dusk brings the same languid trance
Upon the shadowy hills, and in the fields
The waves of fireflies come and go the same,
Making the very flash of light and stir
Vex one like dronings of the shuttles at task.

Give me some change. Must life be only sweet,
All honey-pap as babes would have their food?
And, if my heart must always be adrowse   50
In a hush of stagnant sunshine, give me, then,
Something outside me stirring; let the storm
Break up the sluggish beauty, let it fall
Beaten below the feet of passionate winds,
And then tomorrow waken jubilant
In a new birth; let me see subtle joy
Of anguish and of hopes, of change and growth.

What fate is mine, who, far apart from pains
And fears and turmoils of the cross-grained world,
Dwell like a lonely god in a charmed isle   60
Where I am first and only, and like one
Who should love poisonous savors more than mead,
Long for a tempest on me and grow sick
Of rest and of divine free carelessness!
Oh me, I am a woman, not a god;
Yea, those who tend me, even, are more than I,
My nymphs who have the souls of flowers and birds,
Singing and blossoming immortally.

Ah me! these love a day and laugh again,
And loving, laughing, find a full content;   70
But I know nought of peace, and have not loved.

Where is my love? Does someone cry for me,
Not knowing whom he calls? Does his soul cry
For mine to grow beside it, grow in it?
Does he beseech the gods to give him me,
The one unknown rare woman by whose side
No other woman thrice as beautiful
Could once seem fair to him; to whose voice heard
In any common tones no sweetest sound
Of love made melody on silver lutes,   80
Or singing like Apollo's when the gods
Grow pale with happy listening, might be peered
For making music to him; whom once found,
There will be no more seeking anything?

Oh love, oh love, oh love, art not yet come
Out of the waiting shadows into life?
Art not yet come after so many years
That I have longed for thee? Come! I am here.

Not yet. For surely I should feel a sound
Of his far answer if now in the world   90

He sought me who will seek me—Oh, ye gods,
Will he not seek me? Is it all a dream?
Will there be only these, these bestial things
Who wallow in their sties, or mop and mow
Among the trees, or munch in pens and byres,
Or snarl and filch behind their wattled coops;
These things who had believed that they were men?

Nay, but he *will* come. Why am I so fair,
And marvelously minded, and with sight
Which flashes suddenly on hidden things,   100
As the gods see, who do not need to look?
Why wear I in my eyes that stronger power
Than basilisks, whose gaze can only kill,
To draw men's souls to me to live or die,
As I would have them? Why am I given pride
Which yet longs to be broken, and this scorn,
Cruel and vengeful, for the lesser men
Who meet the smiles I waste for lack of him
And grow too glad? Why am I who I am?
But for the sake of him whom fate will send   110
One day to be my master utterly,
That he should take me, the desire of all,
Whom only he in the world could bow to him.

Oh, sunlike glory of pale glittering hairs,
Bright as the filmy wires my weavers take
To make me golden gauzes—Oh, deep eyes,
Darker and softer than the bluest dusk
Of August violets, darker and deep
Like crystal fathomless lakes in summer noons—
Oh, sad sweet longing smile—Oh, lips that tempt   120
My very self to kisses—oh, round cheeks
Tenderly radiant with the even flush
Of pale smoothed coral—perfect lovely face
Answering my gaze from out this fleckless pool—
Wonder of glossy shoulders, chiseled limbs—
Should I be so your lover as I am,
Drinking an exquisite joy to watch you thus
In all a hundred changes through the day,
But that I love you for him till he comes,
But that my beauty means his loving it?   130

Oh, look! a speck on this side of the sun,
Coming—yes, coming with the rising wind
That frays the darkening cloud-wrack on the verge
And in a little while will leap abroad,

Spattering the sky with rushing blacknesses,
Dashing the hissing mountainous waves at the stars,
'Twill drive me that black speck, a shuddering hulk
Caught in the buffeting waves, dashed impotent
From ridge to ridge, will drive it in the night
With that dull jarring crash upon the beach,   140
And the cries for help and the cries of fear and hope.

And then tomorrow they will thoughtfully,
With grave low voices, count their perils up
And thank the gods for having let them live,
And tell of wives and mothers in their homes,
And children, who would have such loss in them
That they must weep (and maybe I weep too)
With fancy of the weepings had they died.
And the next morrow they will feel their ease
And sigh with sleek content, or laugh elate,   150
Tasting delight of rest and reveling,
Music and perfumes, joyance for the eyes
Of rosy faces and luxurious pomps,
The savor of the banquet and the glow
And fragrance of the winecup; and they'll talk
How good it is to house in palaces,
Out of the storms and struggles, and what luck
Strewed their good ship on our accessless coast.
Then the next day the beast in them will wake,
And one will strike and bicker, and one swell   160
With puffed-up greatness, and one gibe and strut
In apish pranks, and one will line his sleeve
With pilfered booties, and one snatch the gems
Out of the carven goblets as they pass,
One will grow mad with fever of the wine,
And one will sluggishly besot himself,
And one be lewd, and one be gluttonous;
And I shall sickly look and loathe them all.

Oh my rare cup! my pure and crystal cup,
With not one speck of color to make false   170
The entering lights, or flaw to make them swerve!
My cup of truth! How the lost fools will laugh
And thank me for my boon, as if I gave
Some momentary flash of the gods' joy,
To drink where *I* have drunk and touch the touch
Of *my* lips with their own! Aye, let them touch.

Too cruel, am I? And the silly beasts,
Crowding around me when I pass their way,

Glower on me and, although they love me still
(With their poor sorts of love such as they could),   180
Call wrath and vengeance to their humid eyes
To scare me into mercy, or creep near
With piteous fawnings, supplicating bleats.
Too cruel? Did I choose them what they are?
Or change them from themselves by poisonous charms?
But any draft, pure water, natural wine,
Out of my cup revealed them to themselves
And to each other. Change? there was no change;
Only disguise gone from them unawares:
And had there been one true right man of them,   190
He would have drunk the draft as I had drunk
And stood unharmed and looked me in the eyes,
Abashing me before him. But these things—
Why, which of them has even shown the kind
Of some one nobler beast? Pah! yapping wolves,
And pitiless stealthy wildcats, curs, and apes,
And gorging swine, and slinking venomous snakes—
All false and ravenous and sensual brutes
That shame the Earth that bore them, these they are.

Lo, lo! the shivering blueness darting forth   200
On half the heavens, and the forked thin fire
Strikes to the sea: and hark, the sudden voice
That rushes through the trees before the storm
And shuddering of the branches. Yet the sky
Is blue against them still, and early stars
Sparkle above the pine-tops; and the air
Clings faint and motionless around me here.

Another burst of flame—and the black speck
Shows in the glare, lashed onwards. It were well
I bade make ready for our guests tonight.   210

1870

A Castaway

Poor little diary, with its simple thoughts,
Its good resolves, its "Studied French an hour,"
"Read modern history," "Trimmed up my gray hat,"
"Darned stockings," "Tatted," "Practiced my new song,"
"Went to the daily service," "Took Bess soup,"
"Went out to tea." Poor simple diary!
And did *I* write it? Was I this good girl,
This budding colorless young rose of home?

Did I so live content in such a life,
Seeing no larger scope, nor asking it,   10
Than this small constant round—old clothes to mend,
New clothes to make, then go and say my prayers,
Or carry soup, or take a little walk
And pick the ragged robins in the hedge?
Then, for ambition (was there ever life
That could forgo that?), to improve my mind
And know French better and sing harder songs;
For gaiety, to go, in my best white,
Well washed and starched and freshened with new
        bows,
And take tea out to meet the clergyman.   20
No wishes and no cares, almost no hopes,
Only the young girl's hazed and golden dreams
That veil the future from her.

                    So long since:
And now it seems a jest to talk of me
As if I could be one with her, of me
who am . . . me.

                    And what is that? My looking-glass
Answers it passably; a woman, sure,
No fiend, no slimy thing out of the pools,
A woman with a ripe and smiling lip
That has no venom in its touch, I think,   30
With a white brow on which there is no brand;
A woman none dare call not beautiful,
Not womanly in every woman's grace.

Aye, let me feed upon my beauty thus,
Be glad in it like painters when they see
At last the face they dreamed but could not find
Look from their canvas on them, triumph in it,
The dearest thing I have. Why, 'tis my all,
Let me make much of it: is it not this,
This beauty, my own curse at once and tool   40
To snare men's souls (I know what the good say
Of beauty in such creatures), is it not this
That makes me feel myself a woman still,
With still some little pride, some little—

                    Stop!
"Some little pride, some little—" Here's a jest!
What word will fit the sense but modesty?
A wanton I, but modest!

                    Modest, true;
I'm not drunk in the streets, ply not for hire
At infamous corners with my likenesses
Of the humbler kind; yes, modesty's my word—   50
'Twould shape my mouth well too, I think I'll try:
"Sir, Mr. What-you-will, Lord Who-knows-what,
My present lover or my next to come,
Value me at my worth, fill your purse full,
For I am modest; yes, and honor me
As though your schoolgirl sister or your wife
Could let her skirts brush mine or talk of me;
For I am modest."

                    Well, I flout myself:
But yet, but yet—

                    Fie, poor fantastic fool,
Why do I play the hypocrite alone,   60
Who am no hypocrite with others by?
Where should be my "But yet"? I am that thing
Called half a dozen dainty names, and none
Dainty enough to serve the turn and hide
The one coarse English worst that lurks beneath:
Just that, no worse, no better.

                    And, for me,
I say let no one be above her trade;
I own my kindredship with any drab
Who sells herself as I, although she crouch
In fetid garrets and I have a home   70
All velvet and marquetry and pastilles,
Although she hide her skeleton in rags
And I set fashions and wear cobweb lace:
The difference lies but in my choicer ware,
That I sell beauty and she ugliness;
Our traffic's one—I'm no sweet slaver-tongue
To gloze upon it and explain myself
A sort of fractious angel misconceived—
Our traffic's one: I own it. And what then?
I know of worse that are called honorable: 80
Our lawyers, who with noble eloquence
And virtuous outbursts lie to hang a man,
Or lie to save him, which way goes the fee;
Our preachers, gloating on your future hell
For not believing what they doubt themselves;
Our doctors, who sort poisons out by chance
And wonder how they'll answer, and grow rich;

Our journalists, whose business is to fib
And juggle truths and falsehoods to and fro;
Our tradesmen, who must keep unspotted names   90
And cheat the least like stealing that they can;
Our—all of them, the virtuous worthy men
Who feed on the world's follies, vices, wants,
And do their businesses of lies and shams
Honestly, reputably, while the world
Claps hands and cries, "good luck." Which of their
        trades,
Their honorable trades, barefaced like mine,
All secrets brazened out, would show more white?

And whom do I hurt more than they? as much?
The wives? Poor fools, what do I take from them   100
Worth crying for or keeping? If they knew
What their fine husbands look like seen by eyes
That may perceive there are more men than one!
But, if they can, let them just take the pains
To keep them: 'tis not such a mighty task
To pin an idiot to your apron-string;
And wives have an advantage over us
(The good and blind ones have), the smile or pout
Leaves them no secret nausea at odd times.
Oh, they could keep their husbands if they cared,   110
But 'tis an easier life to let them go,
And whimper at it for morality.

Oh! those shrill carping virtues, safely housed
From reach of even a smile that should put red
On a decorous cheek, who rail at us
With such a spiteful scorn and rancorousness
(Which maybe is half envy at the heart),
And boast themselves so measurelessly good
And us so measurelessly unlike them,
What is their wondrous merit that they stay   120
In comfortable homes whence not a soul
Has ever thought of tempting them and wear
No kisses but a husband's upon lips
There is no other man desires to kiss—
Refrain in fact from sin impossible?
How dare they hate us so? what have they done,
What borne, to prove them other than we are?
What right have they to scorn us—glass-case saints,
Dianas under lock and key—what right
More than the well-fed, helpless barn-door fowl   130
To scorn the larcenous wild birds?

Pshaw, let be!
Scorn or no scorn, what matter for their scorn?
I have outfaced my own—that's harder work.
Aye, let their virtuous malice dribble on—
Mock snowstorms on the stage—I'm proof long
　　　since:
I have looked coolly on my what and why,
And I accept myself.

　　　　　Oh, I'll endorse
The shamefullest revilings mouthed at me,
Cry "True! Oh perfect picture! Yes, that's I!"
And add a telling blackness here and there,　　　　　　　　140
And then dare swear you, every nine of ten,
My judges and accusers, I'd not change
My conscience against yours, you who tread out
Your devil's pilgrimage along the roads
That take in church and chapel and arrange
A roundabout and decent way to hell.

Well, mine's a short way and a merry one:
So says my pious hash of ohs and ahs,
Choice texts and choicer threats, appropriate names,
(*Rahabs* and *Jezebels*) some fierce Tartuffe　　　　　　　　150
Hurled at me through the post. We had rare fun
Over that tract digested with champagne.
Where is it? where's my rich repertory
Of insults Biblical? *'I prey on souls'*—
Only my men have oftenest none I think:
'I snare the simple ones'—but in these days
There seem to be none simple and none snared,
And most men have their favorite sinnings planned
To do them civilly and sensibly:
'I braid my hair'—but braids are out of date:　　　　　　　　160
'I paint my cheeks'—I always wear them pale:
'I—'

　　　　　Pshaw! the trash is savorless today:
One cannot laugh alone. There, let it burn.
What, does the windy dullard think one needs
His wisdom dovetailed onto Solomon's,
His threats outthreatening God's, to teach the news
That those who need not sin have safer souls?
We know it, but we've bodies to save too;
And so we earn our living.

　　　　　　　　Well lit, tract!
At least you've made me a good leaping blaze.　　　　　　　　170

Up, up, how the flame shoots! and now 'tis dead.
Oh proper finish, preaching to the last—
No such bad omen either; sudden end,
And no sad withering horrible old age.
How one would clutch at youth to hold it tight!
And then to know it gone, to see it gone,
Be taught its absence by harsh careless looks,
To live forgotten, solitary, old—
The cruelest word that ever woman learns.
Old—that's to be nothing, or to be at best   180
A blurred memorial that in better days
There was a woman once with such a name.
No, no, I could not bear it: death itself
Shows kinder promise . . . even death itself,
Since it must come one day—

                           Oh this gray gloom!
This rain, rain, rain, what wretched thoughts it brings!
Death: I'll not think of it.

                        Will no one come?
'Tis dreary work alone.

                  Why did I read
That silly diary? Now, singsong, ding-dong,
Come the old vexing echoes back again,   190
Church bells and nursery good books, back again
Upon my shrinking ears that had forgotten—
I hate the useless memories: 'tis fools' work
Singing the hackneyed dirge of 'better days':
Best take Now kindly, give the past good-bye,
Whether it were a better or a worse.

Yes, yes, I listened to the echoes once,
The echoes and the thoughts from the old days.
The worse for me: I lost my richest friend,
And that was all the difference. For the world,   200
I would not have that flight known. How they'd roar:
"What! Eulalie, when she refused us all,
'Ill' and 'away,' was doing Magdalene,
Tears, ashes, and her Bible, and then off
To hide her in a refuge . . . for a week!"

A wild whim that, to fancy I could change
My new self for my old because I wished!
Since then, when in my languid days there comes
That craving, like homesickness, to go back
To the good days, the dear old stupid days,   210

To the quiet and the innocence, I know
'Tis a sick fancy and try palliatives.

What is it? You go back to the old home,
And 'tis not *your* home, has no place for you,
And if it had, you could not fit you in it.
And could I fit me to my former self?
If I had had the wit, like some of us,
To sow my wild oats into three-percents,
Could I not find me shelter in the peace
Of some far nook where none of them would come,   220
Nor whisper travel from this scurrilous world
(That gloats, and moralizes through its leers)
To blast me with my fashionable shame?
There I might—oh, my castle in the clouds!
And where's its rent?—but there, were there a
          there,
I might again live the grave blameless life
Among such simple pleasures, simple cares:
But could they be my pleasures, be my cares?
The blameless life, but never the content—
Never. How could I henceforth be content   230
With any life but one that sets the brain
In a hot merry fever with its stir?
What would there be in quiet rustic days,
Each like the other, full of time to think,
To keep one bold enough to live at all?
Quiet is hell, I say—as if a woman
Could bear to sit alone, quiet all day,
And loathe herself and sicken on her thoughts.

They tried it at the refuge, and I failed:
I could not bear it. Dreary hideous room,   240
Coarse pittance, prison rules, one might bear these
And keep one's purpose; but so much alone,
And then made faint and weak and fanciful
By change from pampering to half-famishing—
Good God, what thoughts come! Only one week
          more
And 'twould have ended: but in one day more
I must have killed myself. And I loathe death,
The dreadful foul corruption with who knows
What future after it.

          Well, I came back,
Back to my slough. Who says I had my choice?   250
Could I stay there to die of some mad death?

And if I rambled out into the world
Sinless but penniless, what else were that
But slower death, slow pining shivering death
By misery and hunger? Choice! what choice
Of living well or ill? could I have that?
And who would give it me? I think indeed
If some kind hand, a woman's—I hate men—
Had stretched itself to help me to firm ground,
Taken a chance and risked my falling back,   260
I could have gone my way not falling back:
But, let her be all brave, all charitable,
How could she do it? Such a trifling boon—
A little work to live by, 'tis not much—
And I might have found will enough to last:
But where's the work? More seamstresses than
        shirts;
And defter hands at white work than are mine
Drop starved at last: dressmakers, milliners,
Too many, too, they say; and then their trades
Need skill, apprenticeship. And who so bold   270
As hire me for their humblest drudgery?
Not even for scullery slut; not even, I think,
For governess although they'd get me cheap.
And after all it would be something hard,
With the marts for decent women overfull,
If I could elbow in and snatch a chance
And oust some good girl so, who then perforce
Must come and snatch her chance among our crowd.

Why, if the worthy men who think all's done
If we'll but come where we can hear them preach,   280
Could bring us all, or any half of us,
Into their fold, teach all us wandering sheep,
Or only half of us, to stand in rows
And baa them hymns and moral songs, good lack,
What would they do with us? what could they do?
Just think! with were it but half of us on hand
To find work for . . . or husbands. Would they try
To ship us to the colonies for wives?

Well, well, I know the wise ones talk and talk:
"Here's cause, here's cure"—"No, here it is, and
        here"—   290
And find society to blame, or law,
The Church, the men, the women, too few schools,
Too many schools, too much, too little taught:
Somewhere or somehow someone is to blame;

But I say all the fault's with God himself
Who puts too many women in the world.
We ought to die off reasonably and leave
As many as the men want, none to waste.
Here's cause: the woman's superfluity;
And for the cure, why, if it were the law,   300
Say, every year, in due percentages,
Balancing them with males as the times need,
To kill off female infants, 'twould make room;
And some of us would not have lost too much,
Losing life ere we know what it *can* mean.

The other day I saw a woman weep
Beside her dead child's bed: the little thing
Lay smiling, and the other wailed half mad,
Shrieking to God to give it back again.
I could have laughed aloud: the little girl   310
Living had but her mother's life to live;
There she lay smiling, and her mother wept
To know her gone!

        My mother would have wept.

Oh, mother, mother, did you ever dream,
You good grave simple mother, you pure soul
No evil could come nigh, did you once dream
In all your dying cares for your lone girl
Left to fight out her fortune helplessly
That there would be *this* danger?—for *your* girl,
Taught by you, lapped in a sweet ignorance,   320
Scarcely more wise of what things sin could be
Than some young child a summer six months old,
Where in the north the summer makes a day,
Of what is darkness . . . darkness that will come
Tomorrow suddenly. Thank God at least
For this much of my life, that when you died,
That when you kissed me dying, not a thought
Of this made sorrow for you, that I too
Was pure of even fear.

        Oh yes, I thought,
Still new in my insipid treadmill life   330
(My father so late dead), and hopeful still,
There might be something pleasant somewhere in it,
Some sudden fairy come, no doubt, to turn
My pumpkin to a chariot, I thought then
That I might plod and plod and drum the sounds
Of useless facts into unwilling ears,

Tease children with dull questions half the day,
Then con dull answers in my room at night
Ready for next day's questions, mend quill pens
And cut my fingers, add up sums done wrong   340
And never get them right; teach, teach, and teach—
What I half knew, or not at all—teach, teach
For years, a lifetime—*I*!

                  And yet, who knows?
It might have been, for I was patient once,
And willing, and meant well; it might have been
Had I but still clung on in my first place—
A safe dull place, where mostly there were smiles
But never merrymakings; where all days
Jogged on sedately busy, with no haste;
Where all seemed measured out, but margins broad: 350
A dull home but a peaceful, where I felt
My pupils would be dear young sisters soon,
And felt their mother take me to her heart,
Motherly to all lonely harmless things.
But I must have a conscience, must blurt out
My great discovery of my ignorance!
And who required it of me? And who gained?
What did it matter for a more or less
The girls learned in their schoolbooks, to forget
In their first season? We did well together: 360
They loved me and I them; but I went off
To housemaid's pay, six cross-grained brats to teach,
Wrangles and jangles, doubts, disgrace . . . then this;
And they had a perfection found for them
Who has all ladies' learning in her head
Abridged and scheduled, speaks five languages,
Knows botany and conchology and globes,
Draws, paints, plays, sings, embroiders, teaches all
On a patent method never known to fail:
And now they're finished and, I hear, poor things,   370
Are the worst dancers and worst dressers out.
And where's their profit of those prison years
All gone to make them wise in lesson books?
Who wants his wife to know weeds' Latin names?
Who ever chose a girl for saying dates?
Or asked if she had learned to trace a map?

Well, well, the silly rules this silly world
Makes about women! This is one of them.
Why must there be pretense of teaching them
What no one ever cares that they should know,   380

What, grown out of the schoolroom, they cast off
Like the schoolroom pinafore, no better fit
For any use of real grown-up life,
For any use to her who seeks or waits
The husband and the home, for any use,
For any shallowest pretense of use,
To her who has them? Do I not know this,
I, like my betters, that a woman's life,
Her natural life, her good life, her one life,
Is in her husband, God on earth to her,   390
And what she knows and what she can and is,
Is only good as it brings good to him?

Oh God, do I not know it? I, the thing
Of shame and rottenness, the animal
That feed men's lusts and prey on them, I, I,
Who should not dare to take the name of wife
On my polluted lips, who in the word
Hear but my own reviling, I know that.
I could have lived by that rule, how content:
My pleasure to make him some pleasure, pride   400
To be as he would have me, duty, care,
To fit all to his taste, rule my small sphere
To his intention; then to lean on him,
Be guided, tutored, loved—no, not that word,
That *loved* which between men and women means
All selfishness, all cloying talk, all lust,
All vanity, all idiocy—not loved,
But cared for. I've been loved myself, I think,
Some once or twice since my poor mother died,
But *cared for*, never—that's a word for homes,   410
Kind homes, good homes, where simple children
        come
And ask their mother is this right or wrong,
Because they know she's perfect, cannot err;
Their father told them so, and he knows all,
Being so wise and good and wonderful,
Even enough to scold even her at times
And tell her everything she does not know.
Ah, the sweet nursery logic!

                            Fool! thrice fool!
Do I hanker after that, too? Fancy me
Infallible nursery saint, live code of law!   420
Me, preaching! teaching innocence to be good!—
A mother!

　　　　　　　　Yet the baby thing that woke
And wailed an hour or two, and then was dead,
Was mine, and had he lived . . . why then my name
Would have been mother. But 'twas well he died:
I could have been no mother, I, lost then
Beyond his saving. Had he come before
And lived, come to me in the doubtful days
When shame and boldness had not grown one sense,
For his sake, with the courage come of him,　　　　　　　　430
I might have struggled back.

　　　　　　　　But how? But how?
His father would not then have let me go:
His time had not yet come to make an end
Of my 'forever' with a hireling's fee
And civil, light dismissal. None but him
To claim a bit of bread of if I went,
Child or no child: would he have given it me?
He! no; he had not done with me. No help,
No help, no help. Some ways can be trodden back,
But never our way, we who one wild day　　　　　　　　440
Have given good-bye to what in our deep hearts
The lowest woman still holds best in life,
Good name—good name, though given by the world
That mouths and garbles with its decent prate,
And wraps it in respectable grave shams,
And patches conscience partly by the rule
Of what one's neighbor thinks, but something more
By what his eyes are sharp enough to see.
How I could scorn it with its Pharisees,
If it could not scorn me: but yet, but yet—　　　　　　　　450
Oh God, if I could look it in the face!

Oh I am wild, am ill, I think, tonight:
Will no one come and laugh with me? No feast,
No merriment tonight. So long alone!
Will no one come?

　　　　　　　　At least there's a new dress
To try and grumble at—they never fit
To one's ideal. Yes, a new rich dress,
With lace like this, too, that's a soothing balm
For any fretting woman, cannot fail;
I've heard men say it . . . and they know so well　　　　　　　　460
What's in all women's hearts, especially
Women like me.

No help! no help! no help!
How could it be? It was too late long since—
Even at the first too late. Whose blame is that?
There are some kindly people in the world,
But what can *they* do? If one hurls oneself
Into a quicksand, what can be the end
But that one sinks and sinks? Cry out for help?
Ah yes, and if it came, who is so strong
To strain from the firm ground and lift one out?   470
And how, so firmly clutching the stretched hand
As death's pursuing terror bids, even so,
How can one reach firm land, having to foot
The treacherous crumbling soil that slides and gives
And sucks one in again? Impossible path!
No, why waste struggles, I or anyone?
What is must be. What then? I where I am,
Sinking and sinking; let the wise pass by
And keep their wisdom for an apter use,
Let me sink merrily as I best may.   480

Only, I think my brother—I forgot;
He stopped his brotherhood some years ago—
But if he had been just so much less good
As to remember mercy. Did he think
How once I was his sister, prizing him
As sisters do, content to learn for him
The lesson girls with brothers all must learn,
To do without?

               I have heard girls lament
That doing so without all things one would,
But I saw never aught to murmur at,   490
For men must be made ready for their work,
And women all have more or less their chance
Of husbands to work for them, keep them safe
Like summer roses in soft greenhouse air
That never guess 'tis winter out of doors:
No, I saw never aught to murmur at,
Content with stinted fare and shabby clothes
And cloistered silent life to save expense,
Teaching myself out of my borrowed books,
While he, for some one pastime (needful, true,   500
To keep him of his rank; 'twas not his fault),
Spent in a month what could have given me
My teachers for a year.

'Twas no one's fault:
For could he be launched forth on the rude sea
Of this contentious world and left to find
Oars and the boatsman's skill by some good chance?
'Twas no one's fault: yet still he might have thought
Of our so different youths and owned at least
'Tis pitiful when a mere nerveless girl
Untutored must put forth upon that sea,   510
Not in the woman's true place, the wife's place,
To trust a husband and be borne along,
But impotent blind pilot to herself.

Merciless, merciless—like the prudent world
That will not have the flawed soul prank itself
With a hoped second virtue, will not have
The woman fallen once lift up herself . . .
Lest she should fall again. Oh, how his taunts,
His loathing fierce reproaches, scarred and seared
Like branding iron hissing in a wound!   520
And it was true—*that* killed me: and I felt
A hideous hopeless shame burn out my heart,
And knew myself forever that he said,
That which I was— Oh, it was true, true, true.

No, not true then. I was not all that then.
Oh, I have drifted on before mad winds
And made ignoble shipwreck; not today
Could any breeze of heaven prosper me
Into the track again, nor any hand
Snatch me out of the whirlpool I have reached;   530
But then?

       Nay, he judged very well: he knew
Repentance was too dear a luxury
For a beggar's buying, knew it earns no bread—
And knew me a too base and nerveless thing
To bear my first fault's sequel and just die.
And how could he have helped me? Held my hand,
Owned me for his, fronted the angry world
Clothed with my ignominy? Or maybe
Taken me to his home to damn him worse?
What did I look for? for what less would serve   540
That he could do, a man without a purse?
He meant me well; he sent me that five pounds,
Much to him then; and if he bade me work
And never vex him more with news of me,
We both knew him too poor for pensioners.

I see he did his best; I could wish now
Sending it back I had professed some thanks.

But there! I was too wretched to be meek:
It seemed to me as if he, everyone,
The whole great world, were guilty of my guilt,   550
Abettors and avengers: in my heart
I gibed them back their gibings; I was wild.

I see clear now and know one has one's life
In hand at first to spend or spare or give
Like any other coin; spend it, or give,
Or drop it in the mire, can the world see
You get your value for it, or bar off
The hurrying of its marts to grope it up
And give it back to you for better use?
And if you spend or give, that is your choice;   560
And if you let it slip, that's your choice, too—
You should have held it firmer. Yours the blame,
And not another's, not the indifferent world's
Which goes on steadily, statistically,
And counts by censuses not separate souls—
And if it somehow needs to its worst use
So many lives of women, useless else,
It buys us of ourselves; we could hold back,
Free all of us to starve, and some of us
(Those who have done no ill, and are in luck),   570
To slave their lives out and have food and clothes
Until they grow unserviceably old.

Oh, I blame no one—scarcely even myself.
It was to be: the very good in me
Has always turned to hurt; all I thought right
At the hot moment, judged of afterwards,
Shows reckless.

      Why, look at it, had I taken
The pay my dead child's father offered me
For having been its mother, I could then
Have kept life in me—many have to do it,   580
That swarm in the back alleys, on no more,
Cold sometimes, mostly hungry, but they live—
I could have gained a respite, trying it,
And maybe found at last some humble work
To eke the pittance out. Not I, forsooth,
I must have spirit, must have womanly pride,
Must dash back his contemptuous wages, I,
Who had not scorned to earn them, dash them back

The fiercer that he dared to count our boy
In my appraising: and yet now I think   590
I might have taken it for my dead boy's sake;
It would have been *his* gift.

                           But I went forth
With my fine scorn, and whither did it lead?
Money's the root of evil do they say?
Money is virtue, strength; money to me
Would then have been repentance: could I live
Upon my idiot's pride?

                        Well, it fell soon.
I had prayed Clement might believe me dead,
And yet I begged of him— That's like me too,
Beg of him and then send him back his alms!   600
What if he gave as to a whining wretch
That holds her hand and lies? I am less to him
Than such a one; her rags do him no wrong,
But I, I wrong him merely that I live,
Being his sister. Could I not at least
Have still let him forget me? But 'tis past:
And naturally, he may hope I am long dead.

Good God! to think that we were what we were
One to the other . . . and now!

                         He has done well;
Married a sort of heiress, I have heard,   610
A dapper little madam, dimple-cheeked
And dimple-brained, who makes him a good wife—
No doubt she'd never own but just to him,
And in a whisper, she can even suspect
That we exist, we other women things:
What would she say if she could learn one day
She has a sister-in-law? So he and I
Must stand apart till doomsday.

                           But the jest,
To think how she would look!—Her fright, poor
    thing!
The notion!—I could laugh outright . . . or else,   620
For I feel near it, roll on the ground and sob.

Well, after all, there's not much difference
Between the two sometimes.

                        Was that the bell?
Someone at last, thank goodness. There's a voice,

And that's a pleasure. Whose, though? Ah, I know.
Why did she come alone, the cackling goose?
Why not have brought her sister?—she tells more
And titters less. No matter; half a loaf
Is better than no bread.

                Oh, is it you?
Most welcome, dear: one gets so moped alone.   630

              1870

Sonnets from *Mother and Daughter*
5

Last night the broad blue lightnings flamed the sky;
   We watched, our breaths caught as each burst its way
   And, through its fire, outleaped the sharp white ray,
And sudden dark reclosed when it went by:
But she, that where we are will needs be nigh,
   Had tired with hunting orchids half the day.
   Her father thought she called us; he and I,
Half anxious, reached the bedroom where she lay.

Oh lily face upon the whiteness blent!
   How calm she lay in her unconscious grace!   10
A peal crashed on the silence ere we went;
   She stirred in sleep, a little changed her place,
   "Mother," she breathed, a smile grew on her face:
"Mother," my darling breathed, and slept content.

8

A little child she half defiant came
   Reasoning her case—'twas not so long ago—
   "I cannot mind your scolding, for I know
However bad I were you'd love the same."
And I, what countering answer could I frame?
   'Twas true, and true, and God's self told her so.
   One does but ask one's child to smile and grow,
And each rebuke has love for its right name.

And yet, methinks, sad mothers, who for years,
   Watching the child pass forth that was their boast,   10
Have counted all the footsteps by new fears
Till even lost fears seem hopes whereof they're reft
And of all mother's good love sole is left—
   Is their Love Love, or some remembered ghost?

14

To love her as today is so great bliss
   I needs must think of morrows almost loath,
   Morrows wherein the flower's unclosing growth
Shall make my darling other than she is.
The breathing rose excels the bud I wis,
   Yet bud that will be rose is sweet for both;
   And "by-and-by" seems like some later troth
Named in the moment of a lover's kiss.

Yes, I am jealous, as of one now strange
   That shall instead of her possess my thought,   10
Of her own self made new by any change,
   Of her to be by ripening morrows brought.
My rose of women under later skies!
Yet, ah! my child with the child's trustful eyes!

16

She will not have it that my day wanes low,
   Poor of the fire its drooping sun denies,
   That on my brow the thin lines write good-byes
Which soon may be read plain for all to know,
Telling that I have done with youth's brave show;
   Alas! and done with youth in heart and eyes,
   With wonder and with far expectancies,
Save but to say "I knew such long ago."

She will not have it. Loverlike to me,
   She with her happy gaze finds all that's best,   10
She sees this fair and that unfretted still,
   And her own sunshine over all the rest:
So she half keeps me as she'd have me be,
And I forget to age, through her sweet will.

1895

MATHILDE BLIND

pseud., Claude Lake (1841–1896)

༺⚜༻

After her father (a German banker) died, Mathilde Cohen took the name of her step-father, Karl Blind, with whom she went into exile after the revolution of 1848. Educated first in Germany and Belgium, she settled in England amid a circle of European refugees that included Louis Blanc and Garibaldi; she admired Mazzini, about whom she published reminiscences. Her brother committed suicide when his attempt to assassinate Bismarck failed; he left her his portion of the family inheritance. In later years she was a friend of the painter Ford Maddox Brown.

At twenty-six, under the name Claude Lake, Blind published her first volume of Poems *(1867). Her poetry reflected her political views and later her travels in the Mediterranean. Blind's work included a tragedy about Robespierre; a historical romance in verse; an epic on the violent displacement of Scottish crofters,* The Heather on Fire *(1886); and a Darwinian epic,* The Ascent of Man *(1889). She wrote biographies of George Eliot (1883) and Mme. Roland (1886), edited Shelley and Byron, and translated David F. Strauss's* The Old Faith and the New *(1873), as well as Marie Bashkirtseff's* Journal *(1890). Reviewers praised the melody, color, and delicacy of* Songs and Sonnets *(1893). When* Birds of Passage *(1895) appeared, she was considered "probably more various than any other woman poet in English literature." A believer in women's suffrage and women's higher education, she left an endowment to Newnham College, Cambridge.*

Nûît[1]

The all upholding,
The all enfolding,
The all beholding,
   Most secret Night;
From whose abysses,
With wordless blisses,
The Sun's first kisses
   Called gods to light.

One god undying,
But multiplying,   10
Restlessly trying,
   Doing: undone.
Through myriad changes,
He sweeps and ranges;
But life estranges
   Many in one.

In wild commotion,
Out of the ocean,
With moan and motion,
   Waves upon waves,   20
Mingling in thunder,
Rise and go under:
Break, life, asunder;
   Night has her graves.

1895

Noonday Rest

The willows whisper very, very low
   Unto the listening breeze;
Sometimes they lose a leaf, which, flickering slow,
   Faints on the sunburnt leas.

Beneath the whispering boughs and simmering skies,
   On the hot ground at rest,
Still as a stone, a ragged woman lies,
   Her baby at the breast.

---

1. *Nûît*: One of the names for the primaeval night of Egyptian mythology. She is described as follows in an inscription cut on the front of the mummy case of Mykerinos, the builder of the third great Pyramid: "Thy mother Nûît has spread herself out over thee in her name of Mystery of the Heavens."

Nibbling around her browse monotonous sheep,
　　Flies buzz about her head;　　　　　　　　　　10
Her heavy eyes are shuttered by a sleep
　　As of the slumbering dead.

The happy birds that live to love and sing,
　　Flitting from bough to bough,
Peer softly at this ghastly human thing
　　With grizzled hair and brow.

O'er what strange ways may not these feet have trod
　　That match the cracking clay?
Man had no pity on her—no, nor God—
　　A nameless castaway!　　　　　　　　　　　　20

But Mother Earth now hugs her to her breast,
　　Defiled or undefiled;
And willows rock the weary soul to rest,
　　As she, even she, her child.

HAMPSTEAD HEATH
1895

VIOLET FANE

pseud. of Mary Montgomerie Singleton, née Lamb
(1843–1905)

Lamb took a pseudonym early to avoid parental disapproval of her juvenilia, and continued as Violet Fane or V when she continued writing. She published three novels and numerous essays. Her marriage in 1864 to Henry Singleton, an Irish landowner, produced four children; their comfortable circumstances permitted her to move in fashionable London circles as a latter-day L.E.L. She composed many volumes of fluent verse, including From Dawn to Noon *(1872),* Denzil Place, a Story in Verse *(1875),* The Queen of the Fairies and Other Poems *(1877),* Collected Verses *(1880), and* Autumn Songs *(1889). After the death of Singleton, she married Sir Philip Currie, British ambassador to Turkey; her late poetry,* Under Cross and Crescent *(1896) and* Betwixt Two Seas *(1900), was written in Constantinople and Rome.*

Afterwards

I know that these poor rags of womanhood,
    This oaten pipe whereon the wild winds played,
    Making sad music—tattered and outfrayed,
Cast off, played out—can hold no more of good,
    Of love, or song, or sense of sun and shade.

What homely neighbors elbow me (hard by
    Neath the black yews) I know I shall not know,
    Nor take account of changing winds that blow,
Shifting the golden arrow, set on high
    On the grey spire, nor mark who come and go.   10

Yet would I lie in some familiar place,
    Nor share my rest with uncongenial dead—
    Somewhere, maybe, where friendly feet will tread—

As if from out some little chink of space,
   Mine eyes might see them tripping overhead.

And though too sweet to deck a sepulcher
   Seem twinkling daisy buds and meadow grass;
   And so, would more than serve me, lest they pass
Who fain would know what woman rested there,
   What her demeanor, or her story was—   20

For these I would that on a sculptured stone
   (Fenced round with ironwork to keep secure),
   Should sleep a form with folded palms demure,
In aspect like the dreamer that was gone,
   With these words carved, *"I hoped, but was not sure."*

1880

A Reverie

By the side of a ruined terrace
   I sat in the early Spring;
   The leaves were so young that the speckled hen-thrush
   Could be seen as she sat in the hawthorn bush,
Faltering and faint at the cuckoo's cry;
   The cypress looked black against the green
     Of folded chestnut and budding beech,
       And up from the slumbering vale beneath
   Came now and again the ominous ring
     Of a passing-bell for a village death.   10
Yet a spirit of hope went whispering by,
       Through the wakening woods, o'er the daisied mead,
        And up the stem of the straight Scotch fir:
An insolent squirrel, in holiday brush,
       Went scampering gaily, at utmost speed,
   To gnaw at his fir-apples out of reach.
       All seemed so full of life and stir,
   Of twitter and twinkle, and shimmer and sheen,
       That I closed my book, for I could not read;
       So I sat me down to muse instead,   20
By the side of the ruined terrace,
   In the breath of the early Spring.

Alas that the sound of a passing-bell
   (Only proclaiming some villager's death),
   As it echoes up from the valley beneath,
     Should summon up visions of trestle and shroud!
     And pity it is that yon marble urn,

Fallen and broken, should seem to tell
Of days that are done with and may not return,
Whatever the future shall chance to be!   30
Hollow and dead as the empty shell
Of last year's nut as it lies on the grass,
Or the frail laburnum's withered seed,
That hang like felons on gallows-tree!
This is a truth that half aloud
We may but murmur with bated breath:
How many sat as I sit today,
In the vanished hours of the olden time,
Watching the Spring in her early prime
Beam, and blossom, and go her way!   40
Squirrels that sport and doves that coo,
And leaves that twinkle against the blue,
And green woodpecker and screeching jay,
Ye are purposeless things that perish and pass,
Yet you wanton and squander your transient day—
My soul is sickened at sight of you!
"I had rather be shrouded and coffined and dead"
(To my innermost soul I, sighing, said)
"Than know no pleasure save love and play!"
Then all seemed so full of the odor of death   50
(Though I smelt the gorse-blossom blown from the heath)
That I opened my book and tried to read,
Since my soul was too saddened to muse instead,
By the side of the ruined terrace,
In the breath of the early Spring.

I wonder now if it could be right
For the Great First Cause to let such things be?
To plan this blending of black and white—
(I know, for myself, I had made *all* bright!)
And to mold me, and make me, and set me here,   60
Without my leave and against my will,
With never so much as a word in mine ear
As to how I may pilot my bark through the night?
Was it well, I wonder, or was it ill
That I should feel such a wish to be wise,
And dream of flying, and long for sight,
With faltering footsteps and bandaged eyes,
To be blamed the more that I may not see,
As I stagger about in the wilderness,
And know no more than the worms and the flies?   70
I feel at my heart that it is not right—
"Nothing is right and nothing is just;

We sow in ashes and reap the dust;
I think, on the whole, I would rather be
The wandering emmet, that loses its way
On the desert plain of my muslin dress,
Than be molded as either a woman or man."
(All this I said in my bitterness.)
"Yet who is to help me and who is to blame?"
But just at that moment a hurrying sound,   80
A sound as of hurrying, pattering feet,
In the dry leaves under the hawthorn bush,
Troubled the heart of the speckled hen-thrush,
Whilst the love-sick pigeon that called to her mate
And the green woodpecker and screeching jay
Outspread their wings and flew scared away;
And on a sudden, with leap and bound,
My neighbor's collie, marked black and tan,
Sprang panting into the garden seat,
His collar aglow with my neighbor's name!   90
So my neighbor himself cannot be far,
Ah, I care not now how wrong things are! . . .
I know I am ignorant, foolish, and small
As this wandering emmet that climbs my dress,
Yet I know that now I had answered "Yes"—
(Were I asked my will by the Father of all)
"I desire to be, I am glad to be born!"
And all because on a soft May morn
My neighbor's collie dog, black and tan,
Leapt over the privet-hedge and ran   100
With a rush, and a cry, and a bound to my side,
And because I saw his master ride,
Laying spurs to his willing horse,
Over the flaming yellow gorse.
Awake, my heart! I may not wait!
Let me arise and open the gate,
To breathe the wild warm air of the heath,
And to let in Love, and to let out Hate,
And anger at living, and scorn of Fate,
To let in Life, and to let out Death   110
(For mine ears are deaf to the passing-bell—
I think he is buried now out of the way);
And I say to myself, "It is good, it is well;
Squirrels that sport and doves that coo,
And leaves that twinkle against the blue,
And green woodpecker and screeching jay—
Good morrow, all! I am one of you!"
Since now I need neither muse nor read,

I may listen, and loiter, and live instead,
And take my pleasure in love and play,   120
And share my pastime with all things gay,
By the side of the ruined terrace,
    In the breath of the early Spring.

1880

MICHAEL FIELD

pseud. of Katherine Harris Bradley (early pseud., Arran Leigh)
and her niece, Edith Emma Cooper (early pseud., Isla Leigh)
(Bradley, 1846–1914; Cooper, 1862–1913)

Michael Field was the pseudonym of Katherine Bradley and her niece, Edith Cooper, once called the "double-headed nightingale" because of their collaboration as poets. Their writing was "like mosaic work—the mingled, various product of our two brains." Katherine Bradley lost her father to cancer when she was two, her mother when she was twenty-two. She attended lectures at Newnham College, Cambridge, and the Collège de France in Paris; a brief affair with a French friend's brother ended with his death. Ruskin broke off his correspondence as "Master" with her when he learned that she was reading atheist philosophy and would not submit to his literary dictates.

Following an illness of her married sister, Bradley adopted and educated her niece. As Arran Leigh, Bradley published The New Minnesinger and Other Poems *(1875), which Ruskin didn't bother to read. When Edith reached sixteen, they swore a compact to become lovers and write poetry together: their first production was* Bellerophon, *"by Arran and Isla Leigh" (1881). As Michael Field, they launched a prolific career in drama, writing twenty-seven plays, for the most part historical, whose elegance and force were admired by the critic Lionel Johnson.*

Together they studied classics and philosophy at Bristol; of several languages they mastered, the most important may have been Katherine's Greek, which enabled their poems built around Sappho's fragments. The preface to Long Ago *(1889) explains their audacious attempt: "Devoutly as the fiery-bosomed Greek turned in her anguish to Aphrodite, praying her to accomplish her heart's desires, I have turned to the one woman who has dared to speak unfalteringly of the fearful mastery of love." George Meredith praised the "faultless flow" of this volume, which Robert Browning called "a little collection of poems by a great genius."*

Travels during the 1880s and 1890s in Germany and Italy inspired Sight and Song *(1892), which translated paintings into adventurously sensual words. In Florence they met art critic Vernon Lee (Violet Paget), and in England became close friends with their neighbors the artists Charles Ricketts and Charles Shannon. The compact imagistic lyrics in* Underneath the Bough *(1893) and* Wild Honey *(1908) experiment with metric forms to convey the rhythms and senses of a startlingly frank eroticism. As they explained to Robert Browning, "We have many things to say that the world will not tolerate from a woman's lips." The headstrong Katherine ("Michael") recorded in her diary: "Wild gusts of passion sweep over me, & leave me desolated in body & spirit. At such times, I feel evil as a stray man within me." Their admirers included Browning, George Meredith, Oscar Wilde, Herbert Spencer, George Moore, and Alice Meynell.*

In 1907, they both converted to Catholicism, a shift reflected in the Poems of Adoration *(1912) and* Mystic Trees *(1913). Edith died of cancer in 1913, Katherine eight months later, after publishing* Dedication, *a volume of her niece's early verse. The voluminous diaries they kept between 1888 and 1914 were excerpted by T. Sturge Moore in* Works and Days *(1933). The* Wattlefold, *a collection of unpublished poems, was published by Edith C. Fortey in 1930.*

From *Long Ago*

33

Ταῖς κάλαις ὕμμιν {τό}
νόημα τὦμον οὐ διάμειπτον.

Maids, not to you my mind doth change;
Men I defy, allure, estrange,
Prostrate, make bond or free:
Soft as the stream beneath the plane,
To you I sing my love's refrain;
Between us is no thought of pain,
          Peril, satiety.

Soon doth a lover's patience tire,
But ye to manifold desire
Can yield response, ye know   10
When for long, museful days I pine,
The presage at my heart divine;
To you I never breathe a sign
          Of inward want or woe.

When injuries my spirit bruise,
Allaying virtue, ye infuse
With unobtrusive skill:
And if care frets ye come to me
As fresh as nymph from stream or tree,
And with your soft vitality   20
          My weary bosom fill.

34

Οὐ τι μοι ὔμμες.

"Sing to us, Sappho!" cried the crowd,
    And to my lyre I sprang;
Apollo seized me, and aloud
    Tumultuous I sang.
I did not think of who would hear;
I knew not there were men who jeer;
Nor dreamed I there were mortals born
To make the poet's heart forlorn.

There is a gift the crowd can bring,
    A rapture, a content;   10
Pierian roses scarcely fling
    So ravishing a scent
As that with which the air is stirred
When hearts of heavenly things have heard—
Sigh, and let forth the odor steal
Of that which in themselves they feel.

But now no subtle incense rose;
    I heard a hostile sound
And looked—oh, scornfuller than those
    'Mong men I ne'er have found.   20
I paused: the whistling air was stilled;
Then through my chords the godhead thrilled,
And the quelled creatures knew their kind
Ephemeral through foolish mind.

52

Ἔγων δ' ἐμαύτᾳ
τοῦτο σύνοιδα.

Climbing the hill a coil of snakes
Impedes Tiresias' path; he breaks
His staff across them—idle thrust
That lays the female in the dust
But dooms the prophet to forgo
His manhood and, as woman, know
The unfamiliar, sovereign guise
Of passion he had dared despise.

Ah, not in the Erinnys' ground
Experience so dire were found   10
As that to the enchanter known

When womanhood was round him thrown:
He trembled at the quickening change,
He trembled at his vision's range,
His finer sense for bliss and dole,
His receptivity of soul;
But when love came and, loving back,
He learned the pleasure men must lack,
It seemed that he had broken free
Almost from his mortality.   20

Seven years he lives as woman, then
Resumes his cruder part 'mong men,
Till him indignant Hera becks
To judge betwixt the joys of sex,
For the great Queen in wrath has heard
By her presumptuous lord averred
That, when he sought her in his brave
Young godhead, higher bliss he gave
Than the unutterable lure
Of her veiled glances could procure   30
For him, as balmy-limbed and proud
She drew him to Olympia's cloud.

"In marriage who hath more delight?"
She asks; then quivers and grows white,
As sacrilegious lips reveal
What woman in herself must feel—
And passes an avenging hand
Across his subtle eyelids bland.

Deep-bosomed Queen, fain wouldst thou hide
The mystic raptures of the bride!   40
When man's strong nature draweth nigh
'Tis as the lightning to the sky,
The blast to idle sail, the thrill
Of springtide when the saplings fill.
Though fragrant breath the sun receives
From the young rose's softening leaves,
Her plaited petals once undone,
The rose herself receives the sun.

Tiresias, ere the goddess smite,
Look on me with unblinded sight,   50
That I may learn if thou hast part
In womanhood's secluded heart:
Medea's penetrative charm

Ownst thou, to succor and disarm,
Hast thou her passion inly great,
Heroes to mold and subjugate?
Canst thou divine how sweet to bring
Apollo to thy blossoming
As Daphne; or, as just a child
Gathering a bunch of tulips wild,   60
To feel the flowery hillside rent
Convulsive for thy ravishment?

Thou needst not to unlock thine eyes,
Thy slow, ironic smile replies:
Thou hast been woman, and although
The twining snakes with second blow
Of golden staff thou didst assail,
And, crushing at a stroke the male,
Hadst virtue from thy doom to break
And lost virility retake—   70
Thou hast been woman, and her deep,
Magnetic mystery dost keep;
Thou hast been woman and canst see
Therefore into futurity:
It is not that Zeus gave thee power
To look beyond the transient hour,
For thou hast trod the regions dun,
Where life and death are each begun;
Thy spirit from the gods set free
Hath communed with Necessity.   80
Tilphusa's fountain thou mayst quaff
And die, but still thy golden staff
Will guide thee with perceptive hand
Among the shades to understand
The terrors of remorse and dread
And prophesy among the dead.

63

Ἄγε δη χέλυ δῖά μοι
φωνάεσσα γένοιο.

Grow vocal to me, O my shell divine!
    I cannot rest;
Not so doth Cypris pine
To raise her love to her undinted breast
When sun first warms the earth, as I require
To roll the heavy death from my recumbent lyre.

O whilom tireless voice, why art thou dumb?
    Today I stood
Watching the Mænads come
From a dark fissure in the ilex wood   10
Forth to the golden poplars and the light;
My tingling senses leapt to join that concourse bright.

Passed is the crowd, passed with his buoyant flute
    The Evian King:
My plectrum still is mute
Of beauty, of the halcyon's nest, of spring;
Though deep within, a vital madness teems,
And I am tossed with fierce, disjointed, wizard dreams.

Apollo, Dionysus passes by,
    Adonis wakes,   20
Zephyr and Chloris sigh:
To me, alas, my lyre no music makes,
Though tortured, fluttering toward the strings I reach,
Mad as for Anactoria's lovely laugh and speech.

For thou—where, in some balmy, western isle
    Each day doth bring
Seed-sowing, harvest smile,
And twilight drop of fruit for garnering,
Where north wind never blows—dost dwell apart,
Keeping a gentle people free from grief of heart.   30

Sun god, return! Break from thine old-world bower,
    Thy garden set
With the narcissus flower
And purple daphne! To thy chariot get,
Glorious arise as on thy day of birth,
And spread illuminating order through the earth.

I scan the rocks: O sudden mountain rill,
    That sure hast heard
His footsteps on the hill,
Leaping from crag to crag to bring me word—   40
Lapse quiet at my feet; I hear along
My lyre the journeying tumult of an unbreathed song.

1889

The Sleeping Venus

(Giorgione)

THE DRESDEN GALLERY

Here is Venus by our homes
And resting on the verdant swell
Of a soft country flanked with mountain domes:
She has left her archèd shell,
Has left the barren wave that foams,
Amid earth's fruitful tilths to dwell.
 Nobly lighted while she sleeps
 As sward lands or the cornfield sweeps,
 Pure as are the things that man
 Needs for life and using can   10
 Never violate nor spot—
 Thus she slumbers in no grot,
  But on open ground,
  With the great hillsides around.

And her body has the curves,
The same extensive smoothness seen
In yonder breadths of pasture, in the swerves
Of the grassy mountain-green
That for her propping pillow serves:
There is a sympathy between   20
 Her and Earth of largest reach,
 For the sex that forms them each
 Is a bond, a holiness,
 That unconsciously must bless
 And unite them, as they lie
 Shameless underneath the sky
  A long opal cloud
  Doth in noontide haze enshroud.

O'er her head her right arm bends;
And from the elbow raised aloft   30
Down to the crossing knees a line descends,
Unimpeachable and soft
As the adjacent slope that ends
In checkered plain of hedge and croft.
 Circular as lovely knolls,
 Up to which a landscape rolls
 With desirous sway, each breast
 Rises from the level chest,
 One in contour, one in round—
 Either exquisite, low mound   40

Firm in shape and given
To the August warmth of heaven.

With bold freedom of incline,
With an uttermost repose,
From hip to herbage-cushioned foot the line
Of her left leg stretching shows
Against the turf direct and fine,
Dissimilar in grace to those
    Little bays that in and out
    By the ankle wind about;
    Or that shallow bend, the right
    Curled-up knee has brought to sight
    Underneath its bossy rise,
    Where the loveliest shadow lies!
    Charmèd umbrage rests
    On her neck and by her breasts.

Her left arm remains beside
The plastic body's lower heaves,
Controlled by them, as when a riverside
With its sandy margin weaves
Deflections in a lenient tide;
Her hand the thigh's tense surface leaves,
    Falling inward. Not even sleep
    Dare invalidate the deep,
    Universal pleasure sex
    Must unto itself annex—
    Even the stillest sleep; at peace,
    More profound with rest's increase,
    She enjoys the good
    Of delicious womanhood.

Cheek and eyebrow touch the fold
Of the raised arm that frames her hair,
Her braided hair in color like to old
Copper glinting here and there,
While through her skin of olive-gold
The scarce carnations mount and share
    Faultlessly the oval space
    Of her temperate, grave face.
    Eyelids underneath the day
    Wrinkle as full buds that stay
    Through the tranquil summer hours
    Closed although they might be flowers;
    The red lips shut in
    Gracious secrets that begin.

50

60

70

80

On white drapery she sleeps,
That fold by fold is stained with shade;
Her mantle's ruddy pomegranate in heaps
For a cushion she has laid
Beneath her; and the glow that steeps
Its grain of richer depth is made   90
    By an overswelling bank,
    Tufted with dun grasses rank.
    From this hillock's outer heaves
    One small bush defines its leaves
    Broadly on the sober blue
    The pale cloud bank rises to,
    Whilst it sinks in bland
    Sunshine on the distant land.

Near her resting place are spread,
In deep or greener-lighted brown,   100
Wolds, that, half-withered by the heat o'erhead,
Press up to a little town
Of castle, archway, roof, and shed,
Then slope in grave continuance down:
    On their border, in a group,
    Trees of brooding foliage droop
    Sidelong; and a single tree
    Springs with bright simplicity,
    Central from the sunlit plain.
    Of a blue no flowers attain,   110
    On the fair, vague sky
    Adamantine summits lie.

And her resting is so strong
That while we gaze it seems as though
She had lain thus the solemn glebes among
In the ages far ago
And would continue, till the long,
Last evening of Earth's summer glow,
    In communion with the sweet
    Life that ripens at her feet: 120
    We can never fear that she
    From Italian fields will flee,
    For she does not come from far;
    She is of the things that are,
    And she will not pass
    While the sun strikes on the grass.

1892

A Portrait

(Bartolommeo Veneto)

STÄDELISCHES INSTITUT AT FRANKFURT

A crystal, flawless beauty on the brows
Where neither love nor time has conquered space
On which to live; her leftward smile endows
The gazer with no tidings from the face;
About the clear mounds of the lip it winds with silvery pace,
    And in the umber eyes it is a light
Chill as a glowworm's when the moon embrowns an August night.

She saw her beauty often in the glass,
Sharp on the dazzling surface, and she knew
The haughty custom of her grace must pass: 10
Though more persistent in all charm it grew
As with a desperate joy her hair across her throat she drew
    In crinkled locks stiff as dead, yellow snakes . . .
Until at last within her soul the resolution wakes

She will be painted, she who is so strong
In loveliness, so fugitive in years:
Forth to the field she goes and questions long
Which flowers to choose of those the summer bears;
She plucks a violet larkspur—then a columbine appears
    Of perfect yellow—daisies choicely wide;   20
These simple things with finest touch she gathers in her pride.

Next on her head, veiled with well-bleachen white
And bound across the brow with azure-blue,
She sets the box-tree leaf and coils it tight
In spiky wreath of green, immortal hue;
Then, to the prompting of her strange emphatic insight true,
    She bares one breast, half-freeing it of robe,
And hangs green-water gem and cord beside the naked globe.

So was she painted and for centuries
Has held the fading field-flowers in her hand   30
Austerely, as a sign. O fearful eyes
And soft lips of the courtesan who planned
To give her fragile shapeliness to art, whose reason spanned
    Her doom, who bade her beauty in its cold
And vacant eminence persist for all men to behold!

She had no memories save of herself
And her slow-fostered graces, naught to say
Of love in gift or boon; her cruel pelf
Had left her with no hopes that grow and stay;

She found default in everything that happened night or day,   40
  Yet stooped in calm to passion's dizziest strife
And gave to art a fair, blank form, unverified by life.

  Thus has she conquered death: her eyes are fresh,
  Clear as her frontlet jewel, firm in shade
  And definite as on the linen mesh
  Of her white hood the box-tree's somber braid,
That glitters leaf by leaf and with the year's waste will not fade.
  The small, close mouth, leaving no room for breath,
In perfect, still pollution smiles—Lo, she has conquered death!

             1892

[It was deep April, and the morn]

  It was deep April, and the morn
    Shakespeare was born;
  The world was on us, pressing sore;
  My Love and I took hands and swore,
   Against the world, to be
  Poets and lovers evermore,
  To laugh and dream on Lethe's shore,
  To sing to Charon in his boat,
  Heartening the timid souls afloat;
  Of judgment never to take heed,   10
  But to those fast-locked souls to speed,
  Who never from Apollo fled,
  Who spent no hour among the dead;
    Continually
    With them to dwell,
  Indifferent to heaven and hell.

            1893

[A girl]

A girl,
 Her soul a deep-wave pearl,
Dim, lucent of all lovely mysteries;
 A face flowered for heart's ease,
 A brow's grace soft as seas
 Seen through faint forest trees;
 A mouth, the lips apart,
Like aspen leaflets trembling in the breeze
 From her tempestuous heart.

Such: and our souls so knit,   10
I leave a page half-writ—
The work begun
Will be to heaven's conception done,
If she come to it.

1893

Marionettes

We met
After a year. I shall never forget
How odd it was for our eyes to meet,
For we had to repeat
In our glances the words that we had said
In days when, as our lashes lifted
Or drooped, the universe was shifted.
We had not closed with the past; then why
Did the sense come over us as a fetter
That all we did speaking eye to eye   10
Had been done before and so much better?
I think—but there's no saying—
What made us so hateful was the rage
Of our souls at finding ourselves a stage
Where marionettes were playing:
For a great actor once had trod
Those boards and played the god.

1893

Unbosoming

The love that breeds
In my heart for thee!
As the iris is full, brimful of seeds,
And all that it flowered for among the reeds
Is packed in a thousand vermilion beads
That push, and riot, and squeeze, and clip,
Till they burst the sides of the silver scrip,
And at last we see
What the bloom, with its tremulous, bowery fold
Of zephyr-petal at heart did hold: 10
So my breast is rent
With the burden and strain of its great content;
For the summer of fragrance and sighs is dead,

The harvest secret is burning red,
And I would give thee, after my kind,
The final issues of heart and mind.

1893

[Your rose is dead]

Your rose is dead,
    They said,
The Grand Mogul—for so her splendor
Exceeded, masterful, it seemed her due
By dominant male titles to commend her:
    But I, her lover, knew
That myriad-colored blackness, wrought with fire,
Was woman to the rage of my desire.
    My rose was dead? She lay
Against the sulfur, lemon, and blush-gray   10
Of younger blooms, transformed, morose,
Her shriveling petals gathered round her close,
    And where, before,
Coils twisted thickest at her core,
A round, black hollow: it had come to pass
Hints of tobacco, leather, brass
Confounded gave her texture and her color.
I watched her, as I watched her, growing duller,
    Majestic in recession
    From flesh to mold.   ·   20
My rose is dead—I echo the confession,
    And they pass to pluck another;
While I, drawn on to vague, prodigious pleasure,
    Fondle my treasure.
O sweet, let death prevail
Upon you, as your nervous outlines thicken
And totter; as your crimsons stale,
I feel fresh rhythms quicken,
Fresh music follows you. Corrupt, grow old,
Drop inwardly to ashes, smother   30
Your burning spices, and entoil
My senses till you sink a clod of fragrant soil!

1893

To Christina Rossetti

Lady, we would behold thee moving bright
As Beatrice or Matilda mid the trees,
Alas! thy moan was as a moan for ease
And passage through cool shadows to the night:
Fleeing from love, hadst thou not poet's right
To slip into the universe? The seas
Are fathomless to rivers drowned in these,
And sorrow is secure in leafy light.
Ah, had this secret touched thee, in a tomb
Thou hadst not buried thy enchanting self,   10
As happy Syrinx murmuring with the wind,
Or Daphne, thrilled through all her mystic bloom,
From safe recess as genius or as elf,
Thou hadst breathed joy in earth and in thy kind.

1896

The Mummy Invokes His Soul

Down to me quickly, down! I am such dust,
Baked, pressed together; let my flesh be fanned
With thy fresh breath; come from thy reedy land
Voiceful with birds; divert me, for I lust
To break, to crumble—prick with pores this crust!—
And fall apart, delicious, loosening sand.
Oh, joy, I feel thy breath, I feel thy hand
That searches for my heart, and trembles just
Where once it beat. How light thy touch, thy frame!
Surely thou perchest on the summer trees . . .   10
And the garden that we loved? Soul, take thine ease,
I am content, so thou enjoy the same
Sweet terraces and founts, content, for thee,
To burn in this immense torpidity.

1908

After Soufrière

It is not grief or pain,
But like the even dropping of the rain
That thou are gone.
It is not like a grave
To weep upon,
But like the rise and falling of a wave
When the vessel's gone.

It is like the sudden void
When the city is destroyed,
Where the sun shone: 10
There is neither grief or pain,
But the wide waste come again.

                    1908

A Palimpsest

. . . The rest
Of our life must be a palimpsest—
The old writing written there the best.

In the parchment hoary
Lies a golden story,
As mid secret feather of a dove,
As mid moonbeams shifted through a cloud:

Let us write it over,
O my lover,
For the far Time to discover,   10
As mid secret feathers of a dove,
As mid moonbeams shifted through a cloud!

                    1908

Maidenhair

Plato of the clear, dreaming eye and brave
Imaginings, conceived, withdrawn from light,
The hollow of man's heart even as a cave.
With century-slow dropping stalactite
My heart was dripping tedious in despair.
But yesterday, awhile, before I slept:
I wake to find it live with maidenhair
And mosses to the spiky pendants crept.
Great prodigies there are—Jehovah's flood
Widening the margin of the Red Sea shore—   10
Great marvel when the moon is turned to blood
It is to mortals, yet I marvel more
At the soft rifts, the pushings at my heart,
That lift the great stones of its rock apart.

                    1908

September

But why is Nature at such heavy pause
And the earth slowly ceasing to revolve?
Only the lapping tides abide their laws
And very softly on the sand dissolve.
The fruit is gathered—not an apple drops:
In little mists above the garden bed
The petals of the last gold dahlia shed;
The spider central mid his wreathed dewdrops!
Oh still, oh quiet!—and no issue found;
No laying up to rest of callow things,   10
Or scale, or sheaf, or tissue of armed wings:
Open the tilth, open the fallow ground!
The fragrance of the air that has no home
Spreads vague and dissolute, nor cares to roam.

1908

October

Honeybees by little toneless grapes,
        Bees that starve and cling,
    Flowers that are distorted in their shapes,
        Bees wayfaring
        To their bowers—
    Bees that do not come
    To the flowers a-hum,
That rove quiet, trailing up the napes
        Of the sunken flowers.

1908

Nests in Elms

The rooks are cawing up and down the trees!
Among their nests they caw. O sound I treasure,
Ripe as old music is, the summer's measure,
Sleep at her gossip, sylvan mysteries,
With prate and clamor to give zest of these—
In rune I trace the ancient law of pleasure,
Of love, of all the busyness of leisure,
With dream on dream of never-thwarted ease.
O homely birds, whose cry is harbinger
Of nothing sad, who know not anything   10
Of seabirds' loneliness, of Procne's strife,
Rock round me when I die! So sweet it were

To die by open doors, with you on wing
Humming the deep security of life.

1908

White Madness

White flowers as robes for Solomon fine spun
There are; and others that grow white themselves,
Distraught, made very bashful by the sun,
Turned to particular as gnomes and elves.
Thus a gold daffodil grows white and dumb,
Trembling a little; even for this cause
Mid lusty forest hyacinths a-hum,
One silver cluster into light withdraws;
Untangled from their massy group one sees
Thus from dark bell-heads clear fritillaries: 10
And there beside are violets, so shy
They would not bear the name we love them by,
That in white madness, witless and undone,
Creep through unhaunted hedgerows to the sun.

1908

Festa

A feast that has no wine! O joy intense,
Clear ecstasy in one white river room!
Tonight my Love is with me in the bloom
Of roses—laughing at their redolence:
"A cedar coffer, a miasma dense
With suck of honey." . . . Dote on their perfume,
Find tropes! I, shuddering at thy rescued doom,
Sigh for some wider token to my sense
Of the wonder that I have of thee, my bride,
My feast. . . . The candles burn: they are too few.   10
But, hist! the river night hath heard my sigh:
The candles reappear and multiply,
Procession-wise in filmy lights outside;
And the oar plashes as from singing dew.

1908

Covenant

What is there now betwixt my God and me?
Where is the bond? I do not reach the rim
Of the dark light beyond the seraphim,
Though I have breathed there in simplicity,
Breathing and taking breath of love as free
As the clean flames He feeds that leap to Him:
I am afar, far off; the earth is grim,
Graves in the grass and winter on the tree.
Yet there is this—He has the dead in sight,
Bosoms their sorrows; He is where their eyes   10
Open and smile and weep; He knows their plight,
Mortal and lonely, dimples their new skies,
Makes soft their spring; then turns on me to shed
The glory, the refreshing of my dead.

1908

Possession

Thou hast no grave. What is it that bereaves,
That has bereft us of thee? Thou art gone!
The forest with its infinite soft leaves
May have received thee, or thou wandered'st on,
The tender, wild, exhilarating flowers
Crowning thy broken pathway; or the white
Glare of the torrent smote thee; or the powers
Of the great sculptured country, from their height
Prompted thee upward. Thou hast made no plea
For rest or for possession; and thy hold   10
Is on the land forever: thine the gold
Brimming the crystal crests, the gold that fills
The vales, the valley's fountain purity,
And thine the inmost meadows of the hills.

1908

Falling Leaves

To hush within my heart the beating cry
Up toward thy hills, I cross an English street,
On to a garden where great lindens meet:
The leaves are falling—ah, how free to die!
The leaves are falling, life is passing by,
The leaves are falling slowly at my feet,
And soon with the dead summer, soon—how sweet!—

They will be garnered safe from every eye.
Their honey-mingling life among the trees
Is as it had not been; by twos and threes   10
Wide to the dimming earth they fall, they fall,
Yet, as I watch them dropping, something stills,
Heart of my heart, that over-bitter call,
As for one lost, to thee among thy hills.

1908

Ascending and Descending

Among the tide pools, when the tender shine
Of sunset lit them, whilst a ruffling breeze
Freshened the currents from unrolling seas
    Till the clogged weeds that wave-forsaken pine
Were fanned to plumy forests, coralline
Spread its pink branches, and among the trees,
Clusters of daisy-flowered anemones
Were roused by plashing ripples to untwine
Their starry fingers. In a little space
Apart, a tiny sea bloom I espied,   10
With tranquil tentacles that did not cease
To undulate: and I, meseemed, could trace
The way from that dim pleasure to the peace
Of Isaac musing in the eventide.

1908

Circe at Circæum

How may the drooping poppy leaf abide
                Wreathed in the bladder-weeds
                    Athwart the tide?
Whose are the white-robed, whiter-shadowed limbs
                Within the shaggy rims
                Of the shore's last rock pool?
O Circe, Circe! Is there hope or woe
Can bring her to a mirror set so low?
Deep into it the shadowed poppy bleeds,
                Mid crabs and fishes cool,   10
The poppy on her forehead; and she cooes
Across the shallows toward the deeper sea,
As out from woods; her lips above the swing
Of little tide tracks have a freshet's spring
Of smiles for the vast glitter of the brine.

O Circe, Circe! Do not sorely pine
      For answer to thy call,
      For answer to thy smiles:
It is the slow noontide that bindeth all,
Beguiling further than thy charm beguiles.   20
Her breath removes from lips to her still heart;
No covert in the foldings of a hill
Was ever from all breeze so greatly still
As she with waiting: and, their lids apart,
As lakes that never look from off the sky,
Her eyes are on the sea. Thus noon goes by.

O Circe, Circe, wake, arouse thy magic!
The poppy bud now dribbles from its drop
Through the rock pool, nor will its flowing stop;
Shadows from the heaven breast the sea;   30
The hour is tempered to thy potency.
She breathes as if the rustling ferns set free
The evening dew; she looses from her bosom
A trail of jasmine flower; her breathing stirs
All that bees ravish from auriculas
Of drugged, delicious, smothering meal; she closes
With tremor to the shadowy breeze her lids,
And lets her sweetness overlap the salt.
What coldness in the ocean ooze forbids
A lover to attempt such rare assault?   40
The ripples crease her mirror; from its bed
No spasm waves in coiling current spread
From sudden pressure. Are the sea gods dead?

O suppliant by the sea, are spells in vain?
She rises and a cloud of summer rain
Washes the wave tips as it washed green leaves,
Dashes its dew to sea spray, nestling cleaves
Soft to the barren eddies in their lapse;
And with its beauty and its shower enwraps
The churning bubbles in a rainbow clear.   50

O Circe, Circe! A king died beneath
The poison of thine anger that is death:
Thy weariness recoils on doting kings,
And they turn brutish in their wallowings.
Her rain is gathered in, and the blank sea
Receives a shadow cast immovably.
As thunder rolls along through mountain glens,
Her eyes and lips and nostrils, as from dens,
Give forth their curse. A budded stalk among

The poppies on her forehead reareth strong,   60
No bud head, but a serpent that, by fits,
The sea gust and the sea shine madly hits
With fork on fork, until one moment grows
An imprecation: "Glaucus, thou hast braved
All charms I bring from earth: await its ban.
Thou liest on a breast that is my foe's!
Not by thy closest love shall she be saved."

Ocean heard dumbly. There was poppy seed
Scumming the streamers of the bladder-weed,
Where poppy flowers had vanished from the glass.   70
No one would come out seaward till at dawn
The maiden Scylla to the pool would pass
Across the reefs and bathe amid that spawn
Of steeping poppy seeds. At dead of night
The waves howled once or twice: but day dawned bright.

1914

Second Thoughts

I thought of leaving her for a day
In town, it was such iron winter
At Durdans, the garden frosty clay,
The woods as dry as any splinter,
The sky congested. I would break
From the deep, lethargic, country air
To the shining lamps, to the clash of the play,
And, tomorrow, wake
Beside her, a thousand things to say.
I planned—O more—I had almost started;   10
I lifted her face in my hands to kiss—
A face in a border of fox's fur,
For the bitter black wind had stricken her,
And she wore it, her soft hair straying out
Where it buttoned against the gray, leather snout—
In an instant we should have parted;
But at sight of the delicate world within
That fox-fur collar, from brow to chin,
At sight of those wonderful eyes from the mine,
Coal pupils, an iris of glittering spa,   20
And the wild, ironic, defiant shine
As of a creature behind a bar
One has captured and, when three lives are past,
May hope to reach the heart of at last,

All that, and the love at her lips, combined
To show me what folly it were to miss
A face with such thousand things to say,
And beside these, such thousand more to spare,
For the shining lamps, for the clash of the play—
O madness; not for a single day   30
Could I leave her! I stayed behind.

1925

ALICE CHRISTIANA GERTRUDE MEYNELL

née Thompson (1847–1922)

Alice Thompson spent part of her childhood in Italy, where she was educated thoroughly in English literature by her father and became fluent in Italian and French. Her pianist mother persuaded her family to convert to Catholicism. In 1877, Alice married Wilfred Meynell, a Catholic journalist and literary critic; she bore eight children, seven of whom survived to compete for her attention with household tasks, journalism, and poetry. Among her close male friends were the poets Francis Thompson, Coventry Patmore, and George Meredith. Her open house on Sundays was visited by W. B. Yeats, Oscar Wilde, and Katharine Tynan.

Her creative and critical work for periodicals and newspapers helped support the family: collections of her essays (described as "limpid" by George Meredith) include The Rhythm of Life (1893), The Colour of Life (1896), and The Spirit of Place (1899). She wrote biographies of the Pre-Raphaelite Holman Hunt and of Ruskin; she edited the works of Jean Ingelow, Barrett Browning, Christina Rossetti, and Charlotte Yonge. Her diary at eighteen condemned the evil "selfishness of men that keeps women from work." Later she committed herself to women's suffrage and housing reform, calling herself a "Christian Socialist." Vita Sackville-West found her essays "penetratingly wise," and Virginia Woolf considered her a "true critic, courageous, authoritative, and individual."

Preludes (1875), published before her marriage, was illustrated by her sister Elizabeth Thompson Butler, who achieved fame as a painter of military subjects. In response to this first volume of poems, reminiscent of the metaphysical poets, Ruskin praised the close of "A Letter from a Girl" as among "the finest things I have yet seen or felt in modern verse," and one of Christina Rossetti's brothers thought "Renouncement" "one of the three finest sonnets ever written by women." Later volumes of poems exhibit her characteristic fusion of analytic wit, lyric mysticism, and feminism. She sought to "sing" what she called "intellectual passion." A Father of Women and Other Poems (1917) recorded her response to World War I. In a review, Francis Thompson claimed that "the footfalls of her muse waken not sounds, but silences." Vita Sackville-West singled her out for "the image perfectly married to the thought."

To the Beloved

Oh, not more subtly silence strays
    Amongst the winds, between the voices,
Mingling alike with pensive lays
    And with the music that rejoices,
Than thou art present in my days.

My silence, life returns to thee
    In all the pauses of her breath.
Hush back to rest the melody
    That out of thee awakeneth;
And thou, wake ever, wake for me!   10

Thou art like silence all unvexed,
    Though wild words part my soul from thee.
Thou art like silence unperplexed,
    A secret and a mystery
Between one footfall and the next.

Most dear pause in a mellow lay!
    Thou art inwoven with every air.
With thee the wildest tempests play,
    And snatches of thee everywhere
Make little heavens throughout a day.   20

Darkness and solitude shine for me.
    For life's fair outward part are rife
The silver noises; let them be.
    It is the very soul of life
Listens for thee, listens for thee.

O pause between the sobs of cares;
    O thought within all thought that is;
Trance between laughters unawares:
    Thou art the shape of melodies,
And thou the ecstasy of prayers!   30

1875

A Letter from a Girl to Her Own Old Age

Listen, and when thy hand this paper presses,
O timeworn woman, think of her who blesses
What thy thin fingers touch, with her caresses.

O mother, for the weight of years that break thee!
O daughter, for slow time must yet awake thee,
And from the changes of my heart must make thee!

O fainting traveler, morn is gray in heaven.
Dost thou remember how the clouds were driven?
And are they calm about the fall of even?

Pause near the ending of thy long migration,   10
For this one sudden hour of desolation
Appeals to one hour of thy meditation.

Suffer, O silent one, that I remind thee
Of the great hills that stormed the sky behind thee,
Of the wild winds of power that have resigned thee.

Know that the mournful plain where thou must wander
Is but a gray and silent world, but ponder
The misty mountains of the morning yonder.

Listen: The mountain winds with rain were fretting,
And sudden gleams the mountaintops besetting.   20
I cannot let thee fade to death, forgetting.

What part of this wild heart of mine, I know not,
Will follow with thee where the great winds blow not,
And where the young flowers of the mountain grow not.

Yet let my letter with my lost thoughts in it
Tell what the way was when thou didst begin it
And win with thee the goal when thou shalt win it.

Oh, in some hour of thine, my thoughts shall guide thee.
Suddenly, though time, darkness, silence, hide thee,
This wind from thy lost country flits beside thee,   30

Telling thee: All thy memories moved the maiden;
With thy regrets was morning overshaden;
With sorrow thou hast left, her life was laden.

But whither shall my thoughts turn to pursue thee?
Life changes, and the years and days renew thee.
Oh, Nature brings my straying heart unto thee.

Her winds will join us, with their constant kisses
Upon the evening as the morning tresses,
Her summers breathe the same unchanging blisses.

And we, so altered in our shifting phases,   40
Track one another mid the many mazes
By the eternal child-breath of the daisies.

I have not writ this letter of divining
To make a glory of thy silent pining,
A triumph of thy mute and strange declining.

Only one youth, and the bright life was shrouded.
Only one morning, and the day was clouded.
And one old age with all regrets is crowded.

O hush, O hush! Thy tears my words are steeping.
O hush, hush, hush! So full, the fount of weeping?   50
Poor eyes, so quickly moved, so near to sleeping?

Pardon the girl; such strange desires beset her.
Poor woman, lay aside the mournful letter
That breaks thy heart; the one who wrote, forget her:

The one who now thy faded features guesses,
With filial fingers thy gray hair caresses,
With morning tears thy mournful twilight blesses.

1875

The Visiting Sea

As the inhastening tide doth roll
Home from the deep along the whole
   Wide shining strand and floods the caves
   —Your love comes filling with happy waves
The open seashore of my soul.

But inland from the seaward spaces,
None knows, not even you, the places
   Brimmed, at your coming, out of sight
   —The little solitudes of delight
This tide constrains in dim embraces.   10

You see the happy shore, wave-rimmed,
But know not of the quiet dimmed
   Rivers your coming floods and fills,
   The little pools mid happier hills,
My silent rivulets, overbrimmed.

What! I have secrets from you? Yes.
But, visiting Sea, your love doth press
   And reach in further than you know,
   And fills all these; and when you go
There's loneliness in loneliness.   20

1875

Regrets

As, when the seaward ebbing tide doth pour
   Out by the low sand spaces,
The parting waves slip back to clasp the shore
   With lingering embraces—

So in the tide of life that carries me
   From where thy true heart dwells,
Waves of my thoughts and memories turn to thee
   With lessening farewells;

Waving of hands; dreams, when the day forgets;
A care half lost in cares;   10
The saddest of my verses; dim regrets;
   Thy name among my prayers.

I would the day might come, so waited for,
   So patiently besought,
When I, returning, should fill up once more
   Thy desolated thought,

And fill thy loneliness that lies apart
   In still, persistent pain.
Shall I content thee, O thou broken heart,
   As the tide comes again,   20

And brims the little seashore lakes, and sets
   Seaweeds afloat, and fills
The silent pools, rivers, and rivulets
   Among the inland hills?

                       1875

A Poet of One Mood

A poet of one mood in all my lays,
   Ranging all life to sing one only love,
   Like a west wind across the world I move,
Sweeping my harp of floods mine own wild ways.
The countries change, but not the west-wind days
   Which are my songs. My soft skies shine above,
   And on all seas the colors of a dove,
And on all fields a flash of silver grays.

I make the whole world answer to my art
   And sweet monotonous meanings. In your ears   10
I change not ever, bearing, for my part,
   One thought that is the treasure of my years—

A small cloud full of rain upon my heart
And in mine arms, clasped, like a child in tears.

1875

Renouncement

I must not think of thee; and tired yet strong,
  I shun the thought that lurks in all delight—
  The thought of thee—and in the blue heaven's height,
And in the sweetest passage of a song.
O just beyond the fairest thoughts that throng
  This breast, the thought of thee waits hidden yet bright;
  But it must never, never come in sight;
I must stop short of thee the whole day long.

But when sleep comes to close each difficult day,
  When night gives pause to the long watch I keep   10
    And all my bonds I needs must loose apart,
Must doff my will as raiment laid away—
  With the first dream that comes with the first sleep,
  I run, I run, I am gathered to thy heart.

1882

A Song of Derivations

I come from nothing; but from where
Come the undying thoughts I bear?
  Down, through long links of death and birth,
  From the past poets of the earth,
My immortality is there.

I am like the blossom of an hour.
But long, long vanished sun and shower
  Awoke my breath in the young world's air;
  I track the past back everywhere
Through seed and flower and seed and flower.   10

Or I am like a stream that flows
Full of the cold springs that arose
  In morning lands, in distant hills;
  And down the plain my channel fills
With melting of forgotten snows.

Voices I have not heard possessed
My own fresh songs; my thoughts are blessed
  With relics of the far unknown.

And mixed with memories not my own,
The sweet streams throng into my breast.   20

Before this life began to be,
The happy songs that wake in me
   Woke long ago and far apart.
   Heavily on this little heart
Presses this immortality.

1885

Cradle Song at Twilight

The child not yet is lulled to rest.
   Too young a nurse, the slender Night
So laxly holds him to her breast
   That throbs with flight.

He plays with her and will not sleep.
   For other playfellows she sighs;
An unmaternal fondness keep
   Her alien eyes.

1895

Parentage

*When Augustus Cæsar legislated against the unmarried citizens of Rome,
he declared them to be, in some sort, slayers of the people.*

   Ah! no, not these!
These, who were childless, are not they who gave
So many dead unto the journeying wave,
The helpless nurslings of the cradling seas;
Not they who doomed by infallible decrees
Unnumbered man to the innumerable grave.

   But those who slay
Are fathers. Theirs are armies. Death is theirs—
The death of innocence and despairs;
The dying of the golden and the gray.
The sentence, when these speak it, has no Nay.   10
And she who slays is she who bears, who bears.

1896

To the Body

Thou inmost, ultimate
Council of judgment, palace of decrees,
Where the high senses hold their spiritual state,
    Sued by earth's embassies,
And sign, approve, accept, conceive, create;

    Create—thy senses close
With the world's pleas. The random odors reach
Their sweetness in the place of thy repose,
    Upon thy tongue the peach,
And in thy nostrils breathes the breathing rose.   10

    To thee, secluded one,
The dark vibrations of the sightless skies,
The lovely inexplicit colors, run;
    The light gropes for those eyes.
O thou, august! thou dost command the sun.

    Music, all dumb, hath trod
Into thine ear her one effectual way;
And fire and cold approach to gain thy nod,
    Where thou callst up the day,
Where thou awaitest the appeal of God.   20

            1906

The Launch

Forth, to the alien gravity,
Forth, to the laws of ocean, we,
    Builders on earth by laws of land,
    Entrust this creature of our hand
Upon the calculated sea.

Fast bound to shore we cling, we creep,
And make our ship ready to leap
    Light to the flood, equipped to ride
    The strange conditions of the tide—
New weight, new force, new world: the Deep.   10

Ah thus—not thus—the Dying, kissed,
Cherished, exhorted, shriven, dismissed;
    By all the eager means we hold
    We, warm, prepare him for the cold,
To keep the incalculable tryst.

            1913

TORU DUTT

(1856–1877)

As a child in a family of Hindu converts to Christianity, Dutt was familiar with Bengali mythology and songs recited to her by her mother; she also read her father's preferred works, Milton's Paradise Lost *and the novels of Eliot and Thackeray. Barrett Browning was her favorite poet. Her older brother died young, making their affectionate and literary father particularly dependent on the two surviving girls, Aru and Toru. In 1869 he decided to take his family to Europe; the girls first spent two months in a boarding school in the south of France, then, after visiting Paris, went in 1870 to England, where Dutt and her sister attended the "higher lectures for women" at Cambridge University in 1871. When the family returned to Bengal in 1873, the girls began the study of Sanskrit. Toru wrote on Lecomte de Lisle (1874), and published translations from French into English,* A Sheaf Gleaned, *in 1876. She also translated from French Clarisse Bader's* Woman in Ancient India. *Aru died when she was twenty, followed by Toru at the age of twenty-one. A posthumous volume,* Ancient Ballads and Legends of Hindustan *(1882) gathered Dutt's reworkings of Bengal themes with more topical poems on the war of 1870.*

Sîta

Three happy children in a darkened room!
What do they gaze on with wide-open eyes?
A dense, dense forest where no sunbeam pries
And in its center, a cleared spot. There bloom
Gigantic flowers on creepers that embrace
Tall trees; there, in a quiet lucid lake
The white swans glide; there, "whirring from the brake,"
The peacock springs; there herds of wild deer race;
There patches gleam with yellow waving grain;
There blue smoke from strange altars rises light—

There dwells in peace the poet-anchorite.
But who is this fair lady? Not in vain
She weeps—for lo! at every tear she sheds,
Tears from three pairs of young eyes fall amain,
And bowed in sorrow are the three young heads.
It is an old, old story, and the lay
Which has evoked sad Sîta from the past
Is by a mother sung. . . . 'Tis hushed at last
And melts the picture from their sight away,
Yet shall they dream of it until the day!   20
When shall those children by their mother's side
Gather, ah me! as erst at eventide?

1878

Our Casuarina Tree

Like a huge python, winding round and round
   The rugged trunk, indented deep with scars
   Up to its very summit near the stars,
A creeper climbs, in whose embraces bound
   No other tree could live. But gallantly
The giant wears the scarf, and flowers are hung
In crimson clusters all the boughs among,
   Whereon all day are gathered bird and bee;
And oft at nights the garden overflows
With one sweet song that seems to have no close,   10
Sung darkling from our tree while men repose;

When first my casement is wide open thrown
   At dawn, my eyes delighted on it rest;
   Sometimes—and most in winter—on its crest
A gray baboon sits statuelike alone,
   Watching the sunrise, while on lower boughs
His puny offspring leap about and play;
   And far and near kokilas hail the day;
   And to their pastures wend our sleepy cows;
And in the shadow, on the broad tank cast   20
By that hoar tree, so beautiful and vast,
The water lilies spring, like snow enmassed.

But not because of its magnificence
   Dear is the Casuarina to my soul:
   Beneath it we have played; though years may roll,
O sweet companions, loved with love intense,
   For your sakes shall the tree be ever dear!
Blent with your images, it shall arise

In memory, till the hot tears blind mine eyes!
    What is that dirgelike murmur that I hear,   30
Like the sea breaking on a shingle beach?
It is the tree's lament, an eerie speech,
That haply to the unknown land may reach.

Unknown, yet well known to the eye of faith!
    Ah, I have heard that wail far, far away.
    In distant lands, by many a sheltered bay,
When slumbered in his cave the water wraith,
    And the waves gently kissed the classic shore
Of France or Italy beneath the moon,
When earth lay trancèd in a dreamless swoon: 40
    And every time the music rose, before
Mine inner vision rose a form sublime—
Thy form, O Tree, as in my happy prime
I saw thee, in my own loved native clime.

Therefore I fain would consecrate a lay
    Unto thy honor, Tree, beloved of those
    Who now in blessed sleep for aye repose;
Dearer than life to me, alas! were they!
    Mayest thou be numbered when my days are done
With deathless trees—like those in Borrowdale,   50
Under whose awful branches lingered pale
    "Fear, trembling Hope, and Death, the skeleton,
And Time, the shadow"; and though weak the verse
That would thy beauty fain, oh fain rehearse,
May Love defend thee from Oblivion's curse.

1878

JANE BARLOW
(1857–1917)

Barlow's intense shyness kept her at home under the tutelage of her father, a professor of history and later vice-provost at Trinity College, Dublin. She was trained in classics but made her reputation with Irish dialect poetry, stories, and novels, whose local subjects reflected her sympathy with Irish nationalism.

She met particular success with her short stories, studies in Irish manners and customs that went into numerous editions in England and the United States. One of her first volumes, Irish Idylls (1892), went through eight editions. Other titles were A Creel of Irish Stories (1897), From the East unto the West (1898), At the Back of Beyond (1902), By Beach and Bogland (1905), and Irish Ways (1909). Her novels include Kerrigan's Quality (1893), Flaws (1911), and In Mio's Youth (1917).

Barlow's first volume of tales in verse, Bog-Land Studies (1892), was published by Yeats's mentor, Thomas William Rolleston. There she wittily juxtaposes classical allusion and local observation, or what she calls "eschatology in a bog." A verse narrative, The End of Elfintown (1894), was illustrated by Laurence Housman. Verses reflecting the indirect impact of war on Ireland were gathered in Between Doubting and Daring (1916).

In her studies of daily routine and peasant poverty, "every pebble and blade of grass is seen as through a microscope." Virginia Woolf found that she captures "the charm of the wild and melancholy land, and of the people who scrape a scanty living from it." She received an honorary degree from Trinity College in 1904.

In Higher Latitudes

"A frost," we say, "the stars such keen rays wore
All night; and now against a roughened pane
This dawn-light quivering beats with red-rose stain,
And pearled till noontide lie the meadows hoar."

Yet reck the while of climes where toward earth's core
The fierce cold strikes a thrilling shaft, as fain
To daunt the center's fire, and all the plain
Is monstrous ice and snow for evermore.
   Even so, this spell that half a night can keep
Our senses chilled yet scarce outlingereth   10
The earliest beam, but while long shadows creep
Fades dreamlike from the fields of thought and breath,
We, journeying through a milder zone, call sleep,
Remembering still the arctic sleep of death.

1908

Wayfarers

On yestereve a while in talk I stood
With Norah Doyne beside her shadowy door,
And saw dim twilight fiery rood on rood
Steal from the sunset's shore.
Wide swept the moorland brown, we watched it o'er,
To earth's up-tilting rim; and if we turned
Eastward, again, low-glimmering on her floor
The red embers burned.

"Aye," said the banati, "'tis lonesome lies
This road of ours; full often round and round   10
I look and see scarce emptier are the skies,
Clear of a cloud-breath found.
So seldom a foot goes by to market bound,
Or carrying sods cut yonder past the furze,
'Twixt morn and morn, belike, no step will sound,
And 'tis shadow stirs.

'Troth, 'tis the black road: in the winter's cold,
When cruel blasts are keening by or gray
Grows all the air with sleet, some neighbor old
Happen will fare this way,   20
Feeble, and stooped, and slow; and then the day
Seems weary-long, because the winds that roam
Keep me heart-vexed, till I can reckon and say:
Now the creature's home.

But whiles a vagrant lad comes wandering by,
That makes the lonesome place feel lonelier yet,
So sure I be no sun out of this sky
Shines where his heart is set:
And to the world's end on his face the fret

Bides still. His bit and sup I grudge, God knows,   30
As little as I his woeful look forget
When his way he goes.

For save the drink of milk, and crust of bread,
And kindly word, his share of life outright
Was lost on him, since all his care," she said,
"Hidden was from his sight
In one dark house. And if at dusk grows bright
Some door fast by, that watching folk unbar,
Aye farther from him seems its blink of light
Than the evening star."   40

There, as she spoke, I gazed and doubting spied
A sheeny mote, sunk deep in heaven's domed roof,
Its phantom ray, athwart the mist rose-dyed,
Thrill, very faint, in proof
Of world from world immeasurably aloof:
A quivering thread o'er blank abysses cast,
Where Fate weaves on with magic warp and woof
In the void and vast.

And yet, methought, those starry citadels
That front the shoreless Deep, with straiter bands   50
Hold each to each than haply he who dwells
Yonder, and he who stands
Even at the door. Yea, though he warm his hands,
Lingering a space as by his friend's hearth fire,
None saith o'er what wild seas, in what strange lands,
The flame were kindled to his soul's desire.

                                                          1908

Barred

With lifted latch it stands ajar,
By April breaths 'tis shaken still,
Only a sunbeam slants to bar
Sweet Eileen's door against her will;
Yet shadows creep anear, afar,
And never a step has crossed the sill.

Athwart its gold gleam, brightlier bright,
What sudden glinting diamond slips?
'Twixt hovering flakes that drift and light
Like breeze-blown sails for elfin ships,   10
Oft through the cherry bough foam-white
A twinkle of beaded crystal drips.

O'er dim green wood roofs trailing float
Wan shower-webs, dwindled as they fly;
A dewdrop's clearness in his note
The merle has caught who sings fast by:
The softest step would hush his throat,
But ever his lilt rings loud and high.

Soon shall the earliest glimmering star
Prick down through ray-lorn airs and chill,   20
Where now no sunbeam bides to bar
Sweet Eileen's door against her will.
Then hope must flit afar, afar,
If never a step cross o'er the sill.

1908

AGNES MARY FRANCES ROBINSON
(1857–1944)

Robinson's architect father drew a lively literary circle to his home, where she met Robert Browning and Oscar Wilde. Her schooling at Coventry, Brussels, and University College, London, gave her excellent Greek and made her virtually bilingual in French. The Crowned Hippolytus (1881) contains her translations from Euripides; Arden: A Novel followed in 1883.

She described her poetry as "scattered fragments" from the "ode" of her life that she had imprinted with her friendships and experiences. Her first volume of poetry, A Handful of Honeysuckle (1878), was written for Vernon Lee; The New Arcadia (1884) modeled its pastoral figures on her neighbors in Surrey; for An Italian Garden (1886) she drew many of the scenes and verse forms from her visits to Tuscany. After her marriage in 1888 to a professor of Persian, James Darmesteter, she moved to Paris. He translated her poetry into French, while she translated his work into English. She edited the works of Marguerite de Navarre and Marie de Sévigné and wrote biographies of Emily Brontë (1883) and Marguerite de Navarre (1886), as well as critical studies of the Brownings (1901, 1922) and of Marie Lenéru (1924). When Emily Dickinson received a copy of Robinson's Emily Brontë, she wrote that it was "more electric far than anything since Jane Eyre."

After the death of her first husband in 1894, she married Émile Duclaux and moved from Paris to the French countryside. Her French work was published under the names of Mme. James Darmesteter and Mme. Duclaux. Her later volumes of verse include Songs, Ballads, and a Garden Play (1888), Retrospect and Other Poems (1893), Collected Poems (1902), and Images and Meditations (1923). She aligned her "sober little songs" with the meditative work of "the Minor poet." Women, she argued, "have always been the prime makers of ballads and love songs, of anonymous snatches and screeds of popular song."

Love Without Wings
Eight Songs

I.

I thought: no more the worst endures!
  I die, I end the strife—
You swiftly took my hands in yours
  And drew me back to life!

II.

We sat when shadows darken
  And let the shadows be:
Each was a soul to hearken,
  Devoid of eyes to see.

You came at dusk to find me;
  I knew you well enough . . .
O lights that dazzle and blind me—
  It is no friend, but Love!

III.

How is it possible
  You should forget me,
Leave me forever,
  And never regret me?

I was the soul of you,
  Past love or loathing,
Lost in the whole of you . . .
  Now, am I nothing?

IV.

The fallen oak still keeps its yellow leaves
  But all its growth is o'er!
So, at your name, my heart still beats and grieves
  Although I love no more.

V.

And so I shall meet you
  Again, my dear;
How shall I greet you?
  What shall I hear?

I, you forgot!
  (But who shall say

10

20

30

You loved me not
—Yesterday?)

VI.

Ah me, do you remember still
    The garden where we strolled together,
The empty groves, the little hill
    Starred o'er with pale Italian heather?

And you to me said never a word,
    Nor I a single word to you.
And yet how sweet a thing was heard,
    Resolved, abandoned by us two!   40

VII.

I know you love me not . . . I do not love you;
    Only at dead of night
I smile a little, softly dreaming of you
    Until the dawn is bright.

I love you not; you love me not; I know it!
    But when the day is long
I haunt you like the magic of a poet
    And charm you like a song.

VIII.

O Death of things that are, Eternity
    Of things that seem!
Of all the happy past remains to me,   50
    Today, a dream!

Long blessèd days of love and wakening thought,
    All, all are dead;
Nothing endures we did, nothing we wrought,
    Nothing we said.

But once I dreamed I sat and sang with you
    On Ida's hill.
There, in the echoes of my life, we two
    Are singing still.   60

1886

Neurasthenia

I watch the happier people of the house
    Come in and out, and talk, and go their ways;

I sit and gaze at them; I cannot rouse
　My heavy mind to share their busy days.

I watch them glide, like skaters on a stream,
　Across the brilliant surface of the world.
But I am underneath: they do not dream
　How deep below the eddying flood is whirled.

They cannot come to me, nor I to them;
　But if a mightier arm could reach and save,　　　　10
Should I forget the tide I had to stem?
　Should I, like these, ignore the abysmal wave?

Yes! in the radiant air how could I know
How black it is, how fast it is, below?

　　　　　　　　　　　　　1886

Darwinism

When first the unflowering fern forest
　Shadowed the dim lagoons of old,
A vague, unconscious, long unrest
　Swayed the great fronds of green and gold.

Until the flexible stem grew rude,
　The fronds began to branch and bower,
And lo! upon the unblossoming wood
　There breaks a dawn of apple flower.

Then on the fruitful forest boughs
　For ages long the unquiet ape　　　　　　　　10
Swung happy in his airy house
　And plucked the apple and sucked the grape.

Until in him at length there stirred
　The old, unchanged, remote distress,
That pierced his world of wind and bird
　With some divine unhappiness.

Not love, nor the wild fruits he sought;
　Nor the fierce battles of his clan
Could still the unborn and aching thought
　Until the brute became the man.　　　　　　　20

Long since . . . And now the same unrest
　Goads to the same invisible goal,
Till some new gift, undreamed, unguessed,
　End the new travail of the soul.

　　　　　　　　　　　　　1888

Selva Oscura

In a wood
  Far away,
Thrushes brood,
  Ravens prey,
Eagles circle overhead,
Through the boughs a bird drops dead.

Wild and high,
  The angry wind
Wanders by
  And cannot find
Any limit to the wood
Full of cries and solitude.

1893

DOLLIE RADFORD

née Maitland (1858–1920)

Maitland studied at Queen's College. After her marriage to the writer Ernest Radford in 1883, she lived in Hampstead and moved in Socialist and Fabian circles; she corresponded with D. H. Lawrence. She wrote what she called "little songs" in a fashionably sentimental vein, as well as more acid monologues on modern topics for the Savoy *and* The Yellow Book. *Her books for children include* In Summer Time: A Little Boy's Dream *and* The Young Gardeners' Kalendar *(1904). Other volumes, such as* A Light Load *(1891),* Songs for Somebody *(1893),* Good Night *(1895), and* Songs and Other Verses *(1895), juxtapose children's verse and urbane occasional poems.*

To a Stranger

Last night I lay and dreamed of you,
   Through all the wind and rain,
So close a part I seemed of you,
   I could not wake again;
Sunk in your spirit, deep, so deep,
In the blue caverns of my sleep.

Your face seemed full of love for me,
   You knew my heart's desire,
Vague and unquiet as the sea,
   For which I toil and tire
With prayer and pilgrimage and tears,
Through all the rolling of the years.

You welcomed me with gentle hands,
   As one expected long,
The earth seemed made of golden lands,

And life an angel song,
Fervent and full from rise to fall,
With God's great music through it all.

How came it to be you I sought
In the wide realm of sleep?
Remote from all my waking thought,
As the two ways we keep
Are distant, with dark growths between,
Making each day a surer screen.

And now you draw me with a spell
I have no power to break,
My lonely heart alone knows well
How it must ache and ache:
I pray you do not pass today
Till I have dreamed my dream away!

1895

Nobody in Town

I stand upon my island home,
My island home in Regent Street,
And listen to the ceaseless foam
Of traffic breaking at my feet:
The sky above is clear and sweet,
The summer day is smiling down;
I muse upon it, and repeat
That there is nobody in town.

All day a living metronome
Keeps up a firm relentless beat;
All day the little children roam
Through airless alleys, in the heat;
All day the men and women meet
With tired eyes, and settled frown—
I marvel, in my safe retreat,
That there is nobody in town.

Ah, world beneath the sky's blue dome,
In flannels white, and spotless gown,
Ah, would that such a day might come,
When there was nobody in town.

1895

A Novice

What is it, in these latter days,
Transfigures my domestic ways
And round me, as a halo, plays?
   My cigarette.

For me so daintily prepared,
No modern skill, or perfume, spared,
What would have happened had I dared
   To pass it yet?

What else could lighten times of woe,
When someone says, "I told you so,"   10
When all the servants, in a row,
   Give notices?

When the great family affairs
Demand the most gigantic cares
And one is very ill upstairs,
   With poultices?

What else could ease my aching head
When, though I long to be in bed,
I settle steadily instead
   To my "accounts"?   20

And while the house is slumbering,
Go over them like anything
And find them ever varying
   In their amounts!

Ah yes, the cook may spoil the broth,
The cream of life resolve to froth,
I cannot now, though very wroth,
   Distracted be;

For as the smoke curls blue and thin
From my own lips, I first begin   30
To bathe my tired spirit in
   Philosophy.

And sweetest healing on her pours,
Once more into the world she soars
And sees it full of open doors
   And helping hands.

In spite of those who, knocking, stay
At sullen portals day by day
And weary at the long delay
   To their demands.   40

The promised epoch, like a star,
Shines very bright and very far,
But nothing shall its luster mar,
    Though distant yet.

If I, in vain, must sit and wait
To realize our future state,
I shall not be disconsolate,
    My cigarette!

       1895

From the Suburbs

It rushes home, our own express,
So cheerfully, no one would guess
    The weight it carries

Of tired husbands, back from town,
For each of whom, in festal gown,
    A fond wife tarries.

For each of whom a better half,
At even, serves the fatted calf,
    In strange disguises,

At anxious boards of all degree,   10
Down to the simple "egg at tea,"
    Which love devises.

For whom all day, disconsolate,
Deserted villas have to wait,
    Detached and semi—

Barred by their own affairs, which are
As hard to pass through as the far
    Famed alpine Gemmi.

Sometimes as I at leisure roam,
Admiring my suburban home,   20
    I wonder sadly

If men will always come and go
In these vast numbers, to and fro,
    So fast and madly.

I muse on what the spell can be
Which causes this activity:
    Who of our Sages

The potent charm has meted out
To tall and thin, to short and stout,
      Of varying ages. 30

I think, when other fancy flags,
The magic lies within the bags
      Which journey ever

In silent, black mysterious ways,
With punctual owners all their days
      And fail them never.

In some perhaps sweet flowers lie,
Sweet flowers which shape a destiny
      To pain or pleasure,

Or lady's glove, or ringlet bright, 40
Or many another keepsake light,
      Which true knights treasure.

May be—may be— Romance is rife,
Despite our busy bustling life,
      And rules us gaily,

And shows no sign of weariness,
But in our very own express
      Does travel daily.

          1895

From Our Emancipated Aunt in Town

All has befallen as I say,
The old régime has passed away,
      And quite a new one

Is being fashioned in a fire,
The fervors of whose burning tire
      And quite undo one.

The fairy prince has passed from sight,
Away into the *Ewigkeit*,
      With best intention

I served him, as you know, my dears, 10
Unfalteringly through more years
      Than ladies mention.

And though the fairy prince has gone,
With all the props I leaned upon,
      And I am stranded,

With old ideals blown away,
And all opinions, in the fray,
      Long since disbanded;

And though he's only left to me,
Of course quite inadvertently,   20
      The faintest glimmer

Of humor, to illume my way,
I'm thankful he has had his day,
      His shine and shimmer.

Le roi est mort—but what's to come?—
Surcharged the air is with the hum
      Of startling changes,

And our great "question" is perforce
The vital one: o'er what a course
      It boldly ranges!   30

Strange gentlemen to me express
At quiet "at homes" their willingness
      To ease our fetters,

And ladies in a fleeting car
Will tell me that the moderns are
      My moral betters.

My knees I know are much too weak
To mount the high and shaky peak
      Of latest ethics;

I'm tabulated and I stand,   40
By evolution, in a band
      Of poor pathetics

Who cannot go alone, who cling
To many a worn-out tottering thing
      Of a convention;

To many a prejudice and hope,
And to the old proverbial rope
      Of long dimension.

It is to you to whom I look
To beautify our history book   50
      For coming readers,

To you my nieces, who must face
Our right and wrong and take your place
      As future leaders.

And I, meanwhile, shall still pursue
And that is weird and wild and new,
                    In song and ballet,

In lecture, drama, verse and prose—
With every cult that comes and goes
                    Your aunt will dally.   60

A microscopic analyst
Of female hearts, she will subsist
                    On queerest notions

And subtlest views of maid and wife
Ever engaged in deadly strife
                    With the emotions.

But while you walk, and smile at her,
In quiet lanes, which you prefer
                    To public meetings,

Remember she prepares your way,   70
With many another Aunt today,
                    And send her greetings.

                    1895

A Portrait

In winter days you came to me,
    When sitters all had taken flight,
When I no longer thought to see
    Gay faces by my studio light;
When grave and gay long since had sought
The brightness mine no longer brought.

And when my painting, good and ill,
    Discarded lay amid the gloom,
When only shadows stayed to fill
    The vacant spaces of my room;   10
In such a dreary hour your feet
Came kindly up the lonely street.

Of silks and jewels rarely wed,
    Of flower-hued embroideries,
Your flowing raiment surely shed
    A heavenly fragrance for my ease;
And healing rays for me to see
And paint you by—so gratefully.

And with the cunning of my hand,
  And with the passion of my heart,   20
With all my life at my command
  Did I perform my grateful part,
And beautiful beyond compare,
I set you on my canvas there.

But you, with nought but laughing eyes,
  Went forth again without a word;
From my beseeching prayers and sighs,
  You turned, as though you had not heard,
You would not learn, or stay to see,
The triumph you had made for me.   30

And when the year had changed to spring,
  And idle through the sunny day,
About you I sat wondering,
  You came once more my studio way,
And with a cold indifferent face,
You passed the old familiar place.

With all its former splendor gone,
  In somber folds your raiment fell;
No jewels from its dullness shone
  Of all that I had loved so well;   40
No beauty now nor grace betrayed
Yours was the picture I had made.

Then for my gratitude's sweet sake,
  With firm and patient brush I drew,
And painted out my last mistake—
  The beautiful dear face I knew—
And empty now, whate'er befall,
Your canvas hangs upon my wall.

                    1910

EDITH NESBIT

(1858–1924)

❧

Educated at boarding schools in England, France, and Germany, Nesbit was one of six children in a comfortable family that was reduced to straitened circumstances after her father's death when she was four. By age twenty she had entered a radical circle and decided to leave home. Her marriage in 1880 (when seven months pregnant) to the journalist Hubert Bland was darkened by financial difficulties, several stillbirths, and his many infidelities. Her friend Alice Hoatson became Hubert's mistress and a member of the household, caring for Nesbit's three children and her own two. In this bohemian home Bland's mistresses, Nesbit's lovers, and anarchist politicians rubbed elbows with feminists such as Olive Schreiner, Eleanor Marx, and Beatrice Webb. Bland died in 1914; Nesbit married Thomas Terry Tucker in 1917.

Like countless other women, Nesbit picked up her pen to balance the family budget. With The Story of the Treasure Seekers, *serialized in 1897, she launched a career that eventually produced over forty children's books signed "E. Nesbit." In a single year, she earned £1100 from* The Wouldbegoods *(1901). Her novels thrust groups of well-meaning but inventively mischievous children into far-flung adventures, transported through time by quirky magical beings or tokens. Aside from the light humor with which each child's profile emerges, part of the fascination of these tales lies is their lively re-creation of the atmosphere of Anglo-Saxon England, pharaonic Egypt, or the lost island of Atlantis.*

Nesbit also, however, wrote novels, stories, and poetry for adults; she reviewed poetry and edited several journals. As a child, she had dreamed of becoming a great poet like Shakespeare or Christina Rossetti. For the "tenderness of sentiment," passionate Fabian sympathies, and "dramatic power" in Lays and Legends *(1886),* Leaves of Life *(1888),* Songs of Love and Empire *(1898), and* The Rainbow and the Rose *(1905) she won praise from Algernon Swinburne, Oscar Wilde, and other reviewers. She achieved her finest poetic control, paradoxically, in autobiographical poems about dead children and ironic dramatic monologues about jealousy and infidelity.*

The Depths of the Sea

FOR A PICTURE BY E. BURNE-JONES

I.

> *Habes tota quod mente petisti*
> *Infelix.*

In deep vague spaces of the lonely sea
   She deemed her soulless life was almost fair,
   Yet ever dreamed that in the upper air
Lay happiness—supreme in mystery;
Then saw him—out of reach as you I see—
   Worshipped his strength, the brown breast broad and bare,
   The arms that bent the oar, and grew aware
Of what life means, and why it is good to be;
   And yearned for him with all her body sweet,
   Her lithe cold arms, and chill wet bosom's beat,   10
      Vowed him her beauty's unillumined shrine:
So I—seeing you above me—turn and tire,
Sick with an empty ache of long desire
   To drag you down, to hold you, make you mine!

II.

Attained at last—the lifelong longing's prize!
   Raped from the world of air where warm loves glow,
   She bears him through her water-world below;
Yet in those strange, glad, fair, mysterious eyes
The shadow of the after-sorrow lies,
   And of the coming hour, when she shall know   20
   What she has lost in having gained him so,
And whether death life's longing satisfies.
   She shall find out the meaning of despair,
   And know the anguish of a granted prayer,
      And how, all ended, all is yet undone.
So I—I long for what, far off, you shine,
   Not what you must be ere you could be mine,
      That which would crown despair if it were won.

1886

Bewitched

Attracted, repelled, and heart-sickened
   By rhythmic delight and disdain,
Succeeding each other like wave-beats

On the storm-broken shore of my brain—
I hate you until we are parted,
    And ache till I meet you again!

I would give up my hopes, ah! how gladly,
    If I could take yours, you my part—
I would give up my soul for your loving,
    I would give up my life for your heart;
Drop by drop I would drain all my blood out,
    If each drop fell on you as a smart.

I desire you, despise you, deny you,
    Am false to myself and to you,
I am false to the gods that I worship,
    And could I, I would not be true.
To help you, or hurt you, or hold you,
    There is nothing your fool would not do!

For the depths of the night and the silence,
    Are alive with your dark malign face:
Your voice drowns all solitude's voices,
    And your eyes—oh, your eyes!—are all space;
And yourself is the heaven of my dreaming—
    And the hell of my waking—disgrace.

You are Fate, you are love, you are longing,
    You are music, and roses, and wine,
You are devil, and man, and my lover,
    You are hatefully mine and not mine.
You are all that's infernal in loving,
    And all that in hate is divine.

If raising a hand would efface you,
    Ah! trust me, a hand should be raised!
Ah! had I the tongue that could sting you,
    Who too long and too well have been praised!
Could I kindle the fire in your being,
    That on my life's ruin has blazed!

I hate you, but hate you too little,
    You love me, but love not enough,
And your love, which I never shall quicken
    To a madness like mine, is pale stuff
For a star, yet you see how it leads me,
    Where the way is unlovely and rough.

And all would be nothing to suffer,
    If once at my feet you could lie,
And offer your soul for my loving—

10

20

30

40

Could I know that your world was just I—
And could laugh in your eyes and refuse you,
And love you and hate you and die!

1888

The Things That Matter

Now that I've nearly done my days
    And grown too stiff to sweep or sew,
I sit and think, till I'm amaze,
    About what lots of things I know:
Things as I've found out one by one—
    And when I'm fast down in the clay
My knowing things and how they're done
    Will all be lost and thrown away.

There's things, I know, as won't be lost,
    Things as folks write and talk about:
The way to keep your roots from frost,
    And how to get your ink spots out;
What medicine's good for sores and sprains,
    What way to salt your butter down,
What charms will cure your different pains,
    And what will bright your faded gown.

But more important things than these,
    They can't be written in a book:
How fast to boil your greens and peas,
    And how good bacon ought to look;
The feel of real good wearing stuff,
    The kind of apple as will keep,
The look of bread that's rose enough,
    And how to get a child asleep.

Whether the jam is fit to pot,
    Whether the milk is going to turn,
Whether a hen will lay or not,
    Is things as some folks never learn.
I know the weather by the sky,
    I know what herbs grow in what lane;
And if sick men are going to die,
    Or if they'll get about again.

Young wives come in, a-smiling, grave,
    With secrets that they itch to tell:
I know what sort of times they'll have,
    And if they'll have a boy or gell.

10

20

30

And if a lad is ill to bind
   Or some young maid is hard to lead,
I know when you should speak 'em kind,
   And when it's scolding as they need.   40

I used to know where birds ud set,
   And likely spots for trout or hare,
And God may want me to forget
   The way to set a line or snare;
But not the way to truss a chick,
   To fry a fish, or baste a roast,
Nor how to tell, when folks are sick,
   What kind of herb will ease them most!

Forgetting seems such silly waste!
   I know so many little things,   50
And now the Angels will make haste
   To dust it all away with wings!
O God, you made me like to know,
   You kept the things straight in my head,
Please God, if you can make it so,
   Let me know *something* when I'm dead.

1905

ROSAMUND MARRIOTT WATSON

née Rosamund Ball; pseud., Graham R. Tomson
(1860–1911)

Born in London, Rosamund Ball received a broad literary education that introduced her to contemporary French and German poetry. She married George F. Armytage at eighteen; they had two daughters. Some of her early verse, which echoes Heine and French authors, was signed R. Armytage, but the volume ironically titled Tares appeared anonymously. Legally separated in 1885, she was divorced by Armytage a year later and lost custody of her daughters after she began to live with Arthur Tomson, an artist. When she married Tomson in 1887 she was eight months pregnant. For her next volumes of poetry she took the pseudonym Graham R. Tomson.

The Bird-Bride, a Volume of Ballads and Sonnets (1889), brought her acclaim and introduced her to a fashionable literary acquaintance that over the years included the novelist Thomas Hardy, the poet Laurence Housman, and the "decadent" circle of The Yellow Book, to which she contributed. Her female friends included E. Nesbit, Alice Meynell, Amy Levy, and the feminist journalist Mona Caird, who, like Mary Wollstonecraft, opposed marriage. She edited Sylvia's Journal (1893–94) and edited poetry for the Athenaeum (1904–11). Her later volumes include A Summer Night (1891), Vespertilia (1895), and After Sunset (1904); she edited several anthologies.

In 1895 she fell in love with a young writer, H. B. Marriott Watson, became pregnant, and went through a second divorce. Watson, whom she did not marry although she assumed his name, edited the posthumous edition of her works, including the unpublished collection "The Lamp and the Lute." Some of her poems seek symbolist effects of synesthesia fusing a chromatic and emotional atmosphere in a monotone like the paintings of Whistler, others imitate antique lyrics, French aubades, and Italian stornelli. She has been most admired for her polished and musical ballads, whose macabre evocations of death and sexual violence erupt with glittering force.

Ballad of the Bird-Bride

(Eskimo)

They never come back, though I loved them well;
   I watch the South in vain;
The snowbound skies are blear and gray,
Waste and wide is the wild gull's way,
    And she comes never again.   5

Years agone, on the flat white strand,
   I won my sweet sea-girl:
Wrapped in my coat of the snow-white fur,
I watched the wild birds settle and stir,
    The gray gulls gather and whirl.   10

One, the greatest of all the flock,
   Perched on an ice floe bare,
Called and cried as her heart were broke,
And straight they were changed, that fleet bird-folk,
    To women young and fair.   15

Swift I sprang from my hiding place
   And held the fairest fast;
I held her fast, the sweet, strange thing:
Her comrades skirled, but they all took wing,
    And smote me as they passed.   20

I bore her safe to my warm snow house;
   Full sweetly there she smiled;
And yet, whenever the shrill winds blew,
She would beat her long white arms anew,
    And her eyes glanced quick and wild.   25

But I took her to wife, and clothed her warm
   With skins of the gleaming seal;
Her wandering glances sank to rest
When she held a babe to her fair warm breast,
    And she loved me dear and leal.   30

Together we tracked the fox and the seal,
   And at her behest I swore
That bird and beast my bow might slay
For meat and for raiment, day by day,
    But never a gray gull more.   35

A weariful watch I keep for aye
   Mid the snow and the changeless frost:
Woe is me for my broken word!

Woe, woe's me for my bonny bird,
   My bird and the love-time lost!   40

Have ye forgotten the old keen life?
   The hut with the skin-strewn floor?
O winged white wife, and children three,
Is there no room left in your hearts for me,
   Or our home on the low seashore?   45

Once the quarry was scarce and shy,
   Sharp hunger gnawed us sore,
My spoken oath was clean forgot,
My bow twanged thrice with a swift, straight shot,
   And slew me seagulls four.   50

The sun hung red on the sky's dull breast,
   The snow was wet and red;
Her voice shrilled out in a woeful cry,
She beat her long white arms on high,
   "The hour is here," she said.   55

She beat her arms, and she cried full fain
   As she swayed and wavered there.
"Fetch me the feathers, my children three,
Feathers and plumes for you and me,
   Bonny gray wings to wear!"   60

They ran to her side, our children three,
   With the plumage black and gray;
Then she bent her down and drew them near;
She laid the plumes on our children dear,
   Mid the snow and the salt sea-spray.   65

"Babes of mine, of the wild wind's kin,
   Feather ye quick, nor stay.
Oh, oho! but the wild winds blow!
Babes of mine, it is time to go:
   Up, dear hearts, and away!"   70

And lo! the gray plumes covered them all,
   Shoulder and breast and brow.
I felt the wind of their whirling flight:
Was it sea or sky? was it day or night?
   It is always nighttime now.   75

Dear, will you never relent, come back?
   I loved you long and true.
O winged white wife, and our children three,

Of the wild wind's kin though ye surely be,
    Are ye not of my kin too?   80

Aye, ye once were mine, and till I forget,
    Ye are mine forever and aye,
Mine, wherever your wild wings go,
While shrill winds whistle across the snow
    And the skies are blear and gray.   85

                                        1889

Ballad of the Willow Pool

There was never a face, to my mind, like hers,
    Nor ever a voice so sweet;
I would hearken aye at set o' the sun,
. When the last long furrow was turned and done,
    For her song and her lightsome feet.

'Tween the summer sward and gold of the west,
    Through the quiet air and cool,
She would lead her goats on their homeward way
By the grass-grown road and the sedges gray,
    By the side of the Willow Pool.   10

Cursed and cursed be the Willow Pool,
    And the life that dwells therein!
'Twas never a rival of flesh and blood,
But a chill, unholy fiend of the flood
    That tempted her soul to sin.

What glistering mesh could the Neckan weave
    For a soul so pure and fair?
She would dream all day in the old black boat,
And she wore a circlet about her throat
    Of a single red-gold hair.   20

One summer twilight I saw her lean,
    Low down to the water's edge.
"Farewell," she wailed, "to the old days o'er,
Farewell forever and evermore!"
    And she sank through the waving sedge.

The spell that had bound me snapped and broke,
    I sped to the waterside;
There was never a ring nor a steely track
In the water gleaming cold and black,
    No sound—but a curlew cried.   30

And ever at dusk, as that summer waned
   And the green fields turned to brown,
I would take my pipes to the slope above,
And play the airs that she used to love
   Ere the Neckan lured her down.

There was no star once in the murky sky,
   But a sullen, blood-red moon;
The waters gleamed and the air was still;
The voice of my reeds rang cracked and shrill
   As I strove to shape the tune.   40

But I strove till the reeds sang keen and clear
   As they never had sung before
(Sang till the black pool heaved and stirred),
Sweet as the song of a prisoned bird
   That sings for the Spring once more.

A faint, faint cry rose up through the gloom—
   I watched with a beating heart—
But the voice died out in a strangled wail;
Longing and love could naught avail
   'Gainst the powers of Evil Art.   50

   *   *   *   *   *

The morrow's dawn was dim and gray,
   With a mist like a winding-sheet;
She leaned in the dusk by my open door,
Slid through my arms to the rush-strewn floor,
   Like a drowned corpse at my feet.

There were pale bright gems at her breast and throat—
   Their like had I never known;
She was wrapped in a web of blue and gold,
Her eyes were closed and her lips were cold,
   And her breast like the marble stone.   60

Her folk came up from the harvest fields,
   But they crossed themselves amain;
The mother that bore her turned away,
Shuddered aloof from the poor cold clay
   Of my lass come home again.

So I drew from her limbs the glistering gear
   Where the water dripped and ran,
I wrung the drops from her yellow hair
And wrapped her in linen white and fair,
   White webs that my mother span.   70

And the carven stones and the woven gold
   (Ill meshes of death and dool!),
And the dim blue gown, like a coiling snake,
I flung far out to the sedgy lake,
   To their lord in the Willow Pool.

I took my store in the leathern pouch
   (Laid by for our plenishing),
I sought the priest and I prayed him lay
My lass in the hallowed ground that day,
   Secure from the Evil Thing.   80

He said me nay—"Through the kirkyard gates
   No corpse accursed may win,
Nor ghoul in its semblance—who can tell?
For this is sure, in the deepest Hell
   Bides that soul seared black with sin."

So I digged her grave on a shadowed slope
   Where the poplars sigh and stir,
I laid her down with her face to the west,
With a sprig of the rowan athwart her breast,
   And a cross 'tween the Pool and her.   90

The priest cries shame on my dead white dove
   (May the foul fiend hunt his track!);
If she loved the Neckan?—nay, what then?
Glamour is strong past mortal ken—
   And my piping brought her back.

My heart's like the water, dark and still,
   With a curse for its inmost guest;
The Neckan keepeth his gems and gold,
The priest and his flock are safe in the fold,
   And my truelove lies at rest.   100

1891

MARY ELIZABETH COLERIDGE

pseud., Anodos (1861–1907)

The Coleridge household was a lively literary and musical milieu, visited by Fanny Kemble, Robert Browning, Tennyson, and the painter Millais. Educated at home, Mary Coleridge acted in children's productions of Scott's Waverley *novels. She was encouraged to write poetry and short stories by her father's friend, the poet William Johnson Cory, who became her tutor. The* Quintette, *a group of her women friends, evolved into a reading circle joined by Henry Newbolt, who urged the publication of two of Coleridge's novels:* The Seven Sleepers of Ephesus *(1893) and* The King with Two Faces *(1897), a historical romance about the assassination of Gustavus III of Sweden, which went through ten editions by 1908. "Unwelcome," the beggar's song from this romance, was celebrated in its day. Other novels included* The Fiery Dawn *(1901),* The Shadow on the Wall *(1904), and* The Lady on the Drawing-room Floor *(1906).*

When a friend passed a manuscript volume of her poetry to Robert Bridges, he recognized her artistic insight and made suggestions for revision. Two volumes of poetry by Anodos were the result of his approval, if not his advice: Fancy's Following *(1896) and an expanded version,* Fancy's Guerdon *(1897). "They really do contain that rare and strange quality called poetry," Bridges commented, "though it is not of a lofty kind, it is on the other hand distinctly original." He liked her effects of "intimacy and spontaneity." Coleridge herself regretted that "words cannot express how inadequate I find them." She maintained that "poetry is, by its very derivation,* making, not feeling." *A number of her poems assume a male persona; Henry Newbolt, who responded to her enigmatic poetic ventriloquism, admired the "very deep shadows filled with strange shapes."*

Coleridge wrote essays for the Monthly Review, *the* Guardian, *the* Cornhill Magazine, *and from 1902 onward,* The Times Literary Supplement. *She taught at the Working Women's College for several years. A biography,* Life of Holman Hunt *(1908) and* Poems, New and Old *(1907) were published after her death. In* Gathered Leaves *(1910), a posthumous collection of stories and essays, she observes (never herself having married), "The borderland between Miss and Mrs., especially the extreme verge of the borderland, has an odd fascination. . . . It is, at any rate, a crisis." She died of appendicitis at forty-five.*

The Other Side of a Mirror

I sat before my glass one day
   And conjured up a vision bare,
Unlike the aspects glad and gay
   That erst were found reflected there—
The vision of a woman, wild
   With more than womanly despair.

Her hair stood back on either side
   A face bereft of loveliness.
It had no envy now to hide
   What once no man on earth could guess.   10
It formed the thorny aureole
   Of hard unsanctified distress.

Her lips were open—not a sound
   Came through the parted lines of red.
Whate'er it was, the hideous wound
   In silence and in secret bled.
No sigh relieved her speechless woe,
   She had no voice to speak her dread.

And in her lurid eyes there shone
   The dying flame of life's desire,   20
Made mad, because its hope was gone,
   And kindled at the leaping fire
Of jealousy, and fierce revenge,
   And strength that could not change nor tire.

Shade of a shadow in the glass,
   O set the crystal surface free!
Pass—as the fairer visions pass—
   Nor ever more return, to be
The ghost of a distracted hour,
   That heard me whisper, "I am she!"   30

                    1882 / 1908

A Clever Woman

You thought I had the strength of men,
   Because with men I dared to speak,
And courted Science now and then,
   And studied Latin for a week;
But woman's woman, even when
   She reads her *Ethics* in the Greek.

You thought me wiser than my kind;
   You thought me "more than common tall";
You thought because I had a mind
   That I could have no heart at all;   10
But woman's woman you will find,
   Whether she be great or small.

And then you needs must die—ah, well!
   I knew you not, you loved not me.
'Twas not because that darkness fell
   You saw not what there was to see.
But I that saw and could not tell—
   O evil Angel, set me free!

                       1883

Gone

About the little chambers of my heart
Friends have been coming—going—many a year.
      The doors stand open there.
Some, lightly stepping, enter; some depart.

Freely they come and freely go at will.
The walls give back their laughter; all day long
      They fill the house with song.
One door alone is shut, one chamber still.

               1889 / 1896

[True to myself am I, and false to all]

    "To thine own self be true;
    And it must follow, as the night the day,
    Thou canst not then be false to any man."

True to myself am I, and false to all.
   Fear, sorrow, love, constrain us till we die.
   But when the lips betray the spirit's cry,
The will, that should be sovereign, is a thrall.
Therefore let terror slay me, ere I call
   For aid of men. Let grief begrudge a sigh.
   "Are you afraid?"—"unhappy?" "No!" The lie
About the shrinking truth stands like a wall.
"And have you loved?" "No, never!" All the while,
   The heart within my flesh is turned to stone.   10
Yea, nonetheless that I account it vile,

The heart within my heart makes speechless moan,
  And when they see one face, one face alone,
The stern eyes of the soul are moved to smile.

1889

The Witch

I have walked a great while over the snow,
And I am not tall nor strong.
My clothes are wet, and my teeth are set,
And the way was hard and long.
I have wandered over the fruitful earth,
But I never came here before.
Oh, lift me over the threshold, and let me in at the door!

The cutting wind is a cruel foe.
I dare not stand in the blast.
My hands are stone, and my voice a groan,   10
And the worst of death is past.
I am but a little maiden still,
My little white feet are sore.
Oh, lift me over the threshold, and let me in at the door!

Her voice was the voice that women have
Who plead for their heart's desire.
She came—she came—and the quivering flame
Sank and died in the fire.
It never was lit again on my hearth
Since I hurried across the floor   20
To lift her over the threshold and let her in at the door.

1892 / 1908

On a Bas-relief of Pelops and Hippodameia
Which Was Wrecked and Lay Many Years Under the Sea

Thus did a nameless and immortal hand
  Make of rough stone, the thing least like to life,
  The husband and the wife
That the Most High, ere His creation, planned.
Hundreds of years they lay, unsunned, unscanned,
  Where the waves cut more smoothly than the knife,
  What time the winds tossed them about in strife
And filled those lips and eyes with the soft sand.

Art, that from Nature stole the human form
   By slow device of brain, by simple strength,   10
Lent it to Nature's artless force to keep.
So, with the human sculptor, wrought the storm
   To round those lines of beauty, till at length
A perfect thing was rescued from the deep.

1895

Unwelcome

We were young, we were merry, we were very very wise,
   And the door stood open at our feast,
When there passed us a woman with the West in her eyes
   And a man with his back to the East.

O, still grew the hearts that were beating so fast,
   The loudest voice was still.
The jest died away on our lips as they passed,
   And the rays of July struck chill.

The cups of red wine turned pale on the board,
   The white bread black as soot.   10
The hound forgot the hand of her lord,
   She fell down at his foot.

Low let me lie, where the dead dog lies,
   Ere I sit me down again at a feast,
When there passes a woman with the West in her eyes
   And a man with his back to the East.

1897

The White Women[1]

Where dwell the lovely, wild white women folk,
   Mortal to man?
They never bowed their necks beneath the yoke,
They dwelt alone when the first morning broke
   And Time began.

Taller are they than man, and very fair,
   Their cheeks are pale,
At sight of them the tiger in his lair,
The falcon hanging in the azure air,
     The eagles quail.   10

---

1. From a legend of Malay, told by Hugh Clifford.

The deadly shafts their nervous hands let fly
    Are stronger than our strongest—in their form
Larger, more beauteous, carved amazingly,
And when they fight, the wild white women cry
      The war-cry of the storm.

Their words are not as ours. If man might go
    Among the waves of Ocean when they break
And hear them—hear the language of the snow
Falling on torrents—he might also know
      The tongue they speak.   20

Pure are they as the light; they never sinned,
    But when the rays of the eternal fire
Kindle the West, their tresses they unbind
And fling their girdles to the Western wind,
      Swept by desire.

Lo, maidens to the maidens then are born,
    Strong children of the maidens and the breeze,
Dreams are not—in the glory of the morn,
Seen through the gates of ivory and horn—
      More fair than these.   30

And none may find their dwelling. In the shade
    Primeval of the forest oaks they hide.
One of our race, lost in an awful glade,
Saw with his human eyes a wild white maid,
      And gazing, died.

                    1900

No Newspapers

Where, to me, is the loss
    Of the scenes they saw—of the sounds they heard;
A butterfly flits across,
    Or a bird;
The moss is growing on the wall;
    I heard the leaf of the poppy fall.

                    1900

CAROLINE FITZ GERALD

(fl. 1889)

✦❧✦

Of an American family, Fitz Gerald married Lord Edmund Fitzmaurice (1889) but had the marriage annulled in 1894. Venetia Victrix and Other Poems (1889), dedicated to Robert Browning, includes dramatic monologues and narratives whose local color or antique settings distance the poetic voice.

Hymn to Persephone

Oh, fill my cup, Persephone,
  With dim red wine of Spring,
    And drop therein a faded leaf,
    Plucked from the Autumn's bearded sheaf,
Whence, dread one, I may quaff to thee,
  While all the woodlands ring.

Oh, fill my heart, Persephone,
  With thine immortal pain,
    That lingers round the willow bowers
    In memories of old happy hours,
When thou didst wander fair and free
  O'er Enna's blooming plain.

Oh, fill my soul, Persephone,
  With music all thine own!
    Teach me some song thy childhood knew,
    Lisped in the meadow's morning dew,
Or chant, on this high windy lea,
  Thy godhead's ceaseless moan.

10

1889

AMY LEVY

(1861–1889)

❧

Daughter of an editor, Levy was the first Jewish student at the recently founded Newn-
ham College, Cambridge; she studied philosophy, read both Greek and Latin, and
translated German poetry. Her first poem appeared when she was fourteen. By the age of
twenty, she had demonstrated in Xantippe and Other Poems *(1881) her mastery of*
ironic narrative, her flexible innovations in tight metrical forms, and her feminist con-
cerns. She moved in radical circles in London; among her friends were Beatrice Webb,
Olive Schreiner, and Vernon Lee. Her journalism includes an essay on club women that
defends women's need for a professional environment; she also examined the specificity of
Jewish humor, child-rearing, and attitudes toward women, presenting views that scan-
dalized some in her community.

Levy's dramatic poetry in the voices of Xantippe, Medea, and a "fallen" woman
abandoned by her lover explores the destructiveness of social paradigms for women. Other
poems evoke the "city pageant"; a number revolve around the theme of suicide. An essay of
1888 on Christina Rossetti praises "the delicate, unusual melody of the verse; the rich-
ness, almost to excess of imagery"—qualities that are resonant in her own second volume,
A Minor Poet and Other Verse *(1884). In her last months, she projected a sapphic*
volume of verse, The New Phaon.

Levy published three novellas, Reuben Sachs *(1888),* The Romance of a Shop
(1888), and Miss Meredith *(1889). She revised proofs for her last collection of poetry,*
A London Plane Tree *(1889), just before taking her own life at twenty-eight. To Olive*
Schreiner she wrote, "philosophy can't help me. I am too much shut in with the personal."
Beatrice Webb thought her "brilliant," and Oscar Wilde, who published her work in
Woman's World, *praised the "sincerity, directness, and melancholy" of her work.*

Xantippe

A Fragment

What, have I waked again? I never thought
To see the rosy dawn, or even this gray,
Dull, solemn stillness, ere the dawn has come.
The lamp burns low; low burns the lamp of life:
The still morn stays expectant, and my soul,
All weighted with a passive wonderment,
Waiteth and watcheth, waiteth for the dawn.
Come hither, maids; too soundly have ye slept
That should have watched me; nay, I would not chide—
Oft have I chidden, yet I would not chide   10
In this last hour—now all should be at peace.
I have been dreaming, in a troubled sleep,
Of weary days I thought not to recall;
Of stormy days whose storms are hushed long since;
Of gladsome days, of sunny days; alas!
In dreaming, all their sunshine seemed so sad,
As though the current of the dark To Be
Had flowed, prophetic, through the happy hours.
And yet, full well I know it was not thus;
I mind me sweetly of the summer days,   20
When, leaning from the lattice, I have caught
The fair, far glimpses of a shining sea,
And nearer, of tall ships, which thronged the bay
And stood out blackly from a tender sky
All flecked with sulphur, azure, and bright gold;
And in the still, clear air have heard the hum
Of distant voices; and methinks there rose
No darker fount to mar or stain the joy
Which sprang ecstatic in my maiden breast
Than just those vague desires, those hopes and fears,   30
Those eager longings, strong, though undefined,
Whose very sadness makes them seem so sweet.
What cared I for the merry mockeries
Of other maidens sitting at the loom?
Or for sharp voices, bidding me return
To maiden labor? Were we not apart—
I and my high thoughts, and my golden dreams,
My soul which yearned for knowledge, for a tongue
That should proclaim the stately mysteries
Of this fair world and of the holy gods?   40
Then followed days of sadness, as I grew
To learn my woman-mind had gone astray,

And I was sinning in those very thoughts—
For maidens, mark, such are not woman's thoughts—
(And yet, 'tis strange, the gods who fashion us
Have given us such promptings). . . .

                      Fled the years,
Till seventeen had found me tall and strong,
And fairer, runs it, than Athenian maids
Are wont to seem; I had not learned it well—
My lesson of dumb patience—and I stood   50
At life's great threshold with a beating heart
And soul resolved to conquer and attain. . . .
Once, walking 'thwart the crowded marketplace
With other maidens, bearing in the twigs,
White doves for Aphrodite's sacrifice,
I saw him, all ungainly and uncouth,
Yet many gathered round to hear his words,
Tall youths and stranger-maidens—Socrates—
I saw his face and marked it, half with awe,
Half with a quick repulsion at the shape. . . .   60
The richest gem lies hidden furthest down
And is the dearer for the weary search;
We grasp the shining shells which strew the shore,
Yet swift we fling them from us; but the gem
We keep for aye and cherish. So a soul,
Found after weary searching in the flesh,
Which half repelled our senses, is more dear
For that same seeking than the sunny mind
Which lavish nature marks with thousand hints
Upon a brow of beauty. We are prone   70
To overweigh such subtle hints, then deem,
In after disappointment, we are fooled. . . .
And when, at length, my father told me all,
That I should wed me with great Socrates,
I, foolish, wept to see at once cast down
The maiden image of a future love,
Where perfect body matched the perfect soul.
But slowly, softly did I cease to weep;
Slowly I 'gan to mark the magic flash
Leap to the eyes, to watch the sudden smile   80
Break round the mouth and linger in the eyes;
To listen for the voice's lightest tone—
Great voice, whose cunning modulations seemed
Like to the notes of some sweet instrument.
So did I reach and strain, until at last
I caught the soul athwart the grosser flesh.

Again of thee, sweet hope, my spirit dreamed!
I, guided by his wisdom and his love,
Led by his words, and counseled by his care,
Should lift the shrouding veil from things which be,   90
And at the flowing fountain of his soul
Refresh my thirsting spirit. . . .
                              And indeed,
In those long days which followed that strange day
When rites and song, and sacrifice and flowers,
Proclaimed that we were wedded, did I learn,
In sooth, a-many lessons; bitter ones
Which sorrow taught me, and not love inspired,
Which deeper knowledge of my kind impressed
With dark insistence on reluctant brain—
But that great wisdom, deeper, which dispels   100
Narrowed conclusions of a half-grown mind
And sees athwart the littleness of life
Nature's divineness and her harmony,
Was never poor Xantippe's. . . .
                              I would pause
And would recall no more, no more of life,
Than just the incomplete, imperfect dream
Of early summers, with their light and shade,
Their blossom-hopes, whose fruit was never ripe;
But something strong within me, some sad chord
Which loudly echoes to the later life,   110
Me to unfold the after-misery
Urges with plaintive wailing in my heart.
Yet, maidens, mark; I would not that ye thought
I blame my lord departed, for he meant
No evil, so I take it, to his wife.
'Twas only that the high philosopher,
Pregnant with noble theories and great thoughts,
Deigned not to stoop to touch so slight a thing
As the fine fabric of a woman's brain—
So subtle as a passionate woman's soul.   120
I think, if he had stooped a little, and cared,
I might have risen nearer to his height,
And not lain shattered, neither fit for use
As goodly household vessel nor for that
Far finer thing which I had hoped to be. . . .
Death, holding high his retrospective lamp,
Shows me those first, far years of wedded life
Ere I had learned to grasp the barren shape
Of what the Fates had destined for my life.

Then, as all youthful spirits are, was I   130
Wholly incredulous that nature meant
So little, who had promised me so much.
At first I fought my fate with gentle words,
With high endeavors after greater things;
Striving to win the soul of Socrates,
Like some slight bird who sings her burning love
To human master till at length she finds
Her tender language wholly misconceived
And that same hand, whose kind caress she sought,
With fingers flippant flings the careless corn. . . .   140
I do remember how, one summer's eve,
He, seated in an arbor's leafy shade,
Had bade me bring fresh wineskins. . . .
                                              As I stood
Lingering upon the threshold, half concealed
By tender foliage, and my spirit light
With drafts of sunny weather, did I mark
An instant the gay group before mine eyes.
Deepest in shade and facing where I stood
Sat Plato, with his calm face and low brows
Which met above the narrow Grecian eyes,   150
The pale, thin lips just parted to the smile,
Which dimpled that smooth olive of his cheek.
His head a little bent, sat Socrates,
With one swart finger raised admonishing,
And on the air were borne his changing tones.
Low lounging at his feet, one fair arm thrown
Around his knee (the other, high in air,
Brandished a brazen amphor, which yet rained
Bright drops of ruby on the golden locks
And temples with their fillets of the vine),   160
Lay Alcibiades the beautiful.
And thus, with solemn tone, spake Socrates:
"This fair Aspasia, which our Pericles
Hath brought from realms afar and set on high
In our Athenian city, hath a mind,
I doubt not, of a strength beyond her race;
And makes employ of it, beyond the way
Of women nobly gifted: woman's frail—
Her body rarely stands the test of soul;
She grows intoxicate with knowledge; throws   170
The laws of custom, order, neath her feet,
Feasting at life's great banquet with wide throat."
Then sudden, stepping from my leafy screen,

Holding the swelling wineskin o'er my head,
With breast that heaved and eyes and cheeks aflame,
Lit by a fury and a thought, I spake:
"By all great powers around us! can it be
That we poor women are empirical?
That gods who fashioned us did strive to make
Beings too fine, too subtly delicate,   180
With sense that thrilled response to every touch
Of nature's, and their task is not complete?
That they have sent their half-completed work
To bleed and quiver here upon the earth?
To bleed and quiver, and to weep and weep,
To beat its soul against the marble walls
Of men's cold hearts, and then at last to sin!"
I ceased, the first hot passion stayed and stemmed
And frighted by the silence: I could see,
Framed by the arbor foliage, which the sun   190
In setting softly gilded with rich gold,
Those upturned faces and those placid limbs;
Saw Plato's narrow eyes and niggard mouth,
Which half did smile and half did criticize,
One hand held up, the shapely fingers framed
To gesture of entreaty—"Hush, I pray,
Do not disturb her; let us hear the rest;
Follow her mood, for here's another phase
Of your black-browed Xantippe. . . ."
                                        Then I saw
Young Alcibiades, with laughing lips   200
And half-shut eyes, contemptuous, shrugging up
Soft, snowy shoulders, till he brought the gold
Of flowing ringlets round about his breasts.
But Socrates, all slow and solemnly,
Raised, calm, his face to mine and sudden spake:
"I thank thee for the wisdom which thy lips
Have thus let fall among us: prithee tell
From what high source, from what philosophies
Didst cull the sapient notion of thy words?"
Then stood I straight and silent for a breath,   210
Dumb, crushed with all that weight of cold contempt;
But swiftly in my bosom there uprose
A sudden flame, a merciful fury sent
To save me; with both angry hands I flung
The skin upon the marble, where it lay
Spouting red rills and fountains on the white;
Then all unheeding faces, voices, eyes,

I fled across the threshold, hair unbound—
White garment stained to redness—beating heart
Flooded with all the flowing tide of hopes   220
Which once had gushed out golden, now sent back
Swift to their sources, never more to rise. . . .
I think I could have borne the weary life,
The narrow life within the narrow walls,
If he had loved me; but he kept his love
For this Athenian city and her sons;
And, haply, for some stranger-woman, bold
With freedom, thought, and glib philosophy. . . .
Ah me! the long, long weeping through the nights,
The weary watching for the pale-eyed dawn   230
Which only brought fresh grieving: Then I grew
Fiercer and cursed from out my inmost heart
The fates which marked me an Athenian maid.
Then faded that vain fury; hope died out;
A huge despair was stealing on my soul,
A sort of fierce acceptance of my fate—
He wished a household vessel—well, 'twas good,
For he should have it! He should have no more
The yearning treasure of a woman's love
But just the baser treasure which he sought.   240
I called my maidens, ordered out the loom,
And spun unceasing from the morn till eve;
Watching all keenly over warp and woof,
Weighing the white wool with a jealous hand.
I spun until, methinks, I spun away
The soul from out my body, the high thoughts
From out my spirit; till at last I grew
As ye have known me—eye exact to mark
The texture of the spinning; ear all keen
For aimless talking when the moon is up   250
And ye should be a-sleeping; tongue to cut
With quick incision 'thwart the merry words
Of idle maidens. . . .
                    Only yesterday
My hands did cease from spinning; I have wrought
My dreary duties, patient till the last.
The gods reward me! Nay, I will not tell
The after-years of sorrow; wretched strife
With grimmest foes—sad want and poverty—
Nor yet the time of horror, when they bore
My husband from the threshold; nay, nor when   260
The subtle weed had wrought its deadly work.

Alas! alas! I was not there to soothe
The last great moment; never any thought
Of her that loved him—save at least the charge,
All earthly, that her body should not starve. . . .
You weep, you weep; I would not that ye wept;
Such tears are idle; with the young, such grief
Soon grows to gratulation, as, "Her love
Was withered by misfortune; mine shall grow
All nurtured by the loving" or "Her life   270
Was wrecked and shattered—mine shall smoothly sail."
Enough, enough. In vain, in vain, in vain!
The gods forgive me! Sorely have I sinned
In all my life. A fairer fate befall
You all that stand there. . . .
                                        Ha! the dawn has come;
I see a rosy glimmer—nay! it grows dark;
Why stand ye so in silence? throw it wide,
The casement, quick; why tarry?—give me air—
O fling it wide, I say, and give me light!

                                                        1881

Felo de Se

With Apologies to Mr. Swinburne

For repose I have sighed and have struggled; have sighed and have
        struggled in vain;
I am held in the Circle of Being and caught in the Circle of Pain.
I was wan and weary with life; my sick soul yearned for death;
I was weary of women and war and the sea and the wind's wild breath;
I culled sweet poppies and crushed them, the blood ran rich and red—
And I cast it in crystal chalice and drank of it till I was dead.
And the mold of the man was mute, pulseless in every part;
The long limbs lay on the sand with an eagle eating the heart.
Repose for the rotting head and peace for the putrid breast,
But for that which is "I" indeed the gods have decreed no rest;   10
No rest but an endless aching, a sorrow which grows amain:
I am caught in the Circle of Being and held in the Circle of Pain.
Bitter indeed is life, and bitter of life the breath,
But give me life and its ways and its men, if this be death.
Wearied I once of the sun and the voices which clamored around;
Give them me back—in the sightless depths there is neither light
        nor sound.
Sick is my soul, and sad and feeble and faint as it felt
When (far, dim day) in the fair flesh-fane of the body it dwelt.

But then I could run to the shore, weeping and weary and weak;
See the waves' blue sheen and feel the breath of the breeze on my cheek;   20
Could wail with the wailing wind; strike sharply the hands in despair;
Could shriek with the shrieking blast, grow frenzied and tear the hair;
Could fight fierce fights with the foe or clutch at a human hand;
And weary could lie at length on the soft, sweet, saffron sand. . . .
I have neither a voice nor hands, nor any friend nor a foe;
I am I—just a Pulse of Pain—I am I, that is all I know.
For life, and the sickness of life, and death, and desire to die—
They have passed away like the smoke; here is nothing but Pain and I.

1881

London in July

What ails my senses thus to cheat?
    What is it ails the place,
That all the people in the street
    Should wear one woman's face?

The London trees are dusty brown
    Beneath the summer sky;
My love, she dwells in London town,
    Nor leaves it in July.

O various and intricate maze,
    Wide waste of square and street,   10
Where, missing through unnumbered days,
    We twain at last may meet!

And who cries out on crowd and mart?
    Who prates of stream and sea?
The summer in the city's heart—
    That is enough for me.

1889

Ballade of an Omnibus

> *To see my love suffices me.*
> —*Ballades in Blue China*

Some men to carriages aspire;
On some the costly hansoms wait;
Some seek a fly, on job or hire;
Some mount the trotting steed, elate.

I envy not the rich and great,
A wandering minstrel, poor and free,
I am contented with my fate—
An omnibus suffices me.

In winter days of rain and mire
I find, within, a corner strait;   10
The busmen know me and my lyre,
From Brompton to the Bull-and-Gate.
When summer comes, I mount in state
The topmost summit, whence I see
Crœsus look up, compassionate—
An omnibus suffices me.

I mark, untroubled by desire,
Lucullus' phaeton and its freight.
The scene whereof I cannot tire,
The human tale of love and hate,   20
The city pageant, early and late,
Unfolds itself, rolls by, to be
A pleasure deep and delicate.
An omnibus suffices me.

Princess, your splendor you require,
I, my simplicity; agree
Neither to rate lower nor higher.
An omnibus suffices me.

1889

Borderland

Am I waking, am I sleeping?
As the first faint dawn comes creeping
Through the pane, I am aware
Of an unseen presence hovering,
Round, above, in the dusky air:
A downy bird, with an odorous wing,
That fans my forehead and sheds perfume
As sweet as love, as soft as death,
Drowsy-slow through the summer gloom.
My heart in some dream-rapture saith,   10
It is she. Half in a swoon,
I spread my arms in slow delight—
O prolong, prolong the night,
For the nights are short in June!

1889

To Vernon Lee

On Bellosguardo, when the year was young,
We wandered, seeking for the daffodil
And dark anemone, whose purples fill
The peasant's plot, between the corn shoots sprung.

Over the gray, low wall the olive flung
Her deeper grayness; far off, hill on hill
Sloped to the sky, which, pearly pale and still,
Above the large and luminous landscape hung.

A snowy blackthorn flowered beyond my reach;
You broke a branch and gave it to me there;   10
I found for you a scarlet blossom rare.

Thereby ran on of art and life our speech;
And of the gifts the gods had given to each—
Hope unto you, and unto me despair.

1889

A Ballade of Religion and Marriage

Swept into limbo is the host
        Of heavenly angels, row on row;
The Father, Son, and Holy Ghost,
        Pale and defeated, rise and go.
The great Jehovah is laid low,
        Vanished his burning bush and rod—
Say, are we doomed to deeper woe?
        Shall marriage go the way of God?

Monogamous, still at our post,
        Reluctantly we undergo   10
Domestic round of boiled and roast
        Yet deem the whole proceeding slow.
Daily the secret murmurs grow;
        We are no more content to plod
Along the beaten paths—and so
        Marriage must go the way of God.

Soon, before all men, each shall toast
        The seven strings unto his bow,
Like beacon fires along the coast,
        The flames of love shall glance and glow.   20
Nor let nor hindrance man shall know,
        From natal bath to funeral sod;

Perennial shall his pleasures flow
    When marriage goes the way of God.

Grant, in a million years at most,
    Folk shall be neither pairs nor odd—
Alas! we shan't be there to boast
    "Marriage has gone the way of God!"

1915

MAY KENDALL

penname of Emma Goldworth Kendall (1861–1944)

The child of a Yorkshire Wesleyan minister, Kendall was interested in contemporary politics and science. She playfully dealt with such themes as evolution and women's work in Dreams to Sell *(1887) and* Songs from Dreamland *(1894). Her novels were* From a Garret *(1887),* Such Is Life *(1889) and* White Poppies *(1893). The short stories in* Turkish Bonds *(1898) responded to the massacre of Armenians. She also collaborated with Andrew Lang on* That Very Mab *(1885) and with Seebohm Rowntree on economic treatises:* How the Labourer Lives *(1913) and* The Human Needs of Labour *(1918).*

Lay of the Trilobite

A mountain's giddy height I sought,
    Because I could not find
Sufficient vague and mighty thought
    To fill my mighty mind;
And as I wandered ill at ease,
    There chanced upon my sight
A native of Silurian seas,
    An ancient Trilobite.

So calm, so peacefully he lay,
    I watched him even with tears:
I thought of Monads far away
    In the forgotten years.
How wonderful it seemed and right,
    The providential plan,
That he should be a Trilobite,
    And I should be a Man!

And then, quite natural and free
  Out of his rocky bed,
That Trilobite he spoke to me,
  And this is what he said: 20
"I don't know how the thing was done,
  Although I cannot doubt it;
But Huxley—he if anyone
  Can tell you all about it;

"How all your faiths are ghosts and dreams;
  How in the silent sea
Your ancestors were Monotremes—
  Whatever these may be;
How you evolved your shining lights
  Of wisdom and perfection   30
From Jellyfish and Trilobites
  By Natural Selection.

"You've Kant to make your brains go round,
  Hegel you have to clear them,
You've Mr. Browning to confound,
  And Mr. Punch to cheer them!
The native of an alien land
  You call a man and brother,
And greet with hymnbook in one hand
  And pistol in the other!   40

"You've Politics to make you fight
  As if you were possessed;
You've cannon and you've dynamite
  To give the nations rest;
The side that makes the loudest din
  Is surest to be right—
And oh, a pretty fix you're in!"
  Remarked the Trilobite.

"But gentle, stupid, free from woe
  I lived among my nation;   50
I didn't care—I didn't know
  That I was a Crustacean.[1]
I didn't grumble, didn't steal,
  I *never* took to rhyme:

---

1. He was not a Crustacean. He has since discovered that he was an Arachnid, or something similar. But he says it does not matter. He says they told him wrong once and they may again.

Salt water was my frugal meal,
  And carbonate of lime."

Reluctantly I turned away,
  No other word he said;
An ancient Trilobite, he lay
  Within his rocky bed.   60
I did not answer him, for that
  Would have annoyed my pride:
I merely bowed and raised my hat
  But in my heart I cried:

"I wish our brains were not so good,
  I wish our skulls were thicker,
I wish that Evolution could
  Have stopped a little quicker;
For oh, it was a happy plight,
  Of liberty and ease,   70
To be a simple Trilobite
  In the Silurian seas!"

                                             1887

A Pure Hypothesis

(A lover, in four-dimensioned space, describes a dream.)

Ah, love, the teacher we decried,
  That erudite professor grim,
In mathematics drenched and dyed,
  Too hastily we scouted him.
He said: "The bounds of Time and Space,
  The categories we revere,
May be in quite another case
  In quite another sphere."

He told us: "Science can conceive
  A race whose feeble comprehension   10
Can't be persuaded to believe
  That there exists our Fourth Dimension,
Whom Time and Space forever balk;
  But of these beings incomplete—
Whether upon their heads they walk
  Or stand upon their feet—

We cannot tell, we do not know,
  Imagination stops confounded;
We can but say 'It *may* be so,'

To every theory propounded."   20
Too glad were we in this our scheme
    Of things, his notions to embrace—
But I have dreamed an awful dream
    Of *Three-dimensioned* Space!

I dreamed—the horror seemed to stun
    My logical perception strong—
That everything beneath the sun
    Was *so unutterably wrong.*
I thought—what words can I command?—
    That nothing ever did come right.   30
No wonder *you* can't understand:
    I could not, till last night!

I would not, if I could, recall
    The horror of those novel heavens,
Where Present, Past, and Future all
    Appeared at sixes and at sevens,
Where Capital and Labor fought,
    And in the nightmare of the mind,
No contradictories were thought
    As truthfully combined!   40

Nay, in that dream-distorted clime,
    These fatal wilds I wandered through,
The boundaries of Space and Time
    Had got most frightfully askew.
"What *is* 'askew'?" my love, you cry;
    I cannot answer, can't portray;
The sense of Everything awry
    No language can convey.

I can't tell what my words denote,
    I know not what my phrases mean;   50
Inexplicable terrors float
    Before this spirit once serene.
Ah, what if on some lurid star
    There should exist a hapless race
Who live and love, who think and are,
    In Three-dimensioned Space!

                                              1887

The Philanthropist and the Jellyfish

Her beauty, passive in despair,
    Through sand and seaweed shone,

The fairest jellyfish I e'er
  Had set mine eyes upon.

It would have made a stone abuse
  The callousness of fate,
This creature of prismatic hues
  Stranded and desolate!

Musing I said: "My mind's unstrung,
  Joy, hope, are in their grave:
Yet ere I perish all unsung
  One jellyfish I'll save!"

And yet I fancied I had dreamed
  Of somewhere having known
Or met a jellyfish that seemed
  As utterly alone.

But ah, if ever out to sea
That jellyfish I bore,
Immediately awaited me
  A level hundred more!

I knew that it would be in vain
  To try to float them all;
And though my nature is humane,
  I *felt* that it would pall.

"Yet this one jellyfish," I cried,
  "I'll rescue if I may.
I'll wade out with her through the tide
  And leave her in the bay."

I paused, my feelings to control,
  To wipe away a tear—
It seemed to me a murmur stole
  Out of the crystal sphere.

She said: "Your culture's incomplete,
  Though your intention's kind;
The sand, the seaweed, and the heat
  I do not really mind.

"To wander through the briny deep
  I own I do not care;
I somehow seem to go to sleep
  Here, there, or anywhere.

"When wild waves tossed me to and fro,
  I never felt put out;

I never got depressed and low,
  Or paralyzed by doubt.

"'Twas not the ocean's soothing balm.
  Ah no, 'twas something more!
I'm just as peaceful and as calm
  Here shriveling on the shore.

"It does not matter what may come,
  I'm dead to woe or bliss: 50
I haven't a Sensorium,
  And that is how it is."

1887

Woman's Future

Complacent they tell us, hard hearts and derisive,
  In vain is our ardor, in vain are our sighs:
Our intellects, bound by a limit decisive,
  To the level of Homer's may never arise.
We heed not the falsehood, the base innuendo;
  The laws of the universe, these are our friends.
Our talents shall rise in a mighty crescendo;
  We trust Evolution to make us amends!

But ah, when I ask you for food that is mental,
  My sisters, you offer me ices and tea!   10
You cherish the fleeting, the mere accidental,
  At cost of the True, the Intrinsic, the Free.
Your feelings, compressed in Society's mangle,
  Are vapid and frivolous, pallid and mean.
To slander you love, but you don't care to wrangle:
  You bow to Decorum, and cherish Routine.

Alas, is it woolwork you take for your mission,
  Or Art that your fingers so gaily attack?
Can patchwork atone for the mind's inanition?
  Can the soul, oh my sisters, be fed on a *plaque*?   20
Is this your vocation? My goal is another,
  And empty and vain is the end you pursue.
In antimacassars the world you may smother;
  But intellect marches o'er them and o'er you.

On Fashion's vagaries your energies strewing,
  Devoting your days to a rug or a screen,
Oh, rouse to a lifework—do something worth doing!
  Invent a new planet, a flying-machine.

Mere charms superficial, mere feminine graces,
    That fade or that flourish, no more you may prize;   30
But the knowledge of Newton will beam from your faces,
The soul of a Spencer will shine in your eyes.

Envoy

Though jealous exclusion may tremble to own us,
    Oh, wait for the time when our brains shall expand!
When once we're enthroned, you shall never dethrone us—
    The poets, the sages, the seers of the land!

              1887

In the Toy Shop

The child had longings all unspoken—
    She was a naughty child.
She had "a will that must be broken";
    Her brothers drove her wild.
She read the tale, but skipped the moral.
    She thought: "One *might* be good
If one could never scream and quarrel,
    If one were only wood!"

Meanwhile, the doll: "Ah, fatal chasm!
    Although I've real curls,   10
I am not made of protoplasm
    Like other little girls.
You see on every wooden feature
    My animation's nil.
How nice to be a human creature,
    Get cross, and have a will!"

And what may be the real issue
    There's none hath understood;
But some of us are nervous tissue,
    And some of us are wood.   20
And some to suffering, striving wildly,
    Are never quite resigned;
While we of wood yet murmur mildly
    At being left behind.

             1894

CHARLOTTE MEW

pseud., Charles Catty (1869–1928)

Mew's quiet middle-class existence in Bloomsbury was etched by troubles. She lost three siblings early in life; poverty followed her father's death; and she feared inheriting the same mental illness that had forced the confinement of a brother and sister. Yet while caring for a querulous mother and struggling for a semblance of bourgeois comfort, Mew and her sister Anne were able to pursue careers in writing and painting. She attended lectures at University College, London. A few trips to France alone or with friends were possible; they were fodder for her humorous tales in company and fostered the cosmopolitan touches of French in her poetry. Moving in advanced literary circles in mannish dress, she had a reputation for smoking and swearing, and for witty banter. She said she had "a scarlet soul." During the First World War she worked for the War Pensions Committee as a visitor to needy widows. Depressed after Anne's death from cancer in 1927, she poisoned herself with Lysol.

Mew's stories, essays, and poems began to appear in the '90s in The Yellow Book, *the* Nation, *the* New Statesman, *the* Englishwoman, Temple Bar, *and* The Egoist; *a one-act play in Cornish dialect,* The China Bowl, *was not produced until 1953 by the BBC. George Eliot was one of Mew's favorite authors; in 1904 she published an essay praising the "somber and startling beauty" of Emily Brontë's poetry. May Sinclair, whom she met in 1913, first encouraged her work, then apparently broke off their relationship. Harold and Alida Monro of the Poetry Bookshop published* The Farmer's Bride *in 1916, as well as the posthumous* Rambling Sailor (1929). *The dramatic monologues gathered in her 1916 volume immediately brought her recognition for her innovative lines and the force with which they explore mental illness and physical passion and its denial. Thomas Hardy declared her "far and away the best living woman poet" and recommended her for a civil-list pension in 1923. Virginia Woolf, who had been told Mew was "the greatest living poetess," found her "unlike anyone else." Other readers have praised her concision and thrusting rhythms: For Louis Untermeyer, "her work, like herself, had a deceptive fragility, a cameo cut in steel." A reviewer wrote that her poems "come burning from the printed page."*

Afternoon Tea

Please you, excuse me, good five-o'clock people,
    I've lost my last hatful of words,
And my heart's in the wood up above the church steeple,
    I'd rather have tea with the birds.

Gay Kate's stolen kisses, poor Barnaby's scars,
    John's losses and Mary's gains,
Oh! what do they matter, my dears, to the stars
    Or the glowworms in the lanes!

I'd rather lie under the tall elm trees,
    With old rooks talking loud overhead,   10
To watch a red squirrel run over my knees,
    Very still on my brackeny bed.

And wonder what feathers the wrens will be taking
    For lining their nests next Spring;
Or why the tossed shadow of boughs in a great wind shaking
    Is such a lovely thing.

*c.*1903 / reprinted 1929

In Nunhead Cemetery

It is the clay that makes the earth stick to his spade;
    He fills in holes like this year after year;
The others have gone; they were tired and half afraid,
    But I would rather be standing here;

There is nowhere else to go. I have seen this place
    From the windows of the train that's going past
Against the sky. This is rain on my face—
    It was raining here when I saw it last.

There is something horrible about a flower;
    This, broken in my hand, is one of those   10
He threw in just now: it will not live another hour;
    There are thousands more: you do not miss a rose.

One of the children hanging about
    Pointed at the whole dreadful heap and smiled
This morning, after THAT was carried out;
    There is something terrible about a child.

We were like children, last week, in the Strand;
    That was the day you laughed at me
Because I tried to make you understand

The cheap, stale chap I used to be   20
    Before I saw the things you made me see.

This is not a real place; perhaps by and by
    I shall wake—I am getting drenched with all this rain:
Tomorrow I will tell you about the eyes of the Crystal Palace train
        Looking down on us, and you will laugh and I shall see what you see
                                again.

        Not here, not now. We said, "Not yet
        Across our low stone parapet
Will the quick shadows of the sparrows fall."

        But still it was a lovely thing
        Through the gray months to wait for Spring   30
        With the birds that go a-gypsying
In the parks till the blue seas call.
        And next to these, you used to care
        For the lions in Trafalgar Square,
Who'll stand and speak for London when her bell of Judgment tolls—
        And the gulls at Westminster that were
        The old sea captains' souls.
Today again the brown tide splashes, step by step, the river stair,
        And the gulls are there!

By a month we have missed our day: 40
    The children would have hung about
Round the carriage and over the way
    As you and I came out.

We should have stood on the gulls' black cliffs and heard the sea
    And seen the moon's white track,
I would have called, you would have come to me
    And kissed me back.

You have never done that: I do not know
    Why I stood staring at your bed
And heard you, though you spoke so low,   50
    But could not reach your hands, your little head.
There was nothing we could not do, you said,
    And you went, and I let you go!

Now I will burn you back, I will burn you through,
    Though I am damned for it, we two will lie
    And burn, here where the starlings fly
    To these white stones from the wet sky;
    Dear, you will say this is not I—
It would not be you, it would not be you!

If for only a little while   60
    You will think of it you will understand,
        If you will touch my sleeve and smile
As you did that morning in the Strand,
        I can wait quietly with you
        Or go away if you want me to—
God! What is God? but your face has gone and your hand!
        Let me stay here too.

    When I was quite a little lad
At Christmastime we went half mad
    For joy of all the toys we had,   70
And then we used to sing about the sheep
    The shepherds watched by night;
We used to pray to Christ to keep
    Our small souls safe till morning light—
I am scared, I am staying with you tonight—
        Put me to sleep.

I shall stay here: here you can see the sky;
The houses in the streets are much too high;
    There is no one left to speak to there;
    Here they are everywhere,   80
And just above them fields and fields of roses lie—
If he would dig it all up again they would not die.

                                        1911 / 1916

The Farmer's Bride

        Three summers since, I chose a maid,
        Too young maybe—but more's to do
        At harvesttime than bide and woo.
            When us was wed she turned afraid
        Of love and me and all things human;
        Like the shut of a winter's day.
        Her smile went out, and 'twasn't a woman—
            More like a little frightened fay.
                One night, in the Fall, she runned away.

        "Out 'mong the sheep, her be," they said,   10
        Should properly have been abed;
        But sure enough, she wasn't there,
        Lying awake with her wide brown stare.
    So over seven-acre field and up-along across the down
        We chased her, flying like a hare
        Before our lanterns. To Church-Town

All in a shiver and a scare
We caught her, fetched her home at last
And turned the key upon her, fast.

She does the work about the house   20
As well as most, but like a mouse:
Happy enough to chat and play
With birds and rabbits and such as they,
So long as menfolk keep away.
"Not near, not near!" her eyes beseech
When one of us comes within reach.
The women say that beasts in stall
Look round like children at her call.
I've hardly heard her speak at all.

Shy as a leveret, swift as he,   30
Straight and slight as a young larch tree,
Sweet as the first wild violets, she,
To her wild self. But what to me?

The short days shorten and the oaks are brown,
The blue smoke rises to the low gray sky,
One leaf in the still air falls slowly down,
A magpie's spotted feathers lie
On the black earth spread white with rime,
The berries redden up to Christmastime.
What's Christmastime without there be   40
Some other in the house than we!

She sleeps up in the attic there,
Alone, poor maid. 'Tis but a stair
Betwixt us. Oh! my God! the down,
The soft young down of her, the brown,
The brown of her—her eyes, her hair, her hair!

1912

The Fête

Tonight again the moon's white mat
Stretches across the dormitory floor,
While outside, like an evil cat
The *pion* prowls down the dark corridor,
Planning, I know, to pounce on me, in spite
For getting leave to sleep in town last night.
But it was none of us who made that noise,
Only the old brown owl that hoots and flies
Out of the ivy—he will say it was us boys—

Seigneur mon Dieu! the *sacré* soul of spies! 10
   He would like to catch each dream that lies
      Hidden behind our sleepy eyes:
Their dream? But mine—it is the moon and the wood that sees;
All my long life how I shall hate the trees!

In the *Place d'Armes*, the dusty planes all Summer through
Dozed with the market women in the sun and scarcely stirred
   To see the quiet things that crossed the square—
A tiny funeral, the flying shadow of a bird,
   The hump-backed barber, Célestin Lemaire,
   Old madame Michel in her three-wheeled chair, 20
      And filing past to Vespers, two and two,
      The *demoiselles* of the *pensionnat*.
Towed like a ship through the harbor bar,
   Safe into port, where *le petit Jésus*
Perhaps makes nothing of the look they shot at you:
   Si, c'est défendu, mais que voulez-vous?
It was the sun. The sunshine weaves
A pattern on dull stones: the sunshine leaves
   The portraiture of dreams upon the eyes
      Before it dies: 30
   All Summer through,
The dust hung white upon the drowsy planes
Till suddenly they woke with the Autumn rains.

      It is not only the little boys
      Who have hardly got away from toys,
But I, who am seventeen next year,
Some nights, in bed, have grown cold to hear
      That lonely passion of the rain,
Which makes you think of being dead,
And of somewhere living to lay your head 40
      As if you were a child again,
Crying for one thing, known and near
Your empty heart, to still the hunger and the fear
   That pelts and beats with it against the pane.
      But I remember smiling, too,
At all the sun's soft tricks and those Autumn dreads
   In winter time, when the gray light broke slowly through
The frosted window-lace to drag us shivering from our beds.
   And when at dusk the singing wind swung down
Straight from the stars to the dark country roads 50
      Beyond the twinkling town,
   Striking the leafless poplar boughs as he went by,
Like some poor stray dog by the wayside lying dead,

We left behind us the old world of dread,
I and the wind, as we strode whistling on under the Winter sky.

And then in Spring for three days came the Fair
   Just as the planes were starting into bud
Above the caravans: You saw the dancing bear
   Pass on his chain and heard the jingle and the thud.
       Only four days ago   60
       They let you out of this dull show
To slither down the *montagne russe* and chaff the man *à la tête de veau*—
       Hit, slick, the bull's-eye at the *tir*,
Spin round and round till your head went queer
On the *porcs-roulants. Oh! là là! la fête!*
Va pour du vin, et le tête-à-tête
With the girl who sugars the *gaufres! Pauvrette,*
   How thin she was; but she smiled, you bet,
   As she took your tip—"One does not forget
The good days, Monsieur." Said with a grace,   70
But *sacrebleu!* what a ghost of a face!
   And no fun, too, for the *demoiselles*
Of the *pensionnat*, who were hurried past,
   With their *"Oh, que c'est beau"*—*"Ah, qu'elle est belle!"*
A lapdog's life from first to last!
The good nights are not made for sleep, nor the good days for
              dreaming in,
   And at the end in the big circus tent we sat and shook and
              stewed like sin!

   Some children there had got—but where?
Sent from the south, perhaps—a red bouquet
   Of roses, sweetening the fetid air   80
With scent from gardens by some faraway blue bay.
   They threw one at the dancing bear;
The white clown caught it. From St. Rémy's tower
   The deep, slow bell tolled out the hour;
The black clown, with his dirty grin,
   Lay, sprawling in the dust, as She rode in.

She stood on a white horse—and suddenly you saw the bend
   Of a far-off road at dawn, with knights riding by,
A field of spears—and then the gallant day
Go out in storm, with ragged clouds low down, sullen and gray   90
   Against red heavens: wild and awful, such a sky
   As witnesses against you at the end
Of a great battle; bugles blowing, blood and dust—
The old *Morte d'Arthur*, fight you must . . .
   It died in anger. But it was not death

That had you by the throat, stopping your breath.
She looked like Victory. She rode my way.

She laughed at the black clown, and then she flew
  A bird above us, on the wing
Of her white arms; and you saw through
A rent in the old tent, a patch of sky
With one dim star. She flew, but not so high—
  And then she did not fly;
She stood in the bright moonlight at the door
Of a strange room, she threw her slippers to the floor—
   Again, again
  You heard the patter of the rain,
  The starving rain—it was this Thing,
Summer was this, the gold mist in your eyes—
   Oh God! it dies,
   But after death—
 Tonight the splendor and the sting
 Blows back and catches at your breath,
The smell of beasts, the smell of dust; the scent of all the roses
   in the world, the sea, the Spring,
The beat of drums, the pad of hoofs, music, the dream, the dream,
    the Enchanted Thing!

 At first you scarcely saw her face,
 You knew the maddening feet were there,
What called was that half-hidden, white unrest
To which now and then she pressed
 Her fingertips; but as she slackened pace
 And turned and looked at you it grew quite bare:
  There was not anything you did not dare—
Like trumpeters the hours passed until the last day of the fair.

 In the *Place d'Armes* all afternoon
 The building birds had sung, "Soon, soon,"
The shuttered streets slept sound that night,
  It was full moon:
The path into the wood was almost white,
The trees were very still and seemed to stare;
 Not far before your soul the Dream flits on,
 But when you touch it, it is gone
And quite alone your soul stands there.

Mother of Christ, no one has seen your eyes: how can men pray
  Even unto you?
There were only wolves' eyes in the wood—
  My Mother is a woman too:
Nothing is true that is not good,

100

110

120

130

With that quick smile of hers, I have heard her say . . .
I wish I had gone back home today.
    I should have watched the light that so gently dies   140
    From our high window, in the Paris skies,
            The long, straight chain
    Of lamps hung out along the Seine;
I would have turned to her and let the rain
Beat on her breast as it does against the pane—
    Nothing will be the same again—
There is something strange in my little Mother's eyes,
There is something new in the old heavenly air of Spring:
The smell of beasts, the smell of dust—*The Enchanted Thing*!

All my life long I shall see moonlight on the fern   150
    And the black trunks of trees. Only the hair
Of any woman can belong to God.
The stalks are cruelly broken where we trod—
            There had been violets there—
              I shall not care
As I used to do when I see the bracken burn.

                              1910 / 1914

Fame

    Sometimes in the overheated house, but not for long,
        Smirking and speaking rather loud,
      I see myself among the crowd,
    Where no one fits the singer to his song,
    Or sifts the unpainted from the painted faces
    Of the people who are always on my stair;
    They were not with me when I walked in heavenly places;
          But could I spare,
    In the blind Earth's great silences and spaces,
        The din, the scuffle, the long stare   10
        If I went back and it was not there?
    Back to the old known things that are the new,
    The folded glory of the gorse, the sweetbrier air,
    To the larks that cannot praise us, knowing nothing of what we do
        And the divine, wise trees that do not care
    Yet to leave Fame, still with such eyes and that bright hair!
    God! If I might! And before I go hence,
          Take in her stead,
          To our tossed bed,
      One little dream, no matter how small, how wild.   20
    Just now, I think I found it in a field, under a fence—

A frail, dead, newborn lamb, ghostly and pitiful and white,
    A blot upon the night,
    The moon's dropped child!

                  1913 / 1914

The Forest Road

The forest road,
The infinite straight road stretching away
World without end: the breathless road between the walls
Of the black listening trees; the hushed, gray road
Beyond the window that you shut tonight,
Crying that you would look at it by day—
There is a shadow there that sings and calls
But not for you. Oh! hidden eyes that plead in sleep
Against the lonely dark, if I could touch the fear
And leave it kissed away on quiet lids—   10
If I could hush these hands that are half awake,
Groping for me in sleep, I could go free.
I wish that God would take them out of mine
And fold them like the wings of frightened birds,
Shot cruelly down but fluttering into quietness so soon.
Broken, forgotten things; there is no grief for them in the
      green Spring
When the new birds fly back to the old trees.
But it shall not be so with you. I will look back. I wish I knew
              that God would stand
Smiling and looking down on you when morning comes,
To hold you, when you wake, closer than I,   20
So gently though; and not with famished lips or hungry arms:
He does not hurt the frailest, dearest things
As we do in the dark. See, dear, your hair—
I must unloose this hair that sleeps and dreams
About my face, and clings like the brown weed
To drowned, delivered things, tossed by the tired sea
Back to the beaches. Oh! your hair! If you had lain
A long time dead on the rough, glistening ledge
Of some black cliff, forgotten by the tide,
The raving winds would tear, the dripping brine would rust away   30
Fold after fold of all the loveliness
That wraps you round, and makes you, lying here,
The passionate fragrance that the roses are.
But death would spare the glory of your head
In the long sweetness of the hair that does not die:
The spray would leap to it in every storm,

The scent of the unsilenced sea would linger on
In these dark waves, and round the silence that was you—
Only the nesting gulls would hear, but there would still be
                    whispers in your hair;
Keep them for me; keep them for me. What *is* this singing
                    on the road   40
That makes all other music like the music in a dream—
Dumb to the dancing and the marching feet; you know,
                    in dreams, you see
Old pipers playing that you cannot hear,
And ghostly drums that only seem to beat. This seems to climb:
Is it the music of a larger place? It makes our room too small:
                    it is like a stair,
A calling stair that climbs up to a smile you scarcely see,
Dim, but so waited for; and *you* know what a smile is, how it calls,
How if I smiled you always ran to me.
Now you must sleep forgetfully, as children do.
There is a Spirit sits by us in sleep   50
Nearer than those who walk with us in the bright day.
I think he has a tranquil, saving face: I think he came
Straight from the hills; he may have suffered there in time gone by,
And once, from those forsaken heights, looked down,
Lonely himself, on all the lonely sorrows of the earth.
It is his kingdom—Sleep. If I could leave you there—
If, without waking you, I could get up and reach the door—!
We used to go together— Shut, scared eyes,
Poor, desolate, desperate hands, it is not I
Who thrust you off. No, take your hands away—   60
I cannot strike your lonely hands. Yes, I have struck your heart,
It did not come so near. Then lie you there,
Dear and wild heart, behind this quivering snow
With two red stains on it; and I will strike and tear
Mine out, and scatter it to yours. Oh! throbbing dust,
You that were life, our little windblown hearts!
                    The road! the road!
There is a shadow there: I see my soul,
I hear my soul, singing among the trees!

                                        1914 / 1916

Notes

ANNA BARBAULD

The Rights of Woman

Barbauld's response to criticism by Mary Wollstonecraft.

Washing Day

epigraph: Loosely quoted from *As You Like It* (II.vii.161–63). **line 30** *Guatimozin:* last of the Aztec emperors, tortured by Cortes. **77** *clap and iron and plait:* smooth, iron, and pleat. **82** Joseph and Jacques Montgolfier launched a hot-air balloon in 1783; Barbauld saw a balloon on exhibit in 1784.

Eighteen Hundred and Eleven

As contemporaries noted, the title refers not to an event but to the general political and social climate. The year 1811 was a low point in British politics, when the "financial difficulties" Barbauld prophesied from the war against Napoleon had grown acute, following blockades, labor strife, material shortages, and the porphyria of George III.

    line 10 *obey:* By 1809 most of Europe had capitulated to Napoleon. **49** *ruin:* In 1810 the economy suffered from inflation, bankruptcies, and a growing threat of war against the United States. **73** *Crescent:* Unlike the fall of the Ottoman empire, Barbauld patriotically suggests, the decline of Britain's commercial empire will leave a rich legacy in representative government, the arts, and sciences. Like tourists to Greece, pilgrims will be drawn to visit the homes of Englishmen such as the philosophers John Locke and William Paley, poets John Milton, James Thomson, William Cowper, and Shakespeare, the mathematician Isaac Newton, and the agronomist-historian William Roscoe. **101** *Joanna:* Baillie, whose tragedies *Count Basil* and *Ethwald* Barbauld believes will exert moral influence. **154** *Skiddaw:* Just as worshippers of Shakespeare visit the river Avon, readers of Wordsworth will visit Mount Skiddaw and the waterfall of Lodore, or the ruins at Edinburgh and Melrose Abbey, celebrated by Sir Walter Scott. **178** *silent dead:* Monuments. Lines 177–86 depict St. Paul's in London, with its monuments to Samuel Johnson and John Howard. **191** *Here Chatham:* Future tourists in London, Barbauld prophesies, will visit the Houses of Parliament, theaters, the Royal Institution, and the British Museum to admire the art of Sir Joshua Reynolds, the valor of Lord Nelson and General Moore, and the scientific discoveries of Sir Humphrey Davy, Benjamin Franklin, and Joseph Priestley. 215 *spirit:* Contemporaries took Barbauld to mean the spirit of liberty, civilization, or progress. 249 *Tadmor:* Palmyra. The "Genius" or spirit of progress travels through Palmyra, Carthage, Troy, and Babylon, and the pastoral world of antiquity (l. 260) to inhabit Holland (the Batavian Republic). Poetic gifts pass from Italy's Cicero (Tully) and Virgil (Maro) to Britain. 289 *Bonduca:* Boadicea 309 *exiles:* Persecuted exiles refute the justice of British laws.

ELIZABETH MOODY

To Dr. Darwin

Loves of the Plants: an exposition in verse of the Linnaean system of botanical classification published in 1789.

The Housewife

subtitle *Lysander:* Spartan general. line 52 *beauteous Mother of mankind:* Eve, in Milton's *Paradise Lost.* 56 *Agamemnon:* Greek general, in Pope's translation of Homer's *Iliad.* 120 *Salopia:* Shropshire.

CHARLOTTE SMITH

Thirty-eight

subtitle *Mrs. H——y:* Eliza Hayley, age nineteen, married William Hayley in 1769; they separated permanently in 1789.

To My Lyre

line 11 *drawbacks, bottomry:* tax rebates and a mortgage on commercial shipping. 12 *tare and tret:* allowances for weight of container and for waste. 13 *scrip, omnium, and consols:* stock certificates, an aggregate loan, British government securities. 26 *Bowbells:* the bells of Bow Church. 29 *calipash and calipee:* the prized meat of a tortoise.

Beachy Head

line 40 *dubious spot:* The trading ship is both indistinct visually and dubious morally, since the spice and cotton trade with India and the silk trade with China, like the collection of pearls, depend upon slavery (1.52) and imperialist war. 121 *Neustria:* Normandy. 127 *Drogon, Fier-a-bras, and Humfroi:* As Smith's note explains, three Norman brothers who conquered Sicily. Smith's notes to her own note 9 are inserted in brackets. 128 *Trinacria:* Sicily. 130 *Parthenope:* Naples. 133 *Taillefer:* Troubadour who led the troops of William the Conqueror into battle. 137 *Saxon heptarchy:* England was divided into the seven kingdoms of Kent, South Saxons, West Saxons, East Saxons, East Angles, Mercia, and Northumberland. 143 *Gallia:* France should not conclude from the Norman conquest or the surrender of Italy and Spain that England will yield to Napoleon. 195 *turbary:* peat bog. 220 *charlock:* The family clear the land of wild mustard, thistles, and stones. 237 *"flock" bed:* made of tufts of wool. 239 *"hind":* peasant, rural laborer. 294 *frith:* firth, narrow bay. 306 *wain:* cart. 360 *tump:* hillock. 374 *cal-*

careous soil: the limestone, chalk, or "calx" of the cliffs above the Channel. 389 *weald:* wold, open plain. 401 *wether flock:* rams castrated to facilitate handling and selective breeding. 411 *rapire or excavated fossé:* rampart or trench. 452 *hassock:* tuft of coarse grass. 472 *windmill:* mill for the "white load" of flour. 498 *conqueror:* William the Conqueror.

ANN YEARSLEY

To Mira

line 20 *groat:* small change. 80 *Golconda:* famed copper mines.

Familiar Poem

line 6 *Tellus:* Nisa's husband. 25 *Tarpeian mount:* a Roman cliff. 59 *Tartarean:* underworld. 64 *Phoebus:* Apollo, the sun.

FRANCES O'NEILL

To Mr. Kelly

canto 1, line 16 *Toby:* the uncle in *Tristram Shandy.* 1.22 *fictious:* fictitious. 1.30 *gauldy optics:* perhaps eyes that are *gowlie* (full of secretion) or *gaudy* (beady, full of trickery). 1.134 *skip:* manservant, footman. 2.17 *gabey calf:* fool, dolt, boor in Lancashire dialect. 2.38 *sawney:* simpleton, native of Scotland (derisive). 2.41 *clack:* tongue (contemptuous). 2.84 *dowd-capped:* wearing a nightcap. 2.159 *prog:* food.

MARY ROBINSON

January 1795

line 15 *placemen:* officeholders.

Modern Female Fashions

Retitled "Female Fashions for 1799" in 1806, with many changes in language, omitting stanza 7.
    line 6 *Breastworks of size resisting:* (1806) Like *country clown* enlisting 24 *Otaheitian:* Tahitian.

Modern Male Fashions

Retitled "Male Fashions for 1799" in 1806; like its companion poem rewritten and cut, omitting stanzas 5, 8, and 9.
    line 27 *Beauty:* (1806) Science

The Poet's Garret

line 39 *nothing sad:* not sad that he lacks a fine table setting. 70 *rich:* (1806) sick.

Ode, Inscribed to the Infant Son of S. T. Coleridge

The 116-line version in the *Morning Post* (October 17, 1800), like the "lyrical tales" Robinson wrote in the '90s, experiments with mixed meter, whose irregular stanzas are tied together by repetition in their last line of the phrase "wood-wild harmony." The 1806 version abandons the refrain, cuts melancholy reflections on the sorrows baby Hartley Coleridge might encounter in life, as well as a barb about "bland religion," while adding lines 7–16 on the "Power creative" that infuses meaning into nature.

line 19 *Skiddaw:* Robinson invokes the Cumberland landscape that frames the poems of both Wordsworth and Coleridge, including Skiddaw mountain, the river Lodore, Lake Basenthwaite, Borrowdale, and Keswick, where Coleridge lived and his son Hartley was born.

The Camp

Published August 1, 1800, in the *Morning Post*; reprinted in 1804 as "Winkfield Plain, or a Description of a Camp in the Year 1800," under the name of Robinson's daughter, Maria Elizabeth Robinson, who censored lines 13–18, 21–24, and 39–42, with other minor changes of wording.

line 2 *suttling houses:* supply stores. 13 *petit maîtres:* dandies, fops. 20 *a lover:* (1804) their soldiers. 35 *sociables:* open carriages. 38 *to nobles:* (1804) for money.

ELIZABETH HANDS

Death of Amnon

Amnon, son of David (2 Samuel 13).

canto 1, line 14 *Shechem:* see Genesis 34. 1.77 *Shimeah:* David's brother, uncle of Amnon. canto 4, line 67 *Bathsheba:* To satisfy his lust for her, David arranged that her husband be sacrificed in battle (2 Samuel 11). canto 5, line 40 *returns:* The cycle of days sharpens the "spears" of reflection.

HELEN MARIA WILLIAMS

To Dr. Moore

Williams celebrates the harvest as symbolic fruit of French democracy (on "Gallia's plains"). She rewrote lines in the 1823 edition of *Poems on Various Subjects.*

To the Curlew

This poem was written for the translation of *Paul and Virginia*, by Bernardin de Saint Pierre. Paul here laments the absence of Virginia, who has been sent to Europe.

JOANNA BAILLIE

A Winter's Day

The 1840 edition added fifteen lines and notes to the version of 1790, emphasizing "covenanted worship." Baillie edited the language in detail, removing vernacular terms such as "grumly" (dismal).

line 99 *colworts:* greens.

A Summer's Day

The 1840 edition cut twenty-two lines from "A Summer Day" (1790).

CAROLINA, BARONESS NAIRNE

The Laird o' Cockpen

line 3 *braw:* fine. 4 *fashious:* annoying. 14 *yett:* gate. 15 *ben:* into the parlor. 20 *mutch:* coif, cap.

CHARLOTTE NOOTH

Irregular Lines

Mme. de Staël's *Corinne, or Italy* (1807) presents the exceptional poet whose genius costs her the love of a convention-bound Englishman. Her *De l'Allemagne* (*On Germany*, 1810) examines the interrelationship of literature, politics, and society, and introduced romanticism to France.

A Dish of Tea!

line 16 *meanless:* meaningless

DOROTHY WORDSWORTH

A Sketch

Titled "A Fragment" in several manuscript copies by Dorothy; first printed by Susan Levin in 1987.

Grasmere—a Fragment

Other titles Dorothy used are "A Cottage in Grasmere Vale," "A Winter's Ramble in Grasmere Vale," and "A Fragment."

After-recollection at Sight of the Same Cottage

Equals lines 41–48 of "Grasmere—a Fragment"; first identified as a separate fragment by Susan Levin in 1987.

JANE TAYLOR

Recreation

lines 116–17: (1832) And each reputed virtue hide,— / Till we were fully satisfied!

A Pair

line 10 *Land's End to Johnny Groat's:* tip of Cornwall to tip of mainland Scotland. 12 *William:* Taylor implies that kings are equivalent to her idle middle-class subject. 30 *Tom Thumb:* fairy-tale person who is two inches high. 53 *Gibeon's hill:* Joshua 10.12–14 records that the sun stood still over the hill of Gibeon to allow a battle to be fought. 62 *St. Giles' or James':* a poor parish outside the city walls, where the great plague started, or St. James, a fashionable district.

Accomplishment

lines 23–24: (1832) Sits down to her work, if you duly reward her, / And sends it home finished according to order.

CAROLINE LAMB

A New Canto

Ostensibly another canto by Byron, whose epic *Don Juan*, in comic cantos, began to appear in 1819.

line 7 *impudent reviewer:* "Byron" harks back to a negative review of his youthful *Hours of Idleness* in the *Edinburgh Review*; he "measured stings" with them in *English Bards and Scotch Reviewers* (1809). 9 *Montgomery:* Like Keats, James Montgomery was mistakenly thought to have died as a result of a negative review. 15 *a fancy:* The following stanzas are an apocalyptic vision of the fall of England. 28 *omnium:* for each £100 unit of a government borrowing on the stock exchange, the aggregate of stocks, annuities, etc. guaranteeing the loan. 31 *The Regent raves:* like his father. 31 *Moore:* Thomas Moore, poet and friend of Byron. 36 *Smithfield sort:* the vulgarity of the meat-market contrasts with the soprano of the opera. 42 *the Monument:* Sir Christopher Wren's column, erected to celebrate the Great Fire of 1666 in London. 48 *lapsus linguae:* slip of the tongue. 72 *Kremlin:* Napoleon occupied Moscow in the fall. 1812. The city burned. 75 *Bernadotte:* King of Sweden, who fought Napoleon. 81 *a gallant youth:* Lord Nelson. 89 *deathwatches:* ticking beetles. 112 *conventicle:* chapel of Dissenters. 115 *Wilberforce:* supported abolition. 120 *Seven Dials:* redlight district. 132 *strike them from the rolls:* debar them. 144 *Mr. Harris:* Thomas Harris, owner of Covent Garden. 160 *Horace and James Smith:* parodists. 161 *In rebus modus est:* Measure in all things. 188 *never-quenched desire:* Lamb speaks behind her Byron mask. 206 *Blackwood, Jeffrey, Gifford, Hazlitt:* reviewers and editors. 216 *Kean:* Edmund Kean, a leading actor.

Would I had seen thee dead and cold

Printed posthumously with Byron's *Fugitive Pieces* (1829).

To Harriet Wilson

Possibly Harriette Wilson, a clever demimondaine who claimed a passing acquaintance with Byron, and whom Lamb here derides as a paid courtesan.

FELICIA HEMANS

Properzia Rossi

line 80 *meed:* reward

Corinne at the Capitol

Corinne: Improvisational poet, heroine of a novel by Mme. de Staël **epigraph:** "Women must reflect that this career rarely is of a kind to equal the most obscure life of a woman loved and a happy mother." Mme. de Staël

ELIZABETH BARRETT BROWNING

The Cry of the Children

epigraph: "Do you hear the cry, do you hear the children's cry?" Euripides, *Medea*

To George Sand, A Desire

George Sand was the pseudonym of Aurore Dupin Dudevant (1804–1876), a French novelist who left her husband to pursue her career as a writer. She scandalized contemporaries by cross-dressing and by her affairs with Musset, Liszt, and Chopin. Her early novels attacked laws repressive of women's rights; her later idylls celebrated rural working-class life. Browning considered her the first female genius of any country or age.

Sonnets from the Portuguese

The title alludes to the love poetry of Luis de Camoëns, but Barrett Browning also reverses the hopeless love recorded in the anonymous *Letters from a Portuguese Nun*.

Aurora Leigh

Book I.

line 390 *bene . . . che che:* fine . . . no, no. 392 *collects:* Anglican prayers for specific dates. 394 *Articles:* the 39 principles of the Church of England; *Tracts against the Times:* the reactionary "Tracts for the Times" attacking church reforms. 395 *Buonaventure:* platonistic theologian. 400 *Balzac:* French realist novelist. 407 *Oviedo:* sixteenth-century Spanish historian. 416 *Dr. Johnson:* who commented on a young woman's performance of a difficult piece of music, "Would that it had been impossible." 429 *Tophet:* hell. 424 *Cellarius:* a dance. 454 *tragic poet:* Aeschylus, whose accidental death suggests the killing power of petitpoint. 467 *Brinvilliers:* The Marquise de Brinvilliers, a murderess, was tortured then executed in 1676. Like the water torture, Aurora's forcible education leaves her thirst unquenched.

Book II

line 61 *Caryatid:* column in form of a woman. 83 *Oread:* tree nymph; *naiad:* water nymph. 171 *Miriam:* Miriam's song follows the death of Pharaoh in the sea, Exodus 15.19–21. 176 *sounding brass:* 1 Corinthians 13.1. 209 Cordelia: *King Lear,* 4.7. 413 Hagar: Genesis. 16. 483 *Fourier:* François Charles Fourier, socialist theorist (1772–1837), whose project of communal living in "phalanges" is a model for Romney Leigh.

Book V

line 142 *Payne Knight:* English philologist (1750–1824) who disputed the antiquity of the Elgin marbles and integrity of the *Iliad;* his skepticism blinded him, like fog, and exposed his own defects. 149 *Hector's infant: Iliad* 6.595–601. 207 *Roland: Chanson de Roland.* 213 *Fleet Street:* location of debtor's prison and newspaper offices.

A Musical Instrument

When Syrinx escaped from Pan by her metamorphosis into reeds, he gathered these into panpipes (Ovid, *Metamorphoses,* i).

CHARLOTTE BRONTË

He is gone

Marian Hume sings these stanzas (sometimes printed as "Marian's Song") to the Marquis of Douro, accompanying herself with "a little ivory lyre."

We wove a web

Titled "Retrospection" by later editors.
line 5 *mustard seed:* cf. Matthew 13.31. 6 *almond rod:* cf. Numbers 17. 34 *Aaron's rod:* cf. Numbers 17. **postscript:** *Oh Grave, where is thy sting:* I Corinthians 15:55.

EMILY JANE BRONTË

High waving heather

First printed in 1902 with four additional lines from a fragment, "Woods."

Song

The Gondal notebook indicates the speaker is Lord Eldred W. addressing A.G.A.

Remembrance

Entitled "R. Alcona to J. Brenzaida" in MS. Brontë removed all allusions to the world of Gondal for publication in 1846.

Stars

line 9   *I blessed:* One of several echoes of Coleridge's *Rime of the Ancient Mariner.*

The Prisoner

For publication in 1846 Brontë excerpted lines 13–44 and 65–92 from "Julian M. and A. G. Rochelle," and added a stanza.

GEORGE ELIOT

A Minor Prophet

line 47   *The Vedas—Tripitaka—Vendidad:* Sanskrit and Zoroastrian poems. 79 *Caffrarian:* South African. 271 *Barbarossa:* Frederick I (1122–1190), German emperor.

O May I Join the Choir Invisible

epigraph: "The long stretch of time, when I shall not be, moves me more than this narrow one."

Erinna

A fourth-century B.C. poet from Telos, who died at nineteen. The Greek Anthology preserves three epigrams, one describing a portrait, and two inscriptions for the tomb of Baucis. Eliot cites Erinna's long poem, "The Spindle," or *Strands from the Distaff.* The two fragments she quotes may be translated:

> With this, an empty echo penetrates even to Hades but is silent among the dead, and darkness covers the eyes.

> O thou, companion fish, who bringst sailors a fair voyage, may thou escort from the stern my sweet girl.

JEAN INGELOW

High Tide on the Coast of Lincolnshire, 1571

line 28   *melick:* grass. 73 *scorpe:* scarp, steep slope. 101 *eygre:* a bore, high tidal wave.

ANNE BRONTË

A Prayer

From a music ms., shortened by Charlotte when she printed it in 1850.

Last Lines

Charlotte's note: "These lines written, the desk was closed."
   line 5   *blinding mist:* Anne Brontë typically left alternative wording in her manuscripts. Here for *blinding* she considered *whelming, rolling,* and *gathering.*

DORA GREENWELL

To Elizabeth Barrett Browning in 1851

Perhaps occasioned by Barrett Browning's visit to England in 1851.

The Homeward Lane

epigraph: Do you appear pale? / Take heart! You have reached home.

Demeter and Cora

title: *Cora:* Kore, daughter of Demeter. **line 35** *Cicula:* cicada. **37** *Aïdes:* Hades, lord of the underworld.

CHRISTINA GEORGINA ROSSETTI

A Soul

line 4 *aspic:* the asp smuggled under fruits to Cleopatra in prison for her suicide.

L.E.L.

title: First entitled "Spring," the poem carried a note "*L.E.L.* by E.B.B.," pointing to Letitia Landon's phrase "Do you think of me as I think of you?" and to Barrett Browning's line, "One thirsty for a little love."

Goblin Market

Originally inscribed to Rossetti's sister Maria, with an acknowledgment of Dante Gabriel's "suggestive wit and revising hand."

Monna Innominata, Sonnet 10

epigraphs: "With better course and with better star." (Dante) "Life flees, and stays not an hour." (Petrarch)

EMILY JANE PFEIFFER

The Lost Light

An elegy addressed to George Eliot.

Klytemnestra

Wife of Agamemnon, who avenged the sacrifice of their daughter Iphigenia by taking Aegysthus as her lover, then murdering her husband on his return from Troy; her son Orestes later killed her.

MICHAEL FIELD

Long Ago, Fragment 33

The title numbers echo, but do not correspond to, the numbers conventionally used for the fragments of Sappho that inspired the sequence of poems in *Long Ago*.

epigraph: "To you, fair maids, my mind changes not." (Henry T. Wharton, *Sappho*, fragment #14; Loeb, *Lyra Graeca*, vol.1, #14). Field wrote of the "passionate pleasure Dr. Wharton's book had brought to me," and Wharton in turn quoted excerpts from Field in a revised edition of his *Sappho* (1895).

Fragment 34

epigraph: "You are nought to me." (Wharton, *Sappho*, fragment #23; Loeb #49.)

Fragment 52

epigraph: "And this I feel in myself." (Wharton, *Sappho*, fragment #15; Loeb #15.) According to myth, Tiresias acquired prophetic vision by undergoing metamorphosis into the body of a woman and back. He reported that woman has greater sexual pleasure than man.

Fragment 63

epigraph: "Come now, divine shell, become vocal for me." (Wharton, *Sappho*, fragment #14; Loeb #14.) **line 3** *Cypris*: Aphrodite. **14** *Evian King*: Dionysus.

[It was deep April and the morn]

Sometimes titled "Prologue."

After Soufrière

Soufrière was a city in Guadeloupe destroyed by a volcanic eruption.

Circe at Circæum

An early poem by Edith Cooper, published posthumously in *Dedicated*, edited by Katherine Bradley.

ALICE MEYNELL

To the Beloved

When first printed this and other poems in *Preludes* (1875) carried an epigraph in Italian. Meynell in later editions removed the epigraph and a stanza following line 10:

> Full, full is life in hidden places,
> > For thou art silence unto me.
> Full, full is thought in endless spaces.
> > Full is my life. A silent sea
> Lies round all shores with long embraces.

The Visiting Sea

First entitled "Song" in *Preludes* (1875).

A Poet of One Mood

First entitled "Sonnet" (1875).

A Song of Derivations

Entitled "The Modern Poet" in *Merry England* (August 1885); Meynell changed the title for *Poems* (1893).

TORU DUTT

Sîta

Heroine of the *Ramayana*, Sîta was abducted and upon her return to her husband underwent trial by fire to prove her chastity to her husband, the god Rama.

Our Casuarina Tree

Casuarina is a genus of leafless trees whose twigs resemble cassowary feathers.
     line 18 *kokilas:* songbird. 50 *Borrowdale:* in the Lake Country; a place name in Coleridge's *Christabel.*

JANE BARLOW

Wayfarers

line 9 *banati:* housewife.

DOLLIE RADFORD

From the Suburbs

line 18 *alpine Gemmi:* Swiss pass in the Bernese Alps.

From Our Emancipated Aunt in Town

line 8 *Ewigkeit:* eternity. 25 *le roi est mort:* the king is dead.

EDITH NESBIT

The Depths of the Sea

epigraph: You have what you sought with all your heart, / Unfortunate one. (See Vergil, *Aeneid* IV, 100.)

ROSAMUND MARRIOTT WATSON

Ballad of the Willow Pool

line 16 *Neckan:* nix, water sprite. 72 *dool:* grief.

MARY ELIZABETH COLERIDGE

A Clever Woman

A pessimistic response to Charlotte Yonge's *Clever Woman of the Family* (1865).

Pelops and Hippodameia

Pelops, son of Tantalus, was cut up by his father and served to the gods but restored by Hermes, with an ivory shoulder. He won the hand of Hippodameia with the help of Poseidon at the cost of her father's life; Atreus was one of their children. He renamed the region he ruled Peloponnesus.

AMY LEVY

Felo de Se

The title means felony against oneself, the former legal term for suicide. Levy imitates Swinburne's metrics, using six stresses and heavy alliteration.

Ballade of an Omnibus

epigraph: From Andrew Lang, one model for Levy's use of the ballade in 3 stanzas of seven to ten lines, each ending on a refrain, followed by a short envoy. line 15 *Croesus:* a rich person, like the sixth century king of Lydia. 18 *Lucullus' phaeton:* a van delivering delicacies, like those served by the Roman consul at his banquets.

A Ballade of Religion and Marriage

The title, usually misspelled, refers to the archaic stanzaic form (with refrain and envoy) that Levy used repeatedly.

MAY KENDALL

Lay of the Trilobite

line 7 *Silurian:* of the earliest Paleozoic era. 27 *Monotreme:* lowest order of mammal.

The Philanthropist and the Jellyfish

line 51 *Sensorium:* the nerve center at which impressions are transformed into sensations.

CHARLOTTE MEW

The Fête

line 4 *pion:* monitor, junior master. 10 *Seigneur mon Dieu . . . the sacré soul of spies:* My Lord God; the bloody soul of spies. 15 *Place d'Armes:* Arsenal square. 22 *demoiselles of the pensionnat:* the girls of the boarding school. 24 *le petit Jésus:* baby Jesus. 26 *Si, c'est défendu, mais que voulez-vous?:* Well, yes, it's forbidden, but what do you expect? 62 *montagne russe . . . the man à la tête de veau:* roller coaster; the man with calf's head. 63 *tir:* shooting gallery. 65 *porcs-roulants:* a fairgrounds ride. 65–66 *Oh! là là! la fête! Va pour du vin, et le tête-à-tête:* Ooh! Festivity! Let's go for the wine, and the tête-à-tête. 67 *gaufres! Pauvrette:* waffles! Poor thing. 71 *sacrebleu:* zounds! 74 *Oh, que c'est beau—Ah, qu'elle est belle!:* Oh, how lovely it is—Ah, how pretty she is! 94 *Morte d'Arthur:* cycle of Arthurian legends by Thomas Malory.

INDEXES

Index of Titles
and First Lines

Index of Authors

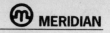